Memoria Romana

Memoirs of the American Academy in Rome

Supplementary Volume X

Support for this publication was provided by the Lucy Shoe Meritt, FAAR '37, '50, Publication Fund of the American Academy in Rome and by the 1984 Foundation.

MEMORIA ROMANA

Memory in Rome

and

Rome in Memory

edited by

Karl Galinsky
University of Texas at Austin

PUBLISHED FOR THE AMERICAN ACADEMY IN ROME
by
The University of Michigan Press
Ann Arbor, Michigan
2014

Copyright © by Karl Galinsky 2014
Published in the United States of America by
The University of Michigan Press
Manufactured in the United States of America
⊗ Printed on acid-free paper

2017   2016   2015   2014   4   3   2   1

A CIP catalog record for this book is available from the British Library.

ISBN 978-0-472-11943-1

Contents

Figures

Contributors

Anna Anguissola is a postdoctoral teaching faculty member at "Distant Worlds: Munich Graduate School for Ancient Studies" of the Ludwig Maximilians University of Munich. She has been an affiliated fellow of the American Academy in Rome and a member of the School of Historical Studies of the Institute for Advanced Study, Princeton, as well as the recipient of a *Memoria Romana* research grant. Her publications include *Intimità a Pompei. Riservatezza, condivisione e prestigio negli ambienti ad alcova di Pompei* (Berlin and New York 2010) and *Difficillima imitatio. Immagine e lessico delle copie tra Grecia e Roma* (Rome 2012).

Diane Favro is Professor of Architecture and Urban Design at UCLA and former President of the Society of Architectural Historians. Her research encompasses Roman architecture and urbanism, digital technologies in the humanities, and women in architecture. As Director of the UCLA Experiential Technologies Center, she has directed numerous digital projects simulating historic buildings and environments, such as the Lighthouse at Alexandria, Temple of Amon at Karnak, and late antique Rome. Her numerous publications include *The Urban Image of Augustan Rome* (Cambridge 1996).

Harriet I. Flower is Professor of Classics at Princeton University, where she also serves as Master of Mathey College. Her research has been in the areas of Roman cultural and social history, epigraphy, and Latin literature, with a special focus on memory, commemoration, and spectacle. She has published *Ancestor Masks and Aristocratic Power in Roman Culture* (Oxford 1996), *The Art of Forgetting: Disgrace and Oblivion in Roman Political Culture* (Chapel Hill 2006), and *Roman Republics* (Princeton 2010). A second edition of her edited volume, *The Cambridge Companion to the Roman Republic* (2004), is due out in 2014.

Bernard Frischer is Professor of Informatics at Indiana University, where he also directs the Virtual World Heritage Laboratory. The mission of the laboratory is to apply 3D technologies to research and instruction in the humanities. In recent years, Frischer has been working on digitizing ancient sculpture and creating a digital simulation of Hadrian's Villa. He earned his B.A. in 1971 from Wesleyan University and his Ph.D. in 1975 from Heidelberg. From 1974 to 1976 he held a postdoctoral Rome Prize Fellowship in Classical Studies at the American Academy in Rome.

Karl Galinsky is the Floyd Cailloux Centennial Professor of Classics and University Distinguished Teaching Professor at the University of Texas at Austin. The range of his publications, including ten books, extends over Roman literature, art, social and cultural history, and reception. In 2009 he was awarded a Max-Planck Prize for International Cooperation for research on memory in ancient Rome. The resulting project, *Memoria Romana*, based at the Ruhr-Universität Bochum, has funded fourteen doctoral students and seventeen postdoc researchers (http://www.utexas.edu/research/memoria).

Karl-J. Hölkeskamp is Professor of Ancient History at the University of Cologne, Germany. He has published extensively on civic society, politics, and law in ancient Greece and the Roman republic. Recent publications include volumes on *lieux de mémoire* of Greek and Roman antiquity (coedited with Elke Stein-Hölkeskamp) and *Reconstructing the Roman Republic: An Ancient Political Culture and Modern Research* (Princeton 2010).

Jessica Hughes is a Lecturer in Classical Studies at The Open University, UK, and recipient of a *Memoria Romana* research grant. Her research focuses on Greek and Roman material culture, and she has particular interests in material religion, classical reception studies, and the body. Her publications include articles on anatomical votives, human-animal hybrids, restorations of ancient sculpture, and receptions of classical ruins in later periods. Her monograph on votive body parts (*The Anatomy of Ritual*) is forthcoming in 2014, and she is currently coediting, with Dr. Claudio Buongiovanni, a volume on receptions of classical antiquity in the city of Naples.

Richard Jenkyns is Emeritus Professor of the Classical Tradition, University of Oxford, and Emeritus Fellow of Lady Margaret Hall. His books are *The Victorians and Ancient Greece* (1980), *Three Classical Poets: Sappho, Catullus and Juvenal* (1982), *Dignity and Decadence: Victorian Art and the Classical Inheritance* (1991), *Classical Epic: Homer and Virgil* (1992), *Virgil's Experience* (1998), *A Fine Brush on Ivory: An Appreciation of Jane Austen* (2004), and *God, Space and City in the Roman Imagination* (2013), and he edited *The Legacy of Rome* (1992). He is now writing a survey of classical literature for the Pelican imprint of Penguin Books.

Daniel Libeskind, B.Arch. M.A. BDA AIA, is an international architect and designer. His practice extends from building major cultural and commercial institutions—including museums and concert halls—to convention centers, universities, housing, hotels, shopping centers, and residential work. Daniel Libeskind's commitment to expanding the scope of architecture reflects his profound interest and involvement in philosophy, art, literature, and music. (He began his career with studying music and became a virtuoso performer before receiving his professional architectural degree in 1970.) Fundamental to Libeskind's philosophy is the notion that buildings are crafted with perceptible human energy and that they address the greater cultural context in which they are built. He has designed such world-renowned projects as the master plan for the World Trade Center in New York and the Jewish Museum, Berlin.

Lisa Marie Mignone is an Assistant Professor in the Classics Department at Brown University. Her special interest is Roman social history of the republic, and she draws her evidence from a wide range of sources, including history, literature, art history, and archaeology. In her studies of the city of Rome, she combines urban theory with comparative evidence from other ancient cities, including Pompeii, where she did field work. She was awarded a Rome Prize from the American Academy in Rome and has also been a fellow at the Scuola Normale Superiore di Pisa.

Gianpiero Rosati is Professor of Latin Literature at the Scuola Normale Superiore di Pisa. He is the author of numerous publications on Ovid (among them *Narciso e Pigmalione*, 1983, and books 4–6 of the commentary on the *Metamorphoses* directed by A. Barchiesi for the Fondazione Valla, 2007–2009) and other Latin authors. He is currently working on Flavian literature and culture.

T. P. Wiseman is Emeritus Professor of Classics at the University of Exeter and a Fellow of the British Academy. His most recent books are *The Myths of Rome* (Exeter 2004), *Unwritten Rome* (Exeter 2008), and *Remembering the Roman People* (Oxford 2009); he hopes soon to complete *The Roman Audience*. A new translation of Ovid's *Fasti* by Anne and Peter Wiseman (*Times and Reasons*, 2011) is now in paperback in the Oxford World's Classics series.

Preface and Acknowledgments

The papers in this volume are based on a conference by the same title that was held at the American Academy in Rome in October of 2011. I am most grateful to all those who contributed to its success. Our endeavor would never have materialized without the Max-Planck Society, which awarded me a generous Research Prize for International Cooperation in 2009 in the specified area of memory studies. The result has been the project *Memoria Romana* (http://www.utexas.edu/research/memoria), based at the Ruhr-Universität Bochum. It is a pleasure to acknowledge the support of some true facilitators there, including its Rektor, Professor Elmar Weiler; the Vice-Rektor for Research, Professor Ulf Eysel; my classical colleagues Professor Reinhold Glei and Dr. Wolfgang Polleichtner; and the Director of the *Reise-Dezernat*, Mr. Peter Sack, who helped us navigate the bureaucratic *mare nostrum*.

In Rome, the American Academy was an ideal host with its distinct combination of professionalism and genuine hospitality. The then Mellon Professor of Classical Studies, Corey Brennan, was instrumental in all stages of planning; the details of the event and his energy and ready accessibility will always be fondly remembered. The two directors of the Academy with whom I worked, Carmela Franklin and Christopher Celenza, could not have been more supportive. Finally, the staff made it all work; I am profoundly grateful to Anne Coulson and her assistants for their tireless efforts and efficient cooperation.

I, too, have been blessed with good assistants. Cornelia Sonnleitner, who has been my German right hand since the beginning of the project, took care of the arrangements, especially for the workshop we organized for the predoctoral grantees in conjunction with the conference. Subsequently, she helped with the *editio princeps* of the manuscripts for this volume. Bartolo Natoli, my assistant at the University of Texas, was an invaluable help in preparing the final version(s) for publication and staying atop many details both large and small. It is a real pleasure, too, to express my profound gratitude to Professor Elaine Gazda, Ellen Bauerle, and Peg Lourie for their extraordinay helpfulness. In their respective capacities as chair of the Academy's Publications Committee, acquisitions editor at the University Press, and managing editor of *MAAR* pubications, they provided expeditious and patient support throughout the entire publication process. It has been a privilege and a pleasure to work with them.

Finally, my great thanks go to the contributors. They generated a spirited conference with many stimulating perspectives and then were most expeditious in producing the expanded versions of their papers for this volume. Living up to the topic, they made our encounters and discussion a truly memorable occasion. It has been a privilege for me to work with them and the many grantees of the *Memoria Romana* project.

Austin, September 2013

Introduction

Karl Galinsky

1. General Perspectives

Memory defined Roman civilization. Latin authors, such as the ever-prolific Cicero, viewed history (*historia*) as the preservation of memory (*memoria*), and such preservation could take on the shape of poetry as well as prosaic historiography.[1] Succinctly—and Cicero could be succinct when he wanted to—he characterized *historia* as *vita memoriae* (*De or.* 2.36), and the convergence, if not the identification, of history and memory persisted well into the nineteenth century.[2] Fittingly, therefore, memory is a pervasive theme in Vergil's quintessential Roman epic, the *Aeneid*, which was the kind of poetic (re)construction of Roman cultural memory that resonated.[3] In contrast to the Homeric epics, for instance, the Muse is asked not to "sing" or "tell" but to "bring back memories" (*memora*; 1.8; cf. 7.645–646). Mnemosyne, of course, was the mother of the Muses, and on the highest citadel of Rome, the *arx* on the Capitoline, there stood the Temple of Juno Moneta (now safely tucked away underneath the Church of Ara Coeli).[4] Moneta is the Latin equivalent of Mnemosyne; the temple was the repository of significant public records, and, providing an apt illustration of the changes of "memory" itself, the name lived on as it was applied to the silver currency minted in the precinct and then to money in general. Memory can live on in a variety of ways.

---

[1] For a concise discussion of some key passages, see Gowing 2005, 7–17 and esp. 11: "For the Romans *historia* is less a genre than a definition of subject matter." It might be added that, while recognizing poetry, such as Ennius's *Annales*, "as a source of legitimate historical information (*Brut.* 57, 60)" and epic poetry as a congenial medium for his own attempts at history, as evidenced by *De consulatu suo*, Cicero also could be aware of different principles (*leges*) guiding *historia* and *poema*: *veritas* for the former, *delectatio* for the latter, although some historians like Herodotus, *pater historiae,* combine both (*Leg.* 1,2,5). Typically, the subject of *memoria* soon enters into the discussion (1.3.8). On the general subject, see also Timpe 1996.

[2] This is not the place to recapitulate the extensive scholarship on this issue, and therefore a few markers may suffice. Halbwachs 1925 posited the incompatibility of history and memory (history begins where and when memory ends), followed to some extent by Nora 1984–1992 and A. Assmann 1999, 314–322, esp. 317: "The spirit of historical research develops at the expense of breaking with traditions and forgetting normative pasts" ("Der historische Forschergeist entwickelt sich auf Kosten von Traditionsbruch und Verges-

sen normativer Vergangenheiten"). Professional historians, too, have continued to stress the dichotomy: Klein, for instance, regards memory as "the therapeutic alternative to historical discourse" (2000, 145). At the same time, the surge of memory studies has contributed to many a searching examination of the contingencies of historical writing; for a short list, see Olick and Robbins 1998, 110–111. Many scholars now occupy a middle ground and view memory and history as complementary; see, e.g., Le Goff 1992, Yerushalmi 1982, Hutton 1993, and Confino 1997. Burke 1989 even echoes Cicero, defining history as social memory. Good surveys of trends are Olick and Robbins 1998 and Erll 2011. The discussion continues in this volume, especially in the contributions of Wiseman and Hölkeskamp.

[3] See my brief comments at http://www.utexas.edu/research/memoria/Virgil/Memory in AeneidA.htm; Seider 2012 and 2013; comprehensive collection of material in Raymond 2011.

[4] See "Iuno Moneta, Aedes" (G. Gianelli) in *Lexicon Topographicum Urbis Romae* 3 (1996) 123–125; cf. F. Coarelli, in ibid., 279–280.

As for the recollection of the history of Rome, it was based, up to the middle republic, not on extensive written accounts, let alone verifiable data, but on what modern scholars like to call "collective" or "cultural" memory; we should note already at this point that it is more appropriate to speak of such memor*ies* as there is nothing monolithic about them. Literacy and writing, shared only by a small portion of the populace at best, never led to the demise of an orally communicated tradition; the ongoing (re)production of memory cut across such posited divides. An outstanding demonstration was provided, on an almost daily basis, by the many practitioners of rhetoric. Much has been made of their mnemotechnic training. Perhaps most famously, Cicero's story of Simonides, who was able to recall the identities of the guests at a banquet, who were killed and disfigured by the building's collapse, by remembering where they had been seated (*De or.* 2.351–353), has become a *locus classicus*, though it may also be another iconic instance of the invention of tradition.[5] The important point is that the practice was not a limited technical phenomenon but played a much larger cultural role as the orators drew on *memoria rerum Romanarum*, "a memory of (and for) Roman history" (*Brut.* 322).[6] It was in the nature of their profession that they would use and shape the historical precedents and information they cited elastically to suit a given purpose. The resulting *memoria rerum Romanarum* was not uniform but a collection of many *memoriae*—here is another dimension of "collective" memory.

It comes as no surprise that an accompanying, if not resulting, phenomenon is the multifaceted semantic spectrum of *memoria*.[7] *Memoria* can be the sum of all traditions (for as long as people can remember). Conversely, it can denote a temporal limit, applying to memories that are present from the perspective of the living. And, of course, *memoria* can stand for the content of such tradited versions; it is significant that *memoria* and writing are viewed as complementary. More narrowly, *memoria* is used for the text of funeral inscriptions; more widely, of course, *memoria* is the obligation to remember the dead. Its reverse, *damnatio memoriae*, has gained wide currency as a scholarly term of convenience, but there never was an actual and comprehensive Roman statute by that name for the various efforts to delete or reduce the memory of an individual.[8] As Harriet Flower has demonstrated, it is more accurate to speak of memory sanctions that were "deliberately designed strategies that aim to change the picture of the past";[9] defined in these terms, the phenomenon was an extensive one for many centuries.

The power of visual commemoration was just as important. Any *monumentum* by definition was a *lieu de mémoire*. As one of the commentators on Horace noted succinctly, the meaning of *monumentum*, beyond its specific purpose such as a *sepulcrum*, is that "everything about it attests and demonstrates memory."[10] Such memory, preserved in stone or bronze, lives up even more to the essence of *mani-moria* (Varro's etymology for *memoria*; *Ling.* 6.49) because it is even more abiding than ever-changing oral or written traditions. The range of monuments was extensive and formed an environment that, in turn, shaped Roman identities: ancestor masks in the house and

[5] For this important concept, see Hobsbawm and Ranger 1983. Discussions of the Simonides anecdote include Farrell 1997; A. Assmann 1999, 35–38; and Bergmann 1994. An excellent source for Roman mnemotechniques in general and the role of *loci* is Small 1997, 95–137.

[6] Rightly emphasized by Gowing 2005, 16–17; cf. Vernant 1965, 51 and, with reference to the hermetic philosophers of the Renaissance, Yates 1966.

[7] Besides the complete documentation in *Thesaurus linguae*

Latinae and *The Oxford Latin Dictionary* s.v. *memoria*, see the concise discussion of Walter 2004, 26–35; cf. Heusch 2011, 23–47.

[8] H. I. Flower's 1998 discussion is essential; cf. Hedrick 2000, 89–130; Varner 2004, 41–43; and Galinsky 2008, 15–16.

[9] H. I. Flower 2006, 2.

[10] Porphyrio on Horace, *Odes* 1.2.15: *monumentum non sepulcrum tantum dicitur, sed omne quicquid memoriam testatur.*

at funerals, an increasing forest of statues especially in the capital city that could be lightened only by radical intervention, victory columns, temples built by *imperatores* from spoils, a plethora of public structures including those in the original Forum and the imperial Fora, and more. Like the head of Janus, which was chosen as the emblem of the American Academy, such memorials (in the largest sense of the word) have a dual function: they both preserve memories of the past and shape the memories of their beholders, present and future (Cicero placed the emphasis on the latter in a letter to Caesar);[11] hence the spirited controversies even in our time about the design of memorials for Civil War sites, the Vietnam Memorial in Washington DC, and the 9/11 Memorial in New York (on which see the concluding essay by Daniel Libeskind in this volume).[12] *Monumenta*, therefore, are not static but keep eliciting different responses and associations, which, of course, are mostly based on the memories of viewers and onlookers.[13]

This complements another, essential characteristic of memory. So far from being archival, static, or a hard drive, the memory of individuals is a continuing process of creation and recreation. That has been established as a basic fact in the cognitive and psychological studies of memory and the entire spectrum of memory research in neuroscience.[14] Given that basis, it is not surprising to see this process paralleled, if not replicated, in what we might call social and historical memory—that is, essentially supra-individual memory as practiced by specific groups. Besides not being homogenous, such memories constantly acquire new layers, evolve, and develop in new directions. Memories of Rome, by Romans and of Romans, offer a rich variety of examples. Already by late antiquity, the city itself had become a palimpsest, a characterization made famous by Freud in *Civilization and Its Discontents*, who looked at Rome from the perspective of even more centuries and used its layering as a metaphor for the human psyche.

The present volume, based on the proceedings of a conference held at the American Academy in October of 2011, explores some of these aspects. It does not aim to be a methodological *vademecum* but, rather, to illustrate a variety of approaches to, and perspectives on, different roles memory could play in ancient Rome and, also, on the palimpsestic Rome. Such variety is appropriate in two ways. First, it has characterized the "memory boom" of the last three decades, a phenomenon that has been fed by many sources and, accordingly, many disciplines, such as social studies, cognitive sciences, humanities, and media studies, along with neurosciences and biopsychology, to mention only the main ones. Despite some brave attempts, especially by German scholars, to tidy things up with the usual academic recourse to extensive categorization and to systematize the sprawl of the memory industry, one abiding forte of scholarly preoccupation with memory has been precisely a lack of orthodoxies, dogmas, and rigid conceptualizations. Like memory itself, then—and that is my second point—whether historical or neurological, memory studies, or *Gedächtnisgeschichte*, are a dynamic and lively work in progress, continuously acquiring new layers and, in fact, arguing about its own definitions.[15] It is all to the good that we are not looking at a static, let alone stale, phenomenon, and in this volume, too, we do not want to lose the rich cultural forest for the taxonomic trees.

[11] *Epist. ad Caes.* fr. 7: "As for the raison d'être of a monument, I am reminded by its very name: it must look more to the memory of posterity than the favor of the present time" (*sed ego quae monumenti ratio sit nomine ipso admoneor: ad memoriam magis spectare debet posteritatis quam ad praesentis temporis gratiam*).

[12] Good selection of examples, from George Washington's statue onwards, in Senie and Webster 1992.

[13] This dimension could be fruitfully added to viewer-response approaches to Roman art, such as Elsner's (1995).

[14] Some basic works include Bartlett 1997; Schacter, Norman, and Koutstaal 1998; Welzer 2005, 19–45; Siegel 2006.

[15] A seminal instance is the polemic by Gedi and Elam 1996, who argue for jettisoning the term *collective memory* altogether because the concept adds nothing new to older formulations such as tradition and historical consciousness.

Some further advantages accrue. When the Max-Planck Society awarded me its generous international research prize for the specified research area of *Gedächtnisgeschichte*, it was not because I had been an active, let alone founding, member of the guild, quite in contrast to the other recipient, Aleida Assmann (whom I greatly admire). Rather, at this stage of the evolution of memory studies it seemed like a good idea to test the insights of this scholarly orientation in comparison with other approaches and methodologies. Given the organic and ubiquitous presence of *memoria* in all areas of Roman culture, there was no need to impose artificial and extraneous constructs on the phenomenon. Memory scholars can choose from a broad and elastic spectrum of approaches and ideas. They range from the recycling of insights into the obvious—yes, the past does live on in the present—to nuanced, culture-specific observations. The thirty-one international grantees in the *Memoria Romana* Project have done exactly that, and I can only restate my joy at the privilege of working with such a talented group. The same applies to the contributors to this conference. The goal, as always, is critical assessment rather than schematic application, and to contribute something new to our understanding of a major cultural force in ancient Rome.

Another benefit for this conference was its locus, the American Academy in Rome. It was deliberately chosen for its wide horizons. Since its inception, the focus of the Academy's residents and students has been not just on the archaeology and history of ancient Rome but on the abiding influence of Rome's culture and memory in a cosmopolitan setting that encourages multiple strands of creativity and pursuits of knowledge. The last two essays of this collection aptly reflect that orientation, dealing with the digital recovery of Roman *lieux de mémoire* to perspectives on memorialization by a leading contemporary architect. The conference was a successful and stimulating reflection of the resulting dialogue that is fostered by the Academy and its ability to overcome compartmentalization.

Behind the concern, if not the obsession, with memory looms the long, dark shadow of oblivion. The dynamic is not a simple one, though the spectrum is wide and allows characters like Achilles to settle firmly at one end of it. For most individuals and societies, however, forgetting and memory/remembrance are complementary. In the succinct formulation of Aleida Assmann: "In order . . . to remember anything, one has to forget: but what is forgotten need not necessarily be lost forever."[16] The rare exceptions of individuals who retain complete recall of everything are clinical cases,[17] and recent findings in the neuroscience of memory seem to indicate that the process of forgetting may be an active neural one, just like memory.[18] When it comes to cultural and social memory, with their effect on shaping identities, the process of selection is just as willful. With typical common sense, Susan Alcock has articulated some of the guiding questions for any inquiry into this central issue: "What was forgotten, and at whose behest? Who formulated and promulgated the dominant commemorative narratives, and how effectively were other versions of the past masked and erased?"[19] Not all these processes were due to the manipulation of the more powerful: there was the realization, too, that civic entities, just like individuals, cannot forever dwell on the past but need to move on. Nietzsche forcefully expressed the general sentiment by calling excessive preoccupation with the past "the gravedigger of the present,"[20] and Tzvetan Todorov's trenchant critique of the memory

[16] From "Canon and Archive," in Olick, Vinitzky-Seroussi, and Levy 2011, 337.

[17] See, e.g., Parker, Cahill, and McGaugh 2006.

[18] See, most recently, Lai, Franke, and Gan 2012.

[19] Alcock 2002, 32.

[20] It is important to note that Nietzsche's concern is the degree (*Grad*) and boundary (*Grenze*) for forgetting the past; he did not utter the absolutist dictum "the past is the gravedigger of the present" that is generally cited (cf. Olick, Vinitzky-Seroussi, and Levy 2011, 73). Nietzsche is notoriously hard to translate; I have therefore relied on the German original (in *Unzeitgemäße Betrachtungen* [chapter 1]: *Vom Nutzen und Nachteil der Historie für das Leben* [section 1]). He goes

boom, which he sees as blinding us to novel challenges of the present and future, is a more recent voice.[21] Sometimes it is for the sake of the common good that not all memories are kept alive, and the motives are anything but sinister. A famous example is the Athenian amnesty decree of 403 that enjoined "not to remember bad things" (*mē mnēsikakein*) after the atrocities of the Thirty Tyrants and the retaliation against them; the precedent was invoked, successfully, by Cicero when he persuaded the Senate, on 17 March 44 B.C., to grant amnesty to Caesar's murderers. Similarly, Octavian looked beyond the horrors of the 30s B.C. when he "burned as many writings as he could concerning the civil strife" already at that time (App. *B Civ.* 5.132); the motivation was a mix of self-interest and the realization that Rome, and he, eventually would need to move beyond that past.[22]

These and similar instances throughout history are, of course, judgment calls that can be, and have been, debated forever. The memories of those times were not suppressed. Rather, the question was the coexistence of maintaining a sense of the past with the imperatives of the present. The larger perspective, in terms of memory studies, is that the subject is anything but simply academic—for reasons such as these, one of the main impulses for the genesis of *Gedächtnisgeschichte* was the Holocaust, especially as the generation that witnessed it started fading away. How does one come to terms with such memories? What is the best way to preserve them? Is there any place for forgetting? Similarly rooted in reality was a second major reason for the turn to memory studies. By the 1980s much writing about history—ancient history happily being excluded for the most part—had become increasingly abstract, focusing on systemic concepts like metahistory, overriding ideas or *Ideologeme*, anemic constructs, and so on. The question arose: where are the people in all this? Memory studies addressed that deficit.[23] In light of these origins, therefore, they do not need to be overtheorized. Nor is their purpose to replace traditional historical inquiry but, rather, to interact with it and complement it. Accordingly, and due to the dominant role of memory in Roman culture, one of our principal tasks is to historicize Roman memory.[24]

2. The Contributions to This Volume

The present contributions aim to do so from a variety of perspectives and to engage the reader in continuing the work and reflect on issues, *sub specie memoriae*, that often appear quite settled. Richard Jenkyns's introductory essay is an excellent example. What role did the actual physical fabric of Rome play in the Romans' own sense and memory of Rome's past? Surprisingly little, it seems. In modern sensibility Rome is the supreme example of the multilayered, palimpsestic city, but in antiquity the view was rather different. The Romans attributed patina and oldness to their habits and institutions, but our sources tell a different story about their concern—or, rather, lack

---

on to say that such degrees and boundaries depend on the "plastische Kraft" (call it "vital ability") of "an individual, a people, a culture" to "develop out of oneself in one's own way." An example of such growth is to be able to "heal wounds." For a recent stimulating discussion of this issue from ancient to modern times, see Meier 2010. Cf. Winston Churchill in his 1946 speech in Zurich advocating the creation of United States of Europe: "There must be an end to retribution. There must be what Mr Gladstone many years ago called 'a blessed act of oblivion'."

[21] Todorov 1995. A counterpoint is Erll's observation that "remembrances are small islands in a sea of oblivion" (2005, 7).

[22] Cf. Galinsky 2012, 180.

[23] Cf. the relevant comments of Connerton 1989, 18–20 and Fentress and Wickham 1992, 200–201. There are additional contemporary agendas; it is no coincidence, for instance, that Nora published his multivolume hodge-podge collection of *lieux de mémoire* (1984–1992) as a beacon for *l'identité française* at a time of massive immigration from former French colonies.

[24] Cf. Confino 1997, 1404.

of it—for original texture of, and the effects of maturation on, the physical structures: the sense of memory a building conveyed was not based on those factors of "authenticity." In contrast to the often obsessive hankering after the old in other areas of aesthetic production, such as literature and sculpture, similar fondness for affecting ancientness is largely absent from their attitude to architecture. Structures in their growing metropolis routinely burned down and were rebuilt or restored in a better way. Such updates were hailed as improvements instead of being faulted for not preserving the old. Sure, these were *lieux de mémoire*, but just as Pierre Nora used the term from the start to give it a wider, and even metaphorical, application, so, in Jenkyns's astute argument, it is, for instance, the atmospheric awe (*religio*) instilled by temples rather than their changing physical fabric that is the main agent in their effecting memory. And, as he points out, "it was not only the buildings of Rome that were changeable; there were the inhabitants, too." *Roma aeterna*, as can be seen, was based on its ability to evolve materially and on its cosmopolitanism. The notion of eternal Rome, such as it was, pointed to the future and not the past. In antiquity, the city was never regarded as a static museum; collections of artifacts, rather than unchanging architectural preservation, provided an avenue there.[25] It is only fitting, of course, that physical *lieux de mémoire* should evolve (and not just in terms of reception) just as memory itself does; it may be because of this more dynamic aspect of Rome's memory, too, and not just the palimpsestic one—Jenkyns credits Vergil with the poetic articulation of the latter—that the memory of Rome became the powerful presence we know.[26]

In a similar vein, Harriet Flower takes a closer look at a phenomenon whose function seems to be self-evident—certainly in modern times—and arrives at new results. Autobiography is an established defense against oblivion and for shaping one's memory for the present and future. As with so many practices of memory, this one, while occurring in most written cultures, is also culture-specific. Romans of the republican period had many traditional ways in which they sought to ensure that their achievements and personal qualities would be remembered after they died. Statues, inscriptions, and monuments of various kinds were designed to recall careers and successes within the setting of the city. Triumphs and funerals were the two related rituals that celebrated a man's highest achievement (and its public recognition by his peers).[27] Eulogistic words were delivered in funeral speeches (*laudationes*) and inscribed on tombs (*elogia*) and portraits of the deceased. By the end of the second century B.C., that was not enough, and autobiographical prose writings began to be published while the authors were still alive. As Flower points out, there were multiple reasons for this development as it was embedded in a specific social, political, and cultural context and its agendas. The multifaceted founding figure that emerges is Lutatius Catulus (consul in 100 B.C.), distinguished both by his political and military vicissitudes and his innovative cultural cosmopolitanism. Did he succeed? Like others, including the autobiography of Augustus (and most writings from antiquity), neither of his accounts—one a lengthy letter to the Roman Senate setting out his case for a triumph, and the other a Greek-inspired memoir—has survived.[28] It is, however, significant for the assessment of memory in Roman times that the letter, or a copy of it, was available for almost three centuries, until the time of Marcus Aurelius. Typically, however, these were not the

[25] See now Rutledge 2012. Cf., from a modern perspective on Paris, Christine Boyer's (2011) concept of the modern city as a text and context of collective memory where multiple pasts and presents commingle.

[26] One of many testimonia is Tacitus's rare compliment to Augustus: he "accommodated certain relics of horrid antiquity to the spirit of the present" (*Ann.* 4.16).

[27] Buildings connected with the triumph served the deliberate purpose of perpetuating the memory of the *triumphator*; see M. Popkin's dissertation (New York University 2012), which the author is now turning into a book.

[28] For the challenge of recuperating basic aspects of content and presentation in that case, see Smith and Powell 2009.

only strategies on which Roman memoir writers relied for projecting their memories beyond the "communicative stage" of two or three generations:[29] as Flower emphasizes, the memoirs need to be read alongside inscriptions and other monuments that record and recall the same man's name in the role of "author" in the eyes of posterity.

In their spirited debate, Peter Wiseman and Karl-Joachim Hölkeskamp take up related and central issues. A concept like cultural or social memory, whether of the Romans or other civilizations, always runs the risk of being reified,[30] while the term *collective memory* tends to lump together, and even homogenize, traditions that are often diverse, varying, and variable. How exactly does the process work, and what do Roman sources tell us about it? Wiseman, who prefers "popular memory" to "collective memory" because it reflects the realities more precisely, succinctly articulates the task: "Somehow, if 'cultural memory' is to be a historically helpful concept, we have to find a way of explaining how the Roman people come to understand its own past." We are looking at the same problem here that exists with regard to "Romanization": both "cultural/collective memory" and "Romanization" can denote both process and result.[31]

Wiseman's resolute focus is on process. To that end, and in the best tradition of British empiricism (cf. Jenkyns), he presents and analyzes a dazzling and informative array of primary literary sources. They tell us, he argues, mainly four things in whose light any conceptualizing generalizations need to be modified. One concerns the memory function of monuments, especially statues: they do not simply speak for themselves, but the memory of events depends largely on the written information provided on them in inscriptions (*tituli*). Such *tituli*, then, can serve as thumbnail memoirs; perhaps presciently, their authors used them to obviate the vagaries of later hermeneutics such as viewer-response approaches, reception aesthetics, or recourse to polysemy. Whereas writing matters here, oral communication—not what the people read, which was negligible, but what they heard—was the major factor in popular memory and its transmission, which included various performances at the festivals, the *ludi scaenici*. "The composite narrative of the usable past" also included recitations in prose (cf. my earlier comments on the orators). For good reasons, the relationship of orality and writing, and its effect on memory, has held a central place, from the start, in the scholarship on memory.[32] By the documentation he provides, one of Wiseman's many contributions is to elucidate the specific cultural milieu of Rome. Finally, his concluding term *landscapes of memory* is apt because the result was multifarious rather than uniform.

In his response, Hölkeskamp takes a different route. In their influential article on the development of social memory studies and their state in 1998, Jeffrey Olick and Joyce Robbins took the multidisciplinary nature of this burgeoning field as their starting point, remarking that "perhaps as a result" it presents itself as "a nonparadigmatic, transdisciplinary, centerless enterprise."[33] In other words, a libertarian's dream. Hence, as I briefly adverted earlier, the perceived need to order the seemingly diffuse and uncoordinated nature of the memory phenomenon with some guiding

[29] Welzer 2005 offers a concise treatment of this issue, which is typically contested in memory studies. He usefully discusses "autobiographic memory" and its pitfalls throughout his book.

[30] Well discussed by Fentress and Wickham 1992, 2–8.

[31] On this definitional shortcoming and others, see, e.g., Revell 2009, 5–7 and Mattingly 2011, 38–41.

[32] J. Assmann 2011 (the German original was published in

1992) and A. Assmann 1999, esp. 179–217, have set much of the tone of the debate. The former's discussion of archaic Greece provides a good example of the necessity for cultural differentiation; (more recent) scholarly references besides Eric Havelock's work could be cited. For Rome, see also the succinct discussion of Walter 2004, 27–28, with some good textual references in n. 64.

[33] Olick and Robbins 1998, 105–106. Overcoming disciplinary compartmentalization was the explicit goal of a pioneer of memory studies, Aby Warburg (1866–1929); cf. Wuttke 1979.

conceptualizations, and *memoria* in Rome is no exception. Fundamental issues of methodology and approach are involved, and Hölkeskamp offers a vigorous defense, arguing for a more comprehensive ensemble of texts and contexts. While fully recognizing the value of Wiseman's engagement with the evidence he presents, Hölkeskamp insists on the necessity of a larger interpretive, methodological, and theoretical framework, given the complexity of possible interrelations of the phenomena and agencies that constitute memory. Such approaches are not extraneous but, as shown in their application to historical memory in various periods and cultures, provide a holistic perspective on the many manifestations of *memoria* in Rome. As for monuments, for instance, "it is a fundamental interpretive strategy [here Hölkeskamp cites Wiseman, whose wide-ranging *oeuvre* has few peers in Roman studies] to uncover the particular sort of 'memory-evoking' or 'memory-generating' capacity of individual monuments within the 'text' or 'con-text' of Roman culture." Hölkeskamp's theoretical horizon is wide and prominently includes cultural theorists such as Clifford Geertz.

As a result, Hölkeskamp's essay touches on some of the central themes of memory studies. He cites from the late Reinhard Koselleck's classic *Futures Past: On the Semantics of Historical Time* (1985): "What turns a *story* into *history* cannot be read from the 'sources' directly and immediately." But do such criteria apply to memory, too, which, though complementary, is differentiated from history today? The Romans frequently identified the two, as we have seen. And whereas Wiseman's focus is Roman popular memory, Hölkeskamp's perspective also includes the cultural leadership of the *nobiles*, whose memory management is more accessible for us because of the nature of its documentation. Did that power of theirs abide and intensify as (or because) other areas of their cultural power, and especially their influence over the control of knowledge, were eroding?[34] The dialogue between these two eminent scholars—Wiseman's chapter, in fact, is a response to Hölkeskamp's in *A Companion to the Roman Republic* (2006)—is an invitation to the readers to join in the discussion and continue it on their own.

The transmission and evolution of cultural memory, then, can take on many forms. Poetry is one of these, and not just in Roman times.[35] Today, we certainly distinguish more sharply than some Romans did (see above) between history proper and its poetic reflections, and here the much debated distinction between history and memory is helpful: poems like Vergil's *Aeneid* do not constitute history but nevertheless are carriers of cultural memory. As we have seen, Vergil programmatically introduced that aspect in his very invocation of the Muse, and subsequent Latin poets took notice. In the poetry of Statius, as Gianpiero Rosati well demonstrates, concern with memory is a constituent element that has several important aspects. To begin with, it establishes a relationship between the epic poet and his readers: the epic poet in particular recalls the memory of great deeds of the past, and the readers are called on to memorize and preserve them as part of their cultural memory or patrimony—a good example of an ongoing dynamic or, in Jan Assmann's words, "connective structure." There are corollary aspects: intertextuality, for example, can usefully be viewed from the perspective of memory because, especially in civic poetry, it "activates a relationship between texts which are an essential part of the cultural past."[36]

Of course, when such activity is undertaken by a court poet like Statius, the much discussed connection between memory and power comes to the fore. Hobsbawm, for instance, and others tend

---

[34] Rome's "cultural revolution": Wallace-Hadrill 2005 and 2008.

[35] See, for instance, A. Assmann 1999, where discussions of poets, such as Carlyle, Wordsworth, Heinrich Heine, and

others, figure prominently. As for antiquity, Homer's role in this regard is self-evident.

[36] In perhaps a more limited way, Ovid uses words such as *meminisse* to signal instances of poetic allusion; see Miller 1993.

to view commemorative practices and traditions as efforts, which are often disingenuous, to secure political power[37]—after all, memory is an important kind of knowledge, and Foucault's ideas have been influential here, too.[38] The situation is certainly applicable to Rome: who shaped and controlled "popular" and "collective" memory and the resulting identities? More generally, as Rosati argues, the memory of a victorious past is a necessity for maintaining power. In this regard, the Flavians and Statius faced a problem: unlike the Julio-Claudians, the Flavians had no mythical ancestry. The problem of memory, the "need for the past," broadly affected Flavian culture and society. The result was a construction of it by recourse to myths such as the Gigantomachy.[39] Finally, in his analysis of the first and programmatic poem of the *Silvae*, which deals with the placement of Domitian's larger-than-life equestrian statue in the Forum, Rosati also continues a central topic debated by Wiseman and Hölkeskamp. The poem, in his view, is "an exemplary case of how a monument may become a 'mnemotope', a physically concrete document of cultural memory and, at the same time, a symbolic place where the identity of a social community is found to be deposited." *Monumenta*, in short, can have several layers, especially when they are refracted in another medium, such as poetry.

Memory, as we all know, does not stand still but constantly evolves. Varro had this much in mind when he succinctly discussed the etymology of *memoria* that I partially cited earlier: "'Remember' derives from memory, since that which has remained in the mind is moved again; *memoria* can be said to come from 'remaining' like 'remainomoria'" (*Ling.* 6.49: *Meminisse a memoria, cum <in> id quod remansit in mente rursus mouetur; quae a manendo ut manimoria potest esse dicta).*[40] With all their emphasis on *topoi* and *loci*, Roman writers on rhetoric, as Diane Favro points out, were keenly aware of a mnemonic system based on movement (she aptly calls it the Memory Walk System). Fittingly, therefore, she vividly analyzes the kinetic occasions connected with memory—that is, processions and, in particular, the moving spectacle of the Roman triumph. The triumph was quintessentially Roman, and its relation to memory is multiple. There was the immediate occasion, unforgettable for all onlookers and participants. As always, the result was not just one memory—until recently, scholarly reconstructions of the triumph posited a grand composite of a largely unvarying ceremony on the basis of diverse literary and material sources, many of them wildly diachronic—but many recollections and remembrances. How, then, would a *triumphator* and his planners go about designing their version of the spectacle? We don't know of any manuals, but even if they existed, they must have been based on memories. Also, given the height and rarity this achievement presented, every attempt was made not to let it fade into the mists of diminishing communicative memory[41] but to memorialize it in art and architecture and thereby make it a part of collective cultural memory.[42] Here we come back to the issue discussed so vigorously by Wiseman and Hölkeskamp: how are some of these monuments

[37] Hobsbawm in Hobsbawm and Ranger 1983, 1–14. Others include Philippe Ariès (1914–1984), who influenced Halbwachs; see Hutton 1993, 91–105.

[38] One of Foucault's direct contributions was his coining of the phrase *contre-mémoire* for the alternative to hegemonic memories (2001, esp. 85).

[39] This also established a connection with Vergil's epic, where the theme figures prominently as a background; see P. Hardie 1986.

[40] Cf. Pfaffel 1987, 213–214. Jaeger 1997, 15 offers an alternative reading: "since there is once again movement back to that which has stayed in the mind." Her first chapter

in particular contains useful observations on the relation between *monumenta* and memory; cf. Häusle 1980, 29–63.

[41] My diction is inspired by Vergil's invocation of the Muses at the beginning of his catalogue of Latin warriors (*Aen.* 7.645–646): *et meministis enim, diuae, et memorare potestis; / ad nos uix tenuis famae perlabitur aura* ("For you remember, goddesses, and are able to bring back memory; to us hardly a weak breeze of past tales is gliding through"). Different media have different guarantors of memory: Muses for the poet, stone for triumphant leaders.

[42] For a comprehensive study of the temples built by triumphing generals and their effect on shaping triumphal memory, see now Popkin 2012.

to be read? Didn't their readings evolve, too? As can be expected, the material witnesses to triumphs are multifaceted and their memory-generating capacity may include even the creation of pseudo-memory; the triumphal scenes on the Arch of Septimius Severus, whom no historian credits with a triumph, are a case in point. Viewers in later times would assume he had actually been triumphant (and in a way he had seen to it that he was). In so many words, memory clearly played a large role at all levels of the Roman triumph, and Favro surveys some of its major ramifications.

Jessica Hughes continues the discussion with a specific analysis, from the perspective of modern and ancient approaches to memory, of a monument that incorporates many triumphal elements, the Arch of Constantine. Her chapter is a paradigm of the utility especially of modern cognitive research: its insights do not impose an artificial dimension on our understanding of Roman artifacts and monuments but add a deeper understanding and enrich our work. Memory is an intrinsic aspect of *spolia*, which involve transfer and reworking, and a more specific focus on memory can give us fresh insights into how the monument functioned in antiquity in both its immediate present and the time that followed. Scholarly treatments of a monument like Constantine's Arch often tend to posit or construct an ideal learned viewer who possessed the requisite knowledge of the multiple borrowings and adaptations at work in the resulting ensemble. Few such experts existed among the ancient viewers; instead, both individual and group responses based on particular or shared memories were operative in the responses a monument could evoke. Neither, as Hughes makes clear (reemphasizing another continuing theme in this volume), is there just one "collective memory." The notion is too static and belies the dynamic process of engagement. Modern insights from research on memory also shed a suggestive light on the arrangement of the reliefs on this arch: the juxtaposition between a historic past in the form of single, separate images and a recent past presented in the form of a continuous narrative is analogous to the structures of human autobiographical memory—a perspective that holds interest for other periods of artistic production in Rome, too.[43]

Another major area of Roman art in which memory plays an obvious role is copies. "Obvious," as so often, does not mean that much scholarly attention has been focused on this aspect amid more positivistic approaches. Anna Anguissola is filling that gap and pointing the way to future work. Copying, as she elucidates, was not a simple phenomenon in either production or reception. Even replicas were recontextualized, and the layering was yet richer and more nuanced in the many more creative adaptations. Evocations of memory ranged over a wide spectrum, including the fashioning of identity in both the private and public realm. How are we to interpret the funerary altar of one Tiberius Octavius Diadumenus, proudly featuring a descendant of the Polykleitan statue on its pedestal? And there is the overlay of commemoration and remembrance, another starting point (and still an important subject) for memory studies.[44] In the public domain in Rome, Greek masterpieces could be reshaped for multiple identities. Here it is important to realize, once more (and connecting with a persistent theme in this volume) that public art, such as the many works in the Baths of Caracalla, reached a much larger audience than even literature in recital. We come back to the basic issue of how memory worked here, and the process, as always, was far from uniform: "Copies, more than any other artifacts, functioned as the true palimpsests resulting in multiple layers of understanding, judgment, and meaningful reuse." Visual recollections, which are often cued, evolve into an "aesthetic" memory that provides a collective frame for the construction of

[43] An obvious example would be the Altar of Augustan Peace: icons from Rome's past are shown on individual panels, whereas the processions of the imperial family and the senatorial nobility reflect the recent past and the present. As Zanker 1987 has demonstrated, individual *Andachtsbilder* ("images for reflection") rather than extensive narrative (battle) friezes are characteristic of Augustan art; many of them focus on subjects from Rome's historic past.

[44] See, e.g., Le Goff 1992, Castelli 2004, Diefenbach 2007.

individual memories. A diachronic memory of the masterpieces and their creators intersected with a synchronic Roman memory of their sculptural styles—Quintilian and others famously align them with styles of rhetoric—as embodied in their replicas. Perspectives from memory again complement, rather than supplant, other approaches by moving, for instance, beyond mere viewer response, but even such responses, as we have already observed, are predominantly rooted in memory, whether individual or social.

With Lisa Mignone's chapter we enter into the world of memories of ancient Rome in modern times and the interplay between the two. The plebeian secession to the Aventine was fashioned as an icon of the quest for liberty in both Roman times and modern France, Italy, and Latin America; in fact the topic was bandied about—somewhat incorrectly, as it turned out (but then Premier Berlusconi was a main player)—at the very time of our conference. Due to its longer existence and greater global reach, "Remember the Aventine" acquired a wider currency than "Remember the Maine" or "Remember the Alamo." Here we return to the theme of history and memory: investigating the historical basis for it all in republican Rome, Mignone shows the Aventine secession of the plebs to be a case study of the invention of a tradition.[45] Sometimes history does copy itself: the stirring story of Simon Bolivar's oath on Rome's Monte Sacro (the other locale of the secession besides the Aventine) may be exactly the same kind of invention. But, as one commentator has observed, "if this did not happen, it is not important: *it should have happened.*"[46] Does this encapsulate the difference between history and memory and between doing historical research and pursuing memory studies? Hardly. Rather, Mignone's vivid account illuminates another aspect of memory: sometimes it is the *lieu* that generates *mémoire*, but at other times, *mémoire* searches for (and finds) a suitable *lieu*; Maurice Halbwachs's *La topographie légendaire des Évangiles en Terre Sainte* (1941) is still a classic on this phenomenon. Back in ancient Rome, a contributory factor to the dramatization of the event can be seen, as Mignone points out, in the emphasis of Roman theorists of memory, such as the *Rhetorica ad Herennium*, on the novel, the marvelous, and the extraordinary because those qualities created something more memorable—another significant aspect, besides those we already have noted, of the impact of Roman orators on Roman cultural memory.

That passage also figures in the wide-ranging contribution by Bernard Frischer on one of the current frontiers of the preservation and (re)construction of memory, that is "virtual" archaeology by means of digital technology. What sets Frischer's discussion apart from others in this rapidly growing and exciting field is a horizon that is so much larger than a mere recital of technological ways and means. Instead, his insightful approach is informed by many perspectives that relate to memory. They range from the need to balance subjectivity and objectivity in the use of "external memory" and the recreation of the material world to the latest neuroscientific research on memory and, ultimately, the applied learning process of students—the work that is done invariably interests and reaches a large audience today just as artifacts and monuments did in ancient Rome, as we have observed repeatedly. Combining his pioneering technical expertise with his broad humanistic interests, Frischer draws on a wide range of authors and thinkers, including the late Ernst Cassirer, and usefully applies Kandel's notion of "the mental time travel provided by memory" to his work with new 3D digital technologies. The "virtual archaeologist" has tremendous responsibilities because he or she also significantly shapes memories for the future; hence a code of professional ethics has been established that mandates the listing of all possible variants and their paradata—that is, the ways of arriving at them. Frischer's three case studies—the polychromy of the *Prima Porta Augustus*, the

[45] The title and subject of the seminal work of Hobsbawm and Ranger 1983.

[46] Rotker 1998, 42, as cited by Mignone.

portrait of Epicurus, and Hadrian's Villa at Tivoli—exemplify the many steps and considerations that are operative in the recovery of their cultural memory and its continuance. As in the case of Roman copying of Greek originals (Anguissola in this volume), the distinction between "replica" and "model" is essential, while the issue of the spatialization of knowledge has its counterpart in memory functions of the brain. In many ways, as Frischer notes, "we might consider virtual world technology an updated form of mnemotechnics," and writings such as the *Rhetorica ad Herennium* retain their relevance even in the digital age.

Another fruitful dialogue is that with professionals who do not study memory from an academic or scientific perspective but deal with it in their daily practice. We were privileged, therefore, to have Daniel Libeskind as our concluding speaker, whose *oeuvre* prominently includes the design, and at times redesign, of many landmark memorial sites and structures. By what kind of considerations is an architect guided? What are the aims, what is the vision? Libeskind's presentation of some of his signature works is as engaging, insightful, and compelling as it is lacking in pretense. Memory is a dimension that is ever-present and ubiquitous: "I think all architecture is guided by memory, informing our sense of space, of orientation, and of course relationships with each other." Libeskind eschews didacticism; instead, in his essay he leads us step by step through some of his creations and the thinking behind them just as he does, without being present, when we actually visit and go through these buildings. They are not there "to convey a singular message"; instead, they ask us to make our own associations (which, again, have a lot to do with our memories) and give visitors "the chance to make interpretations as they wish." Memory, as we saw earlier, is not just an archive or hard drive but is wired to respond to new impulses, acquire new layers, and keep working. At their best, as shown by Libeskind's work, museums and memorials reflect these aspects and thereby keep memory—and memories—vital. Memory, then, leads from the past to the future, and that is another dimension that distinguishes Libeskind's creations. And just as memory is culture-specific and requires the same consideration from its scholarly interpreters, so does each architectural *lieu de mémoire* have its own meaning and context that challenges the architect to express and convey them. It need not be a specific event; the Jewish Museum in Berlin, for instance, is embedded in a larger, more complex fabric that elicits, through its unique and stunning design, even more evocations.

In so many words, memory, by means of its many representations—speech, texts, art, and monuments—constantly invites ongoing dialogue. I am happy to say that this is exactly what happened at our conference in Rome, and I heartily invite the readers of this collection to continue that dialogue—not only with our observations and discussions but especially with Rome and her many facets and layers of memory.

PART I

ROME:

MEMORY AND MEMOIRS

1 ◆ The Memory of Rome in Rome

Richard Jenkyns

Distance lends enchantment, so they say. There is distance in time as well as space, and men have sometimes been seized by a passion for the past, which has spread an imaginative coloring over eras long gone. Whatever the ancient Romans themselves felt, their city has in more recent centuries been a conspicuous object of such sentiment. Rome, said Henry James, is "the natural home of those spirits . . . with a deep relish for the element of accumulation in the human picture and for the infinite super-positions of history."[1] In similar vein, Freud took the archaeological layers of Rome as a metaphor for the structure of human memory.[2] For us Rome is the supreme example of the city as palimpsest: Gibbon ended his *Decline and Fall* with Poggio Bracciolini, in the fifteenth century, climbing the Palatine and looking down elegiacally on grass growing and cattle grazing in the ruins of the Forum. This peroration was as much a palimpsest as the place itself, for Poggio had in turn fed on Vergil, recalling how he had described the cows and bushes on the site of Rome centuries before its foundation and looked forward from that primitive time to the imperial grandeur on which the humanist now looked back. Walter Pater gave the hero of his *Marius the Epicurean* a relish for accumulation already in the second century A.D.:

> Much which spoke of ages earlier than Nero lingered on, antique, quaint, immeasurably venerable, like the relics of the medieval city in the Paris of Lewis XIV; the work of Nero's own time had come to have that sort of old-world and picturesque interest which the work of Lewis has for ourselves; while . . . we might perhaps liken the architectural *finesses* of the archaic Hadrian to the more excellent products of our own Gothic revival.[3]

It may seem tempting to suppose such a sensibility already present in the classical city. But was it really so?

The fifth book of Cicero's *De finibus*, set in Athens at the time of the author's youth, begins with a discussion of the sentiment of place, the feelings aroused by walking on historic ground, where great men once trod. The work is a dialogue; Piso, one of the participants, remarks that our emotions are more stirred when we see the places where famous men have been; he is moved at this moment by being on the site where Plato discoursed. Even Rome—we should note the significance of that "even" (*etiam*)—has this effect: "For my part, as I looked on our own Curia . . . I used to ponder Scipio, Cato, Laelius, above all my own grandfather; such is the power of exhortation (*vis admonitionis*) inherent in places."[4] Piso is claiming, in other words, that this associative power is

[1] Henry James, *Roderick Hudson*, ch. 5.

[2] Freud 1961, 69–71.

[3] Walter Pater, *Marius the Epicurean*, ch. 11. Some other post-classical ideas of Rome are discussed by Edwards and Liversidge 1996, 7–16.

[4] Cic. *Fin.* 5.2.

something that distinguishes Athens, and a source of emotion richly available there is only scantily to be had in Rome. He refers only to the recent past of his own city; he could have evoked Numa or Cincinnatus, but he does not. He is like an American in Florence saying that he is stirred by standing where Dante and Michelangelo once stood, but back in Boston there is the memory of John F. Kennedy. A little later Lucius Cicero, the orator's cousin, takes up the theme, revealing that he has visited Pericles's tomb and the seashore where Demosthenes practiced declamation: "But such things are endless in this city; for wherever we walk, we plant our footsteps on some piece of history."[5] Writing to a friend in Athens, Cicero expressed the thought that the wise man accounts it no misery to die; "But," he added, "you are in that city in which the very walls might seem able to speak these sentiments" (*Fam.* 6.3.3 [243 Shackleton Bailey]). Seeing Rome was what inspired Gibbon to write Roman history: "Each memorable spot where Romulus stood, or Tully spoke, or Caesar fell, was at once present to my eye."[6] But Tully himself had discovered that style of feeling elsewhere.

This is indeed surprising. The *imagines* in a gentleman's house reminded him daily of his family's past. The city was full of commemorative inscriptions, sculptures, and arches. The statues of top men that Augustus placed around his Forum were perhaps an attempt to render in stone an idea of the flow and process of history, across many generations, which is a pervading theme of the *Aeneid*. Perhaps the sentiment of pilgrimage is felt more easily abroad than at home: the Londoner may be more likely to reflect that he is walking in the steps of Beethoven in Vienna, or Balzac in Paris, than to recall Shakespeare or Turner as he plods the pavements of his own town. But there may also be other reasons, as we shall discover.

Our ways of appreciating old buildings are related to our attitudes to other works of art. In the case of paintings and sculpture, the modern world has an extreme concern for authenticity: is that picture a Rembrandt or not? The enormous amount of money that hangs on the answer is a symptom and not a cause of this concern, for it depends on a belief that the purely aesthetic value of the real thing is vastly greater than even the best reproduction. Connoisseurship thus becomes highly important, and today it can draw on a wide range of techniques; it was different for the Romans (cf. Anna Anguissola's essay in this volume). How could they judge? There were no photographs, so that direct comparison was impossible, and travel was difficult. When Martial praises an antique bowl, he wonders whether it is the work of Myron, Mys, Mentor, or Polyclitus, artists who must surely have differed considerably.[7] And indeed it is hard to see how he or anyone could have known for sure that it came from a particular master's hand.

The Elder Pliny recognized the problem, recording that Phidias was said to have let his pupil Agoracritus pass as the author of several of his own works, that the maker of even a notable Venus recently dedicated by Vespasian was unknown, and that it was uncertain whether Scopas or Praxiteles was the author of the Niobe group in the Temple of Apollo.[8] It is true that descriptions of works of art often praise the maker's fabulous technique; the story of the birds trying to peck at the grapes painted by Zeuxis is a case in point, and accounts of statues constantly celebrate their

---

[5] Cic. *Fin.* 5.5. Wrenched from its context, the passage gets misunderstood. Gowers 1995, 23 puts Piso's and L. Cicero's remarks together, without ellipsis, and refers them to Rome, writing of "Cicero unable to walk the streets without walking on some piece of history"; she thus has him saying more or less the opposite of what he actually says. Edwards 1996, 29 quotes Piso, assuming that what he applies to Athens he applies equally to Rome. Ash 2007 uses L. Cicero's words as an epigraph to an article on Rome, without comment and

so without indication that they refer to the special quality of Athens.

[6] Gibbon 1897, 267.

[7] Mart. 8.50.1–2.

[8] Plin. *HN* 36.4.17, 26, 28.

lifelike realism. That might seem to suggest a special capacity possessed by only a very few artists, who would be appropriately commemorated, but in practice even superlative works often remained anonymous, and there was little concern to preserve the memory of their creators. Pausanias named the sculptors of the pediments at Olympia and gave one of them as Phidias, but he was wrong; the style and date make the attributions impossible.[9] That reminds us of another likelihood: that anonymous works got attributed to famous sculptors, as houses to Wren and witticisms to Wilde.

The idea that seeing an actual Bernini or Velasquez is much better than even the finest reproduction or the most expert photograph draws partly on the belief that the master's brush or chisel is unique and inimitable, partly on the faith that the object in itself, present to the eye, offers an intensity of experience unobtainable at second hand. Such an outlook also encourages a concern for texture, patina, and the effects of maturation, a concern that affects the appreciation of buildings also. As a common attitude, it may be comparatively recent. When Ruskin asserted that no building was at its prime until several centuries had passed over it, he meant to provoke complacency; when he preferred rugged walls and moldering sculpture to "the beautiful new parapet by Mr Scott, with a gross of Kings sent down from Kensington," he was setting himself against the most successful architect and restorer of his time.[10] William Morris founded the Society for the Preservation of Ancient Buildings to resist destructive restoration and the scraping of church interiors—in other words, to guard the texture that buildings have acquired through time. Ironically, whereas Morris's forward-aspiring socialism now seems dated, his sense of the past looks ahead to the taste of the twentieth century.

We might expect that societies which possess few old things would have an especial care for their authentic oldness, but in practice it seems that a critical mass is needed before much appreciation of accretion and the texture of time can develop. Americans, for example, have not always treated their most historic buildings with the tenderness that we might have anticipated. In Boston, Paul Revere's house, which survived into the twentieth century, somewhat altered, is now externally a modern replica of the supposed original, neither authentic nor appealing to the eye. The Governor's Palace at Santa Fe, with origins supposedly in the seventeenth century, and again much altered, now has a modern façade not even in adobe but in concrete pretending to be adobe. The authentic eighteenth-century ordonnance of the College of William and Mary at Williamsburg was replaced by a reproduction of an earlier and inferior design, attributed to Wren. The Romans did not share this taste for replication: they did not have the evidence for it, and they assumed that a new building would be better than the old. What they did lack, for the most part, was the feeling that the scars and wrinkles of age were a proper part of a building's maturation.[11]

And yet *antiquus*, "ancient," was commonly a term of praise. It could be attached approvingly to living people: *homines antiqui* were men of the good old stamp.[12] Ennius had declared, in a famous line, *moribus antiquis stat res Romana virisque* ("Rome stands upon its ancient manners and men").[13] *Antiquus* here qualifies both nouns: it is upon the combination of oldness in the people and in their institutions that national greatness rests. Age imparted respect, venerability, and even

[9] Paus. 5.10.

[10] John Ruskin, *The Seven Lamps of Architecture*, ch. 6, para. 16; *The Stones of Venice* vol. 2, ch. 4, sect. 10, footnote added to the Travellers' Edition.

[11] The Renaissance popes had no qualms about pulling down the Basilica of St. Peter's, a thousand years old, for the sake of something bigger. The most ancient part of Canterbury Cathedral, the eleventh-century northwest tower, was demolished in the 1840s and replaced with a replica of the southwest tower for symmetry's sake. Half a century later the sacrifice would probably have seemed unendurable.

[12] Cic. *Rosc. Am.* 26.

[13] Enn. *Ann.* 156 Sk.

sanctity. Cicero referred to "the most ancient and eminent men" as though the two adjectives made a natural pair, like eggs and bacon.[14] He described the Temple of Juno on Samos as "most ancient and most noble"; its sack was therefore the more shocking.[15] Again, the two epithets have a natural kinship. He expressed outrage that Verres had looted statues from Apollo's temple on Delos, a place *tam antiquo tam sancto tam religioso* ("so ancient, so sacred, so holy").[16] The audience at a trial, he said, expect the advocate to draw "examples from old memories, from monuments and letters, full of dignity, full of antiquity," for these have the greatest authority and give most pleasure.[17] He told Atticus that the *patria* was "our most ancient and sacred parent"; and in a philosophical work he declared that "antiquity approaches nearest to the gods."[18]

Sometimes the love of the past acquired a romantic tinge. In his *Fasti*, Ovid enjoyed the thought of *sacra . . . annalibus eruta priscis* ("sacred matters dug up from annals of yore");[19] the influence of Vergil, with his sense of the depth of the past, is strong upon him here. Statius appealed to "early Story and the secret Oldness of the world" (*Fama prior mundique arcana Vetustas*) to inspire his tale.[20] Livy confessed that as he wrote about bygone events his spirit in some way became ancient (*antiquus*), and a *religio* restrained him from regarding what olden sages had thought worth attention as undeserving of record in his own annals.[21] There is perhaps a touch of ambivalence here; there is at least a recognition that an antique mind needs some defending. And indeed the pervading fondness for the old did stir protest from time to time. Tacitus ended a book of his *Annals* with the reflection that "we exalt the old, incurious about recent times."[22] Horace chafed at readers' unthinking preference for earlier poetry, as for ancient laws and moldering documents: "So greatly sanctified (*sanctum*) is every old poem."[23] Where would we be, he adds, if the Greeks had hated newness as we do?[24] Indeed, the Greeks had a sense of their recentness: Plato relates that an Egyptian priest told Solon, "You Greeks are always children. . . . You are all young in your souls, and have in them no ancient belief handed down by old tradition nor any knowledge that is hoary with age."[25] By contrast, the Romans laid weight upon *mos* or *mores*—custom, habit, tradition—with Ennius's line asserting *antiqui mores* as the basis of their state and Vergil presenting Roman governance as a work of accretion, building *mos* upon peace.[26]

Did the Romans' fondness for affecting the ancients ever affect their attitude to architecture? In one place Martial seems to say so. Comparing the fashionable preference for older writers over contemporaries to people's attitude to buildings, he wrote, "Thus we seek out the old shade of the insensible Pompey, thus old men praise Catulus' cheaply built temple."[27] But the poem is tendentious, and besides, Martial is presenting an outlook that he offers up to ridicule. His epigram may indicate the rarity of the attitude that he ascribes to those elderly gentlemen rather than its ubiquity. When a building was genuinely ancient, the fact was not always noticed: despite Cicero's appeals

[14] Cic. *Verr.* 2.3.210 (*antiquissimorum clarissimorumque hominum*).

[15] Cic. *Verr.* 2.1.50 (*antiquissimi et nobilissimi*).

[16] Cic. *Verr.* 2.1.47.

[17] Cic. *Verr.* 2.3.209.

[18] Cic. *Att.* 9.9.2; *Leg.* 2.27.

[19] Ov. *Fast.* 1.7.

[20] Stat. *Theb.* 4.32.

[21] Livy 43.13.2.

[22] Tac. *Ann.* 2.88.

[23] Hor. *Epist.* 2.1.22–27, 54, 63–65, 76–78.

[24] Hor. *Epist.* 2.1.90–92.

[25] Pl. *Ti.* 22b.

[26] Verg. *Aen.* 6.850.

[27] Mart. 5.10.5–6.

to the emotional force of antiquity in his speeches against Verres, when he came to the Temple of Minerva at Syracuse, already three and a half centuries old, he did not mention its age.[28] And when writers expressed a taste for the simplicity of ancient shrines, the feeling was usually moral rather than aesthetic: "It is worthwhile," wrote Sallust, "after you have made yourself acquainted with town and country houses built up in the form of cities, to visit the temples of the gods made by our ancestors, the most religious of mankind. Those men adorned the gods' shrines with their piety, their houses with their glory."[29] The historian gives no sign of taking visual pleasure in those simple sacred places: their value lies in the abstract fact of devotion, not in its rude expression in plaster, wood, or stone. In the metropolis itself Romulus's Cottage held a special place: its smallness, humility, and the supposed antiquity of its origins expressive amid so much grandeur, but there is little sign that people found it charming. Its physical form will not have breathed antiquity; being made of reeds, it regularly needed to be restored after damage by time and weather.[30]

By the fourth century A.D., Rome possessed historic monuments of the grandest kind, and yet it is still hard to find a sense of multiplied accumulation. Ammianus describes Constantius's visit to Rome: the emperor surveys the city's wonders; nothing that he sees is new and nothing extremely old.[31] The earliest building that Ammianus names is the Theater of Pompey; otherwise everything comes from that era which runs from the Flavians to the Antonines. The narrative depicts a progress through the city, and so nothing is said about interiors; that may account, at least in part, for the historian's near silence about some great works that did not make so much outward show: there is a brief reference to the vastness of the bathhouses, but none is named, and there is not a word on the Christian basilicas (though these were dispersed at the edges of the city). The most striking omission, to the modern reader, is the Basilica of Maxentius, today dominating the Forum. Somehow Constantius—or Ammianus—appears barely to see the massive monuments of modernity. But though the imperial visitor seems almost to ignore the present, his mind does not plunge into the abyss of time either. There had been, in this conception, a single great age of Roman architecture; the idea that Rome had been formed, layer by layer and through many centuries, is absent. The concept of the eternal city (a phrase recurrent in Ammianus) is a concept of indefinite duration in the future, not of a past unfathomably deep. Meanwhile, it is the great works of one century, rather than the multiplied imagining of many, that stirs the eminent spectator's heart.

Dionysius of Halicarnassus wrote that the austere style, found in Pindar and Thucydides, allowed "harsh and dissonant juxtapositions . . . as when stones are selected and laid together in buildings, with their sides not squared off or polished smooth, but remaining unworked and coarse-hewn"; this style is grand and unadorned "and its beauty lies in its quality of antiquity (ἀρχαϊσμός) and its patina (πίνος)."[32] Here is a feeling both for rugged texture on buildings and for the charms of the ageing process. The two feelings do not exactly come together, as the metaphor shifts from architecture to sculpture;[33] buildings are nobly rude and statues nobly old. Nevertheless, this is a sensibility that finds visual pleasure in roughness and the work of time. Yet it does not emerge in Dionysius's history of Rome, a city that he praises instead for a different kind of newness: the constant influx of other peoples. A feeling for the patina of age is implicit in Vergil's encapsulation of the essence of Italy, "rivers flowing below ancient walls," and in another way perhaps in Lucretius's

---

[28] Cic. *Verr.* 2.4.122.

[29] Sall. *Cat.* 12.3.

[30] Dion. Hal. *Ant. Rom.* 1.79.11.

[31] Amm. Marc. 16.10.13–15.

[32] Dion. Hal. *Synth.* 22. He applies the metaphor of patina to Pindar again at *Dem.* 39.

[33] Hornblower 2004, 359.

image of the flower growing between the stones: so many of the deeds of men are forgotten, "nor do they bloom anywhere, grafted in the eternal monuments of fame."[34] But such notes are not common.

Augustus's boast that he had found Rome brick and left it marble showed a concern with surface, not oldness or patina.[35] An exception to the sleekness of his public works was the Temple of the Great Mother, rebuilt in tufa, without marble facing, as a sign, it would seem, of the peculiar and hispid character of her cult.[36] Ovid wrote that under Augustus "shrines feel no age (*senectus*)"; it was meant for praise.[37] Elsewhere in the *Fasti* he did allow Janus to appreciate antiquity, but only while praising modernity the more: we gods delight also in these new golden temples, however much we approve the old ones—such majesty befits a god; we praise the years of old but make use of present years; each is a habit equally worthy to be kept.[38] Seneca wrote of Augustan Rome, "Public works were ravaged by fire, but better ones arose than those consumed."[39] He knew of a Greek who hated Rome but was sorry to hear about fires there because finer buildings would arise from the ruins. Such optimism about the construction business stands in striking contrast to that harking back to the good old days which infuses so much Latin prose. Cicero had assured Catulus that his rebuilding of the Capitol was very beautiful and indeed more magnificent than what had perished; and just as the restoration had surpassed the original, he should decorate it more richly, so that the flames might seem to have been of divine origin, ordained not to destroy the Temple of Jupiter Best and Greatest but so that the place might be nobler and more glorious than before.[40] Of course, the desire to flatter may distort, but Cicero was addressing Catulus in a public speech, and his words needed to have a broad appeal; it remains notable that he should describe the temple's destruction as an opportunity for improvement, with no sense of irremediable or indeed of any loss.

Tacitus lamented that the great fire in Nero's reign had destroyed things of most ancient sanctity (*vetustissima religione*), among which were Servius Tullius's Temple of Luna, Evander's Altar of Hercules, Romulus's Temple of Jupiter Stator, the Palace of Numa, and the shrine of Vesta with the Penates of the Roman people.[41] It is the sheer oldness of these holy places and of the associations clinging to them that makes the sense of violation; the feeling is sacral and patriotic rather than aesthetic. The historian does not refer to the age of the actual structures that had been obliterated; they cannot have been as old as the legendary names attached to them: rather, it is their *religio* that stretches back so deep into the past. Many examples of Greek art won by conquest perished, he continues (and here there is indeed an expression of artistic loss), as well as "ancient and undamaged monuments of genius," by which he seems to mean books burnt in the library, "so that for all the great beauty of the newly arising city older people remembered much that could not be repaired."[42] And what were these irrevocable losses? Statues and pictures, it seems, literature, venerable objects and associations; but architecture, as such, is missing from the list. Indeed, even those elderly nostalgics concede the beauty of the reconstruction. The ravaged area was rebuilt, Tacitus adds, with broad and regular streets and edifices of good stone: "These things, accepted for their utility, also

[34] Verg. *G.* 2.157; Lucr. 5.328–329 (cf. West 1969, 2).

[35] Suet. *Aug.* 28.3.

[36] Beard, North, and Price 1998, 1:198. Columns of peperino are attributed to the Augustan rebuilding (Coarelli 2007, 136).

[37] Ov. *Fast.* 2.61.

[38] Ov. *Fast.* 1.223–226.

[39] Sen. *Ben.* 6.32.3.

[40] Cic. *Verr.* 2.4.69.

[41] Tac. *Ann.* 15.41.

[42] Tac. *Ann.* 15.41.

made the new city handsome."[43] If anyone missed a former picturesqueness or familiar irregularity, Tacitus does not record it.

Cicero told his fellow citizens that their ancestors had awarded statues to many, tombs to few: "But statues perish through tempest, violence and age, whereas the sanctity of tombs is in the very soil . . . and so, as other things are blotted out, tombs become the more sanctified by their age."[44] The orator's interest is in memory and association rather than visible form: the place of ancient burial is hallowed; the statue's weathered aspect is not venerable, merely regrettable. In his *Republic* he made much of Ennius's line about Rome's good old men and customs. Again, it is the antiquity of tradition, not the oldness of objects, that he celebrates. Indeed, he compares the state to a beautiful painting now fading with age, *iam evanescentem vetustate.*[45] That may sound to us romantic, but Cicero does not mean it so: he rebukes the present generation for not having renewed it in its original colors. Brightness and newness are preferred to both the authenticity of the work itself and the charm of time's action upon it.

The Younger Pliny observed that old age (*senectus*) was "venerable in a man, sacred in cities." Sure enough, he was writing to a friend who was going to Greece, and he advised how to respond to that glamorous and historic land: "You should pay honor to antiquity, to mighty deeds, even to legends."[46] Events, story, and memory are the things to stir the spirit, it seems, rather than the visible appearance of the past. Indeed, if we press the comparison with human life, it implies decline, and Rome would be too vigorous to be likened to senescence. When Pliny was told by soothsayers to rebuild a temple of Ceres in bigger and better style, he observed that the existing structure was "old and cramped enough" and looked forward to acting "liberally and religiously" in putting up the most beautiful temple that he could, ordering marble for floor, walls, and columns; he would also need a new statue of the goddess, he added, as the old wooden one had bits broken off.[47] He shows no sense that the ancient image might wear the sanctity of time or have earned affection through long familiarity; there is none of the battered teddy-bear feeling. Later, as governor of Bithynia, he wrote to the emperor for advice on a very ancient temple that needed to be rebuilt or moved. Could it be shifted without religious impropriety?[48] It was the theology of the matter that troubled him, not the loss of visible antiquity.

Given their taste for antiquity and tradition, we may be surprised that the Romans did not make more of their capital as the habitation of historic memory. In part it may have been that for them Rome was a temporary and changeable city; houses and even temples were frequently consumed by fire, and Roman authors time and again write about the collapse of buildings as a regular feature of urban life, in the assumption that the sight will be well known to any reader.[49] In Rome, moreover, it was not only the minor buildings and the ordinary street scene that were in constant flux. In modern Europe great cities have usually retained some ancient and prominent monuments at their heart. For that matter, when Cicero and Horace were in Athens, they could lift their eyes to an Acropolis already several centuries old. But if Cicero looked up at the Temple of Jupiter, he saw Catulus's reconstruction, and if Horace looked up at the Palatine, he saw its skyline reshaped by Augustus

[43] Tac. *Ann.* 15.43.

[44] Cic. *Phil.* 9.14.

[45] Cic. *Rep.* 5.1–2.

[46] Plin. *Ep.* 8.24.

[47] Plin. *Ep.* 9.39.

[48] Plin. *Ep.* 10.49.

[49] The fire in Nero's reign is the most famous, but for other major conflagrations, see, e.g., Livy 30.26.5 and 35.40.8; Dio Cass. 55.26; Vell. Pat. 2.130; Suet. *Clau.* 18, *Vesp.* 8, *Tit.* 8, *Dom.* 5.

When Tacitus wrote his *Annals*, the Temple of Jupiter had been remade yet again. Below the hills, the newer the constructions, on the whole the more interesting they were. Strabo, inspecting Rome with an outsider's eye in the reign of Augustus, devoted almost all his space to the recent works on the Campus Martius, after which one sentence is enough for what he calls "the old Forum."[50]

Other lands, perhaps, were different. Later Romans were keenly conscious that their ancestors' expansion into the Greek south of Italy had been an exciting and unsettling experience, introducing them to high culture and luxury, to elegances and temptations barely known before. The taking of Tarentum and the capture of Syracuse had been critical moments. Livy described the victor's gaze over Syracuse: "When Marcellus entered the walls and could see from the higher ground about the most beautiful of all cities of that time laid out before his eyes, he is said to have wept, partly with joy at having performed so great a feat, partly at the city's ancient (*vetustus*) glory."[51] Although Livy does not directly say that Marcellus grieved at the fate of beauty, he surely implies as much; in the case of the city's glory it seems to be length of history, the fact of age itself, that provokes those tears. Is there any hint of the beauty and patina of antiquity? We might say that the loveliness of the city's form is one matter, the duration of its power another, and that the historian keeps them apart. Alternatively, we might feel that his picture of Syracuse is a broad romantic evocation of age and beauty and that it is artificial to hold the one thing separate from the other. It is hard to tell. A hundred years later, Silius Italicus, in his versified account of Marcellus at Syracuse, does pronounce, *hic sancta vetustas artificum manibus* ("Here oldness was sanctified by the work of artists' hands").[52] After extolling the magnificence of the city's monuments, parks, and palaces, the poet praises the fabulous works of painting, sculpture, and the applied arts, not brought from abroad and yet matching Corinth, Babylon and Tyre, Pergamum and Egypt. Readers will have felt the contrast with Rome, which had needed to import so much of its splendor.[53] In Livy's version a citizen of Syracuse had told Marcellus, "The gods have given you the glory of capturing the noblest and most beautiful of Greek cities."[54] Silius too recreates the impact of Greece upon a Roman of the third century. It was in Magna Graecia, in Rome's "near abroad," that oldness was beautified and sanctified by art.

At least until the later first century A.D. a passion for the physical city of Rome was not chiefly a passion for its visible fabric but a testimony to the pure potency of place. Cicero was appalled when Pompey's strategy for fighting Julius Caesar in 49 B.C. led to his quitting the capital. Again and again in his letters to Atticus at this time he insisted that *urbs* is *patria*, and that the abandonment of Rome was the supreme disgrace.[55] He imagined the argument between Pompey and himself: "'The state', he says, 'does not consist of walls.' But it does consist of altars and hearths."[56] In Cicero's mind, the other man's claim that the walls and houses of the city were not the nation missed the point: what mattered was the presence of Rome as place and possession, something at once more abstract and more actually and solidly permanent, both public and private, domestic and spiritual. One of the spurious letters of Brutus to Cicero argues against the orator: it is the condition of affairs, not the place, that ought to matter. The supposed Brutus takes the high philosophical line: "I cannot be an exile anywhere as long as I hate to be a slave . . . wherever I may live as a free man, that I will consider to be Rome for me."[57]

[50] Strab. 5.3.8; *arkhaios* is his word.

[51] Livy 25.24.11.

[52] Sil. *Pun.* 14.643–644.

[53] Sil. *Pun.* 14.641–664.

[54] Livy 25.29.5.

[55] Cic. *Att.* 7.21.2, 8.2.2, 8.3.3, 9.6.2.

[56] Cic. *Att.* 7.11.3.

[57] *Ep. Brut.* 1.16.6, 8.

Similarly, Lucan imagined the defeated Pompey telling the people of Lesbos what their island, which had given refuge to his wife, had meant to him: "Here were my sacred home and my dear household gods; here for me was Rome."[58] But this way of speaking carries the germ of its own refutation, like Vergil's petulant Corydon telling himself, "You will find another Alexis if this one disdains you."[59] The shepherd's language reveals that, in truth, only Alexis will do; and so it was with Rome. Indeed, Vergil understood this mysterious power of presence. Aeneas receives two visions of the future: he is shown the great men of Rome in the underworld, and he sees action and movement in the city—the triumphal procession of Caesar Augustus, depicted on the shield—but not the towers, temples, and palaces of Augustus's capital; the only such structure that is specifically mentioned is the new Temple to Apollo (8.720). On the other hand, it is profoundly important, in some obscure way, that he should walk upon the site of Rome, and the poet arranges for him to be brought there by means that show almost ostentatiously that his visit lacks a practical purpose. Rome will be its own place, not Troy reborn; Vergil invites us to contrast Helenus, earlier in the poem, who has made his new town into a mimic Troy, with a replica of the town and the Scaean Gate (smaller than the original), a tomb of Hector (empty of his body), and a poor stream dignified with the name Xanthus.[60] This thin nostalgia illustrates the futility of trying to create a lost home elsewhere; a city's being is inseparable from the ground on which it stands.

It was not only the buildings of Rome that were changeable; there were the inhabitants too. Other states boasted, if they could, that their people were primordially indigenous, even born of the earth, like the first men and women of Athens and Thebes.[61] By contrast, it was an old idea that Romulus had populated his town with outcasts and refugees. Other Italian places treasured a deep continuity. Recalling the Perusine War, Propertius lamented the "hearths of the ancient Etruscan people overthrown."[62] Livy drew pathos from the expulsion of the people of Alba from the place that had been their home for four hundred years.[63] Dionysius has the Albans declare the contrast: their race has continued the same from their foundation, whereas the Romans have corrupted their purity by admitting Tuscans, Sabines, and others. The Romans reply that far from being ashamed of the fact, they are proud of having opened up their city to outsiders.[64]

Whereas Livy turned to Alba for the evocation of perennity, Vergil looked to the countryside, representing the farmer's life as eternal, in contrast to perishable kingdoms and the affairs of Rome.[65] Cicero found the strongest sense of duration in his hometown; his family's truly ancient roots, he said, were in Arpinum.[66] Juvenal's Umbricius was brought up on the Aventine.[67] It is part of the outrage that this poem enjoys that the native Roman is driven out while the foreigner thrives, but the poet makes no play with the idea that his family had been there for generations. Rather, the idea that the young Umbricius had been "nurtured on the Sabine olive" may suggest that, like Cicero and like Juvenal himself, he had an ancestry in one of the country towns of Italy.[68]

---

[58] Luc. 8.132–133.

[59] Verg. *Ecl.* 2.73.

[60] Verg. *Aen.* 3.302–305, 349–351.

[61] Purcell 1994, 650–651.

[62] Prop. 2.1.29.

[63] Livy 1.29.6.

[64] Dion. Hal. *Ant. Rom.* 3.10.4–5, 3.11.4.

[65] Verg. *G.* 2.495–498, 513, 532–538.

[66] Cic. *Leg.* 2.3.

[67] Juv. 3.84.

[68] Juv. 3.85.

For an analogy to the way in which the city of Rome lived in the ancient mind, we should not turn to the Rome of today or to those other cities where the past most extensively survives. We might sooner think of London, a very old city whose oldness is only occasionally perceptible, or of New York, which though new by Old World standards is rather old by the standard of the New. Yet it has preserved little from before 1850 and almost nothing from before 1800. Instead, its tradition is to be untraditional, and its most enduring characteristic has been dynamic change. In its own way, Rome was for centuries quite like that. Aelius Aristides described the megalopolis of the second century A.D. as not only "poured over" the ground but rising up into the air, its edifices like cliffs, built up like a strong man carrying another on his shoulders. Vergil had evoked the new city of Carthage, its towers thrusting up, its walls rising, its fortifications huge and threatening, its cranes reaching to the sky.[69] This is an excited and delighting picture, presenting one poet's view of how a great and growing city should be imagined.

It is with Vergil too that the palimpsestic idea of Rome originates. As Poggio and Gibbon knew, we can fix the moment of that beginning: in the 20s B.C., when Vergil wrote the eighth book of the *Aeneid.* Already in the *Georgics* he had shown a feeling for the past and for process; his celebration of Italy captures its quality in two brief pictures:[70]

> *tot congesta manu praeruptis oppida saxis*
> *fluminaque antiquos subterlabentia muros.*

So many towns piled up by man's hand on precipitous rocks and rivers gliding below ancient walls.

Here nature and culture, man and landscape are brought together; the flow of waters, changeless and yet changing with every moment, passes under walls grown ancient through the flow of time. Later in the poem we read, *multosque per annos stat fortuna domus et avi numerantur avorum* ("the fortune of the house stands firm for many years and grandfathers' grandfathers are numbered up").[71] This describes, of all things, a beehive; but indeed through this idea of the changing generations in their unchanging abode the poet likens these insects' history to human experience. In the *Aeneid* the Trojans go to cut down some trees: *itur in antiquam silvam, stabula alta ferarum* ("They go into the ancient wood, the deep lairs of beasts").[72] It is a simple enough action, but Vergil gives it a solemn resonance. His verb is impersonal (literally "there is a going"), the woods are *altus,* that word meaning both "high" and "deep." He conveys an awareness that movement in space can also seem like movement in time, into ancientness. He also feels the romance of the past. Homer had invoked the Muses before his catalogue of the ships, asserting that they are present and know everything, whereas we know nothing.[73] Before his own catalogue of the Italian forces Vergil softens that sharp distinction: the Muses remember and recall (even for them these events are bygone), whereas "to us there wafts only a thin breeze of tale."[74] There is a pleasing melancholy in that thought, along with a sense of great distance.

When the Trojans reach the mouth of the Tiber, they see forest and hear birdsong, the river bursting out from the shadowed thickness of the trees.[75] In Vergil's time this was one of the world's

---

[69] Aristid. 26.8; Verg. *Aen.* 1.437, 4.86–489.

[70] Verg. *G.* 2.156–157.

[71] Verg. *G.* 4.208–209.

[72] Verg. *Aen.* 6.179.

[73] Hom. *Il.* 2.485–486.

[74] Verg. *Aen.* 7.646.

[75] Verg. *Aen.* 7.29–36.

busiest places: Ostia was the palimpsest that man had inscribed upon the primeval landscape. When Aeneas and his party row upstream, they again penetrate a deep woodland, and the notoriously turbulent Tiber has been stilled by miracle; thus in two separate ways the river familiar to the poet's Roman readers has been made strange.[76] When Evander takes the hero over what neither of them knows will be the site of future Rome, we are repeatedly reminded of the contrast between past and present: the massive wood on the flanks of the Palatine, the Capitol now golden but then rough scrubland, and those cattle in the Forum.[77]

Meanwhile, Vergil has also been evolving an awareness of the many layers of the past. In the traditions that he inherited, Latinus was a warrior; he altered the story, changing the king into an old man, past fighting age. And he associates Latinus with a deeper past, introducing him as son of Faunus, who is son of Picus, who is son of Saturn, that deity older than Jupiter himself. His palace, likewise, expresses antiquity and origins: it contains images of ancient kings, Italus and Sabinus, founders of their peoples, and again Picus and primeval Saturn. Yet it has long been recognized that the description also suggests Rome and the future Temple of Jupiter on the Capitol. This palace contains not only objects but also memory and history, stretching both forward and back from the poem's present.[78] The stories of Evander, another old man, sound the depths of time, telling of an age of bleak, primitive habitation even before Saturn came to Italy, of Saturn's reign there and his disappearance, of Albula, the "true name" of the Tiber, lost long ago.[79]

The idea that Vergil developed in the *Georgics*, and especially in the seventh and eighth books of the *Aeneid*, of the interrelationship between man, land, nature, nation, locality, identity, time, and history is among his most original achievements. It has endured as a permanent element of the inheritance of the West, to be rediscovered by later generations from time to time. Aspects of it enchanted the other poets of his own day. Let us look closer at that irresistible detail—the cows:[80]

passimque armenta videbant
Romanoque Foro et lautis mugire Carinis.

And they saw all around cattle lowing in the Roman Forum and the smart Carinae.

The words blend simple humor with sophisticated expression: the charm lies partly in the piquancy of *lautus*, "chic" or "smart," a word from the prose of modern life, dropped like a dash of tabasco into the epic idyll, partly in the running together of different ages, so that the ancient livestock seem to roam in the modern city.

The passage was to be echoed by Propertius and Tibullus immediately, later by Ovid three times[81] (and by Statius; see Rosati in this volume). The odd thing is that none of these elegists matches the epic poet's lightness of touch, for they all spoil what they have taken by again separating the two epochs that Vergil had collapsed into one, spelling out that cattle then occupied what is now urban Rome, and thus losing half his wit. But they were mesmerized: Vergil had found a new way of imagining Rome so entrancing that they had to make it their own. Ovid first introduced those cattle in the *Art of Love*, contrasting the rude simplicity of the past with the cultivated, golden Rome of

---

[76] Verg. *Aen.* 8.86–96.

[77] Verg. *Aen.* 8.337–361.

[78] Verg. *Aen.* 7.47–49, 7.177–179 (on allusion to the Capitoline Temple, Camps 1959, 54; Camps 1969, 153–154).

[79] Verg. *Aen.* 8.314–332.

[80] Verg. *Aen.* 8.360–361. On the diction of *lautus*, Eden 1975, ad loc.

[81] Prop. 4.1.3–4, 4.9.19–20; Tib. 2.5.25, 55–56; Ov. *Ars am.* 3.119–120, *Fast.* 1.243–244, 5.93–94.

his own day: "The Palatine that now shines, with Phoebus and our leaders upon it, what was it but pasture for oxen bred for the plough?"[82] Whatever an author's outlook, Vergil's cows had become inescapably part of his conception of the city.

What these poets do understand is that Vergil's contrasts of golden Rome with its humble prehistory are not moralistic; he does not harry us into agreeing that the decent poverty of the past was better than the splendor of the present, or the reverse. Indeed, one of the minor pleasures of the passage is that, despite the play of a delighted fancy over the scene, and although we feel the impress of an original and personal sensibility, the poet remains at once individual and opaque. His concern is not to manipulate the reader but to show that history's transformations are interesting for their own sake, and to convey the fascination of feeling the bones beneath the skin. A further attraction for other poets was the delicacy of his tone—a genuine affection for a vanished world, an admiration that does not exclude touches of quaintness and humor. He was original in his feeling for the many strata of the past, those multiplied superpositions in which Henry James's hero would one day rejoice. He also set the prehistory of Rome against the present with a new kind of charm and vividness. What he does not quite do is to bring these two things together. He applies the idea of multiplicity to story, society, customs, and events. His picture of physical Rome itself is more like a palimpsest in the strict sense: two layers only, one written on top of the other. He does not see the element of accumulation in the visible fabric of the city; it was not yet there to be seen. Poggio and Gibbon and Pater could draw upon Vergil but also upon more than a millennium and a half of further history, during which Rome had gone through vicissitudes that the poet could not have imagined, while its built inheritance had been immeasurably and diversely enriched. Vergil invented many things, but even he could not invent the future.

---

[82] Ov. *Ars am.* 3.119–120.

2 ◆ Memory and Memoirs in Republican Rome

Harriet I. Flower

In memory of Ernst Badian (1925–2011)[1]

> It took a ruthlessly ambitious and socially impregnable man to write openly *de vita sua*.
>
> Badian 1966, 23

In what follows I will explore a time when autobiographical writing first emerged in republican Rome.[2] It is not easy for most of us to imagine a world in which politicians did not write their autobiographies, often hefty tomes produced soon after the events they describe and characterized by intricate personal details. In Roman republican culture, however, self-representation had not traditionally taken the form of a published narrative centered on the life of an individual. Rather, the ultimate accolades an elite Roman aspired to were expressed in the words of others and reached a definitive climax in the funeral oration (*laudatio*) proclaimed by a relative from the speakers' platform in the Forum. This paper will examine when, how, and why the publication of an autobiographical account in Latin first happened. In a specific and singular context, at the very end of the second century B.C., a Roman politician decided to write about his life; writing his own story was both a literary and political innovation.

1. Background

The culture of the Roman office-holding families (the *nobiles*) consistently valued accountability in the sense of "giving an account" of one's actions and values.[3] Such "accounts" were to be found in speeches delivered by magistrates in office, whether before the people, the Senate, or the soldiers.[4] Accounts of achievements were common at the end of a year in office or of a military campaign, especially when the distinctive honor of a triumph was being requested. The earliest speeches to be published were funeral eulogies (*laudationes*) that described the deeds of the recently deceased and delineated his place amongst the office holding members of his family.[5] Such summaries of

---

[1] Badian 1966, 37 n. 135 dismisses Catulus's work as insignificant. Although my argument is very different, I dedicate this essay as a tribute to his memory.

[2] I would like to thank the following for their help and encouragement: Francis Cairns, Denis Feeney, Michael Flower, Karl Galinsky, Alain Gowing, Stephen Hines, John Marincola, Chris Pelling, Christopher Smith, and Peter Wiseman. Versions of this chapter were delivered at the University of Washington (Seattle), University of Indiana (Bloomington), American Academy in Rome, and Florida State University (Tallahassee). I have greatly benefited from audience discussion in each venue.

[3] Walter 2004 is the best general overview, but see H. I. Flower 2004 on the culture of spectacle and Baier 2005, 123, 142 on avoiding autobiography in traditional Roman self-representation.

[4] Malcovati 1976 is the standard edition of the fragments. See Morstein-Marx 2004 for the *contio*.

[5] See Kierdorf 1980 for the fragments and H. I. Flower 1996, 128–158 for discussion.

careers were also used to compose the inscriptions on tombs and the labels for wax ancestor masks (*imagines*) in the *atria* of family houses.[6] In other words, a politician would advertise his political career and its high points in a variety of rhetorical venues during his lifetime; after his death his family would commemorate his accomplishments in traditionally Roman settings.

Meanwhile, autobiographical elements can be traced from the very beginnings of Latin literature. Early historical writing was dominated by politicians, many of whom had played a direct role in some of the events they described. Fabius Pictor and Cincius Alimentus, who were the first Romans to write prose histories in Greek, had both served against Hannibal and witnessed key moments of the Second Punic War in person.[7] They wrote "history" from the vantage point of privileged participants about the experiences of their own generation of Romans. Cato the censor was the author of the first historical work composed in Latin, the *Origines*.[8] Despite its nominal focus on local history in Italy, this sprawling work contained a number of autobiographical sections and speeches given by Cato. It is striking how much detailed information survives about Cato, including many direct quotations, which makes his life the best documented in the second century B.C. Yet even he did not write an account of his life as a discrete topic in its own right.

In the late second century B.C., autobiographical elements could be found in the works of leading writers, notably L. Calpurnius Piso Frugi (cos. 133 B.C.), C. Fannius (who fought against Carthage side by side with Tiberius Gracchus), and perhaps most notably the satirist Lucilius, who developed a new genre of personal commentary on contemporary society in poetic form. Consequently, a variety of ways to use personal voice, tone, and perspective preceded the publication of an actual "memoir." There is, however, no explicit ancient evidence for any autobiographies being published in the second century B.C.[9]

All of these considerations about Roman political and literary culture raise the question of who actually was the first to publish his own account of his life. When did he publish, and what forms did his work take? What were the political and cultural contexts for his decision to tell his story directly in its own right and in his own words?

2. Chronology

Several early autobiographies in Latin are attested, but only meager fragments survive of the works by three senators of the highest rank, M. Aemilius Scaurus (cos. 115), P. Rutilius Rufus (cos. 105), and Q. Lutatius Catulus (cos. 102).[10] The first full-scale memoir we can really get a good idea of is Sulla's monumental but unfinished autobiography, which was an important source for Plutarch's

---

[6] See H. I. Flower 1996 for the wax ancestor masks, 159–184 for the tomb inscriptions and the labels on the masks in the *atrium*.

[7] For Fabius Pictor and Cincius Alimentus, see Beck and Walter 2001, 55–147 and Chassignet 1996, 16–59.

[8] For the fragments of Cato's *Origines*, see Chassignet 1986 and Beck and Walter 2001, 148–224. Baier 2005, 126–128 calls the seventh book the first Roman autobiography. For further discussion of the emergence of autobiographical elements in second-century authors, see Misch 1949; Bardon 1952, 115–124; Lewis 1991b; Lewis 1993, 659–660; and especially Cornell 2009. Polybius also inserts himself and his experiences into several of his books.

[9] See Tac. *Agr.* 1.2–3 with Chassignet 2004, lxxxvi–lxxxvii. Gaius Gracchus wrote a biography of his brother Tiberius (Cic. *Div.* 1.36, Plut. *Ti. Gracch.* 8.9). On the question of genre, see Marincola 1999 and Pelling 2009. Letters in Greek addressed to Hellenistic kings (such as Philip V) by leading Romans of the earlier second century B.C. clearly served a different function and reached a different audience; see Candau 2011, 121–127.

[10] Chassignet 2004 is the standard text with introduction and commentary. The best recent overview is Walter 2003. Lewis 1993, 669 claims that Augustus wrote the first full-scope autobiography in the first person.

biography of the dictator.[11] Sulla's unfinished memoir, dedicated to L. Licinius Lucullus (cos. 74), was published in twenty-two books soon after his death in 78 B.C. There can be no doubt that Sulla developed the concept of the monumental memoir and that his writings were very influential, both in finding a wide readership (by ancient standards) and in shaping the accounts that other writers gave of his life and times. Scaurus, Rufus, and Catulus published before Sulla but on a much more modest scale, ranging from a single book to five books. Sulla, therefore, eclipsed his predecessors in what had previously been barely a genre in its own right.

In the standard editions, the fragments of the three early memoirists have traditionally been arranged according to the birthdate of each author (and consequently also according to their seniority in holding the supreme office of consul).[12] This chronological arrangement is well established and represents a logical method for dealing with fragmentary ancient authors. It comes as no surprise that we do not have enough evidence to arrange the fragments of Roman historical writing of the republican period by actual publication dates. However, the present order of these early memoirists misrepresents who published first. Because an arrangement by the birthdate of the author has been the accepted pattern, even experts have allowed the received methodology to dictate their analysis of early autobiographical writing in Latin. Accordingly, Aemilius Scaurus is consistently named in first place, with Rutilius Rufus coming next. Catulus is mentioned last in a canonical order. In fact, establishing a clear chronology is essential for any analysis of how autobiography developed in a distinctive and dynamic historical context and in relation to contemporary literature in Latin. There is every reason to believe that Q. Lutatius Catulus, despite being younger than Scaurus and Rufus, published his memoir first.[13]

A closer examination of the lives of these three men will make my argument clearer. M. Aemilius Scaurus, who enjoyed a stellar career and great personal influence (cos. 115, cens. 109, *princeps senatus*), wrote three books, entitled *de vita sua* and dedicated to L. Fufidus, a friend of praetorian rank.[14] Scaurus (whose widow Caecilia Metella soon married Sulla) died some time between 90 and 88 B.C., around the age of seventy-five. The commonly held opinion, that his account was written near the end of his life and published around the year 90 B.C. (if not posthumously in the 80s), has much to recommend it. P. Rutilius Rufus, also a patrician like Scaurus, published under the same title (*de vita sua*) but more extensively in five books.[15] While in exile, he wrote his memoirs in Latin (as well as a history in Greek). Rutilius was motivated to write about his life in order to justify himself after he was convicted in a criminal trial on a charge of embezzlement in the year 92 B.C. It is most

---

[11] For Sulla's memoirs, see Chassignet 2004, 172–184, xcix–civ, 240–247 with Suerbaum 2002, 453–456 no. 173. For discussion, see Lewis 1991a, Giardina 2003, Thein 2009, and Smith 2009. Lewis 1991b, 3650 sees Sulla as Scaurus's heir both in politics and in autobiographical writing.

[12] Peter established the canonical order of the authors in his 1870 first edition (see Peter 1914 for the second edition). He is followed by (for example) Rawson 1985, 227; Suerbaum 2002, 450; and Chassignet 2004. Lewis 1993, 636 is the only previous scholar to notice that Catulus may have published first, but he then omits him from his discussion at 660. Fantham 2004, 153 also reverses the usual order without any comment.

[13] For Q. Lutatius Catulus's fragments, see Suerbaum 2002, 447–453 no. 172 with Chassignet 2004, 170–171, xii–xxiii, xcvii–xcix. Baier 2005, 134–138 dismisses Catulus's work as

not really autobiographical and just a sketch produced for Furius. It is also possible that Catulus published sometime in the 90s, for example to coincide with the dedication of either his portico or his temple.

[14] M. Aemilius Scaurus (*RE* 140 Klebs, ca. 163–ca. 88 B.C., patrician, consul 115 B.C.): Suerbaum 2002, 440–443 no. 170 with Chassignet 2004, 161–163, lxxxviii–xciii (lxxxvi "le premier autobiographe connu"). See also Flammini 1977; Lewis 1993, 660–662; Lewis 2001. The fragments attest Scaurus's use of the first person.

[15] P. Rutilius Rufus (*RE* 34 Münzer, ca. 156–after 78 B.C., patrician, consul 105 B.C.): Suerbaum 2002, 443–447 no. 171, Chassignet 2004, 164–169, 240, xciv–xcvi, with Lewis 1993, 662–665. Use of the first person is not as evident in these fragments.

likely that he published in the 80s, although he was still alive in 78. Both of these works seem to have used a first-person voice in their narratives.

By contrast, Catulus is credited by Cicero with a single book, described as being about his consulate and his achievements (*de consulatu et de rebus gestis suis*), dedicated to the poet A. Furius (Antias).[16] This volume makes most sense very soon after the end of Catulus's term in office. His consulship fell in 102, and he served as proconsul in 101, continuing to command the same army. He was back in Rome and out of office in the tumultuous year 100. Subsequently, in the 90s, Catulus was a leading politician and associate of Scaurus. He went on to serve in the Social War at the age of about sixty and committed suicide in 87 B.C. when threatened with a criminal prosecution by the tribune Marius Gratidianus after Rome had been seized by Cinna and Marius.

In other words, the chronological argument put forward here is straightforward. As many scholars have already noted, Catulus had most to gain politically from his memoir in 100, soon after he had celebrated a joint triumph with Marius for the decisive victory over the Cimbri that they had won on 30 July 101 B.C. at Campi Raudii in northern Italy. Despite the shared triumph and the generous apportioning of booty (Catulus seems to have received more than Marius), the dispute between the two former friends, who were kinsmen and political allies, was notorious and bitter.[17] In the 90s, each man worked to gain attention for his personal achievements by means of an opulent building plan in the city. Despite suffering a political eclipse after the violence and chaos of his sixth consulship in 100 B.C., Marius did not publish either an account of his accomplishments or a formal justification of any of his actions. By contrast, Catulus countered Marius's unprecedented prominence in Rome and his own dubious military record by circulating his version of his consulship and his subsequent part in the victory against the Cimbri.

3. Genre and Voice

What, then, did Catulus write about his life? We have two references to memoirs in later Roman authors (Cicero and Fronto), as well as some indications that Plutarch used Catulus's account (as cited by Sulla) in his life of Marius. Cicero was a great admirer of Catulus, whom he refers to and uses as a character in his writings, as well as being a political ally of Catulus's influential son of the same name (cos. 78 B.C.).[18] Cicero mentions a memoir by Catulus in his *Brutus*, which was published in 46 B.C.:

> *Iam Q. Catulus non antiquo illo more, sed hoc nostro, nisi quid fieri potest perfectius, eruditus. Multae litterae, summa non vitae solum atque naturae sed orationis etiam comitas, incorrupta quaedam latini sermonis integritas; quae perspici cum ex orationibus eius potest tum facillime ex eo libro quem de consulatu et de rebus gestis suis conscriptum molli et Xenophontio genere sermonis misit ad A. Furium poetam, familiarem suum; qui liber nihilo notior est quam illi tres, de quibus ante dixi, Scauri libri. (Brut. 132)*

[16] Münzer in *RE* 7 (1927) is still the best account of Catulus's life, career, and family connections.

[17] Catulus had a family connection to Marius through his mother's second marriage. Marius married Julia (*RE* 541), daughter of Gaius Julius Caesar (*RE* 129), paternal aunt of the dictator Caesar. Catulus's mother Popilia (*RE* 32 Volkmann) married as her second husband L. Julius Caesar (*RE* 141 Münzer, first cousin of Julia's father Gaius) and had two

sons with him, L. Caesar (*RE* 142 Münzer) and C. Caesar Strabo (*RE* 135 Diehl), who were a decade younger than Catulus but very friendly with him. See Münzer's family tree (*RE* Iulius 183–184) and Badian 1957.

[18] Cic. *Rab. Perd.* 26, *Mur.* 36, *Planc.* 12. Cicero uses Catulus as a discussant in *De or.* 2 and 3, set in 91 B.C. (Fantham 2004, 152–160). He also wrote a lost philosophical work titled *Catulus* (*Div.* 2.1).

At that same period Quintus Catulus was a learned speaker, not in that antique manner but in this style of ours, but even better, if such a thing is possible. He was well read; he displayed the greatest affability not only in his life and his nature but also in his speaking style, there was a certain matchless purity to his spoken Latin. These qualities can be seen clearly in his (published) speeches but even more easily in that book which he wrote about his consulship and his achievements, in a smooth style reminiscent of Xenophon, and sent to Aulus Furius the poet, his friend. This book is no better known than those three that I spoke about before, the books by Scaurus.

Cicero seems to be paraphrasing rather than quoting the actual title of Catulus's book, which provided the raw material for an epic poem about the Cimbric war by its addressee Aulus Furius (Antias).[19] Regardless of its exact title (*de bello Cimbrico?*), we can be sure that Catulus's account will have covered more than the consular year of 102 B.C. since his victory and triumph fell in the following year of 101 B.C. Cicero's comparison with Xenophon is a general stylistic one that does not refer to a particular work, but the *Anabasis* comes to mind as the most obviously autobiographical account. In that book, Xenophon famously refers to himself in the third person and does not introduce himself until the third book.[20] Catulus's memoir may have been more focused on himself as the central character but was written in a plain, unadorned style and perhaps in the third person.

By publishing his own account after his triumph, Catulus was making an unusual move to extend the discussion and debate about his achievements after his peers in the Senate had already voted him the ultimate accolade of the triumphal procession into the city. In traditional republican culture, the triumph represented the pinnacle of a politician's career, and its celebration established a man's outstanding credentials; earlier debates about his achievements, no matter how contentious, became irrelevant once he had joined the most coveted circle of Roman generals, the *triumphatores*. It is striking that Catulus continued to seek new ways to advertise and to explain his achievements beyond the traditional ones that had been so prized in republican culture for so long.

At the same time, Catulus was also anticipating, in his own words, the kinds of things that would be said about him by his son at his funeral. In terms of Roman political culture, Catulus was making a bold departure by publishing his own prose account (especially if it was narrated in a seemingly "objective" third-person voice) rather than simply letting his friend Furius write an epic poem, as Ennius had done for M. Fulvius Nobilior in an earlier generation. The succinct format in a single book is reminiscent of a *libellus* (like a political pamphlet), such as Gaius Gracchus's short account of his brother Tiberius's life.[21]

The second reference to Catulus's self-representation comes much later, in a letter written by the rhetorician Fronto in A.D. 163 to his former pupil Lucius Verus (co-emperor with Marcus Aurelius):

> . . . *verum omnes, uti res postulat, breves nec ullam rerum gestarum expeditionem continentes. in hunc autem modum, quo scripsisti tu, extant Catuli litterae, quibus res a se iac<turi>s a<tque d>amni<s> sane gestas, at lauro merendas, <historico exemplo exposuit>; ve<rum> turgent elate <p>rolata teneris prope <v>erbis.* (Van den Hout 1988, 124–125)

---

[19] For A. Furius (Antias), see Courtney 2003, 97–98 with Propertius 2.1.24. Catulus's title might well have been about the Cimbric war rather than about his life (cf. Julius Caesar's *De bello Gallico*).

[20] Rawson 1985, 228 draws a parallel between Catulus and Xenophon's *Anabasis*. See also Marincola 1999, 317. For the *Anabasis*, see M. Flower 2012 for a full discussion of style and narrative techniques. For Xenophon, see also Pelling forthcoming.

[21] See Cic. *Div.* 1.36; Plut. *Ti. Gracch.* 8.9, presumably written shortly after his death. Tiberius did not have a funeral with *imagines* or a *laudatio*.

> But [the letters] were all short, as the subject demands, and did not contain any exposition of
> deeds that had been done. In the style, however, of your letter there is extant a letter of Catulus,
> in which he has recounted in the manner of a historian his own accomplishments, which were
> accompanied by losses and failures but still deserving of the laurel (i.e. of a triumph). But there
> is some bombast in the way [the letter] goes on at length in almost effeminate words.

Since the 1870s most scholars have considered Fronto's words to be a reference to the same single book alluded to by Cicero.[22] In other words, Catulus is imagined as having written one book of memoirs (focused on the events of 102–101 B.C.) in the form of a letter addressed to his friend, the poet Aulus Furius.

There are, however, two reasons to doubt this interpretation. The letter that Fronto refers to seems to be a version of Catulus's request for a triumph in 101 B.C., which would traditionally have included a precise account of losses suffered by his army in comparison with the number of the enemy that were killed. This request would definitely not have discussed Catulus's consulship in the previous year, which is clearly referred to by Cicero as being a central focus of the book that he had read. Similarly, Fronto's description of the style of Catulus's writing in his letter as long-winded and ornate does not match Cicero's characterization as smooth and reminiscent of Xenophon. Consequently, Cicero and Fronto seem most logically to be referring to two separate accounts of his personal achievements written by Catulus.

From these considerations, Catulus emerges as a bold innovator who was simultaneously experimenting with (at least) two different autobiographical forms, each recounting his victory at Campi Raudii but in different styles and with varying emphases. One was published in a single papyrus roll and dedicated to A. Furius; this memoir covered both his consulship and his proconsulship, perhaps ending with his triumph. It was written in a plain style that imitated Xenophon, a Greek author who was widely read and admired by literate Romans. Cicero claims that this book was not well known. The other work was in the form of a letter, probably an edited version of Catulus's official letter to the Senate requesting a meeting outside the *pomerium* to vote him a triumph.[23] This letter, which was perhaps written in an elaborate and bombastic style, contained the formal details that the Senate traditionally asked about in considering the award of a triumph. The letter was still extant for Fronto to read more than 260 years later.

Catulus was most probably writing soon after the events in 101 or 100 B.C., in a time of political crisis and violent dissension and in a culture in which the publication of such an autobiographical account was quite new. He had at his disposal the more traditional option of simply publishing his speeches, which would essentially have covered this same material; he may have availed himself of this option at the same time. Cicero refers to published speeches by Catulus that were circulating in the mid-first century B.C.[24] Catulus, however, felt the need for further venues and means of self-representation, even as he was experimenting with different styles of writing his story. Both Cicero and Fronto seem to suggest that Catulus used a third-person voice rather than the first person that is so effective in his two surviving verse epigrams. At the same time, Catulus was inviting Furius to write about his exploits in an epic form. Catulus's search for a variety of autobiographical formats can be compared with the two different types of buildings he erected in Rome to commemorate

---

[22] Jordan 1872 first suggested this equation, which has been commonly accepted.

[23] Pelikan Pittenger 2008, 35–36 describes the formal procedures for requesting a triumph.

[24] Cic. *Brut.* 132 with Malcovati 1976, no. 63 and Suerbaum 2002, 449 no. 172.

his victory, namely a round temple in the Campus Martius and a portico to display his booty on the Palatine Hill.

4. Contexts

While we are not in a position to recover Catulus's prose, except in occasional paraphrases, we can say more about the various contexts, both political and cultural, in which he was inspired to write. The political and military crisis that led to the exceptional prominence of C. Marius was obviously a major factor in putting pressure on many *nobiles* to position themselves in relation to Rome's new savior.[25] Catulus and his deputy Sulla were particularly subject to being eclipsed by Marius, despite and because of the close and collegial relationship each man had previously enjoyed with him. Indeed Catulus would eventually be forced to kill himself under pressure from Marius's political associates.[26] Meanwhile, Catulus's broadly Hellenizing tastes, which extended from art and architecture to literature and culture, also served as an inspiration for the forms that his innovative self-representation took.

POLITICS

In the late second century, wars on several fronts and repeated setbacks over more than a generation put an immense strain on Rome's traditional class of officeholders.[27] The first Roman defeat by the northern invaders came in 113 B.C. and was followed in 105 B.C. by the catastrophic loss at the battle of Arausio, Rome's most significant military disaster in more than a century.[28] The Cimbri were not finally defeated until the battle at Campi Raudii in 101 B.C., after they had occupied Italy north of the Po. In these same years, Rome encountered challenges and political strife over a war against Jugurtha in Numidia, a large-scale slave revolt in Sicily, and a campaign against pirates in the eastern Mediterranean. The decade before the final defeat of the Cimbri was especially difficult. Even after victories put an end to these various wars, Romans experienced political murder, gang violence, and an episode of full-scale civil war within their city during the year 100 B.C.[29] It was this last decade of the second century B.C. that saw the startling rise of the "new man" Gaius Marius, who held the consulship an unprecedented six times between 107 and 100 B.C.

Although we do not know many details of Catulus's career before his consulship of 102 B.C., he was closely involved with and directly affected by many of the most tumultuous events of these years. Catulus was defeated in three bids to be elected to the consulship and seems not to have run at all in 104 B.C., after the disastrous defeat of his kinsman Caepio at the battle of Arausio.[30] In other words, his career had stopped short of the highest office, since he had been resoundingly rejected by the voters, and he was further compromised by the aftermath of a military disaster, for which

[25] Carney 1961 is still the classic discussion of all the sources.

[26] Val. Max. 9.12.4; Vell. Pat. 2.22.3; Cic. *Tusc.* 5.56.

[27] Linke 2005 gives a crisp survey of the period. Sampson 2010 offers an incisive military analysis of the wars with the Cimbri and Teutoni and with Jugurtha, including maps and a thorough consideration of the sources. Brizzi 2010 gives a different reconstruction of the battle at Campi Raudii.

[28] The battle of Arausio (Orange, Vaucluse) happened on 6 October 105 B.C. See Sampson 2010, 133–141 for a detailed analysis.

[29] Badian 1984 analyzes the year 100 B.C. in detail.

[30] Q. Servilius Caepio (*RE* 49 Münzer, patrician, consul 106 B.C.) was the brother of Catulus's wife Servilia (*RE* 98 Münzer) and the son of the consul of 140 B.C. The tensions between Caepio and Cn. Mallius Maximus (cos. 105 B.C.) that led to disaster on the battlefield seem partly to have been the result of Mallius's defeat of Catulus in his second bid for the consulship.

his relative and political ally Q. Servilius Caepio bore much of the public blame. At the elections in 103 B.C., Marius was the presiding consul (since his colleague L. Aurelius Orestes had died), as well as being elected again himself for a fourth time, thanks to the help of his friend the tribune Saturninus.[31] In what is described as a strong field of candidates and at a moment when there was a real chance to win glory in the field, Marius clearly helped Catulus to gain the consulship against all personal and political odds. Catulus was an in-law of Marius's patrician wife Julia, whom he had married around 110 B.C. Marius must have been on good terms with Catulus and must have had faith in Catulus's ability as a general at a time when Rome faced a formidable military threat that would require both consuls to be in the field defending Italy.

However, Catulus failed miserably and lost all of Italy north of the Po to the Cimbri without so much as a fight.[32] News of his chaotic retreat reached Rome at about the same time as word of Marius's complete victory over the Teutoni (allies of the Cimbri) at Aquae Sextiae in Provence. Marius was elected consul again for 101 B.C. but refused to celebrate a triumph over the Teutoni.[33] Instead, he opted to join Catulus, whose command had been extended as proconsul, to deal with the Cimbri in northern Italy. After the decisive victory over the Cimbri in 101 B.C., Marius and Catulus both triumphed and were both greatly enriched by booty.[34] In other words, Marius and the Senate each continued to support Catulus and gave him a "second chance" to defeat the Cimbri. Catulus clearly owed his consulship and his eventual triumph in no small part to Marius's patience and patronage.[35]

This very debt may have exacerbated the relationship between the two commanders. Despite Marius's political and military support against a formidable enemy, who significantly outnumbered even the combined consular armies, Catulus was concerned that Marius would get all the credit. Catulus's men were ordered to write their commander's name on their spears (and other weapons?) in order to allow credit to be measured accurately after the battle.[36] In the end, Catulus seems to have succeeded in laying claim to more booty than Marius, presumably through a variety of such "proofs" of his solders' accomplishments. Both Catulus and Sulla accused Marius of bad faith during this battle. Yet Marius, who had command over a larger number of soldiers on the field, was surely the architect of the winning battle strategy. It was also Marius who received most popular acclaim and spontaneous divine honors from ordinary Romans immediately after the victory.[37]

---

[31] Plut. *Mar.* 14 with Livy *Per.* 67.

[32] Plut. *Mar.* 23 seems ultimately to be derived from Catulus (cf. Livy *Per.* 68). There is no archaeological evidence for the battle. For analysis, see Lewis 1974, Marasco 1984, and now especially Sampson 2010, 167–168. The problems created by having two commanders in the same field of battle recall the difficulties at Arausio (only four years before), which apparently caused the catastrophic defeat.

[33] Itgenshorst 2005 (CD catalogue), 316 suggests, on the basis of Plut. *Mar.* 24.1, that Marius was voted a triumph *in absentia* and without having made a request, which would have been unprecedented.

[34] Presumably they celebrated two adjacent triumphs for the same victory rather than sharing a single celebration, which would have been unprecedented. The triumphal *fasti* for these years are lost. See *MRR* for 101 B.C. and Itgenshorst 2005 (CD catalogue), 314–320, nos. 234 and 235. Marius,

however, was celebrating two victories, while Catulus could only claim one.

[35] It is hard to say how far Marius was generous to Catulus. Normally, Marius would have celebrated a triumph after his victory at Aquae Sextiae and would not have held any office in the subsequent year (101), let alone the one after (100). Plut. *Mar.* 27 suggests that Catulus's soldiers forced Marius to share the eventual triumph with Catulus. Pelikan Pittenger 2008, 67–83 makes clear that joint campaigns usually ended with two triumphs, one for each general. McDonnell 2006, 286–288 traces the tensions around the triumph (fall 101 B.C.) and into the following year.

[36] See Plut. *Mar.* 27 with Sampson 2010, 169–178. Much more in Plutarch's *Marius* may go back to Catulus, directly or indirectly.

[37] For the divine honors for Marius, see Val. Max. 8.15.7 and Plut. *Mar.* 27.9 with H. I. Flower 2006, 89–90. Marius

The seeds of hatred sown by this competition for recognition led eventually to a series of terrible outcomes: the rift between Marius and Sulla (Catulus's deputy at the time), Catulus's enforced suicide, the outlawing of Sulla, the destruction of Sulla's house by Marius's partisans, Sulla's desecration of Marius's grave, and the barbaric execution of Marius Gratidianus on Catulus's grave. Rome was saved from the threat posed by the invasion from the north but at a terrible political price because even two Romans who were related and who had won election as political colleagues could not find a way to share the credit and celebrate a joint victory. This situation of political and personal strife is the essential background to Catulus's self-presentation.

CULTURAL CAPITAL

Cicero singles out Catulus's consulship in 102 B.C. as a time of intensely Hellenizing influence.[38] Catulus himself was personally known for his appreciation of Greek culture and his learned interests in art, philosophy, and poetry. Catulus has also been associated with the introduction in Rome of the revolutionary "second style" of wall painting as a pattern of masonry blocks in simple colors gave way to elaborate frescoes with scenes in perspective.[39] He paid Aemilus Scaurus a famously high price for the learned slave Daphnis, who went on to become his freedman and his literary collaborator. Either Catulus or Daphnis (or perhaps both working together?) was responsible for an historical work entitled *communes historiae*, a learned treatment of early Rome and Aeneas in at least four books.[40] At the same time, Catulus befriended Greek literary figures in Rome such as Antipater of Sidon and Archias of Antioch.[41]

Unfortunately, we have very little of what Catulus wrote, and we cannot recover the relative chronology of his works. He is the first *nobilis* we know of to have written Latin epigrams in a Greek style.[42] One of his two surviving poems extolls the famous actor Q. Roscius, who was also a close associate (Cic. *Nat. D.* 1.79):

> *constiteram exorientem Auroram forte salutans*
> *cum subito a laeua Roscius exoritur,*
> *pace mihi liceat, caelestes, dicere uestra,*
> *mortalis uisus pulchrior esse deo.*

By chance, I had taken up my position to face the Dawn in prayer, when suddenly Roscius came up from the left; may I be permitted by your allowance, o heavenly deities, to declare that he, though a mortal, appeared more beautiful than a god.

---

is described as drinking from a *kantharos* in imitation of the triumphant god Dionysus (Val. Max. 3.6.6). The coins of 101 B.C. minted by C. Fundanius (*RRC* 326), which show scenes of a triumph and of a victory adorning a trophy, have been referred specifically to Marius, but why could these coins not just as easily recall Catulus or the two triumphing generals together?

[38] See Cic. *Arch.* 5 with Grüner 2004, 24–28 and McDonnell 2006, 264 for the Hellenism of Catulus and his generation.

[39] See Sauron 1999 and 2001, with Grüner 2004, 31–33.

[40] Q. Lutatius Daphnis (*RE* 15 Münzer): Suet. *Gram.* 3 and Plin. *HN* 7.128. For the *communes historiae*, see La Penna 1979; Chassignet 2004, 6–12; and Walter 2009.

[41] Antipater of Sidon: Cic. *De or.* 3.194. Archias of Antioch: Cic. *Arch.* 6 with *Schol. Bob.* 176,12. *Arch.* 19 mentions an epic poem Archias wrote about the Cimbric war (Fantham 2004, 155). For Catulus as a patron, see Stroup 2010, 289–290.

[42] See Blänsdorf 1995, 94–96 for a text with Courtney 2003, 75–78 for commentary and Grüner 2004, 20–23. Perutelli 1990 gives a detailed analysis of the language of Catulus, whom he describes as a sophisticated, innovative, and subtle poet. The epigram about Roscius probably dates before 100 B.C., given that Roscius died at an advanced age in 62 B.C. (Cic. *Arch.* 17).

The personal and homoerotic tone of these epigrams is striking. Catulus is considered a leading predecessor of the neoteric love poets of the first century B.C.

He is also mentioned as the first Roman to give a formal funeral oration in public for a woman, his mother Popilia, perhaps in the year of his consulship.[43] The Lutatii Catuli did not have many distinguished ancestors to put on show at a funeral. Popilia, however, came from a much more distinguished family with many *imagines*. Moreover, her second marriage to L. Iulius Caesar had given Catulus two distinguished half-brothers, to whom he was close. He may well have paraded the *imagines* of the patrician Iulii at his mother's funeral. It was typical of Catulus to organize such an unusual funeral as an opportunity to present himself in a special way to the inhabitants of Rome.

In the context of his literary interests and innovation in several fields, it is not surprising, therefore, to learn that Catulus also tried his hand at two types of autobiographical writing: a letter to the Senate that rehearsed his formal claim to the triumph he had shared with Marius and a memoir in one volume of his time as a general fighting against the Cimbri, written in the style of Xenophon. Each of these formats would have afforded him a different way of representing himself and his career.

Who exactly his intended audience was, and whether he had different people in mind for each text, is very difficult to say. Whether or not he aimed to reach beyond his fellow senators (and the restricted circle of the reading public in Rome) will have depended on occasions when his works could have been read aloud, in private or public settings. In any case, his original aims seem to have been immediate, inspired by the complex and violent politics of the year 100 B.C.

Consuls had traditionally used letters to communicate with the Senate and with foreign governing bodies or kings.[44] In other words, a consul would use the letters for military purposes and for diplomacy. Such letters would be read aloud in the Senate and sometimes in public. The letters, decorated with the traditional laurel, which were sent to report a victory, were famous, typically Roman artifacts that had a role to play before a triumph. The format and tone of such official letters were by definition public rather than personal. However, some private letters were also in circulation at the end of the second century B.C., most notably the famous collection of letters written by Cornelia, mother of the Gracchi, referred to by Cicero.[45]

Fronto's brief allusion to the letter of Catulus indicates a formal letter about his achievements, addressed to the Senate as a body.[46] The letter's possibly ornate and boastful style would, therefore, presumably belong to an edited version. Catulus could have adapted the letter he wrote reporting his victory and requesting a Senate meeting outside the *pomerium* to vote on a triumph, by including further elements from the subsequent speeches he delivered, first at that Senate meeting and then the public speech he would have made to the people in Rome at the time when he celebrated his triumph (*contio triumphalis*). Catulus's public and open (Roman-style) letter to the Senate can and probably should be contrasted with his more personal (Greek-style) memoir dedicated to Furius.

A memoir in the plain style of Xenophon was a completely new kind of publication for a Roman statesman and general. Given Catulus's learning, he may also have been familiar with other

---

[43] For Popilia's *laudatio* (*RE* 32 Volkmann), see Cic. *De or.* 2.11.44 with H. I. Flower 1996, 122 and Hillard 2001.

[44] Cugusi 1970 gives the references to and fragments of lost Latin letters. Suerbaum 2002, 437–440 connects such letters to autobiography. See also Lewis 1993, 633–634.

[45] For the letters of Cornelia (known to Cicero and Quintilian), see Suerbaum 2002, 456–457 no. 174. The fragments preserved in a manuscript of Nepos are problematic: Horsfall

1987 and 1989, 41–43, 125–126. For further discussion, see Petrocelli 2001, 48–51; Hemelrijk 2004, 193–197; and Dixon 2007, 26–29.

[46] Van den Hout 1999, 298–299 notes the poor condition of the text in this passage and the hypothetical nature of the restorations. Nevertheless, he equates this reference to the Cicero passage about the book dedicated to Furius. The original letter from a general to the Senate would presumably have been on a single, folded wax tablet.

autobiographical works in Greek, such as Plato's Seventh Letter and Aratus of Sikyon's ambitious memoir (in more than thirty books).[47] But Xenophon was his chosen model. The dedication to a poet rather than to a political figure also set a particular tone. Not unlike Xenophon himself on his Persian expedition, Catulus had had to contend with significant setbacks, initial defeat, and situations in which the overall command of the whole army was not his. Xenophon's themes of endurance, faith in the gods, reversals of fortune, and ultimate perseverance in the face of daunting odds could provide many points of reference for Catulus to shape his own narrative. Both Xenophon's smooth style and the content of his various works would have been familiar to Catulus's peers.[48] The simple rhetorical style and narrative quality could also have made the memoir suitable for reading aloud to a broader audience. Meanwhile, the Xenophontic features of Catulus's prose would have contrasted nicely with Furius's epic in hexameters. To Roman readers, Catulus's memoir may not have appeared generically the same as the more formally autobiographical writings of Scaurus, Rutilius, Sulla, or even Augustus.[49]

Yet Catulus's self-presentation was mainly defined by his ambitious building program on the Palatine and in the Campus Martius. Any consideration of commemoration and image making must take into account the simple fact that more people in Rome will have seen his buildings than will ever have heard or read his literary works. Catulus was an ambitious and essentially self-made man, whose wealthy plebeian family had not had a distinguished record in politics in the second century. A combination of the challenges he faced in his career with his well-developed cultural tastes led him to seek publicity in a wide variety of venues, both old and new.

Usually there was only a single general and therefore a single vow leading to one temple in Rome that corresponded to a given victory and its associated triumph. Marius and Catulus each vowed temples to separate (and contrasting) deities before the final battle against the Cimbri. Marius's temple was dedicated to *Honos* and *Virtus*, while Catulus favored the unusual *Fortuna Huiusce Diei* (Fortune of this day). In other words, Marius honored abstract deifications of the concepts of "honor" and "manly courage," both qualities of personal valor and achievement.[50] Meanwhile, Catulus attributed success to divinely inspired good fortune specific to a given day (in this case 30 July, the day of the victory over the Cimbri).[51] These temples (as well as the other victory monuments) enshrined the competition between these two bitter political rivals.[52]

Marius's dedication recalled the existing Temple of Honos and Virtus, vowed by M. Claudius Marcellus as consul in 222 B.C. after his great victory over the Gauls at Clastidium, not far from the site of the recent battle at Campi Raudii (Vercellae). Marcellus had himself killed the Insubrian leader Viridomarus and dedicated his armor as *spolia opima* in the Temple of Jupiter Feretrius on the Capitol.[53] Marius was inviting a direct comparison between himself and Marcellus, the great plebeian general who had been elected to five consulships, the most held by any Roman before

[47] Aratus seems to have written in a careless and offhand style, unlike what Cicero sees in Catulus's writing (Plut. *Arat.* 3.3 = *FGrHist* 231 T6).

[48] Rawson 1985, 46, 223.

[49] See Pelling 2009 on autobiography as a "genre" in republican Rome.

[50] See Palombi in Steinby 1993–2000, with McDonnell 2006, 274–280 and Clark 2007, 124–128, 214.

[51] Gros in Steinby 1993–2000, with F37 on the Severan

Marble Plan of Rome (http://formaurbis.stanford.edu/). For discussion, see Coarelli 1997, 288–289; Grüner 2004, 28–31; Stamper 2005, 75–81; McDonnell 2006, 280–285, and Clark 2007, 129–130, 177.

[52] Marius also hung Cimbric shields on some shop fronts in the Forum (Cic. *Orat.* 2.266, *Quinct.* 6.3.38 with Papi in Steinby 1993–2000 under *Tabernae Argentariae*). Note also the clash between Catulus's son and Julius Caesar (Pelling 2011, 157–158 and 173–174).

[53] For M. Claudius Marcellus (*RE* 220), see H. I. Flower forthcoming.

Marius himself. The implication was that Marius indeed deserved the credit for the recent victory that had saved Rome from another Gallic invasion. Similarly, Marcellus had eclipsed his consular colleague Cn. Cornelius Scipio Calvus and celebrated a triumph to mark the end of a significant war.

Catulus's Temple of Fortuna has been identified as the round temple (B) in the sacred area of the Largo Argentina, which was excavated in the 1920s.[54] Although of modest dimensions, this temple was unusually fine and inspired by Hellenistic design (unlike Marius's Italic-style temple). Fragments of its monumental cult statue of Parian marble have suggested that Skopas Minor was the artist. If this identification is correct, then Catulus's statue of Fortuna is a very rare example of a "Hellenistic" work of art commissioned for a Roman context and by a Roman patron.[55] The statue's iconography mirrors that of Demeter at Eleusis. Pliny the Elder speaks of an array of older Greek statues displayed in front of this temple in his own day.[56] The unusual round temple was the most recent in a traditionally sacred area, which may have been enclosed by a new *porticus* shortly before in 107 B.C. Temple A, next to Catulus's, has been attributed to one of his ancestors in the decisive naval victory at the end of the First Punic War.[57] Catulus, therefore, in putting his new round temple adjacent to a traditional rectangular structure that was nearly 150 years old, invited a visual comparison between his victory and the Roman victory over Carthage (in 241 B.C.) that won Sicily as the first overseas province under direct Roman rule. This juxtaposition commemorates a fine tradition of family achievements in war (such as the new man Marius could only evoke indirectly by representing himself as the successor of Marcellus), even as its contrast in style only made Catulus's Hellenism seem all the more avant-garde.

Not content with his Greek-style victory monument, Catulus chose to display his Cimbric booty elsewhere in the city, in a new purpose-built portico on the Palatine next to a house that would later be bought by Cicero.[58] Most triumphing generals deposited their booty in or around the temple each built in fulfillment of a vow on the battlefield. Indeed it was only natural to honor the deity being thanked for the victory with the gift of related spoils and items from the triumph, which would further enhance the celebration of the annual festival of that temple's birthday. Catulus, however, wanted an elaborate display of Celtic spoils in a completely separate commemorative setting, which overlooked the Forum. In other words, Catulus wanted both his Greek temple and his Celtic booty monument.[59]

Catulus seems to have been able to pull off this unusual move because he had a family connection with the prime location where his portico was built. Moreover, the land was empty and had associations with an earlier display of Celtic booty put up by his in-law M. Fulvius Flaccus (cos. 125 B.C.).[60] Flaccus's house had stood on this spot but had been demolished after his involvement with the fall of Gaius Gracchus. Catulus's portico, therefore, removed an erasure imposed as a

[54] For the Largo Argentina sacred area, see Coarelli 2007, 275–281; Claridge 2010, 241–246.

[55] For the suggestion of Skopas minor as the artist, see Coarelli and Sauron 1978, 724.

[56] Cic. *Verr.* 4.126 and Plin. *HN* 34.54.

[57] For temple A as the Temple of Juturna dedicated by C. Lutatius Catulus (*RE* 4) in thanksgiving for his decisive victory over the Carthagininans at Arginusae in 241 B.C., see Coarelli in Steinby 1993–2000.

[58] No ancient source puts this portico next to Catulus's house

(Coarelli in Steinby 1993–2000 with Carandini 2008). For the portico, see Papi in Steinby 1993–2000 with Krause 2001 and 2004.

[59] Marius had several monuments in Rome: Reusser in Steinby 1993–2000 with Sehlmeyer 1999, 192–193.

[60] For M. Fulvius Flaccus's house (*RE* 58 Münzer), see Cic. *Dom.* 38, Val. Max. 6.3.1c with Papi in Steinby 1993–2000; Cerutti 1997, 422–424; H. I. Flower 2006, 76–77. Flaccus's daughter Fulvia (whose two brothers had died along with her father in 121 B.C.) was already married to L. Julius Caesar (cos. 90 B.C., cens. 89 B.C., *RE* 142 Münzer), a half-brother of Catulus, at the time when the portico was being planned.

memory sanction, even as he took advantage of a prime piece of property that had stood empty for some twenty years.[61] Consequently, Catulus's commemorative building plan was grand and carefully designed to convey multiple messages in various venues to a range of audiences.

5. Conclusion

In sum, the subsequent civil war and the dictatorship of his former legate Sulla (amongst other factors) have tended to obscure the figure of Q. Lutatius Catulus, his novel literary achievements, and his role as a patron of the arts. As I have tried to show, it was Catulus, innovator in a range of cultural fields, who was the first to experiment with writing a memoir in Latin, in two contrasting styles and formats, both perhaps making use of the third person to shape his narrative. These literary attempts make best sense around the year 100 B.C. or soon after. They can be classified as reactions to and attempts to cope with the exceptional prominence of Marius, by now six times consul, former political patron of Catulus but recently his bitter rival for the glory of the final victory over the northern invaders. But these first attempts at memoir were more than merely anti-Marian propaganda. A number of factors are relevant to an appreciation of Catulus's literary purposes.

The continued struggle with the Cimbri, which culminated in their occupation of Italy north of the Po, had loomed very large for the Romans for more than a decade. A series of devastating Roman defeats made this northern threat seem as bad as any invasion these Romans could remember.[62] It was Catulus himself who had failed to stop this invasion. Where other generals had suffered defeat, he and his men had nearly all retreated without so much as a fight. When a leader of his cavalry unit returned to Rome, his father would not receive him, and the young patrician committed suicide.[63] Yet Catulus's command was renewed, and he was given another chance to fight the Cimbri but only in unison with Marius as general with overall command of the combined Roman armies.

Catulus now had to contend both with his own desperate need for a victory and with the highly unusual position of Marius as his senior colleague in the field. The result was a total defeat of the Cimbri and the popular acclamation of Marius as the savior of Rome. How could Catulus explain his previous miserable failure and still claim a share in Rome's eventual victory? The answer he proposed was in a particularly theological narrative linked to the goddess Fortuna, who brought defeat one day but victory on another, more auspicious occasion.[64] This explanation painted Catulus as a pious man, whose vicissitudes were caused by bad timing and by the will of the gods rather than being a result of his own lack of skill or courage. It was the need to expound his version of events and a related worldview that inspired Catulus to tell his own story.

As Cicero noted, Catulus's memoir was not much read in the next generation. However, there can be little doubt of his decisive influence on Sulla, who cited Catulus by name in his own

[61] For the *area flaccitana*, see Cic. *Dom.* 38, 102, 114 and Val. Max. 6.3.1.

[62] The two most notorious examples of invasions of Italy were by the Gauls in the early fourth century and by the Carthaginians led by Hannibal in the late third century, both devastating for the Romans.

[63] The youth was a younger son (*RE* 137) of M. Aemilius Scaurus (*RE* 140 von der Mühll). See Lewis 1974, 108, who notes, by contrast, that Opimius's son distinguished himself

in single combat. See Brizzi 2010 for further development of the arguments of Hinard 1987.

[64] For the theology of Fortuna, see Hinard 1987; Royo 1989; McDonnell 2006, 268–271, 294; and especially Clark 2007, 214. Plutarch's *Marius* has much glossing and word play on both "virtue" and "fortune," presumably taken (at least partly) from his sources (e.g., 14.8 Marius is elected for both his ability and his good fortune; 19 Fortune helps Marius in his battle at a river).

autobiography and who also broke with Marius after their joint victory.[65] Like Catulus, Sulla kept company with actors and wrote epigrams in a Hellenistic style. Sulla also famously cultivated the goddess Fortuna, believed in a concept of the fortuitous moment for spontaneous action (καιρός), and devoted his retirement to writing detailed memoirs that gave a vivid and highly partisan account of his life, characterized by divine interventions. After Sulla had written up the events both men had taken part in, there was no need to read Catulus's much briefer and sparer version, but Catulus's autobiographical idea and his theology of divine favor were developed and handed on by Sulla.[66]

[65] Badian 1966, 37 n. 135 sees Sulla as critical of Catulus at Plut. *Sull.* 3 and doubts that he used Catulus as a source.

[66] Catulus will also have influenced many others, including his famous son, Q. Lutatius Catulus Capitolinus (cos. 78 B.C.) and Cicero, whose attempts to represent his consulship surely owed much to Catulus. Note also Caesar's simple style and use of the third person. Eventually Augustus would build his own portico on the Palatine and would write an autobiography in thirteen books that ended with the Cantabrian war in 25 B.C.

PART II

MEMORIA

IN ANCIENT ROME

3 ◆ Popular Memory

T. P. Wiseman

> The collective memory helps a group or a society as a whole to articulate an awareness of its defining characteristics and its unity, and therefore forms an essential basis for its self-image and identity. . . . The spectrum of forms, institutions, and places through which a cultural memory may find its articulation and permanence, the relative importance of these forms and, above all, the specific, synergetic connections of media and locations that result in "systems" or "landscapes" of memory are characteristic of a specific society. In fact, they are themselves integral components of its cultural memory.

Immediately before and after this passage, in his important essay on history and collective memory in the middle republic, Karl-Joachim Hölkeskamp names two inspirational forerunners: Jan Assmann, author of *Das kulturelle Gedächtnis*, and Pierre Nora, author of *Les lieux de mémoire.*[1] As he drily notes, discussion of their work has been largely "a phenomenon of 'Old Europe'."[2] But he himself has done much to bring it to the attention of anglophone scholarship, and I hope he will not mind if I use his essay as an exemplary statement of how their ideas can be applied to Roman memory.

In particular, I want first to draw attention to the idea of "monumental memory," "a cityscape of *memoria* in stone," in which temples, statues, and monuments form a "landscape fraught with political, historical, sacral, and mythical meanings and messages"—a landscape, moreover, that can be "'read' like a text, since it stores the full spectrum of myths . . . and other stories."[3] Citing Nora again, Hölkeskamp concludes that

> the *populus Romanus* and its political elite formed a great, collective *milieu de mémoire*: a vibrant, evolving community of memory. In the midst of this community, there was a complex pattern or landscape of *lieux de mémoire*: these concrete traces and marked spaces of remembrance retained, continually reproduced, and indeed re-enforced their meanings and messages over time.[4]

At the risk of perpetuating national stereotypes,[5] I would like to see these metaphors and abstractions translated into empirical evidence.

Hölkeskamp takes the view that in the last twenty-five years or so the discipline of ancient history has "begun to break out of the 'ghetto' of its traditional fixations and restrictions"; in particular, it is

---

[1] Hölkeskamp 2006a, 481, citing J. Assmann 1992 and Nora 1984–1992.

[2] Hölkeskamp 2006a, 492, alluding to Donald Rumsfeld's offensive comment of 22 January 2003.

[3] Hölkeskamp 2006a, 482–483; cf. 487 ("locations of memo-

ry"), 489 ("landscape of memory"), 491 ("memorial space").

[4] Hölkeskamp 2006a, 491.

[5] Carandini 2000, 98: "Gli Inglesi sono empiristi accaniti e questa loro arcaica stramberia è un loro carattere nazionale."

"slowly emancipating itself from its one-sided methodological fixation upon a conservative classical philology."[6] Perhaps so. But it could equally well be argued that a proper understanding of Roman memory requires more, not less, attention to the detail of the ancient sources and emancipation not from classical scholarship but from unexamined concepts and grand abstractions.

That, at any rate, is the premise on which the following argument is based.[7] I shall concentrate on primary sources, presenting texts (numbered for ease of reference) from which I hope reliable inferences can be drawn. And I begin with those monuments that are supposed to embody the community's memory.

1

The clearest ancient evidence for the Nora/Hölkeskamp hypothesis about monuments carrying memory may be Vitruvius's dedication to *imperator Caesar* of his treatise on architecture, some time in the 20s B.C.:

1. *haec tibi scribere coepi, quod animaduerti multa te aedificauisse et nunc aedificare, reliquo quoque tempore et publicorum et priuatorum aedificiorum, pro amplitudine rerum gestarum ut posteris* memoriae *traderentur, curam habiturum.*

    I have started to write this for you, because I observed that you have constructed many buildings and are now constructing more, and that in future too you intend to take care for both public and private buildings according to the greatness of your achievements, that they may be handed on to memory for later generations. (Vitr. *De arch.* 1 pref. 3)

He may have had the Palatine complex in mind, where both the Temple of Apollo and the *uestibulum* of Augustus's house were decorated with spoils of war.[8] That *spolia* were an important means of preserving the memory of the past is implicit in Suetonius's account of the great fire of A.D. 64, which also juxtaposes public and private buildings:

2. *tunc praeter immensum numerum insularum domus priscorum ducum arserunt adhuc spoliis adornatae deorumque aedes ab regibus ac deinde Punicis et Gallicis bellis uotae dedicataeque, et quidquid uisendum atque* memorabile *ex antiquitate durauerat.*

    Besides a huge number of apartment blocks, the houses of historic leaders burned at that time, still adorned with spoils of war, and temples of the gods that had been vowed and dedicated by the kings or in the Punic and Gallic wars, and everything else noteworthy and memorable that had survived from the past. (Suet. *Ner.* 38.2)

On the basis of these two passages, let us look in turn at the evidence for public buildings (temples) and private buildings (houses).

Some temples were named after the men who had had them built. One might refer to "Catulus's temple," "Pompey's temple," "Metellus's temple,"[9] or to "the Marian temple of Honos," "the

---

[6] Hölkeskamp 2010, 125–126.

[7] I have tried to avoid too much repetition from previous studies, which I hope are still worth consulting: Wiseman 1986 = 1994, 37–48; 1987 = 1994, 98–115; 2007.

[8] Temple (dedicated 28 B.C.): Verg. *Aen.* 8.720–722. House: Ov. *Tr.* 3.1.33–38.

[9] Varro, *Rust.* 3.5.12; Plin. *HN* 34.57, 36.40; also 36.26 (*delubrum Cn. Domitii*).

Aemilian temple of Hercules";[10] or an adjectival name might be attached to the deity, like Hercules Pompeianus, Apollo Sosianus, Diana Planciana, Diana Cornificiana.[11] Cicero and Tacitus show what it meant in practice:

3. *hoc loco, Q. Catule, te appello; loquor enim de tuo clarissimo pulcherrimoque monumento . . . tui nominis aeterna* memoria *simul cum templo illo consecratur.*

   At this point I call on you, Quintus Catulus; for I speak of your most famous and most splendid monument. . . . With that temple is consecrated the everlasting memory of your name. (Cic. *Verr.* 2.4.69, on the Capitoline Temple of Jupiter).

4. *Lutatii Catuli nomen inter tanta Caesarum opera usque ad Vitellium mansit.*

   Among the great works of the Caesars, the name of Lutatius Catulus survived right up to Vitellius. (Tac. *Hist.* 3.72.3, on the burning of the temple in A.D. 69)

Literally, it was the name that survived, inscribed in the marble. If you wanted to know who built a temple, you looked at the inscription.[12] However, that might only tell you who *re*built it, as in Ovid's mention of the arrival of Magna Mater in 204 B.C.:

5. *Nasica accepit. templi non perstitit auctor;*
   Augustus nunc est, ante Metellus erat.

   Nasica received her. The founder of the temple has not survived. It is Augustus now, it was Metellus before. (Ov. *Fast.* 4.347–348)

According to Livy, the Magna Mater Temple was dedicated by a Marcus Iunius Brutus; it was twice destroyed by fire, and no doubt Augustus, the second rebuilder, did not want to perpetuate the name of his father's assassin.[13]

Even when the inscription survived, it might not tell you very much. Ovid's account of the Temple of Minerva Capta is not encouraging for those who believe in *lieux de mémoire*:

6. *nominis in dubio causa est. capitale uocamus*
   ingenium sollers: ingeniosa dea est.
   an quia de capitis fertur sine matre paterni
   uertice cum clipeo prosiluisse suo?
   an quia perdomitis ad nos captiua Faliscis
   uenit? et hoc signo littera prisca docet.
   an quod habet legem, capitis quae pendere poenas
   ex illo iubeat furta reperta loco?

   The reason for the name is in doubt. We call ingenious talent "capital," and the goddess is full of talents. Or is it because, without a mother, she is said to have leapt forth from the top of her father's head, complete with shield? Or is it because she came to us as a captive after the Faliscans had been vanquished? This too is what the old inscription on the statue tells us. Or

[10] Val. Max. 1.7.5; Festus 282L; cf. Plin. *HN* 36.163 (*aedes Fortunae quam Seiani appellant*).

[11] Vitr. 3.3.5; Plin. *HN* 13.53; *CIL* 6.2210, *AE* 1971.31–32; *CIL* 6.4305, *Forma urbis Romae* fr. 22.

[12] Ov. *Fast.* 6.212, on the temple of Hercules Custos in the Circus Flaminius: *si titulum quaeris, Sulla probauit opus.*

[13] Livy 36.36.4 (191 B.C.); the fires were in 111 B.C. and A.D. 3 (Val. Max. 1.8.11), so "Metellus" may be Q. Metellus Numidicus, cos. 109.

is it because she has a law which orders capital punishment to be exacted for receiving things stolen from that place? (Ov. *Fast.* 3.839–848)

If the temple had really carried Rome's collective memory, there would have been no reason for doubt; but what Ovid's poem shows is that the inscription on the cult statue offered just one explanation among many.

A similar argument can be made about statues of mortals. They of all things were meant to embody memory,[14] as Pliny makes clear:

7. *in omnium municipiorum foris statuae ornamentum esse coepere propagarique* memoria *hominum et honores legendi aeuo basibus inscribi, ne in sepulcris tantum legerentur. mox forum et in domibus priuatis factum atque in atriis: honos clientium instituit sic colere patronos.*

    Statues began to ornament the forum of every town, the memory of men began to be perpetu-ated, and honors to be read forever began to be inscribed on the bases, so that they shouldn't be read only on tombs. Soon a forum was made in private houses and *atria* as well; the respect of clients began to honor their patrons in this way. (Plin. *HN* 34.17)

But here too, memory depended on the name inscribed in stone: without an inscription to be read, the attribution of an honorary statue could be as uncertain as the meaning of Minerva Capta.[15]

Mention of statues in houses brings us conveniently to the private sphere, and again it is Pliny who explains things best:

8. *aliter apud maiores in atriis haec erant, quae spectarentur; non signa externorum artificum nec aera aut marmora: expressi cera uultus singulis disponebantur armariis, ut essent imagines quae comitarentur gentilicia funera, semperque defuncto aliquo totus aderat familiae eius qui umquam fuerat populus. stemmata uero lineis discurrebant ad imagines pictas. tabulina codicibus implebantur et monimentis rerum in magistratu gestarum.*

    In the *atria* of our ancestors, on the other hand, portraits were to be looked at. They weren't statues by foreign artists, they weren't bronze or marble, but faces molded in wax and set out in individual cabinets. The purpose was to have likenesses to accompany family funerals, and every time anyone died, all the members of the family that there had ever been were present. There were even family trees, with lines in different directions connecting painted portraits, and the archive rooms were full of codices and documents of the acts of magistrates. (Plin. *HN* 35.6–7)

The use of *imagines* at aristocratic funerals features as Hölkeskamp's first example of the ways the Romans "renew[ed] the inseparable link between past and present,"[16] and for good reason. There is clear and explicit contemporary evidence not only for the obvious commemorative function of the *imagines*[17] but also for how they could stimulate the memory of the past. Sallust writes:

9. *nam saepe ego audiui Q. Maximum P. Scipionem <alios> praeterea ciuitatis nostrae praeclaros uiros solitos ita dicere, quom maiorum imagines intuerentur, uehementissume sibi animum ad*

---

[14] See Tac. *Ann.* 6.2.1 on the disgrace of Livia Iulia, with measures taken *in effigies quoque ac memoriam eius.*

[15] E.g., the bronze statue on a column at the Volcanal (Coarelli 1983, 174–175): an actor who had been struck by lightning (Festus 370L) or Horatius Cocles (Gell. 4.1.1–4)?

[16] Hölkeskamp 2006a, 483 (also 483–487 on triumphs, dedi-cation of temples, display of spoils, honorific statues); for full details on funerals and *imagines*, see H. I. Flower 1996.

[17] Cic. *Verr.* 2.5.36 (*ius imaginis ad memoriam posteritatemque prodendae*); *Rab. Post.* 16 (*imago ipsa ad posteritatis memo-riam prodita*).

uirtutem incendi. scilicet non ceram illam neque figuram tantam uim in sese habere, sed memoria *rerum gestarum eam flammam egregiis uiris in pectore crescere . . .*

I have often heard that Quintus Maximus, Publius Scipio, and other famous men among our citizens used to say that when they were looking at their ancestors' images, their minds were powerfully fired up towards excellence; not of course that the mere wax or the likeness had such power in itself, but that that flame grows in the hearts of excellent men by the memory of past achievements. (Sall. *Iug.* 4.5–6)

But how could portraits alone preserve a memory of events? For Pliny, the *res gestae* were preserved not by the *imagines* but by the documents in the *tabulinum*, and it may be that Sallust too had something similar in mind.[18]

It is important to try to imagine what people did when they were admitted to the *atrium* of a noble house. While waiting their turn to approach the great man's chair, they would admire the tortoiseshell inlay, the Corinthian bronzes, the gold thread in the tapestries,[19] and of course they would look at the portraits and read the inscriptions below:

10.   *perlege dispositas generosa per atria ceras:*
                  contigerunt nulli nomina tanta uiro.

> Read through the wax images displayed throughout noble *atria*: no man has achieved so great a name. (Ov. *Fast.* 1.591–592, on the name "Augustus")

11.   *non tua maiorum contenta est gloria fama*
                  nec quaeris quid quaque index sub imagine dicet.

> Your glory is not content with your ancestors' fame, and you don't ask what the inscription says under each image. (*Panegyricus Messallae* 30–31)

Yet again, as with the temples and the statues, it was not the marble, bronze, or wax in itself that carried the message but the written word. And if the written word was false, then so was the memory:

12. *nec facile est aut rem rei aut auctorem auctori praeferre. uitiatam* memoriam *funebribus laudibus reor falsisque imaginum titulis, dum familiae ad se quaeque famam rerum gestarum honorumque fallente mendacio trahunt; inde certe et singulorum gesta et publica monumenta rerum confusa.*

> It is not easy to put one account before another or one authority before another. I believe that memory has been corrupted by funeral orations and false inscriptions on images, as the respective families claim for themselves, by deceitful falsehood, a story of great deeds and honors; certainly it is from this source that the careers of individuals and the public record of events have alike been thrown into confusion. (Livy 8.40.3–5)

Livy does not often stop to argue about conflicting evidence, but when he does, he takes it for granted that families expanded or invented their ancestors' achievements in the inscriptions below their *atrium* portraits.[20]

---

[18] A. J. Woodman's translation (Penguin Classics 2007) renders *memoria rerum gestarum* as "through the recording of historical affairs."

[19] Verg. *G.* 2.463–464, no doubt from experience. Chair: Cic. *De or.* 3.133, *Leg.* 1.10 (*sedens in solio*).

[20] Livy 4.16.4 on 439 B.C. (*falsum imaginis titulum*), 22.31.11 on 217 B.C. (*augentes titulum imaginis posteros*).

A statue or a wax portrait can remind you what a person looked like, but it cannot tell you what he did in life. Our sources are consistently interested in *res gestae* (items 1, 8, 9, 12)*,* but material objects alone could hardly transmit a memory of events. That, it seems, was something that had to be *read*, whether in an inscription (items 7, 10, 11) or in an archival document (item 8). As Ovid puts it (item 6), *littera prisca docet*.

                                                   2

Our first conclusion, then, must be that the idea of "monumental memory" is perhaps less helpful than it seems. The evidence that can be adduced for it turns out to imply that the memory of events depended less on the monuments themselves than on the *written* information they provided.

There is a further problem: all the suggested *lieux de mémoire* were reminders of individual Roman aristocrats, insofar as their achievements were inscribed on the temples they founded, the bases of their statues, or below their portraits in the ancestral *atrium*. That does not fit very well with the definition of Roman history as "the deeds of the Roman people"—a phrase current from the very beginnings of Latin historiography,[21] and one that could serve as a translation of "the cultural memory of the Romans." Here too we come back to writing:

13. *statui res gestas populi Romani carptim, ut quaeque* memoria *digna uidebantur, perscribere . . .*

     I decided to write out the deeds of the Roman people, selectively, as each seemed worthy of memory. (Sall. *Cat.* 4.2)

14. *Facturusne operae pretium sim si a primordio urbis res populi Romani perscripserim nec satis scio nec, si sciam, dicere ausim . . . utcumque erit, iuuabit tamen rerum gestarum* memoriae *principis terrarum populi pro uirili parte et ipsum consuluisse.*

     I am not sure whether I shall be doing something worth the effort if I write out the deeds of the Roman people from the origin of the city, and if I were sure, I would not venture to say so . . . but be that as it may, it will in itself be a pleasure to have made an honest contribution to the memory of the achievements of the people that is foremost in the world. (Livy, pref. 1–3)

Somehow, if "cultural memory" is to be a historically helpful concept, we have to find a way of explaining how the Roman people came to understand its own past.

Were Sallust and Livy writing for the Roman people? Well, Sallust had been a *popularis* tribune, in the year the Roman people burned down the Senate house,[22] and at least one well-informed reader thought that Livy's history was for the people's benefit:

15. *profiteor mirari T. Liuium auctorem celeberrimum in historiarum suarum quas repetit ab origine urbis quodam uolumine sic orsum, satis enim sibi gloriae quaesitum et potuisse se desidere ni animus inquies pasceretur opere. profecto enim populi gentium uictoris et Romani nominis gloriae, non suae, composuisse illa decuit; maius meritum esset operis amore, non animi causa, perseuerasse et hoc populo Romano praestitisse, non sibi.*

     I confess I admire the famous author Titus Livius for beginning one of the volumes of the history

---

[21] Cato, *Orig.* fr. 1 Chassignet (Pompeius *Commentum artis*   [22] Asconius 33C, 37C, 49C; Cass. Dio 40.49.2–3.
Donati 5.208K): *populi Romani gesta discribere*.

he composed from the origins of the city by saying that he had already achieved fame enough, and could relax, if his restless mind did not feed on the labor. For it was certainly proper that he should have composed it not for his own glory but for that of the people that rules the world, and the name of Rome. It would be more deserving to have persevered from love of labor, not his own satisfaction, and to have done it not for himself but for the Roman people. (Plin. *HN* pref. 16)

But how could that be? Books were luxury items. The typical price of a volume of poetry was about three days' pay for a legionary soldier;[23] with more text to copy, a prose volume would be dearer than that;[24] and Livy's history consisted of 142 volumes. In the Roman republic, the only libraries were in the country villas of the rich;[25] it was not until 39 B.C., when Pollio founded his library in the *atrium Libertatis*,[26] that books became available to that minority of the Roman people who had the habit of reading.[27]

How negligible a minority it was may be seen from two related episodes of the early principate. In A.D. 19, and again in A.D. 64, an allegedly Sibylline prophecy terrified the city's population:[28]

> When thrice three hundred years have come and gone,
> Then civil conflict shall destroy the Romans . . .

The people were clearly unaware of the long tradition of Roman historians, from Quintus Fabius to Marcus Varro, who had fixed the foundation of the city at various dates ranging from 754/3 to 729/8 B.C.,[29] and it did not occur to them to read the *ab urbe condita* dates regularly set out on Augustus's great summary of Roman history, the list of consuls and triumphs on his triumphal arch.[30] Reading was not what they did. They listened to prophets,[31] and nine hundred years must have sounded close enough to cause panic.

Because our literary sources were created by people who *did* read books, and because our scholarly interpretation of them often assumes that their world was as bibliocentric as our own, it may seem self-evidently impossible to find a way into the "cultural memory" of a citizen body that was largely unlettered. The search for sources of memory in the fabric of the city itself is a brave attempt to escape the dilemma, but as we have seen above, it still requires the reading of texts. So where else can we turn?

I take it that popular memory (to use an adjective more precise than "cultural") was the "memory" of events that were believed to have happened and therefore consisted, in some sense, of narrative stories. That being so, and since the oral tradition is long extinct, there is no escape:

[23] Martial 1.66.4 (6 or 10 *sestertii* = 24 or 40 *asses*); Tac. *Ann.* 1.17.4 (10 *asses* per day).

[24] In Diocletian's Price Edict (7.1–12; see Giacchero 1974, 150–151) a copyist's charge for two hundred lines equaled a day's pay for a skilled artisan.

[25] Cic. *Fin.* 3.7–8 (Lucullus at Tusculum), 3.10 (Cicero at Tusculum); *Att.* 4.4a.1 and 8.2 (Cicero at Antium), 4.10.1 (Faustus Sulla at Cumae). Also in the palaces of Hellenistic kings: Plin. *HN* 13.70, 35.10 (Ptolemy, Eumenes); *Suda* E3801, 2.478 Adler (Antiochus). For libraries as war booty, see Plut. *Aem.* 38.11 (Macedon, 168 B.C.), Strabo 13.1.54, C609 (Athens, 86 B.C.).

[26] Plin. *HN* 7.115, 35.10 (*qui primus bibliothecam dicando ingenia hominum rem publicam fecit*). *Atrium Libertatis*: Ov. *Tr.* 3.1.71–72; cf. Livy 43.16.13, Festus 277L, Granius

Licinianus 28.35 (record office). The library had been Caesar's project (Suet. *Iul.* 44.2).

[27] On literacy, see Harris 1989, esp. 171–174 and 222–229 for readers of literature.

[28] Cass. Dio 57.18.4–5, 62.18.3; for the background, see Wiseman 2008, 46–48.

[29] Dion. Hal. *Ant. Rom.* 1.74.1–2 (Cincius, Fabius, Cato); Solinus 1.27 (Cincius, Fabius, Nepos, Lutatius, Atticus, Cicero); Censorinus, *DN* 21.5–6 (Varro).

[30] *CIL* 1².1.1–50; Degrassi 1947, 1–87.

[31] Cic. *Div.* 2.149 (cf. Lucr. 1.102–109) for *uatem audire* as part of *superstitio*.

the surviving texts are all we have. But there are so many of them, concerned with so many different things, that relevant information may still be found. Even authors far removed from the world view of the Roman people may by a casual comment reveal something otherwise unknown to us.

Here for instance is M. Piso, a character in one of Cicero's philosophical dialogues, making the point that intellectual curiosity is innate in human nature:

16. *quid quod homines infima fortuna, nulla spe rerum gerendarum, opifices denique delectantur historia? maximeque eos uidere possumus res gestas audire et legere uelle qui a spe gerendi absunt confecti senectute.*

What of the fact that people of humble station, with no expectation of a public career, and even artisans, take pleasure in history? We can see that the people most eager to hear and read about historical events are those whose age deprives them of the opportunity to take part in them. (Cic. *Fin.* 5.52)

Piso was evidently appealing to something his fellow disputants would take for granted. For us it is precious evidence, perhaps the nearest we can get to the reality of popular memory. But how did those poor people and artisans have access to their history?

The key must be in the next sentence, where Piso refers to people who hear about *res gestae* as well as those who read about them. And at this point another Ciceronian *obiter dictum*, on the superiority of sense perception over belief, may come to our aid:

17. *nam sensus nostros non parens, non nutrix, non magister, non poeta, non scaena deprauat, non multitudinis consensus abducit; at uero animis omnes tenduntur insidiae . . .*

In the case of our senses no parent or nurse or teacher or poet or stage show distorts them, nor does popular opinion lead them astray; for our minds, however, all kinds of traps are laid. (Cic. *Leg.* 1.47)

Popular opinion, "the consensus of the multitude," is just what we are looking for. It was formed by individual childhood influences—parent, nurse, teacher—but also by the communal experience of the *ludi scaenici*, where the audience was always defined as the Roman people itself.[32] What that experience was like is not easy for us to reconstruct; but again, we may get a hint if we listen carefully enough to what our sources say.

In the summer of 45 B.C. the six-year-old daughter of Cicero's friend Atticus was unwell. To help her convalescence, her father took her to the *ludi Apollinares*, and wrote to Cicero about it. Cicero wrote back:

18. *de Attica probo. est quiddam etiam animum leuari cum spectatione tum etiam religionis opinione et fama.*

Good decision about Attica. It's important for the mind to be lifted too, not only by watching the show but also by the general opinion of its religious significance. (*Att.* 13.44.2, ca. 28 July 45).

The games were held in the Circus Flaminius piazza in front of the temple of Apollo the Healer.[33] The other annual *ludi* were those named after Magna Mater, Ceres, Flora, and Victoria, and the

---

[32] Cic. *Sest.* 106, 116–118, *Har. resp.* 22–25, *Pis.* 65, *Att.* 2.19.3, 14.3.2, *Phil.* 1.36; Phaedrus 5.5.34; Plin. *HN* 36.119–120.

[33] Livy 40.51.3 and 6: *theatrum et proscaenium* at the temple of Apollo Medicus.

ludi Romani and *plebeii* that honored Jupiter Optimus Maximus; but in all the multifarious modern scholarship about Roman drama and Roman festivals, religious significance comes a poor second to aristocratic exploitation.[34] Cicero understood the latter very well; but what his letter implies is that the Roman people, including perhaps Atticus and his little girl, saw things differently.

The religious significance of the *ludi* matters for our purposes because there is also evidence, if we care to look for it, that the shows helped the Roman people to understand their own past and the part the gods had played in it. As Mercury says in the prologue of Plautus's *Amphitruo*:

19.
> *nam quid ego memorem (ut alios in tragoediis*
> *uidi, Neptunum Virtutem Victoriam*
> *Martem Bellonam commemorare quae bona*
> *uobis fecissent) quis benefactis meus pater,*
> *deorum regnator, architectust omnibus?*

Why should I—as I've seen other gods in tragedies, Neptune, Virtus, Victoria, Mars, Bellona, relate what good things they've done for you—why should I tell you what benefactions for everyone my father, ruler of the gods, is the deviser of? (Plaut. *Amph.* 41–45)

Ovid's treatment of Q. Claudia and the reception of Magna Mater at Ostia in 204 B.C. is also relevant:

20.
> *dixit, et exiguo funem conamine traxit;*
> *   mira sed et scaena testificata loquar:*
> *mota dea est, sequiturque ducem laudatque sequendo.*

She spoke, and with a tiny effort pulled the rope. I shall speak of wonders, but they are attested also by the stage: the goddess is moved, and follows her guide and in following praises her. (Ov. *Fast.* 4.325–327)

3

So this is the second conclusion: that popular memory consisted not of what the people read, which was negligible, but of what they heard (and saw). Our next task is to think about "the poet and the stage show" (item 17).

As far back as our information goes, it was the bard's song that transmitted knowledge of the past. When Demodocus in Phaeacia sings of the Trojan War, Alcinous comments: "The gods brought this about, and spun a thread of doom for men, that they may be a song for those to come." Six centuries later, Horace knew that without the sacred bard there was only oblivion.[35] The Homeric bard is taught by the Muse to sing the famous deeds of men, and in Hesiod the Muses are the

[34] For a good example of modern ambivalence, see Bernstein 2007, 232–233: "As an integral part of the public cult and festival order, the *ludi publici* were intended to secure the favor and assistance of the gods. However, at the same time, the nobility developed the public games into a universal instrument of their internal and external policy. . . . This ruling elite made the games into a comprehensive means of political influence, because they were at the same time intended to help the community to become aware of itself, and to accentuate and sustain its identity." So which mattered more, religion and identity or elite manipulation?

[35] Hom. *Od.* 8.579–580; cf. *Il.* 6.357–358 (Helen and Paris). Hor. *Carm.* 4.9.25–28. Cf. Cic. *Att.* 10.1.1, *Fam.* 13.15.2, applying to himself Hector's words at *Il.* 22.304–305: "Let me not die without a struggle and without glory, but having done some great deed that those to come may hear of."

daughters of memory, Mnemosyne.[36] At the birth of Latin literature in the third century B.C., the two notions were combined:

21.   *nam diua Monetas filia docuit.*

> For the divine daughter of Memory has taught them. (Liv. Andron. *Od.* fr. 21 Buechner [= *Odyssey* 8.480–481, on bards like Demodocus]).

Moneta is Mnemosyne, "she who calls to mind" as well as "she who warns."[37]

We need not suppose that this was news to the Romans in Livius's time. There is abundant evidence for knowledge of the Hellenic cultural world in archaic Latium;[38] what was new in the third century was the preservation of song and performance in written texts. Since written literature depended on the availability of papyrus, it may be relevant that Roman diplomatic relations with Ptolemaic Egypt began about 273 B.C.[39] In the long run it was an innovation of immense importance (without it we would have no textual evidence), but at the time it probably made little difference to the way popular memory worked.

The first named Latin bard of the new era was Gnaeus Naevius with his *Carmen belli Poenici*, and by good fortune we happen to have evidence, indirect but not to be ignored, about how it reached the Roman people. In his account of the origins of Roman literary scholarship, Suetonius begins with the lectures and discussions held by Crates of Mallos during his stay in Rome, perhaps in the 160s B.C. Then, he says, the Romans themselves followed Crates's example:

22. *hactenus tamen imitati, ut carmina parum adhuc diuulgata uel defunctorum amicorum uel si quorum aliorum probassent diligentius retractarent ac legendo commentandoque etiam ceteris nota facerent: ut C. Octauius Lampadio Naeui Punicum bellum, quod uno uolumine et continenti scriptura expositum diuisit in septem libros.*

> But they imitated him only to this extent, that they carefully rehandled poems that had not yet been circulated, the work either of their own deceased friends or of any others they approved of, and by reading and commenting on them they made them known to everyone else as well—as Gaius Octavius Lampadio did with Naevius's *Punic War*, set out in one volume of continuous text, which he divided into seven books. (Suet. *Gram.* 2.2)

Retractare is an ambiguous word (I deliberately translate it as literally as possible), and it is not certain what Suetonius meant by it. But even so, the clear implication of the whole passage is that poets at this time did not distribute written copies of their work; its delivery must have been oral, and would die with them unless they bequeathed their one performance script to friends who would publicize it. That is evidently what Lampadio did with Naevius's epic; his division of the master text into seven books enabled it for the first time to be copied and "published" as a work to be read. But what matters for popular memory is the original oral delivery, not the newly fashionable circulation of expensive texts.

Naevius's poem taught the Romans about the origins of their city (Romulus the grandson of Aeneas) as well as the great war against Carthage that he himself had fought in. Long after his time,

---

[36] Hom. *Od.* 8.73, 481, 488, cf. 1.338; Hes. *Theog.* 50–55, 915–917.

[37] Hyg. *Fab.* pref. 27: *ex Ioue et Moneta Musae.* Warning: Cic. *Dic.* 1.101, 2.69.

[38] For a summary, see Wiseman 2008, 231–235.

[39] Livy, *Epit.* 14 (*societas*), Dion. Hal. 20.14, Cass. Dio fr. 41 (ὁμολογία).

epic poetry continued to be a main source of information about the Roman past. Here is Servius in the late fourth century A.D., discussing the generic identity of Vergil's *Aeneid*:

23. *est autem heroicum quod constat ex diuinis humanisque personis, continens uera cum fictis; nam Aeneam ad Italiam uenisse manifestum est, Venerem uero locutam cum Ioue missumue Mercurium constat esse compositum.*

It is "heroic," because it is made up of divine and human characters, and contains both truth and fiction; for Aeneas's journey to Italy is plain fact, whereas Venus's conversation with Jupiter and the mission of Mercury are agreed to be invented. (Serv. *Praef.*)

Of course Vergil is a special case, a classic author who was taught in schools. But his work too was created in the first instance for oral performance, and it was in the theater that the Roman people applauded him for it.[40]

Although Vergil didn't like being a celebrity, he did sometimes recite to big audiences, mainly to try out passages he was not certain about, to see how they would be received.[41] And that was not unusual, as we learn from another passing comment of Cicero's. In his treatise on duties, he urges his son to take advice about moral decisions:

24. *ut enim pictores et ii qui signa fabricantur et uero etiam poetae suum quisque opus a uulgo considerari uult, ut si quid reprehensum sit a pluribus id corrigatur, iique et secum et ex aliis quid in eo peccatum sit exquirunt, sic aliorum iudicio permulta nobis et facienda et non facienda et mutanda et corrigenda sunt.*

For just as painters, sculptors, and indeed poets too, all want their work to be assessed by the public, to enable anything criticized by the majority to be put right, and they ask themselves and others where the fault lies, so it is frequently by the judgment of others that we should act, refrain from acting, and change or correct what we do. (Cic. *Off.* 1.147)

Even in a period of literature that we think of as firmly text-based, it is clear that poets first performed to the Roman people (*uulgus*, as Cicero puts it here), and only then thought of committing their final version to papyrus copies.

Epic poets were not the only source of popular memory. To identify our next category, we must go back to the fourth century B.C., and the literature of Athens:

25. εὕροι δ᾽ ἄν τις ἐκ μὲν τοῦ πολέμου τοῦ πρὸς τοὺς βαρβάρους ὕμνους πεποιημένους, ἐκ δὲ τοῦ πρὸς Ἕλληνας θρήνους ἡμῖν γεγενημένους, καὶ τοὺς μὲν ἐν ταῖς ἑορταῖς ᾀδομένους, τῶν δ᾽ ἐπὶ ταῖς συμφοραῖς ἡμᾶς μεμνημένους.

You will find that from war against the barbarians hymns have been made, from war against Greeks we have made laments; the former are sung at festivals, but the latter we have recalled in times of trouble. (Isoc. *Paneg.* 155)

Likewise, Plato comments on those who doubt the existence of the gods:

26. οὐ πειθόμενοι τοῖς μύθοις οὓς ἐκ νέων παίδων ἔτι ἐν γάλαξι τρεφόμενοι τροφῶν τε καὶ ἤκουον καὶ μητέρων,

---

[40] Tac. *Dial.* 31.2; cf. Donat. *Vit. Verg.* 26.90–91 (*Eclogues* on stage), 29.96–99 (Vergil's voice and delivery).

[41] Donat. *Vit. Verg.* 33.112–114: *recitauit et pluribus, sed neque frequenter et ea fere de quibus ambigebat, quo magis iudicium hominum experiretur.*

οἷον ἐν ἐπῳδαῖς μετά τε παιδιᾶς καὶ μετὰ σπουδῆς λεγομένων καὶ μετὰ θυσιῶν ἐν εὐχαῖς αὐτοὺς ἀκούοντές τε, καὶ ὄψεις ὁρῶντες ἑπομένας αὐτοῖς ἃς ἥδιστα ὅ γε νέος ὁρᾷ τε καὶ ἀκούει πραττομένας θυόντων.

They don't believe the stories that they heard as babes in arms from their nurses and mothers, stories like spells that were told both in fun and in earnest; they heard them in prayers at sacrifices, and saw the visual representations that follow, the part of the sacrifice ceremony that a child most loves to see and hear. (Pl. *Leges* 887d)

This evidence for the narrative content of hymns and prayers is particularly important to notice because it helps to make sense of three neglected but significant details in Dionysius's history of early Rome. First about Faunus:

27. ἐτύγχανε δὲ τότε τὴν βασιλείαν τῶν Ἀβοριγίνων παρειληφὼς Φαῦνος, Ἄρεος ὥς φασιν ἀπόγονος, ἀνὴρ μετὰ τοῦ δραστηρίου καὶ συνετός, καὶ αὐτὸν ὡς τῶν ἐπιχωρίων τινὰ Ῥωμαῖοι δαιμόνων θυσίαις καὶ ᾠδαῖς γεραίρουσιν.

It happened that at that time Faunus had inherited the kingship of the Aborigines. Descended, they say, from Ares, he was a man of prudence as well as energy, and the Romans honor him in sacrifices and songs as one of their native gods. (Dion. Hal. *Ant. Rom.* 1.31.2)

Then on Romulus and Remus:

28. οἱ δὲ ἀνδρωθέντες γίνονται . . . οἵους ἄν τις ἀξιώσειε τοὺς ἐκ βασιλείου τε φύντας γένους καὶ ἀπὸ δαιμόνων σπορᾶς γενέσθαι νομιζομένους, ὡς ἐν τοῖς πατρίοις ὕμνοις ὑπὸ Ῥωμαίων ἔτι καὶ νῦν ᾄδεται.

They grew up . . . as one would expect boys to become who were born of royal stock and believed to be of the seed of gods, as is sung even nowadays by the Romans in their traditional hymns. (Dion. Hal. *Ant. Rom.* 1.79.10)

And finally on Marcius Coriolanus:

29. ἐτῶν δὲ μετὰ τὸ πάθος ὁμοῦ τι πεντακοσίων ἤδη διαγεγονότων εἰς τόνδε τὸν χρόνον οὐ γέγονεν ἐξίτηλος ἡ τοῦ ἀνδρὸς μνήμη, ἀλλ' ᾄδεται καὶ ὑμνεῖται πρὸς πάντων ὡς εὐσεβὴς καὶ δίκαιος ἀνήρ.

Though nearly five hundred years have already passed after what happened to him down to the present time, the memory of the man has not become extinct, but he is sung and hymned by all as a pious and just man. (Dion. Hal. *Ant. Rom.* 8.62.3)

Dionysius was very interested in Roman religious ceremonies,[42] and we may be sure that he listened carefully to what was sung for Faunus on the Tiber Island on 13 February, for Pales on the Palatine on 21 April, and for Fortuna Muliebris on the Via Latina on 6 July.[43]

Hymns in the ancient world were normally sung by a chorus. Our evidence allows us only fleeting glimpses of such *choroi* in the Roman world—the boys and girls for Hymenaeus at a wedding,[44] the ladies for Bona Dea at her sanctuary below the Aventine,[45] the eunuch Galli for Magna Mater at the

---

[42] Eyewitness testimony: 7.72.12 (funeral processions), 7.72.18 (prayers and sacrifices). Autopsy implied for "customs surviving to my time": 7.72.2 (*ludi* procession), 7.72.5 (musical instruments used), 7.73.2 (*ludi circenses*).

[43] Faunus: Livy 33.42.10–11, Ov. *Fast.* 2.193–194. Pales and

the Parilia: Varro, *Rust.* 2.1.9, Ov. *Fast.* 2.721–862. Fortuna Muliebris: Val. Max. 1.8.4, Dion. Hal. *Ant. Rom.* 8.55.5.

[44] Catull. 61.36–45 and 114–123, 62.1–19.

[45] Prop. 4.9.23–34, Juv. 6.314–326.

ludi Megalenses,[46] the *mimae* for Flora at the *ludi Florales*,[47] the boys and girls for Apollo and Diana at the *ludi saeculares*.[48] In the first and last of those examples we happen to know who wrote the words; but there must have been poets for all of them, at every festival, just as there were pipers to play the music. What they wrote, and the choir sang, was what stayed in the mind of the Roman people.

If we think only of literature, we may miss the significance of that regular sequence of festivals through the year. It must have been, among other things, an important source of information for the ordinary citizen who did not read books. That was still the norm two centuries after Dionysius, when most Athenians believed that Theseus had founded their democracy:

30. λέγεται μὲν δὴ καὶ ἄλλα οὐκ ἀληθῆ παρὰ τοῖς πολλοῖς οἷα ἱστορίας ἀνηκόοις οὖσι καὶ ὁπόσα ἤκουον εὐθὺς ἐκ παίδων ἔν τε χοροῖς καὶ τραγῳδίαις πιστὰ ἡγουμένοις.

That is an example of the false beliefs that the majority of people state, since they are ignorant of history and consider trustworthy whatever they have heard since childhood in choruses and tragedies. (Paus. 1.3.3)

Like Cicero's "poets and stage shows" (item 17) and Plato's "visual representations" (item 26), Pausanias's juxtaposition of choruses and tragedy reminds us of the performance element in ancient ritual, and thus brings us back to drama. Polybius noted that one of the strengths of the Roman republic was the people's fear of the gods, which he thought was deliberately instilled in them for reasons of control:

31. ἐπὶ τοσοῦτον γὰρ ἐκτετραγῴδηται καὶ παρεισῆκται τοῦτο τὸ μέρος παρ' αὐτοῖς εἴς τε τοὺς κατ' ἰδίαν βίους καὶ τὰ κοινὰ τῆς πόλεως, ὥστε μὴ καταλιπεῖν ὑπερβολήν . . . ἐπεὶ δὲ πᾶν πλῆθός ἐστιν ἐλαφρὸν καὶ πλῆρες ἐπιθυμιῶν παρανόμων, ὀργῆς ἀλόγου, θυμοῦ βιαίου, λείπεται τοῖς ἀδήλοις φόβοις καὶ τῇ τοιαύτῃ τραγῳδίᾳ τὰ πλήθη συνέχειν.

It is impossible to exaggerate the extent to which this matter is turned into tragedy and brought both into their private lives and into the public business of the city. . . . Since every populace is fickle and full of lawless desires, unreasoning anger, and violent passion, the only way of controlling it is by hidden terrors and other such tragedy. (Polyb. 6.56.8, 11)

He may mean "tragedy" literally rather than metaphorically, since we know from contemporary evidence (item 19) that Roman tragedians used the gods to instruct the audience.

Of all rituals, the *ludi scaenici* must have had the greatest impact on the minds of Rome's citizens, as the lavish *apparatus* of the stage enabled them to see their great ancestors act out the heroic past before their eyes.[49] I hope it is no longer necessary to counter the idea that plays on historical subjects were rare in Rome, or to amass once again the evidence for them.[50] Their texts may not often have been found in libraries; but their spectacle was common in Roman theaters, and we should not let the disdain of literary purists blind us to its power:

[46] Varro, *Sat. Men.* 132 (Astbury), Catull. 63.28–30.

[47] Ov. *Fast.* 5.347–352 (*meretricia turba, plebeius chorus*).

[48] Hor. *Carm.* 4.6.31–44, *Carm. saec.* 1–8 and 73–76.

[49] For *apparatus* as the *mot juste*, see Cic. *Sest.* 116, *Pis.* 65, *Fam.* 7.1.2, *Att.* 15.2.3, 15.12.1, *Phil.* 1.36, *Off.* 2.55, *Tusc.*

5.9; Livy 1.9.7, 27.6.19, 27.31.1, 31.49.4, 31.50.2, 32.7.14, 40.45.6, 45.32.8; Phdr. 5.5.14, Val. Max. 2.4.2, Tert. *De spect.* 4.4, 10.2, Ulp. *Digest* 7.1.15.5. Cf. Livy 7.2.13: *hanc uix opulentis regnis tolerabilem insaniam.*

[50] See Wiseman 2008, 205–208 for a brief statement of the argument. One text survives, by a fluke: the pseudo-Senecan *Octavia.*

32.   *quattuor aut pluris aulaea premuntur in horas,*
dum fugiunt equitum turmae peditumque cateruae;
mox trahitur manibus regum fortuna retortis,
esseda festinant, pilenta, petorrita, naues,
captiuum portatur ebur, captiua Corinthus.

The curtains are kept down for four hours or more, while cavalry squadrons and infantry companies take to flight; later, unlucky kings are dragged in with their hands bound behind them; there's a hurry of chariots, carriages, coaches, ships; captured ivory is carried along, and captured Corinth [145 B.C.]. (Hor. *Ep.* 2.1.189–193)

The stage was the only mass medium the ancient world knew.

Even the classic tragedies of Athens were assumed to report historical fact, although, as with epic poems, one had to discount the supernatural.[51] As Plutarch remarks on Phaedra:

33.   τὰς δὲ περὶ ταύτην καὶ τὸν υἱὸν αὐτοῦ δυστυχίας, ἐπεὶ μηδὲν ἀντιπίπτει παρὰ τῶν ἱστορικῶν τοῖς τραγικοῖς, οὕτως ἔχειν θετέον ὡς ἐκεῖνοι πεποιήκασιν ἅπαντες.

As for the misfortunes concerning her and [Theseus's] son, since what the historians say does not conflict with the tragedians, we must suppose that they took place as all those authors have made them. (Plut. *Thes.* 28.2)

And that remained true of the classic tragedy of later centuries, the dance-drama sometimes called *pantomimus*.[52] As Lucian pointed out, the dancer "taught many things about the past," and his repertoire covered the whole history of the world, from the emergence from Chaos to the death of Cleopatra.[53] The sequence is spelt out by Libanius, discussing the tragic poets' ancient role as teachers of the *demos*:

34.   ἐπειδὴ δὲ οἱ μὲν ἀπέσβησαν, τῆς δὲ ἐν μουσείοις παιδεύσεως ὅσον εὐδαιμονέστερον ἐκοινώνησε, τὸ πολὺ δὲ ἐστέρητο, θεῶν τις ἐλεήσας τὴν τῶν πολλῶν ἀπαιδευσίαν ἀντεισήγαγε τὴν ὄρχησιν διδασχήν τινα τοῖς πληθέσι παλαιῶν πράξεων.

But when they died out, and only the wealthy participated in cultural education and the masses were deprived of it, one of the gods took pity on the uneducated multitude and brought in the dance instead, as a sort of instruction for the populace in the events of the past. (Lib. 64.112)

In terrestrial terms, that took place in the early years of Augustus, when the new art form was pioneered by Pylades and Bathyllus; and though our main sources for it are Greek (Lucian and Libanius), and naturally concentrate on the Greek-tragedy repertoire, there is also early evidence for Roman themes danced in togas.[54]

In the fifth book of his astronomical poem, written probably in the late years of Augustus, Manilius reveals the characteristics of those born as the constellation Cepheus rises. Such a man may be a dramatist, or failing that an actor or a *pantomimus* dancer:

---

[51] Cf. Serv. Dan. 1.235: Phaedra is *historia*, but Pasiphae (presumably because of the bull) is *fabula*.

[52] For "pantomime" as ἔνρυθμος τραγῳδία, see the epigraphical sources cited by Lada-Richards 2008, 292.

[53] Lucian, *Salt.* 36–37 (ἡ δὲ πᾶσα τῷ ἔργῳ χορηγία ἡ παλαιὰ ἱστορία ἐστίν), 72 (ὄρχησις…διδάσκουσα πολλὰ τῶν πάλαι).

[54] Plin. *HN* 7.159 on Stephanio, *qui primus togatus saltare instituit*; he performed at both the 17 B.C. and the A.D. 48 Secular Games. Cf. Suet. *Ner.* 54 (Vergil's Turnus), Tert. *De spect.* 17.2 (*fabula Atellana*).

35.   *nunc uoce poetis*
                    nunc tacito gestu referensque affectibus ora,
                    et sua dicendo faciet, scaenisque togatos   480a/482b
                    aut magnos heroas aget, solusque per omnis   482a/480b
                    ibit personas et turbam reddet in uno;   481
                    omnis fortunae uultum per membra reducet,   483
                    aequabitque choros gestu cogetque uidere
                    praesentem Troiam Priamumque ante ora cadentem.

> Now with his voice, now by silent gesture and by rendering them with feeling, in speeches he
> will make the words of poets his own, and on stages he will play Romans in togas or great he-
> roes, and alone will proceed through all the characters and in his one person represent a crowd;
> through his limbs he will recall the appearance of every vicissitude, and match the choruses
> with gesture, and make you see Troy and the fall of Priam present before your eyes. (Manilius,
> *Astronomica* 5.478–485, text as in G. P. Goold's Loeb edition, 1977)

The star dancer performed silently before a chorus that sang the narrative.[55] Those who wrote the
libretti were not regarded highly,[56] but the audience they commanded was enormous (and hard for
the authorities to control).[57] Their work too, like those of their more famous colleagues, helped to
form the mental world of the Roman people from Augustus onward.

4

The third conclusion is that poetry in the Graeco-Roman world was not a merely literary phenomenon but continued to be embedded in the oral culture of the general population. The great majority
of Romans did not read books; they learned what they needed to know at the *ludi scaenici* and the
other festivals of their gods, where epic bards, hymnodists, dramatists, and dance librettists created
that composite narrative of the past that we may define as popular memory.

But was poetry all they listened to? When Cicero referred to ordinary working people obsessed
by history (item 16), it is not self-evident that he was thinking of history as told by poets and dramatists. Were prose forms also embedded in the oral culture?

In the beginning, they certainly were. Herodotus presented his *apodexis* orally:[58]

36.   Ἡροδότου Ἁλικαρνησσέος ἱστορίης ἀπόδεξις ἥδε, ὡς μήτε τὰ γενόμενα ἐξ ἀνθρώπων τῷ χρόνῳ ἐξίτηλα
      γένηται, μήτε ἔργα μεγάλα τε καὶ θωμαστά, τὰ μὲν Ἕλλησι τὰ δὲ βαρβάροισι ἀποδεχθέντα, ἀκλεᾶ
      γένηται.

> This is the demonstration of the researches of Herodotus of Halicarnassus, so that what men
> have done should not become extinct, and that the great and wonderful deeds demonstrated
> by both Greeks and barbarians should not become without glory. (Hdt. 1 pref.)

[55] Phdr. 5.7.23–26, Lucian, *Salt.* 68 (ᾀδόντων ὁμοφωνίαν);
cf. Philo, *De legatione* 96, Aur. Vict. *Caes.* 3.12, Sen. *De ira*
1.20.8 for Caligula acting as a *pantomimus* dancer with a
chorus of his own.

[56] Sen. *Suas.* 2.29 on the "pollution of his talent" by Abronius
Silo; Ovid insisted that he never wrote for the stage, even
though poems of his were danced (*Tr.* 5.7.25–28, cf. 2.519).

Later, Lucan and Statius both wrote *fabulae salticae* (*Vita
Lucani,* Juv. 7.86–87).

[57] Riots and bloodshed: Vell. 2.126.2, Val. Max. 2.4.1; Tac.
Ann. 1.54.2, 1.77.1–3, 4.14.3; Cass. Dio 56.47.2, Macrob.
Sat. 2.7.19.

[58] For instance at Olympia (Lucian, *Herodotus or Aëtion* 1–2).

And even Thucydides, who cared more about the written copy as a permanent resource, took it for granted that history was something an audience listened to:

37. καὶ ἐς μὲν ἀκρόασιν ἴσως τὸ μὴ μυθῶδες αὐτῶν ἀτερπέστερον φανεῖται · ὅσοι δὲ βουλήσονται τῶν τε γενομένων τὸ σαφὲς σκοπεῖν καὶ τῶν μελλόντων ποτὲ αὖθις κατὰ τὸ ἀνθρώπινον τοιούτων καὶ παραπλησίων ἔσεσθαι, ὠφέλιμα κρίνειν αὐτὰ ἀρκούντως ἕξει. κτῆμά τε ἐς αἰεὶ μᾶλλον ἢ ἀγώνισμα ἐς τὸ παραχρῆμα ἀκούειν ξύγκειται.

For an audience, perhaps the unmythical nature of the material will appear rather unpleasing; but if those who wish to look at the clarity both of the past and of events that will happen sometime in the future in much the same way, according to human nature, should judge it useful, that will be enough. It is set down as a permanent possession rather than as a competitive display for immediate hearing. (Thuc. 1.22.4)

When Isocrates in the *Panegyricus* hopes to improve on his fellow orators in style rather than substance, he notes that "the actions that took place in the past have been left to all of us in common."[59] *All* the Athenians, not just those who read books.

The same assumption applied two and a half centuries later. Here is Polybius, describing Flamininus's declaration of the freedom of Greece:

38. τηλικοῦτον συνέβη καταρραγῆναι τὸν κρότον ὥστε καὶ μὴ ῥᾳδίως ἂν ὑπὸ τὴν ἔννοιαν ἀγαγεῖν τοῖς νῦν ἀκούουσι τὸ γεγονός.

Such a shout broke out that those today who hear what happened would not easily be able to bring it into their minds. (Polyb. 18.46.9)

We should not read too much into a mere passing phrase; but even so, Polybius's first thought here—that this event of two generations ago will be *heard*, not just read about—is consistent with some of his more considered observations about the nature of history. Take for instance the programmatic passage in book 3 where Polybius insists on the value of knowledge of the past for a man in public life. He goes on:

39. διόπερ οὐχ οὕτως ἐστὶ φροντιστέον τῆς αὐτῶν τῶν πράξεων ἐξηγήσεως, οὔτε τοῖς γράφουσι οὔτε τοῖς ἀναγινώσκουσι τὰς ἱστορίας, ὡς τῶν πρότερον καὶ τῶν ἅμα καὶ τῶν ἐπιγινομένων τοῖς ἔργοις. ἱστορίας γὰρ ἐὰν ἀφέλῃ τις τὸ διὰ τί καὶ πῶς καὶ τίνος χάριν ἐπράχθη, καὶ τὸ πραχθὲν πότερα εὔλογον ἔσχε τὸ τέλος, τὸ καταλειπόμενον αὐτῆς ἀγώνισμα μὲν, μάθημα δὲ οὐ γίγνεται · καὶ παραυτίκα μὲν τέρπει, πρὸς δὲ τὸ μέλλον οὐδὲν ὠφελεῖ τὸ παράπαν.

For this reason both those who write histories and those who read them should pay attention to the narrative, not just of the events themselves but also of what preceded, accompanied, and followed them. For if one takes away from history the questions why, how, and for what purpose something was done, and whether it had the expected outcome, what is left of it becomes just a competitive display, not something one can learn from, and though it pleases for the moment, it is of no use at all for the future. (Polyb. 3.31.11–13)

Polybius clearly refers to people *reading* history—indeed, he goes on to point out how much easier and more convenient it is to have just his forty volumes of interconnected narrative rather than

[59] Isoc. *Paneg.* 9: αἱ μὲν γὰρ πράξεις αἱ προγεγενημέναι κοιναὶ πᾶσιν ἡμῖν κατελείφθεσαν.

trying to read or obtain the books of the various authors who dealt with all the different regional events. But he is referring only to his sort of history, that which provides a μάθημα by spelling out the reasons for events, the circumstances associated with them, and the consequences that followed from them; any other kind of history is just an ἀγώνισμα that pleases for the moment.

Obviously, he thinks of himself as a Thucydides (item 37): on the one hand, the audience at a one-off oral performance; on the other, the future readers of that permanent possession, the written text. So he proceeds to justify his type of history:

40. ὅσῳ διαφέρει τὸ μαθεῖν τοῦ μόνον ἀκοῦσαι, τοσούτῳ καὶ τὴν ἡμετέραν ἱστορίαν ὑπολαμβάνω διαφέρειν τῶν ἐπὶ μέρους συντάξεων.

I consider that my [universal] history is as much superior to the partial ones as acquiring knowledge is superior to simply listening. (Polyb. 3.32.10)

And he returns to the subject in the proem to book 9, this time with a more fleeting allusion to his great predecessor:

41. οὐκ ἀγνοῶ δὲ διότι συμβαίνει τὴν πραγματείαν ἡμῶν ἔχειν αὐστηρόν τι, καὶ πρὸς ἓν γένος ἀκροατῶν οἰκειοῦσθαι καὶ κρίνεσθαι, διὰ τὸ μονοειδὲς τῆς συντάξεως.

I am aware of the fact that my work has a certain austerity, and is suited to and approved by only one type of audience, because the composition is of a single type. (Polyb. 9.1.2)

As he goes on to explain, other historians use various different modes, and thus "attract many to make the acquaintance of their work."[60] Among those who may enjoy such non-Polybian history is the man who just likes to *listen*, and Polybius knows that his "pragmatic" history of politics and war will be unattractive to most types of listener.[61]

It is particularly interesting that both here and elsewhere Polybius refers to the recipients of his own history as ἀκούοντες.[62] Liddell and Scott gloss that as "readers," but Polybius was quite capable of writing ἀναγινώσκοντες if he had wanted to, and I think we must recognize that even this most reader-centered of historians also assumed an audience for history, among whom those who appreciated his work, the "lovers of learning,"[63] would be in a minority.

The three types of audience member identified by Polybius in the preface to book 9 were the φιλήκοος, who just likes a story, the πολυπράγμων καὶ περιττός, who collects information for its own sake, and the πολιτικός, who is capable of drawing lessons from the past. A century later, Dionysius of Halicarnassus also presented a tripartite analysis, in terms that both allude to Polybius and make clear his own more inclusive approach:

42. σχῆμα δὲ ἀποδίδωμι τῇ πραγματείᾳ οὔθ' ὁποῖον οἱ τοὺς πολέμους μόνους ἀναγράψαντες ἀπεδεδώκασι ταῖς ἱστορίαις οὔθ' ὁποῖον οἱ τὰς πολιτείας αὐτὰς ἐφ' ἑαυτῶν διηγησάμενοι οὔτε ταῖς χρονικαῖς παραπλήσιον, ἃς ἐξέδωκαν οἱ τὰς Ἀτθίδας πραγματευσάμενοι· μονοειδεῖς τε γὰρ ἐκεῖναι καὶ ταχὺ προσίστανται τοῖς ἀκούουσιν· ἀλλ' ἐξ ἁπάσης ἰδέας μικτὸν ἐναγωνίου τε καὶ θεωρητικῆς καὶ διηγηματικῆς, ἵνα καὶ τοῖς περὶ τοὺς πολιτικοὺς διατρίβουσι λόγους καὶ τοῖς περὶ τὴν φιλόσοφον ἐσπουδακόσι θεωρίαν καὶ εἴ τισιν ἀοχλήτου δεήσει διαγωγῆς ἐν ἱστορικοῖς ἀναγνώσμασιν ἀποχρώντως ἔχουσα φαίνηται.

---

[60] Polyb. 9.1.3: πολλοὺς ἐφέλκονται πρὸς ἔντευξιν τῶν ὑπομνημάτων.

[61] Polyb. 9.1.4 (τὸν φιλήκοον), 9.1.5 (τῷ πλείονι μέρει τῶν ἀκροατῶν).

[62] E.g., Polyb. 1.13.6, 9.1.6.

[63] οἱ φιλομαθοῦντες (Polyb. 2.56.11–12, 9.2.5).

The plan I have given to my work is not like the one those who write only of wars have given to their histories, or those who narrate just the constitutions themselves, nor is it like the chronicles that the authors of the *Atthides* have produced (for those are of a single type and soon offend listeners), but it is a combination of every kind—political, theoretical, and narrative—so that it may seem adequate to those who are concerned with political speeches, to those who devote themselves to philosophical speculation, and to any who may want undisturbed entertainment in their historical readings. (Dion. Hal. *Ant. Rom.* 1.8.3)

Again, we see the easy slippage between listening and reading. Dionysius was a professor of rhetoric, used to engaging with an audience, but he also ranked himself with "those who have chosen to leave monuments of their own mind to posterity."[64] Both stages of "publication" were equally important.

Two of Dionysius's three categories, the political and the philosophical, recur in the preface to his eleventh book, and the third is clearly implied. He claims that his history will appeal to practically everyone,[65] and he brings in the entertainment factor as he explains why he has dealt at length with the struggle between the patricians and the *plebs*:

43. ἥδεται γὰρ ἡ διάνοια παντὸς ἀνθρώπου χειραγωγουμένη διὰ τῶν λόγων ἐπὶ τὰ ἔργα, καὶ μὴ μόνον ἀκούουσα τῶν λεγομένων ἀλλὰ καὶ τὰ πραττόμενα ὁρῶσα. οὐδέ γ᾽, ὅταν πολιτικὰς ἀκούουσι πράξεις, ἀρκοῦνται τὸ κεφάλαιον αὐτὸ καὶ τὸ πέρας τῶν πραγμάτων μαθόντες.

     Everybody's mind takes pleasure in being conducted through words to deeds, and in not only hearing what was said but seeing what was done. And when people listen to political events, it is not enough for them just to learn the outline and outcome of what was done . . . (Dion. Hal. *Ant. Rom.* 11.1.3)

"Seeing what was done" evidently refers to the oratorical technique of *enargeia*, putting the events vividly before the listener's eyes.[66] Not everyone will share Dionysius's view that his history is entertaining, but it is clear enough that he hoped to be able to engage a large and varied audience.

Things become much clearer when we come forward another two centuries to Lucian's essay on how to write history. He spells it out quite explicitly:

44. ὅλως πῆχυς εἷς καὶ μέτρον ἀκριβές, ἀποβλέπειν μὴ εἰς τοὺς νῦν ἀκούοντας ἀλλ᾽ εἰς τοὺς μετὰ ταῦτα συνεσομένους τοῖς συγγράμμασιν.

     In short, the one yardstick and exact measure is to look not to those who are listening to you now but to those who hereafter will make the acquaintance of your writings. (Lucian, *Hist. conscr.* 39)

Historians are like any other literary artists; Lucian's contemporary Aelius Aristides puts them "between the poets and the orators," and at one point calls Thucydides a ποιητής.[67] Like poets and orators, they both perform to the crowd (remember all those bad historians Lucian had heard) and then, if they're lucky, find a readership for their written texts.

The two stages of "publication" were normally taken for granted as something everyone knew, but explicit evidence can sometimes be found. Take, for instance, Lucian's essay "Intellectuals for Hire," about which he imagines his friend Sabinus making this comment:

[64] τοὺς προαιρουμένους μνημεῖα τῆς ἑαυτῶν ψυχῆς τοῖς ἐπιγιγνομένοις καταλιπεῖν (Dionysius 1.1.2).

[65] ἅπασι μὲν ὡς εἰπεῖν ἀνθρώποις (Dionysius 11.1.1).

[66] The *locus classicus* is Quin. *Inst.* 6.2.31–32.

[67] Aelius Aristides, *Orationes* 28.68 and 72–73.

45. πάλαι μὲν, ὦ φιλότης, ὡς εἰκός, εὐδοκίμηταί σοι τουτὶ τὸ σύγγραμμα καὶ ἐν πολλῷ πλήθει δειχθέν, ὡς οἱ τότε ἀκροασάμενοι διηγοῦντο, καὶ ἰδίᾳ παρὰ τοῖς πεπαιδευμένοις ὁπόσοι ὁμιλεῖν αὐτῷ καὶ διὰ χειρὸς ἔχειν ἠξίωσαν.

"As you'd expect, my dear friend, this piece of yours has long been admired, both when it was performed before a great crowd, as those who heard it then have told me, and privately among those of the educated who have seen fit to make its acquaintance and have it in their hands." (Lucian, *Apologia* 3)

This was not some innovation of the "Second Sophistic" but how literature had always worked. Lucian's "educated" are the same sort of people as Polybius's "lovers of learning" and those who wanted to "look at the clarity" in Thucydides's Athens (item 37). But they were not the only people who mattered: from first to last, historians might also be keen to command a big popular audience.

All this evidence comes from the Greek-speaking world, but the same must have applied in Rome, where history was the *res gestae* of the Roman people (items 13–14), and Livy wrote it for their sake, not his own (item 15). The enthusiastic history fans mentioned by Cicero (item 16) are recognizable as Polybius's φιλήκοοι,[68] and it is possible that the *commissiones* where Augustus told the praetors to control the use of his name were like the ἀγωνίσματα mentioned by Thucydides and Polybius (items 37 and 39).[69]

The Roman people had the opportunity to listen to prose writers as well as poets. As so often, the evidence is unobtrusive, mentioned in passing by an author with other priorities:

46.   *scribimus inclusi, numeros ille, hic pede liber,*
              grande aliquid quod pulmo animae praelargus anhelet.
              scilicet haec populo pexusque togaque recenti
              et natalicia tandem cum sardonyche albus
              sede leges celsa . . .

Behind closed doors we write—one in verse, another prose—something grand for a huge lungful of air to puff out. This is for the people, of course, and eventually you'll read it from a high position, well combed, all white in a fresh toga, wearing the sardonyx you got for your birthday. (Pers. 1.13–17)

What attracts the satirist is the writer-performer's self-importance. But you had to look impressive if you wanted to command an audience in the middle of the Forum, or in the theater or some other public place.[70] Historians were "between orators and poets," and that man on the platform in the dazzling toga and the sardonyx ring could easily be Livy, deploying his famous eloquence on the moral lessons of history.

Like Vergil, and perhaps less unwillingly, Livy was a celebrity.[71] It is worth remembering what he was celebrated for, as explained by a professor of rhetoric:

[68] Cic. *Fin.* 5.52: *quid cum uolumus nomina eorum qui quid gesserint nota nobis esse, parentes patriam multa praeterea minime necessaria?* Polyb. 9.1.4: τὸν μὲν γὰρ φιλήκοον ὁ γενεαλογικὸς τρόπος ἐπισπᾶται.

[69] Suet. *Aug.* 89.3: *admonebat praetores ne paterentur nomen suum commissionibus obsolefieri.* The reference is probably to the *ludi,* for which the praetors were made responsible in 22 B.C. (Cass. Dio 54.2.3–4).

[70] Hor. *Sat.* 1.4.74–75 (*medio foro*), 1.10.38–39 (theater), *Ep.* 1.19.41–42 (theater); Petron. *Sat.* 3.1, 6.1 (portico in *horti*), 90.1 (portico in temple precinct), 90.5 (theater). Persius's satire assumes a public audience for literature: 1.42 (*os populi meruisse*), 63 (*quis populi sermo est?*).

[71] Plin. *Ep.* 2.3.8 (his *nomen* and *gloria*); *Suda* K2098, 3.158 Adler (his πολὺ καὶ κλεινὸν ὄνομα). He was on good terms with Augustus and his family (Tac. *Ann.* 4.34.3, Suet. *Claud.* 41.1).

47. *neque indignetur sibi Herodotus aequari T. Liuium, cum in narrando mirae iucunditatis claris-*
    simique candoris, tum in contionibus supra quam enarrari potest eloquentem; ita quae dicuntur
    omnia cum rebus tum personis accommodata sunt; adfectus quidem, praecipueque eos qui sunt
    dulciores, ut parcissime dicam, nemo historicorum commendauit magis.

    Nor would Herodotus complain that Titus Livius is put at his level, a man of extraordinary charm
    and lucid clarity in his narrative, and in his speeches eloquent beyond description; everything
    said is so appropriate both to the circumstances and to the speaker, and none of the historians
    (to put it most sparingly) has done more to commend the emotions, especially the more agree-
    able ones. (Quin. *Inst.* 10.1.101)

Since his virtues were those of the orator, in particular the richness of display oratory rather than
the cut and thrust of the courtroom,[72] it is surely inconceivable that his work was written only to
be read on papyrus.

It is true that more select venues were available—what another satirist called "audiences of fine
gentlemen"[73]—and the historians Pliny knew evidently read their works indoors to invited friends
and acquaintances.[74] But the fact that we are well informed about the custom of *recitationes* in
private houses should not tempt us to think that literature was only for the "elite"—whatever we
choose to mean by that slippery word. Some Roman historians drew big crowds, others (like Livy)
small and discerning ones, but there is no reason to doubt that for Romans, as for Lucian's Greeks,
history was "displayed in public."[75]

OUR FINAL conclusion, then, is that popular memory ("collective memory," "cultural memory") was
an amalgam of what the Roman people heard and saw in their rich oral-performance culture of song
and story, prose and verse, drama and narrative. The "landscape of memory" to which Karl-Joachim
Hölkeskamp rightly draws attention served as a reminder of stories the people knew, but could not
in itself generate the knowledge.

In making this argument I have deliberately, and perhaps tediously, insisted on the detail of
ancient sources. This was in order to bring out the easily missable evidence for something that seems
to me too important to ignore: in Rome, as in the cities of the Greek world, an ordinary person could
get a decent literary and historical education without ever having to open a book.

[72] Quint. *Inst.* 8.1.3 (*mira facundia*), 10.1.32 (*lactea ubertas*);
Sen. *Suas.* 6.21–22 (*benignus, candidissimus aestimator*);
Suet. *Dom.* 10.3 (volume of excerpted speeches). Cf. Cic.
Orat. 66 on the closeness of history to epideictic oratory, *De
or.* 2.60 on historians (unlike philosophers) wanting to be
understood by the *uulgus*.

[73] Varro, *Sat. Men.* fr. 517 (Astbury) (*acroasis bellorum hominum*), cf. *Antiquitates Diuinae* fr. 8 Cardauns (*intra parietes
in schola* rather than *extra in foro*), both with reference to
philosophy; Cic. *Att.* 15.17.2 (*in acroasi legere*); Suet. *Aug.*
85.1 (*in coetu familiarium uelut in auditorio recitauit*). It

cannot be literally true that Asinius Pollio was "the first of
all the Romans to recite his works to an invited audience"
(Sen. *Controv.* 4 pref. 2).

[74] Plin. *Ep.* 1.13.3 (Servilius Nonianus), 7.17.3, 9.27 (Tacitus?).

[75] Suda K2098 (3.159 Adler): τοῦ μὲν Κορνούτου παμπλείστους
ἀκούειν ... τοῦ γε Λιβίου ὀλίγους, ἀλλὰ ὧν τι ὄφελος ἦν ἐν κάλλει
ψυχῆς καὶ ἐν εὐγλωττίᾳ. Lucian, *History* 5 (ἐν τῷ κοινῷ δέδεικται
ἡ ἱστορία), cf. 10 (audiences include τὸν συρφετὸν καὶ τὸν
πολὺν δῆμον).

4 ◆ In Defense of Concepts, Categories, and Other Abstractions: Remarks on a Theory of Memory (in the Making)

Karl-J. Hölkeskamp

In the initial statement mapping out the program of his brilliant survey of media and messages of Roman "popular memory," Peter Wiseman "would like to see . . . metaphors and abstractions" such as "monumental memory," the urban topography of the *urbs Roma* "read" "as a cityscape of *memoria* in stone,"—that is, as "a landscape fraught with political, historical, sacral, and mythical meanings and messages," "translated into empirical evidence."[1] Very well.

He takes issue with my (admittedly polemical) statement that the "discipline of ancient history has 'begun to break out of the "ghetto" of its traditional fixations and restrictions'." In particular, it is "slowly emancipating itself from its one-sided methodological fixation upon a conservative classical philology."[2] On the contrary, he proposes "that a proper understanding of Roman memory requires *more*, not *less*, attention to the detail of the ancient sources and emancipation not from classical scholarship but from *unexamined* concepts and *grand* abstractions" (my italics).[3] Not quite so well.

First of all, I hasten to make clear that Wiseman's own well-known way of doing "classical scholarship" in the full inter- and transdisciplinary sense of the term was certainly not the target of my polemical side glance; on the contrary. What he sees as a strictly empirical approach to "reading" the evidence on monuments (such as those of the "resplendent Aemilii" or the *columna Minucia*)[4] is part and parcel of the indispensable methodological underpinning of my theory of Roman memory in the making—in other words, it is a fundamental interpretive strategy[5] to uncover the particular sort of "memory-evoking" or "memory-generating capacity" of individual monuments within the "text" or "con-text" of Roman culture. I borrow these concepts from the art historian Aby Warburg on the one hand, and from Clifford Geertz on the other, and I will return to them shortly.[6] I certainly share Wiseman's ultimate goal, namely "to illustrate the complex processes that created the historical tradition on republican Rome"—the stuff that "collective" or "cultural memory" is

These comments and suggestions were delivered as a rejoinder to Peter Wiseman's contribution at the conference. I have added a few observations and the necessary documentation but not changed the particular character of the text.

I should like to thank Karl Galinsky for the invitation and encouragement (at this memorable event as well as on other occasions), Peter Wiseman for an inspiring exchange of ideas and his generous way of agreeing to disagree, and Elke Stein-Hölkeskamp for a critical reading of the final version.

[1] Wiseman in this volume, p. 43.

[2] Hölkeskamp 2010, 125 and 126. Cf. also the rejoinder to Crawford 2011: Hölkeskamp 2011b.

[3] Wiseman in this volume, p. 44.

[4] Wiseman (1993) 1998 and (1996) 1998.

[5] Cf. also Wiseman 1995 and 2004 as well as his other seminal contributions to our understanding of Rome's "(memorial) culture" in Wiseman 1979, 1994, 2008, and 2009.

[6] Cf. on the new (or renewed) interest in, and the debates on, "(collective) memory," "collective mentalities," etc., the underlying intellectual traditions and their relation to modern "cultural history," e.g., Hutton 1988, Confino 1997, Olick and Robbins 1998, and Klein 2000, all with ample bibliography.

made of; and I think that his approach to "the investigation of the history and pseudo-history"[7] of families like the Minucii and the Aemilii by reading the multilayered allusions, meanings, and messages of their monuments behind a garbled tradition is particularly promising.

It is against this backdrop that I do not understand Wiseman's claim that—if a monument (such as the Temple of Minerva Capta) "had really carried Rome's collective memory, there would have been no reason for doubt" or ambivalence or heterogeneity[8]—after all, as Wiseman himself has explicitly emphasized and brilliantly shown in his own readings of monuments and their mytho-historical meaning(s), we must always "allow for the fact that archaic monuments were interpreted, or misinterpreted, in various ways by later generations."[9] I quote just one particularly pertinent example: the *lacus Curtius* in the central area of the Forum Romanum. Does this "monument" not carry a considerable "memory-generating capacity" just because there are completely different, indeed unrelated myths connected with it? After all, the *lacus* marked a very special space in the midst of the politico-sacral topography of the *urbs Roma*—a space literally laden with symbolic meanings and mythical-historical allusions.[10] The pious *fabula* of the *devotio* of a young warrior named Marcus Curtius, who, mounted and armed, rode his horse into the chasm that had opened right here in the center of the Forum, was certainly "memorable" enough: according to the legend, the chasm closed immediately—the demand of the gods of the underworld that what the *populus Romanus* valued most, namely *arma* and *virtus* of a *civis fortissimus*, be offered to them was now fulfilled, the *imperii fundamenta* were thus made secure, and the *res publica* could become *perpetua*.[11] The other myth—the miraculous escape of the Sabine *vir fortissimus* Mettius Curtius from the thick of battle between Romans under Romulus and Sabines under Titus Tatius[12]—also had a claim to "memorability," namely part of the master narrative of the foundations of the *imperium* and Rome's long way to become the *caput mundi*. A monument like this could always be, and perhaps even necessarily had to be, "read" as an open text, open to different explanations and interpretations at different times, in different contexts, and even by different people—and that is just the reason why it acquired a particularly long-lasting aura: in the early empire, Romans used to throw coins into the *lacus* to discharge vows for the safety and well-being of the *princeps*.[13]

Secondly, I don't know whether the "abstractions" in question are "grand"—it would be, to say the least, a little presumptuous, as it were, to subsume them under the same category as the concepts and models put forward by such icons of "grand theory" as those from Jacques Derrida, Michel Foucault, and Thomas Kuhn to the *Annales* historians, treated in the masterful contributions to the volume on the *Return of Grand Theory in the Human Sciences*, edited and masterminded by Quentin Skinner.[14] In other words, I do not believe that these "abstractions" can or should lay claim to the same epistemological status as, for example, Kuhn's concept of "change of paradigm" or the idea of a "longue durée" and the universalist pattern of historical processes and structures, and I am not proposing yet another "turn"—a sort of "memorial turn" after the "linguistic," "cultural," "iconic," and "spatial turns."

[7] Wiseman (1996) 1998, 105.

[8] Wiseman in this volume, p. 45.

[9] Wiseman (1996) 1998, 93.

[10] Varro, *Ling.* 5.148–150 has no fewer than three versions of the origins. Cf. Richardson 1992, 229–230 s.v. and now the detailed discussion by Oakley 1998, 96–102.

[11] Varro, *Ling.* 5.148; Livy 7.6.1–6; Dion. Hal. *Ant. Rom.* 14.11.1–5; Val. Max. 5.6.2; Plin. *HN* 15.78; Cass. Dio fr. 30.1–2; Zonar. 7.25.1–6; (Paul). Fest p. 42 Lindsay s.v. Curtilacum.

[12] Calpurnius Piso, fr. 6 (Peter) = fr. 8 (Beck and Walter) = Varro, *Ling.* 5.149; Livy 1.12.2–10; 13.5; 7.6.5; Dion. Hal. *Ant. Rom.* 2.42.2–6; Plut. *Vit. Rom.* 18.5–6. Cf. Vasaly 1993, 43–45.

[13] Suet. *Aug.* 57.1.

[14] Skinner 1985.

However, I do admit that Jan Assmann and his seminal book on the "cultural memory" on the one hand[15] and the magisterial multivolume collection of the French national *Realms of Memory*, masterminded by Pierre Nora, on the other[16] are "two inspirational forerunners." Both could (with much more justification than I can hope for) lay claim to be counted among the protagonists of innovative "grand theories" or "changes of paradigm" in the Kuhnian sense of the concept. I gladly admit that Assmann's concept of a (long-range) "cultural memory" versus a (short-range) "communicative memory" in my opinion offers an interesting and indeed promising explanatory potential as a starting point for a theory of memory "Roman-style": the former comprises the whole range of strategies and media of the selective and stylized preservation of "memorable" events of the remote past—such as the myths around the *lacus Curtius*; the latter is in the full sense of the term "present in the present" as it retains only recent "(hi)stories" of the preceding two or three generations. And Nora's sort of invitation to embark on an intellectual glassbead game by playing on the explicit and implicit, literal and metaphorical meanings of *lieu(x)* and *milieu(x) de mémoire* (playing with the double entendre of singular and plural is part of the game) on the other was too much of a temptation for me.[17]

However, they are not the only ones: I name but a few other "forerunners" to whom my reconstruction of what I still call "collective" or "cultural memory"—I'll come back to this decision in due course—owes different, but invariably huge, debts. First of all, theory should and does matter—and not only to the ancient historian and not only in a rather general way, as formulated by the late Reinhart Koselleck in his classic book *Futures Past: On the Semantics of Historical Time*: "what turns a *story* into *history* cannot be read from the 'sources' directly and immediately." As Koselleck put it in his typical style, we need "a theory of possible histories in order to make our sources speak." In other words: any "source"—or rather: "any relic that we turn into a source and thus into 'evidence' by our questions"—refers us to "a (hi)story that is something more or less, but at any rate something other than the relic itself."[18] It is these questions that lead us beyond or beneath the surface of individual acts, facts, and dates, "traités et batailles,"[19] to the underlying contexts and interdependencies, structures, long-range developments and processes—and to ways of thinking, judging, and distinguishing between right and wrong, to the repertoire of values, binding rules, and prevalent norms of past or historical societies, and last but not least to the ways and means, media and strategies, explicit or implicit, of constructing and reproducing their collective identity in the shape of shared memory or memories. These questions call for reflection, not only on methods and models, concepts and categories but also on what we want to do in "classics" and history (ancient as well as modern) and the humanities in general. That means that we are in need of a theory (or even a repertoire of theories) in a broad sense of the concept.[20]

Among my "inspirational forerunners," who have explicitly asked such questions or—by case studies and the like—have implicitly provided concepts, categories, or models to deal with these questions or at least suggestions how to formulate them in the first place, I must count Hubert Cancik's article on

[15] J. Assmann 1992 = 2011 and 2000 = 2006; cf. also A. Assmann 1999 = 2011.

[16] Nora 1984–1992 = 1996–1998. Cf. Hölkeskamp and Stein-Hölkeskamp 2011, with further references.

[17] Hölkeskamp (2001) 2004a, 138–144, 164–165; 2006a, 480–483 and passim.

[18] Koselleck 1979, 204–206 (my translation, or rather paraphrase).

[19] Cf. on the (polemical) concept of "histoire traités-et-batailles" Veyne 1976, referring to Febvre (1947) 1953. Cf. also Morstein-Marx 2009 on the "changing character of political history" from "historical positivism to political culture"; Hölkeskamp 2010, chs. 3–5, 9, and passim.

[20] I have argued my case in a few other concrete contexts: Hölkeskamp 2006c, 2009a and b, 2010, 2011b, and 2013a. Important contributions to the debate on (the necessity of) theories and methodological reflection include Flaig 2003, Jehne 2006, Morstein-Marx 2009, and Roller 2010, all with further references.

"Rome as a Sacral Landscape"[21] in a rather arcane periodical by the interesting title *Visible Religion*; Diane Favro's work on the urban image of Augustan Rome, the urban impact of triumphs, and, last but not least, on the Forum Romanum and Roman Memory;[22] Harriet Flower's seminal contributions on the "spectacular" dimensions of Roman political culture;[23] Egon Flaig's "readings" of symbolic gestures, the politics of ritual(s), and practices of *memoria*;[24] and (once again last but not least) Tonio Hölscher's fundamental work on the "language" of images in the broadest sense of the concept, on the "semantics" of monuments, on what he calls "representative art" as the single most important medium of the politics of public memory,[25] and, in particular, on theoretical and methodological approaches to make this art "readable."[26] I may ask the reader's indulgence and also mention my own contributions on *exempla* and *mos maiorum* and Capitol, Comitium, and Forum as public spaces and memorial landscapes, both (just as the works by my "inspirational forerunners" from modern classics) replete with empirical evidence for the character, interrelated politico-sacral and symbolic-memorial functions of public spaces, the meanings and messages of temples, trophies, and statues as well as of pomp, processions, and other performances *in* public as well as under the eyes of the *populus as* public and as addressee of its meanings and messages.[27] Therefore, I would like to contradict the dismissal of this conceptual framework as "unexamined" in the sense of "empirically untested."

My approach is based on a concept—not unexamined but tried and tested in a broad range fields—by yet another "inspirational forerunner" (with a legitimate claim to a place among Quentin Skinner's masters of "grand theory"), namely Clifford Geertz: he proposed to take culture as a "web of significance," as an "ensemble of texts, themselves ensembles," which by their inseparable interdependence form a whole or "web" that is more than the sum of its constituent parts (or "texts")—and it is this complex web, according to Geertz, "which the anthropologist strains to read over the shoulders of those to whom they properly belong."[28]

It goes without saying that the ancient historian (or the "classicist") cannot hope to decode the full complexity of Roman (republican) culture—but we can and should try to follow Koselleck's advice and formulate a theory or at least a framework of questions, concepts, and categories in order to make some historical or "cultural" sense of the "relics" that we do have. Peter Wiseman himself has taken the lead here, when he expounded an astonishing range of such "relics"—apparently isolated items of information on potential sources of a "popular memory" in the shape of all sorts of songs and performances originally designed for oral delivery, from plays and "dance drama" to epic poetry, hymns, and prayers; and, in fact, he takes them as "texts" in an "ensemble of texts," which he aptly describes as the "rich oral-performance culture of song and story, prose and verse, drama and narrative."[29]

It was this culture that made it possible for the *plebs Romana* (to put it in Nicholas Horsfall's admirably pointed phrase) to look "rather further than bread and circuses, bed, booze, and bawdy."[30] Moreover, it was part and parcel of this culture that political oratory in the *contiones*—which Cicero rightly defined as *oratoris maxima scaena*—as well as on the similarly public "stage" provided by

---

[21] Cancik 1985–1986.

[22] Cf. Favro 1996, 1994, and 1988 respectively.

[23] Flower 1996 and 2004.

[24] Flaig 1993, 1995, and 2003.

[25] Hölscher 1978, 1980, 1984, 1990, 2001a, and 1987 = 2004.

[26] Cf. especially Hölscher 1992, 2000, and 2001b.

[27] Hölkeskamp (1996) 2004a and (2001) 2004a, cf. also Hölkeskamp 2006a, 2008, 2011a, and 2012.

[28] Geertz 1973, 5, 452 (quotations); cf. also Geertz 1983; Roller 2010, 238 and passim.

[29] Wiseman in this volume, p. 62.

[30] Horsfall 1996, 117; cf. Horsfall 2003, 99; Morstein-Marx 2004, ch. 3 (on "civic knowledge").

political trials had a central function as a medium of collective *memoria*. Public speech in the broad sense of the term was replete with historical allusions of all sorts and in the broadest sense of the term—preferably allusions to events and *exempla*, men, and also, once again, monuments that are the "talk of the Town," well known to the *populus* (and the *suffragatores*) in attendance, in Cicero's words, not only *ex sermone hominum* but also *ex memoria vestra ac patrum vestrorum*,[31] that is, in the "communicative memory," as defined by Jan Assmann. Moreover, orators would regularly make use of the most concrete and palpable way of conjuring up men and (hi)stories, even myths and indeed monuments *in vestro conspectus*—just as Cicero did on a *contio* in early January 43, when he denounced the series of statues honoring Marcus Antonius's younger brother Lucius, especially the gilded equestrian statue dedicated by "the 35 tribes": What an "incredible impudence" to style himself the patron of the whole *populus Romanus*, victor and master of the world"—and then, for good measure, he draws an implicit but telling comparison by theatrically pointing to the equestrian statue of Q. Marcius Tremulus *in foro ante templum Castoris*, "who had vanquished the Hernici,"[32] thus evoking certain elements of the implicit master narrative of the early stages of Rome's rise to power, inscribed in the collective (or rather cultural) memory of the Roman people, which was fed, nurtured, administered, and controlled by an educated sociopolitical elite, but obviously shared to a large extent by the elusive "man in the Roman street." In other words, as Robert Morstein-Marx put it with reference to Cicero's allusion to the statue of Tremulus: "a reference such as this suggests that a much wider and deeper stratum of historical and civic knowledge is likely to lie hidden or half-submerged beneath the surface of the oft-cursory explicit allusions in our texts." Such an allusion not only "looks more like an attempt to exploit a variety of civic associations evoked by a familiar monument, including some awareness of a wider narrative to which the man and his statue belonged, than a strained effort to use the unnoticed statue of a forgotten patriot to denigrate a contemporary"; above all, it should be "inserted into its topographic setting and related to specific and well-known social and political practices"[33]—in now familiar metaphors, it should be read as a "text" in an "ensemble of texts," inscribed in the vibrant *milieu de mémoire* of the *populus Romanus*.

These *social and political practices* are indeed themselves a highly complex "ensemble of texts"—namely an "ensemble" that not only consists of the particularly rich repertoire of rituals and ceremonies such as the *pompae* (above all but not only the triumph, the public funeral, the *pompa circensis*) and the spate of other processions and religious practices, games and festivals, pomp and pageantry.[34] Moreover, this "ensemble" also includes the symbolic and expressive side of formal, seemingly exclusively rational procedures such as voting in elections as well as the aforementioned specific rules and contexts of political oratory: the traditional address of the crowd *in contione* as *Quirites*, as it were, conjures up what Tom Habinek has called the "imagined community" of the *populus Romanus*,[35] its majesty as sovereign in assembly, and thus evokes the same kind of "communal experience" as at the *ludi scaenici* in the theater, according to Wiseman, "where the audience was always defined as the Roman people itself."[36]

---

[31] Cic. *Mur.* 16; *Scaur.* 46; *Rab. perd.* 15. Cf. Vasaly 1993, Morstein-Marx 2004, Hölkeskamp (1995) 2004a, Hölkeskamp and Stein-Hölkeskamp 2011.

[32] Cic. *Phil.* 6.12–15, cf. Livy 9.43.22; Plin. *HN* 34.23. Cf. Hölkeskamp (1996) 2004a, 174; 2012.

[33] Morstein-Marx 2004, 82 (with reference to David 1980, 72f.).

[34] Beacham 1999, Flaig 2003, Bell 2004, Flower 2004, Sumi 2005. Cf. also Hölkeskamp 2006b, 2008, and recently Hölkeskamp and Stein-Hölkeskamp 2011, Hölkeskamp 2011a, all with ample bibliography. Cf. also Hölkeskamp, reviews of Beard 2007 and Pittenger 2008, in *Gnomon* 82 (2010) 130–136 and 714–720 respectively (also with references to previous work) and Hölkeskamp 2013b.

[35] Habinek 1998, 44–45; cf. Dugan 2009, 180–181; Hölkeskamp 2013b.

[36] Wiseman in this volume, p. 50.

The very same audience was also the addressee of a culture-specific, indeed very Roman variant of public oratory, namely the *laudatio funebris*—the centerpiece of a spectacular ritual in which the leading families under the eyes of their peers as well as of the *populus* as public displayed their accumulated "symbolic capital" in the shape of a procession of ancestor masks:[37] the ritual syntax or choreography was strictly focused, as it were, on the "magisterial" record (in the literal as well as metaphorical sense of the word) of the family, the *honores* (again in both meanings of the word) of its past members and their *res gestae* in their (senior) "magisterial" functions as contributions to the glorious history of republic and empire.

Moreover, the very same audience was also—and at the same time—the addressee of the typically Roman republican "*representative*"—that is, *public* or *state art*, its particular "quality of communal address," its specific imagery, which "stressed shared communal experience," and its "extraordinary attention" to what Ann Kuttner has aptly described as "historical images," which already by the late fourth century show "graphically sophisticated visual codes for intensely detailed narratives." In concrete terms, these images typically show "uniquely identifiable events, like particular battles" on the one hand and "generic important ones, like magisterial ceremonies" such as the census and other "civilian and military rituals" such as the triumph and "sacrificial processions" on the other, invariably led by figures of togate magistrates and/or priests.[38] In other words, according to Kuttner, "Roman historical art is overwhelmingly an art about crowd scenes, and participatory rituals, intended to energize participatory looking by the living crowd. And it is often, and strikingly, an art about talking—parley, tribunal meetings, priestly prayers." Togate orators throw their right arm out "in direct rhetorical address"[39]—it is a "magisterial" or even imperious gesture, demanding the full and undivided attention of the addressees and indeed reverence, acceptance of, and deference to superior *dignitas* and *auctoritas*. It is a telling kind of gesture, which—in combination with the elevated position of the orator vis-à-vis the *contio*—epitomizes the hierarchical distance between the constituent parties in this typical communicative setup.[40]

The omnipresent principle of steep hierarchy and the asymmetry of power relations is inscribed in the aforementioned collective communal experience. As a result of the "intense monumentalization of the republican city over time," the "populace"—or the notoriously elusive "man in the Roman street"—"walked under a kind of city in the sky, where roof sculptures, honorific column portraits, and arch groups gave high place to the highly placed,"[41] as did, in a particularly demonstrative way, the *fornix Scipionis* overarching the end of the *clivus Capitolinus*, its counterpart at the entrance of the Sacra Via, the *fornix Fabianus* with its array of portrait statues,[42] and—last, but not least—the *columnae rostratae* from the one in honor of Duilius, consul 260, who went down into history (or memory) as the first Roman to have celebrated a *triumphus navalis*, to the similar monument in honor of Octavianus erected in the 30s.[43] The monument as such brings across the message in a nonverbal but invariably unmistakeable way.

---

[37] Flower 1996, with full references; Flaig 1995 and 2003, 49–68; Walter 2004, 84–108; Hölkeskamp 2006b, 347–351; 2008, 104–107.

[38] Kuttner 2004, 310–311. Cf. also Walter 2004, 148–154.

[39] Kuttner 2004, 310 and 312.

[40] Hölkeskamp (1995) 2004a, 233–247; Hölkeskamp and Stein-Hölkeskamp 2011; Hölkeskamp 2013b. Cf. also Morstein-Marx 2004, passim; Sumi 2005, 17–22.

[41] Kuttner 2004, 320 and 318.

[42] Sehlmeyer 1999, 124–125, 168–170, with full references; Hölkeskamp (2001) 2004a, 153–155.

[43] Sehlmeyer 1999, 117–120, 255–257; Hölkeskamp (2001) 2004a, 151–152.

Indeed, "the whole city's ancestral actors, in the form of statues" took center-stage: these statues were not only "described by texts, coins and engraved gems as well as copies in other media"[44] but were also referred to, or even dramatically called up, in the speeches of the living magistrates in their central sociopolitical role as "togate orators" and in other forms of public discourse. Among these forms, a particular epigraphic habit has to take pride of place. It was a habit of interconnecting the formulaic inscriptions on statues in public places with those in different contexts (and lower degrees of publicity) such as funerary inscriptions. They all at least implicitly or even as explicitly and demonstratively as the inscriptions on the sarcophagi of the Cornelii Scipiones *père* and *fils*— texts that proudly declared that they had been consuls, censors, and aediles *apud vos*[45]—address the very same audience: the *populus Romanus*, who had made them consuls, holders of *imperium*, and generals, whose successes in the field add to the accumulated rank of the family as well as the glory of the *res publica* and the greatness of the *gens togata*. This was the stuff that rank and reputation, *dignitas* and *auctoritas*, and the quasi-hereditary status of an aristocrat of the first water was made of. These very same *honores* and *res gestae* were destined to be called up time and again, and not only in the *laudationes* of future Cornelii Scipiones on the occasion of their ritual joining of the long line of ancestors but also in the traditional self-serving sermons of living scions of this noble house on the occasion of taking up the high office.

The underlying ideological construct, therefore, does fit very well (*pace* Wiseman),[46] with the definition of Roman history as "the deeds of the Roman people" (and as the cherished core of what we may well call "the cultural memory" of the Romans). After all, the aristocratic claim to shape and represent this history and, as it were, to administer and cultivate its memory is omnipresent—in more than just one meaning of the word: the "power" (in Foucault's sense) over the collective discourse on what history is or should be, over the contents as well as the media, textual as well as visual, over the language and semantics of monuments as well as over the syntax of rituals and ceremonies and their meanings and messages is indeed part and parcel of the collective social, political, and cultural leadership of the senatorial aristocracy and the *nobiles* as its elite, permanently reproducing itself, as it were, by its memory-focused strategies of self-fashioning.

The "city in the sky" mentioned above also provided the *topographic context* for this extraordinarily rich "culture of memory"—and that means, it was the spatial environment of its "memory in stone" in the shape of monuments and all sorts of visual markers of memory and (hi)stories. From early on, there were even conscious efforts to use "illusionistic sculpture to depict an event at the place where it has occurred, setting and image together reenforcing memory"—just remember the "stories" and symbolic messages of the *lacus Curtius*. Moreover, "just as triumphal images clustered along—and, atop arches, above—triumphal routes," Capitol, Comitium, and Forum Romanum, Campus Martius, Circus Maximus, and innumerable other spaces of religious, symbolic, "memorial," or otherwise "cultural" relevance also (and at the same time) "made a performative stage for living rituals of communality"[47]—that is, the equally rich repertoire of civic rituals with all their pomp and pageantry that served to cultivate the "cultural memory" and its cherished contents in the shape of *exempla maiorum*, "exemplary" stories and histories of men of old, their glorious deeds

---

[44] Kuttner 2004, 319. Cf. also Sehlmeyer 1999 and 2000 and above all Hölscher 1978, 1980, 1984, 1990, and 2001a; Walter 2004, 131–148.

[45] Kruschwitz 2002, no. 2 (32–57) and no. 3 (58–70), with texts, translations, commentary, and full bibliography.

[46] Wiseman in this volume, p. 47.

[47] Kuttner 2004, 318–319 and 313; cf. Favro 1988 and 1994; Hölkeskamp (2001) 2004a, 147–163; Flower 2004.

as well as *mores* of old,[48] ranging from triumphs to all sorts of religious festivals, *ludi*, and dramatic reenactments of these contents to funerals.

The key concept is *interdependence*—it is the complex interplay of written texts and oral tradition in a variety of genres and shapes; of symbolically charged places and spaces, monuments, and other visual markers of memory, as well as of rituals and other performative reenactments that constitute the specific Roman "memorial culture" as a unique variant of a premodern "cultural memory."[49]

In other words, the "ensemble of texts" constituted by ephemeral performances of these civic rituals and their potential for actors and addressees to participate as "co-actors," a participation in different degrees but invariably invaluable in a sociopolitical system based on the reproduction of the oligarchy by the active assent of the ruled in the shape of voting and elections on the one hand; and the "ensemble of texts" constituted by the monumentalization of cultivated memory as the basis of the legitimacy of this oligarchy and their ideology of indefatigable service to *populus*, *res publica*, and empire by permanent markers of memory of great deeds of awe-inspiring ancestors on the other form a highly complex, inseparably interrelated "web of significance."

However, there is still more to it. We have to take into account that there was yet another "ensemble of texts," based on interdependence on another, "secondary" or "abstract" level: Rome was a typical Mediterranean open-air culture of direct interaction, which I have tried to describe as "city-statehood,"[50] a culture of visibility, of seeing and being seen, of orality (or "audibility") and of performativity, as individuals acting out *in persona* their different social and political roles, as actors and co-actors, magistrates, commanders, priests, and patrons on the one hand and ordinary citizens and voters in the *comitia*, legionaries, and clients on the other. That is why the urban topography of the *urbs* had to serve not only as sacral and memorial landscape—it was anything but a museum of past greatness. It was also, and always at the same time, the topographic setting of everyday politics, from the frequent *contiones* to regular (and themselves highly ritual) procedures of voting and elections. In fact, sacral, memorial, and political landscape were in a permanent process of interchanging functions and thus superimposing themselves on one another—and this process guaranteed the permanent and vivid "presence of the past in the present."[51] To put it in other words one last time: the collective or cultural memory of the Roman people (as well as their ephemeral and elusive communicative memory) was permanently "in the making"—and so is the (sort of) theory and its framework of concepts, categories, and other "abstractions," which are indispensable for fully understanding the phenomenon and its complexity.

My play with Clifford Geertz's spinning metaphors has now come full circle. Confronted with the complexity of possible interrelations, we need a sort of theoretical as well as methodological framework to analyze and possibly or hopefully decide in which way the different factors, communicative media, and strategies are interrelated—and whether there is a sort of hierarchy of importance or relevance. In sum, and that is the gist of the "political-culture" paradigm, it is the systemic correlation of all these levels that generates these particularly dense "webs of significance," which in turn are part of a specific and complex cultural system in the Geertzian sense of the concept—and this "ensemble of texts, themselves ensembles" is a whole that is more than the sum of its constituent parts (or "texts").

[48] Cf. Hölkeskamp (1996) 2004a; David 1980; Roller 2004 (on "exemplarity in Roman culture"); Walter 2004, 374–407; and the case studies on prominent figures in Coudry and Späth 2001.

[49] Cf. also Walter 2004.

[50] Hölkeskamp 2009b, 44–48; 2010, 67–75, both with further references.

[51] Obviously, I use this phrase in a different sense than Maurice Bloch, who had coined it: Bloch 1977.

5 ♦ Memory, Myth, and Power in Statius's *Silvae*

Gianpiero Rosati

1. Memory and Poetry

As Statius himself well knows—since his highest ambitions are entrusted to his great epic poem, the *Thebaid*—tradition assigns to the epic the specific responsibility for memory, the task of recalling (*memorare*) great feats or warlike exploits. He jokingly points this out to his friend, the poet Arruntius Stella, who makes the opposite choice, opting for the elegiac genre, love poetry (*Silvae* 1.2.95–99):

> *noster comes ille piusque*
> *signifer armiferos poterat* memorare labores
> claraque facta virum *et torrentes sanguine campos;*
> *sic tibi plectra dedit, mitisque incedere vates*
> *maluit et nostra laurum subtexere myrto.*

> He is our companion, our loyal standard-bearer. He could have told of martial toils, famous deeds of heroes, fields streaming with gore; but he gave his quill to you, preferring to walk softly in his poesy and twine his bay in our myrtle.[1]

Memorare is a specific reference to the beginning of the *Aeneid*, where Vergil asks the Muse to "recall into memory" the reasons for Juno's anger that led to Aeneas's *labores*. More generally, or generically, the subject of epic poetry is *clara facta virum* (the Homeric κλέα ἀνδρῶν), and Statius returns to the specific task of this literary genre at the conclusion of the *Thebaid*, his great epic poem (his second epic work, the *Achilleid*, as is well known, remained little more than a project). However, while the reference to Stella is somewhat generic (almost a repetition of Horace's definition of epic poetry as *res gestae regumque ducumque et tristia bella*, "the exploits of kings and captains and the sorrows of war"),[2] here Statius is much more precise, defining the function of epic poetry in the context of a social group: by positioning the *Thebaid* in the wake of the *Aeneid*, he claims for himself the role of the national bard of contemporary Rome, the new Vergil of the Flavian age, thanks to two requisites that confirm his status as a classic: the recognition of political power and the "memorization" of the new epic work by young students (*Theb.* 12.812–815):

> *iam certe praesens tibi Fama benignum*
> *stravit iter coepitque novam monstrare futuris.*
> *Iam te magnanimus dignatur noscere Caesar,*
> *Itala iam studio discit* memorat*que iuventus.*

[1] Translations from Statius are by D. R. Shackleton Bailey.   [2] Hor. *Ars P.* 73.

Already, 'tis true, Fame has strewn a kindly path before you and begun to show the new arrival
to posterity. Already great-hearted Caesar deigns to know you, and the studious youth of Italy
learns you and recites.

Even though the reader may harbor doubts about the educational function and the "exemplary"
nature of a work whose subject is the horrors of the civil war, for Italic youth,[3] it is clear that Statius
assigns to his epic poem a formative, didactic function for the new ruling class.[4]

He thus establishes a relationship between the epic poet and his readers, based on memory: the
two "acts of memory"—that of the poet who fixes the great actions of the past in poetry and that of
the reader who memorizes, acquires, and preserves them in his own cultural patrimony—guarantee a
continuity (it is repetition that is at the basis of the "connective structure," borrowing a key concept
from J. Assmann),[5] the continuity that serves to preserve and to transmit the memory of heroic feats,
that is the cultural memory. And furthermore—another essential point—this operation of "defense
of the memory" seems to take place under the guardianship of a power (*Caesar* 814), that is to say,
thus confirming the existence of an "alliance between power and memory" (J. Assmann), and that
"power is a strong motivation for memory."[6]

2. Memory and Power

Statius's intention to establish a link with political power (*Caesar*), and to see his role of *vates* recognized by it, is clear not only at the end of the *Thebaid* but throughout all his career (which also
explains the incurable trauma of his defeat in the Capitoline Games). In proudly placing himself
among the Latin classics, he recalls the analogous claim made by Horace (*Carm.* 4.3.13–15: *Romae,
principis urbium,* / dignatur *suboles inter amabilis* / *vatum ponere me choros*, "the youth of Rome,
queen of cities, sees fit to give me a place in the well-loved choir of lyric poets"; trans. Rudd): he
thus presents himself as the greatest poet of Rome under Domitian, esteemed and appreciated by
the Roman senatorial elite (cf. also *Silv.* 5.2.160–161: *sed coetus solitos si forte ciebo* / *et mea Romulei
venient ad carmina patres*, "but if perchance I summon my wonted gatherings and the Romulean
Fathers come to hear my songs"; 5.3.216–217: *Latios quotiens ego carmine patres* / *mulcerem*,
"whenever I soothed the Latin Fathers with my song"). His father, the late Papinius Statius, had
previously been the educator of that same elite and had fulfilled this role by acting as a "guardian
of memory," that is to say, by transmitting to the younger generations the memory of the *mores et
facta* of their ancestors (5.3.146 ff.):[7]

> *Hinc tibi vota patrum credi generosaque pubes*
> *te monitore regi,* mores et facta priorum
> discere . . .

[3] It is in fact a rare case of "negative epics" (somehow similar
to Lucan's poem)—that is, illustrating models of behavior
that are exemplary in their destructive negativity, paradigms
to be rejected: cf. Bessone 2011, 75–101 ("un mito da
dimenticare").

[4] In addition to the explicit reference to Vergil's epics, Statius
is here implicitly evoking another great model of Roman
"civic" poetry (cf. Rosati 2011, 21)—that is, the last book of
Horace's *Odes* (cf. below).

[5] J. Assmann 1997, xiii.

[6] J. Assmann 1997, 43.

[7] On "exemplarity," of great deeds as well as of *mores* of old
venerable men, as typical feature of Roman cultural memory,
cf. Hölkeskamp in this volume; cf. also Farrell 1997, 375
("memories are not things handed down unchanged from the
past to the future, but rather are patterns of cognition and
behavior by which the past creates the future").

Hence parents' hopes were entrusted to you and noble youth governed by your guidance, as they learned the manners and deeds of men gone by.

Thus the poet-*vates*—that is, the poet who aims at performing a civil function, in particular the epic poet (who may deal with either historical or mythological subjects)—is a specialized promoter and repository of the cultural memory: he elaborates it and preserves it, passing it on to the following generations; in a word, he supervises the phase of its formation and its subsequent consolidation by transmitting it, thus contributing to the creation of a tradition. Also significant is the literary form, the way in which Statius expresses his intention to make a contribution to the cultural memory of Rome: the allusion to Horace, to the "civil Horace" of the fourth book of the *Odes*, is in itself an act of cultural memory, like the many intertextual relationships that Statius creates with Horace, and above all with Vergil (e.g. *Theb*. 10.445–448). Literary intertextuality—like all kinds of intertextual practice—is a form of cultural memory because it activates a relationship between texts that are an essential part of the cultural past, of the tradition in which the readers of Statius recognize themselves (all the more when the "intertextual chain" involves specifically civic texts, as Horace's *Odes* 4 or Vergil's *Aeneid*). Statius's self-representation in the act of composing poetry before the sepulcher of his master Vergil emphasizes the connection of his inspiration with the greatest Latin epic poet, whose *Aeneid* is the chief literary monument of Roman cultural memory, and the rootedness of his own poetry in the country (Naples, Statius's own homeland) where Vergil had been living and writing for many years:[8]

> *en egomet somnum et geniale secutus*
> *litus ubi Ausonio se condidit hospita portu*
> *Parthenope, tenues ignavo pollice chordas*
> *pulso Maroneique sedens in margine templi*
> *sumo animum et magni tumulis adcanto magistri.*

Look! Pursuing sleep and the genial shore where stranger Parthenope found refuge in Ausonian haven, I idly strike the slender strings; sitting on the verge of Maro's shrine, I take heart and sing at the tomb of the great master. (*Silv*. 4.4.51–55)

As regards the importance of the cultural memory, Statius tells us a lot; not only his epic poetry but also the *Silvae*, an extraordinary document that reveals the network of relationships in which the poet moves and the social rites of the Flavian elite (their public and private occasions, their ceremonies, their festivities, etc.) and also the physical contexts and settings, the scenery where they take place and communicate their meaning (cultural memory, as we know, "needs places").[9] For example, the first composition of the entire collection is the one that illustrates the equestrian statue of Domitian erected in the Forum, the *lieu de mémoire par excellence* in Rome, the place-symbol that condenses the collective memories of the city within its locations and its monuments. Statius insists on the network of ideas stirred up in the spectator by the presence of the emperor in the heart of the Forum, the center of the memories of the city, thus evoking the mythological-historical roots of Rome. Domitian's gigantic monument is a magnet that not just draws to itself the people's gaze but also stirs up the memory, becoming the climactic point of reference in the outline of Roman history. But it is clearly the poet himself, through the reading-interpretation of the monument

---

[8] On the "Vergilian gaze" in Statius's representation of Campania, cf. Hinds 2001, 247ff.

[9] Cf. the seminal demonstration by Halbwachs 1941 (2008) with reference to the legendary topography of the Holy Land.

that the ekphrasis represents,[10] who takes upon himself the task of stimulating those memories, and first of all, the legendary figure of Manlius Curtius, the eponymous hero of the *lacus Curtius* (*Ipse loci custos, cuius sacrata vorago / famosique lacus nomen memorabile servant*, *Silv.* 1.1.66–67), who sacrificed his life, by the ritual practice of *devotio*, for the salvation of the city.[11] In awakening Curtius from his eternal repose, a repose protected in the depths of the city for which he gave his life, Statius effectively "literalizes" Cicero's idea:[12]

> *nemo qui memoriam rerum Romanarum teneret, ex qua, si quando opus esset, ab inferis locuple-*
> *tissimos testes excitaret.*

> no one who knew thoroughly Roman history, from which as occasion demanded he could sum-
> mon as from the dead most unimpeachable witnesses. (*Brut.* 322, trans. Hendrickson)

Curtius emerges from the world of the distant memories of the Urbs to render homage to Domitian, and thus to include also the current emperor in the long mythological tradition of Rome. The commendatory interpretation that Statius gives of the monument, which is perfectly integrated into the physical landscape of the Forum (*par operi sedes*, 22, "the setting matches the work"), and whose construction saw the participation of the entire social community (61ff.), traces a line of continuity that goes back from Domitian to the mythical Curtius, and even further because the construction of the monument to Domitian symbolically sanctions the new "foundation" of the city in the name of the modern Romulus.[13]

But Statius's description enriches this "memory chain" by introducing another significant event in the long history of Rome.[14] This is how he described the noise produced by the work for the erection of the monument, which interrupts the sleep of Curtius (66–70):

> *Ipse loci custos, cuius sacrata vorago*
> *famosique lacus nomen memorabile servant,*
> *innumeros aeris sonitus et* verbere crudo
> ut sensit mugire forum, *movet horrida sancto*
> *ora situ meritaque caput venerabile quercu.*

> The guardian of the place in person, whose name the sacred chasm and the famous pool preserve
> in memory, hears the countless clashes of bronze and the Forum resounding with harsh blows.
> He raises a visage stark in holy squalor and a head sanctified by well-earned wreath of oak.

The metaphor of the "bellowing in the Forum" (indicating the noise of the construction work, as it is usually interpreted) also has a proper and specific meaning, indicating the literal bellowing of cattle recounted by a famous legend, particularly popular in Augustan literature, regarding the myths of the origins (e.g., in the "archaeological walk" of *Aeneid* 8; cf. Jenkyns in this volume): this was the lowing of the cattle that the monster Cacus stole from Hercules, who, thanks to the bellowing of the animals, discovered the theft and meted out exemplary punishment to the guilty party, thus reestablishing order and justice. The memory of this act of civilization by Hercules is

---

[10] On the (already ancient) metaphor of "reading" a monument, cf. Lowrie 2009, 317 n. 35.

[11] On this "monument" of the Roman Forum, cf. also Hölkeskamp in this volume.

[12] Cf. the remarks of Gowing 2005, 16.

[13] On the adoption of this model by Domitian (who in turn follows in Augustus's wake), cf. Rosati 2012, 448 n. 22.

[14] Cf. Rosati 2012.

recorded in the name of the historic *Forum Boarium*, the area originally surrounding the marsh of Velabrum (evidently so called because it was destined to be a cattle market): the mythical aetiology of that space in the Forum, which is frequently mentioned by the Augustan poets (e.g., Ov. *Fast.* 1.582 and 6.478)[15] and which Statius obliquely recalls (that is the reason why it has escaped the attention of modern readers), is thus an exemplary case of how cultural memory is concretely transferred into the landscape, becoming topography, consolidated in the daily life of those who inhabit an actual *lieu de mémoire*.[16] Artists and architects can so construct a memorial landscape, but beside the concrete and *visible* memories that can be activated, through monuments or images, in a landscape, a garden, or a villa, there are other memories that, as we will see below, can only be evoked indirectly, through an allusive language that aims at suggesting what is kept, even unconsciously, in the repositories of cultural memory.

The first poem of the *Silvae* is thus an exemplary case of how a monument may become a "mnemotope," a physically concrete document of cultural memory, and at the same time a symbolic place where the identity of a social community is found to be deposited. But I would like to insist here on two other aspects, privileging them in the context of a work that can tell us much more about cultural memory. The first aspect concerns the above-mentioned relationship of cultural memory to political power, and how the new Flavian dynasty tries to create its own "foundation myth" to legitimate its leadership;[17] the second is the "construction of the past" as an instrument of social distinction, an operation in which the *Silvae* is specifically engaged.[18]

3. In Search of a Past

Let us examine the first point. An ancient tradition, which goes back to Hesiod, established a close relationship between the Muses, the daughters of Mnemosyne and thus goddesses of memory themselves, and a specific theme that is the subject of their song: the theme of the Gigantomachy, that is to say, the primordial clash between the Titans-Giants and the gods of Olympus, who crush the rebellion of the sons of the Earth and reestablish cosmic order under the power of Zeus-Jupiter. In Hesiod's *Theogony*, the Muses are said to "rejoice the mind of Zeus, singing of the powerful Giants" (lines 50–52), that is to say, we may presume, the story of their defeat by Zeus himself; analogously, in Pindar's first *Pythian* (12ff.) the Muses' song is said to strike fear into the "enemies of Zeus" (antonomastically identified as Typhoeus-Typhon), evidently because they tell the story of the defeat of the Giants, led by Typhoeus (who was punished by being buried beneath Sicily), and thus they are a warning to anybody having subversive intentions against the power of the Olympian gods. The Gigantomachy is the foundation myth of the gods of Olympus and Zeus-Jupiter, and the pleasure that he takes in listening to the story told by the Muses evidently derives from seeing the memory of the exploits that create and legitimate his renewed and celebrated power.

---

[15] Another significant passage (pointed out to me by Marco Fucecchi) on this Hercules's presence rooted in the soil of the Roman Forum is in Sil. *Pun.* 7.50 (*maximaque Herculei mugivit numinis ara*).

[16] Remarkable in this sense the *Silvae* 3.5, which reads the Neapolitan landscape in order to catch in it the traces of the cultural memory that Statius claims as the foundation of his own identity: cf. Rosati 2011, esp. 26ff.

[17] Here and in the following pages I obviously refer to the concept of "invention of tradition" as defined by the key work Hobsbawm and Ranger 1983. On the diffusion in republican Rome of practices aimed to this purpose, see the passage of Livy (8.40.3–5) pointed out in this volume by Wiseman, p. 47 (and cf. Oakley 1997, 30–33).

[18] Cf. Zeiner 2005.

This pleasure that the mighty take from memory is a widely used topos, with the image of the gods during their banquets, who love to listen to the Muses or Apollo telling the story of their victory: following in the wake of a famous "Roman ode" by Horace, *Carm.* 3.4.37ff. (especially *Caesarem altum . . . Pierio recreatis antro*, "you refresh our exalted Caesar within a Pierian grotto," and the long section dedicated to the Gigantomachy in lines 42–58), we find it, for instance, among the Flavian poets, such as in Valerius Flaccus or in Statius, both in his *Thebaid* and in the *Silvae:*

> *tunc adsuetus adest Phlegraeas reddere pugnas*
> *Musarum chorus et citharae pulsator Apollo.*

Then the choir of Muses and Apollo, striker of the lyre, whose wont it is to tell of the Phlegraean fight, appear, and the Phrygian henchman bears round the heavy bowl. (*Arg.* 5.692–693, trans. Mozley)

> *interea cantu Musarum nobile mulcens*
> *concilium citharaeque manus insertus Apollo*
> *Parnasi summo spectabat ab aethere terras*
> *. . .*
> *orsa deum, nam saepe Iovem Phlegramque suique*
> *anguis opus fratrumque pius cantarat honores.*

Meanwhile Apollo was soothing the noble company of the Muses with his song, and with hands upon his lyre watched the earth from Parnassus' ethereal summit . . . for often had he piously sung of Jupiter and Phlegra and the serpent, his own achievement, and the praises of his brothers. (*Theb.* 6.355–359)[19]

> *dux superum secreta iubet dare carmina Musas*
> *et Pallenaeos Phoebum laudare triumphos.*

The leader of the High Ones bids the Muses sing secret songs and Phoebus laud Pallene's triumphs. (*Silv.* 4.2.55–56)

But perhaps it is Ovid who offers the most explicit formulation of this motif (*Trist.* 2.69–72):

> *fama Iovi superest: tamen hunc sua facta referri*
> *et se materiam carminis esse iuvat,*
> *cumque Gigantei* memorantur *proelia belli,*
> *credibile est laetum laudibus esse suis.*

Jupiter has more than enough of glory: yet is he pleased to have his deeds related and himself become the theme of song, and when the battles of his war with the Giants are told, we may believe that he finds pleasure in his praises. (trans. Wheeler)

The *memoria* of his own triumph, entrusted in the world of myth to the Muses (who are the daughters of Memory) and in concrete earthly reality to poets, who are inspired by them, is the foundation on which Jupiter (and his counterpart on earth, the emperor) legitimates his right to command.

---

[19] Editors (though not all of them) postulate after 357 a minor lacuna; in any case, it does not affect the general sense (cf. Pavan 2009, 171).

The past, a glorious past to appeal to, and to maintain fresh in the memory, is thus a necessity for power. And it is for the Flavians, too: it is not surprising, therefore, if they too have their Gigantomachy, that is to say, if they interpret in this key the conflict against Vitellius,[20] which opens the way to imperial power for Vespasian (the clash was not exactly a triumphant victory, but Flavian propaganda chose to ennoble it as such).[21] Domitian himself, who, as is well known, had literary ambitions, seems to have composed a *Bellum Capitolinum*;[22] and Statius presents that episode, at various points in his work, as the *bella Iovis* in the apostrophe to Domitian in the proem of his *Thebaid* (*aut defensa prius vix pubescentibus annis / bella Iovis*, 1.21–22, "or, earlier yet, Jove's warfare warded off in years scarce past childhood") and in the first *Silvae* (1.1.79),[23] or as the "Phlegraean wars" (from Phlegra-Pallene, the locality in the Chalcidean peninsula where the Gigantomachy was usually set), which Statius's father Papinius had also described in his times:[24]

> *talia dum celebras, subitam civilis Erinys*
> *Tarpeio de monte facem Phlegraeaque movit*
> *proelia.*

Such was your occupation when the Fury of civil war suddenly raised her torch from the Tarpeian mount and stirred battles as of Phlegra. (*Silv.* 5.3.195–197)

But Martial, too, does not fail to render homage to Domitian, recalling his youthful participation in the "war of Jupiter," which took place in Rome (*adseruit possessa malis Palatia regnis, / prima suo gessit pro Iove bella puer*, 9.101.13–14, "he freed the Palatine held under evil dominion, and in boyhood waged his first war for his Jupiter").[25]

In other words, the Flavians too need their "foundation myth," a glorious past that legitimates their leadership. And we know that this "need of a past" was a serious political problem for the family that, at the end of the civil war of the "year of the four emperors," had succeeded the glorious Julio-Claudian dynasty (which the myth of Aeneas traced back to divine origins): a family that was *obscura . . . quidem ac sine ullis maiorum imaginibus* (Suet. *Vesp.* 1.1, "an unknown family without any ancestral portraits"; trans. Edwards).[26] The problem of the lack of *auctoritas*, of "a past," is the

[20] Whose supporters, as Stefano Rebeggiani points out to me, were mostly from Germany and thus lent themselves to being seen as savage encroachers (just as the Galatian invaders, defeated by Attalus I, had been allegorically represented in the Gigantomachy frieze of the Great Altar of Zeus at Pergamon: cf., e.g., Hardie 1986, 120ff.; Stewart 2000, 40; Marszal 2000).

[21] Cf. Gibson 2006, 343–344.

[22] Cf. Mart. 5.5.7 *Capitolini caelestia carmina belli*, where to the other connotations of *caelestia* pointed out by Canobbio 2011, 115 (with further bibliography) I would add a possible allusion to Gigantomachy as *caelestia . . . bella* (Ov. *Am.* 2.1.11), or *bella . . . superum* (Ov. *Met.* 5.319, with my note in Rosati 2009), or similar.

[23] Of course, the encomiastic context of the two passages is by no means irrelevant (as Ovid says, "Jupiter" loves listening to his own triumph on rebel Giants).

[24] According to Hardie 1983, 76, who points out the emphasis on the theme of Statius's father's religious *pietas* (200–202,

excisis cum tu solacia templis / impiger et multum facibus velocior ipsis / concinis ore pio captivaque fulmina defles), it must have been "a kind of *monodia* plus consolation for the destruction and sacrilege"; in any case the following lines (*mirantur Latii proceres ultorque deorum / Caesar, et e medio divum pater annuit igni*, 203–204) insist on the recovery of order by the emperor *ultor deorum* (where the plural, "hyperbolical" according to Gibson 2006, 345, is to be explained just as an allusion to "their" battle *par excellence*).

[25] The assimilation to the mythical *bella Iovis* is facilitated by the fact that the Vitellians (as well as the Gauls in 390 B.C.) besieged the Capitoline, where Vespasian's supporters had barricaded themselves, and burned the Temple of Jupiter Optimus Maximus (Tac. *Hist.* 3.71–72). The paradigm of the celebration of Jove's triumph over the Giants by the Olympian gods, as allegory of Rome's joy for the Flavians' victory, is explicitly recalled by Martial, too, in the epigram 8.49(50).

[26] This lack of *imagines* as Vespasian's weak spot in comparison with his rival Galba is also a point made by Mucianus in Tac. *Hist.* 2.76.2 (*cessisti etiam Galbae imaginibus*).

one that concerns Vespasian most of all, immediately after his unexpected rise to power (*Auctoritas et quasi maiestas quaedam ut scilicet inopinato et adhuc novo principi deerat*, *Vesp*. 7.2, "Recently and indeed unexpectedly made emperor, he still lacked a certain dignity and majesty").

But the problem of memory, of a relationship with the past, is not limited to Vespasian and his family: it is a deeply felt characteristic of the Flavian age and culture, whose ruling class has to construct, or redefine, its identity in relation to the past. The "new aristocracy of power,"[27] created above all by Vespasian (who, however, concurrently succeeded in conquering the support of certain sectors of the Senate that were initially hostile toward him:[28] he evidently appreciated the importance of *imagines* and of consolidated power structures), also "needed a past," and it is the *Silvae* by Statius that illustrate their active involvement in the search for this social distinction.[29]

4. The Memory of Myth

This search for a past takes various forms: from the fashion of Greek-style houses, decorated with statues and frescoes, to the display of a consumption of cultural products, to the manifestation of a material culture that, in its allusive language, evokes a consciously Hellenizing lifestyle. Also the widespread ostentation of marble in villas and gardens is a part of this mentality, and Statius's text insists on this point:[30] marble, the most typical material of which a *monumentum* is made, resists the wear and tear of time and is the very emblem of memory. Marble is memory and power because it preserves the commemoration of the past and at the same time expresses the power of the empire (almost all the precious kinds of marble are imported, especially from the East): this is also a political message because it expresses closeness to the center of power and therefore participation in it or, in other words, support for it and testimony to the prosperity that it ensures.[31]

In this "conquest of the past," the practice of collecting works of art stands out; this is a theme at the center of *Silvae* 4.6, whose protagonist is Novius Vindex, a character of the Flavian elite who is a lover of culture. He is a poet himself, but above all he is an art critic and a master of expertise (his name is wittily interpreted by Statius as the appropriate hallmark for a person who exposes forgers and "claims" works of art for their authors). *Silvae* 4.6 is the ekphrasis of a little bronze statue believed to be the work of the great Greek sculptor Lysippus (fourth century B.C.), representing *Hercules at table* (that is to say, ἐπιτραπέζιος, a refined Hellenism evoking that cultural tradition).[32] The prestige of the statue is greatly enhanced by the fact that it has a glorious (and, probably, invented) pedigree behind it: it originally belonged to Alexander and then became the property of Hannibal and subsequently of Sulla; finally it arrived in the hands of Novius Vindex, in whose house it has the function of an ornament for the table, where it is exhibited to the admiration of his guests. Apart from the authenticity of the work, which is much debated,[33] what confers prestige on it (a prestige that is obviously wholly transferred to its possessor) is its great past, as is shown by the parallel epigram dedicated to the statue by Martial, who extols the same glorious "genealogy"

---

[27] I am referring to Mellor 2003.

[28] Mellor 2003, 96ff.

[29] Zeiner 2005 is devoted to this specific theme.

[30] Cf. Zeiner 2005, 84ff.

[31] Newlands 2009 provides a good assessment of the political dimension of the *Silvae*.

[32] On the epithet's possible meanings and nuances, see Bonadeo 2010, 29–39.

[33] See the detailed discussion in Bonadeo 2010, 24–42 and passim.

(9.43.5–10).[34] The search for *vetustas* is evidently a diffusely shared aspiration: this is reflected by the wide-ranging circulation of copies and fakes, which aim to satisfy this general "need of a past," as a mark of cultural distinction,[35] in particular a Greek past.[36] Also, the authority recognized for the expertise of Vindex in unmasking the "false antiquity" of artworks confirms the importance of the social competition based on this "conquest of memories" (4.6.20–24):

> *Mille ibi tunc species aerisque eborisque* vetusti
> *atque locuturas mentito corpore ceras*
> *edidici. Quis namque oculis certaverit usquam*
> *Vindicis, artificum* veteres *agnoscere ductus*
> *et non inscriptis auctorem reddere signis?*

> There it was and that then I learned of a thousand shapes of bronze and antique ivory and of false bodies in wax, ready to speak. For who would ever rival Vindex' eyes in recognizing the hands of old masters and restoring its maker to an untitled statue?

Distinguishing the true antique from the fake means assigning not only the correct value to objects but also the correct social and cultural position to their possessors.[37]

The statue of Hercules exhibited by Vindex is part of the general appropriation of Greek culture and its symbols; one of the characteristic aspects of this phenomenon is the acquisition of myth, its symbols and its language, in the private and domestic spaces, in the villas and gardens, of the elite that Statius represents. The spread of images of divinities, nymphs, and characters of myths, as decorations for gardens or the insides of houses, in the form of statues or frescoes or works of art, is a fundamental aspect of the visual culture of the period; and it is the premise for the analogous operation that Statius's poetry performs in the description of Flavian society and the cultural context surrounding it. Statius "mythicizes" the Flavian world,[38] ennobling the daily life of his friends-protectors, surrounding it with the halo of Greek myth and creating in them the impression of being part of a more-than-human reality: the dissemination of domestic frescoes of mythological subjects, considered the most precious kind,[39] reveals this intention of "bringing myth into the home," creating in its inhabitants the illusion of living among gods and demigods, as happened in the golden age, in the remote period that preceded history. The myth of the golden age as a paradigm of the prosperity and harmony brought by Domitian's regime is an encomiastic theme privileged by Flavian poetry:

> *i nunc saecula compara, Vetustas,*
> *antiqui* Iovis *aureumque tempus:*
> *non sic libera vina tunc fluebant*
> *nec tardum seges occupabat annum.*
> *una vescitur omnis ordo mensa,*

[34] Cf. Zeiner 2005, 195ff.

[35] On these themes, see, e.g., Bartman 1991; Zeiner 2005, 94–95; the best material and observations are found in several contributions by Andrew Wallace-Hadrill, esp. 2008. Cf. Jenkyns in this volume.

[36] The search alone for object-symbols of Greek culture is a specific marker of Romanness; see Bartman 1991, 78; cf. also Barchiesi 2005, 289; Barchiesi 2009, 101–102. For an exem-

plary discussion (with relevant bibliography) of this topic, see now Anguissola in this volume and Anguissola 2012a.

[37] On the importance of pedigree, see Zeiner 2005, 206ff.

[38] For this crucial aspect of Statius's poetry, see Rosati 2006; cf. also Fabbrini 2007.

[39] Cf. Fredrick 1995.

parvi, femina, plebs, eques, senatus:
libertas reverentiam remisit.

Antiquity, compare if you will the ages of ancient Jove and the golden time: not so freely did
wine flow then, not thus would harvest forestall the tardy year. Every order is seated at one
table: children, women, populace, Knights, Senate. Freedom has relaxed reverence. (1.6.39–45)

The remote *vetustas* of the myth of the ideal world, that is to say, of the golden age, has become
reality again thanks to Domitian, whose leadership is inspired by that model and makes it possible.[40]

The poet of the *Silvae* thus assumes the task of *memorare* the civil exploits of Domitian's
aristocracy, and at the same time that of transforming a series of individual experiences into a
social dimension, making public documents out of them and giving them a political significance:
making them the object of a cultural memory.[41] For example, consider how Statius introduces the
description-celebration of the villa of Manlius Vopiscus through the memory of his visit and the
emotions that it arouses in him:

> *O longum* memoranda *dies! quae mente reporto*
> *gaudia, quam lassos per tot miracula visus!*
> *ingenium quam mite solo, quae forma beatis*
> *ante manus artemque locis! non largius usquam*
> *indulsit natura sibi;*
> *. . . .*
> *Vidi artes veterumque manus variisque metalla*
> *viva modis. Labor est auri* memorare *figuras*
> *aut ebur aut dignas digitis contingere gemmas . . .*

Day long to be remembered! What joy does my mind bring back, what weariness of vision amid
so many marvels! How gentle the nature of the ground! What beauty in the blessed spot before
art's handiwork! Nowhere has Nature indulged herself more lavishly . . . (1.3.13–17) Works of
art I saw, creations of old masters, metals variously alive. 'Tis labour to list the golden figures
or the ivory or gems fit to adorn fingers . . . (47–49)

The same technique is used to introduce the story of the dinner, which is a veritable cultural experience for the poet, at the house of Novius Vindex (4.6.17–19):

> *o bona nox iunctaque utinam Tirynthia luna!*
> *nox et Erythraeis Thetidis signanda lapillis*
> *et* memoranda *diu geniumque habitura perennem!*

What a night that was! Would it had been Tirynthian with double moon! A night to be marked
with Thetis' Erythraean gems, long to be remembered, whose spirit will live for ever.

We may observe that the memory of that dinner is guaranteed by Statius's composition, in which
the subjective memory of the poet is crystallized and made available to the whole community of his

---

[40] In this sense Statius's addressees are invited to "enact" that myth (cf. Farrell 1997, 383: "the Romans . . . were to a very large extent in the habit not of storing memories but of performing them").

[41] Cf. Bodel 1997, 17: "What was new was the notion that the domestic environment in which a gentleman cultivated his leisure was itself worthy of poetic commemoration."

readers.[42] Something similar happens in *Silvae* 2.3, which "mythicizes" the landscape around the villa of Atedius Melior, supplying an *aition* capable of explaining the curious shape of the tree rising from the waters of a lake. The words of the wish that Pan expresses to the tree, at the moment when (following the Ovidian model of Apollo and Daphne) he sees the sudden vegetable metamorphosis of the nymph who is the object of his frustrated desire, are to be read in association with those that the poet addresses shortly afterward to the dedicatee, Atedius Melior, which are the complement of that wish, as they declare Statius's awareness of the immortality of his text:

> *vive diu nostri pignus memorabile voti,*
> *arbor, et haec durae latebrosa cubilia nymphae*
> *tu saltem declinis ama, preme frondibus undam.*

Live long, tree, memorable token of my desire; and do you at least stoop down and love this hidden couch of the cruel Nymph, press the water with your foliage. (2.3.43–45)

> *Haec tibi parva quidem genitali luce paramus*
> *dona, sed ingenti forsan victura sub aevo.*

Such is the gift I make you on your birthday, small indeed but perhaps destined to live through vast stretch of time. (62–63)

In conclusion, it is the poetry of Statius that ensures the memory of the mythological *aition.* He succeeded in constructing it around the curious natural phenomenon representing a reason for the attraction of the villa of his friend-protector. In so doing, the poet enriches with a cultural halo what is simply a natural object and confers distinction on the addressee.[43]

In all these examples, through the memory of his own private, personal experience, the poet is able to *memorare* the object of his poetry for the benefit of his readers. Just as we have seen in his epic poetry, it is the filter of poetry that makes it possible to capture the object of the poet's personal memory and to insert it into a wider dimension, the cultural patrimony of the community, thereby perpetuating its memory. The poet, in sum, carries out the essential role of a mediator in the construction of a communal cultural memory: he is the one who raises up private and contingent facts to a public and lasting dimension.

A professional poet like Statius, conscious and proud of his role of *vates*, the new Vergil and *poeta laureatus* of the Flavian society, lays claim to the function of poetry, of his own poetry, as a primary instrument of the Roman cultural memory.

---

[42] Some good thoughts on this point, in particular on the intrinsic competition between poet and *patronus* for the title of "guarantor of memory," are to be found in Bonadeo 2010, 189–190; cf. also Barchiesi 2005, 300.

[43] The sense of Statius's proud claim is of course powerfully heightened by the intertextual network, mainly of Ovidian matrix (most of all the Apollo and Daphne episode), into which the entire *silva* fits (on this theme Hardie 2006 is relevant).

PART III

MEMORIA

IN ROMAN ART

AND TOPOGRAPHY

6 ◆ Moving Events:
Curating the Memory of the Roman Triumph

Diane Favro

On many days of the year, Roman state processions streamed through ancient Rome like rivers. A major ritual parade poured over the cityscape, damming traffic, ebbing away from some monuments and locales while flowing toward others. The sights, sounds, smells, and activities overwhelmed the senses of urban residents. Then the event ended. People relived the parade for months in conversations, until the participatory memories slowly began to fade. The animated, collectively experienced urban parade became memorialized in more durable interpretive texts, artwork, and urban monuments. These enduring objects have, in turn, become the primary data sources for research on ancient urban parades, emphasizing processional composition and route, cultural meaning, and historical evolution.[1] As valuable as these inquiries are, the reliance on fixed objects is problematic on several counts. Post-event, secondary depictions of ancient movement were by nature highly interpretive and selective, with different aspects privileged by wealthy, literary elite donors for political, religious, artistic, and personal reasons. Equally important, their very fixity shifts the emphasis of analysis away from the dynamic, erratic liveliness of the original procession and its relation to the realities of moving through a hilly, crowded cityscape.

1. Meaning in Movement

Movement had meaning for the ancients. Famously, Zeno of Elea in the fifth century B.C. philosophized about kinetic experience in his famous paradox of motion in which fleet-footed Achilles could not overtake a tortoise.[2] During the following century, ancient schools of philosophy advocated walking as essential for thinking. Aristotle's followers were known as the Peripatetics; those of Zeno as the Stoics referencing an ambulatory setting. The Romans, too, associated mobility and mental activity, utilizing such kinetic metaphors as "arriving at an idea" or "entering into (or moving away from) an opinion."[3] At the same time, they literalized the meaning of walking, reversing the metaphoric use of movement to understand thinking. Thus, Seneca underscored that a person's gait revealed his thinking mind (*Ep.* 114.3). This reorientation of the metaphor was obvious for a society in which status, power, and fame resulted from being seen publicly. To move was a performance of identity. In a single glance, the speed, bearing, gestures, escorts, route, and time of day revealed a Roman's position in society—or his aspirations. The pace of a plebeian client hurrying

---

[1] Beard 2007, 71–75.

[2] *Arist. Ph.* 6.9.239b10 and 239b15. For modern analyses of memory and movement, see Casey 2000, 89–90; Schine accessed 2011.

[3] O'Sullivan 2011, 4–10, 111; Short 2008, 106–109. On the connections among Roman language, memory, and movement, see Spencer 2012. The Roman notion of the leisurely walk (*ambulation*) was primarily an extra-urban activity and is not discussed here; O'Sullivan 2011, 78–79.

in the morning along the back alleys toward the house of his patron was decidedly different from that of a patron decorously processing with his retinue on major streets leading to the Forum later in the day. Fast movement conveyed subservience, disorderliness, a lack of clear thinking, and overall low status; unhurried, modulated walking with admiring followers conveyed refinement.[4] The Romans applied the same spatio-kinetic tropes to public processions. Solemn funeral parades moved slowly from the urban abodes of the living to their eternal homes outside the city. In contrast, those honoring the god Bacchus (Dionysus) were disorderly, undirected, unlocalized affairs that underscored the god's uncivilized foreign origins. With anthropological clarity, Strabo acknowledged that ideas about walking were culturally determined; he belittled the barbarian Vettonians of Spain for foolishly not recognizing the high value of ambulation displayed by the more civilized Romans (Strabo, *Geog.* 3.4.16).

Roman notions of movement informed ancient memory studies. Mnemotechnics developed rapidly in the late second century B.C., in response to a dramatic increase in written materials and urban populations, and to the escalating performative importance of urban movement.[5] While Greek philosophers utilized *topoi* to help organize and recall thoughts, these "places" lacked physical and spatial character and thus were related sequentially rather than kinetically.[6] In contrast, Roman rhetoricians fashioned a mnemonic system based on movement through familiar built environments known as the Memory Walk System. Three ancient authors provide the primary information about the memory technique that developed: the so-called Auctor ad Herennium and Cicero in the first century B.C., and Quintilian in the first century A.D.[7] In this Roman system a speaker mentally placed symbolic images (*imagines*) representing interrelated concepts in specific places (*loci*), exploiting the built form to maintain connections and sequences while also avoiding disjunctions and dead ends. For example, the symbol for a minor, preceding notion might be situated in an antechamber, while that for a major, culminating idea logically resided in a grand room. When giving a speech, the rhetorician envisioned strolling mentally (*permeare, pervagari, percurrere*) through the spaces, encountering the *imagines* in sequence. The envisioned architectural setting allowed for maximum flexibility. A speaker could vary his path in response to audience reactions, knowing that the imagined spatial layout maintained content relationships. For a different speech, he simply redecorated, removing one set of *imagines* and inserting another.

Roman discussions on writing emphasized the content and visual aspects rather than the kinetic process of creation and retrieval, perhaps because the moving of the stylus on a wax tablet and reading were too obvious to merit mention, and in large part predetermined. The same was true for descriptions of mnemotechnics that generally omitted explanations of the imagined movement from one *locus* to another, even though the kinetic linkage of *imagines* was essential and defining. Authors described objects and meaning and only implied kinetic characteristics. For example, they recommended *loci* be placed at regular intervals, a modulation that echoed the slow walking associated with upper-class ambulation and the measured rhythms of ritual dancers (Cic. *De or.* 2.87.357–358).

[4] Sen. *Brev. vit.* 14.3–4. Positioning also conveyed status, with the ideal situation being higher than others. For further analysis of Roman cultural attitudes to walking, see Corbeill 2003.

[5] Kennedy 1972, 124. Ancient mnemotechnics are thoroughly discussed in Yates 1966, 1–49 and Small 1997.

[6] The Greeks preferred to memorize using lists, fingers, and groupings as memory aids in contrast to the spatialized systems of the Romans; Small 1997, 81–116.

[7] Modern scholars have given the Roman system many different names, including *Loci* System, House of Memory, Journey System, and Memory Palace. I prefer the Memory Walk System to emphasize the conceptualization of motion by an individual. The effectiveness of this mnemonic technique is in part due to the integrated stimulation of the hippocampus, which spatializes memory, and the parietal cortex and retrosplenial cortex, which organize memory and navigation; O'Keefe and Nadel 1978.

The Memory Walk System calls out for comparison with public processions in Rome. Both exploited familiar environments and movement as the connective narrative force between meaning-bearing images.[8] Yet the lived-in world posed specific challenges not faced in the conceptual realm. Rhetoricians could carefully curate their envisioned environments. For example, the Auctor recommended spaces in the memory system be uncluttered to allow for pure, unadulterated readings of *imagines*, noting in particular that, "the crowding and passing to and fro of people confuse and weaken the impress of the images, while solitude keeps their outlines sharp."[9] With a population of close to one million and almost as many eye-catching memorials, Rome's cityscape could not be uncluttered. In addition, the participants in a live parade did not always move according to script. At the same time, many memories competed for dominance. During the hours of the event, an animated parade wove together specific places and images, but such kinetic associationism soon blurred.[10] Once the event ended, competing *loci* and *imagines* reasserted themselves with the kinetic overlay of the next procession. The movement of only the most notable, repeated processions became imprinted on the collective memory.

2. Moved by the Moving Roman Triumph

The grand *pompa triumphalis* snaking its way through Rome reflected and shaped collective memory and has continued to define Roman culture over the centuries.[11] The elaborate triumphal procession served numerous purposes: catharsis for blood spilled, justification for military hegemony, homage to Jupiter, glorification for the victorious general, and celebration of newly conquered territory. Tied to collective identity of the state, the event could only be awarded by the Senate and only occur in the capital city, Rome. A plethora of recent publications has expanded understanding of this potent urban ritual, especially by clarifying the limited available source materials from antiquity and subsequent post-antique misinterpretations.[12] Evidence comes primarily from ancient authors who wrote for educated, upper-class audiences; most had not personally seen the events they described.[13] Focusing on political concerns, these elite writers had little to say about the kinetic experience of the moving event. Like the authors describing the Memory Walk System, those writing on the triumphal parade relied on standard tropes (animated dancers or marching soldiers) rather than the animated movement or the overall processional flow.

Each triumphal procession was unique, varying in composition, length, duration, and choreography, but it is useful to provide a generalized sketch. The procession was headed by magistrates,

[8] Favro 1993. A number of Roman authors exploited the act of walking through cities to generate narratives, explain monuments, and, ultimately, to animate history; Verg. *Aen.* 8; Edwards 1996, 27–43.

[9] *Propterea quod frequentia et obambulatio hominum conturbat et infirmat imaginum notas, solitudo conservat integras simulacrorum figuras (Rhet. Her. 3.19).*

[10] Forgetting had significant connotations in the Roman world, as affirmed by the practice of *damnatio memoriae*; Flower 2006. Cicero was not sympathetic with the Athenian politician Themistocles, who, blessed with the ability to remember everything, longed to be able to forget; *De or.* 2.84.299.

[11] The triumphal procession was fully integrated into the Romans' collective psyche, as evidenced by the retrojection of the first celebration to the time of Romulus (ca. 752 B.C.). The frequency of triumphs declined after the republican period, yet the event remained vital in social memory. Due to the limited and sporadic data, this study must of necessity generalize, with most examples based on imperial materials.

[12] Künzl 1988, Favro 1994, Brilliant 1999, Hölkeskamp 2006d, Beard 2007, and La Rocca 2008.

[13] Beard 2003, 32.

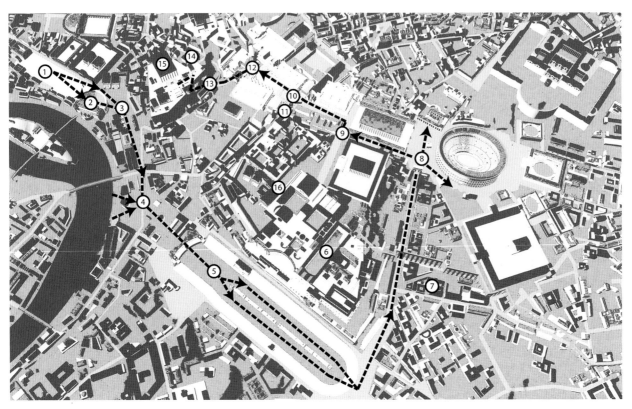

Fig. 6.1. Map of triumph with generalized route of the pompa triumphalis *through late antique Rome (image by Marie Saldaña): 1. Circus Flaminius area, 2. Theater of Marcellus, 3. Forum Holitorium, 4. Forum Boarium, 5. Circus Maximus, 6. Palatine Hill, 7. Caelian Hill, 8. Arch of Constantine and Meta Sudans, 9. Arch of Titus, 10. Portico across entry to Forum, 11. Arch of Augustus, 12. Area in front of Curia, 13. Clivus Capitolinus, 14. Capitoline Hill, 15. Temple of Jupiter Optimus Maximus, 16. Temple of Apollo.*

who were followed by tangible evidence of the value of war, including wagons and floats (*fercula*) overflowing with booty, painted and live recreations of battles, chained captives, and models of captured cities, along with animals for sacrifice, musicians, and dancers (see fig. 6.3). The triumphant general appeared in the middle of the parade, standing in luxurious display atop a magnificent horse-drawn triumphal chariot. In the final section marched row after row of soldiers, who shouted cries of triumph and bawdy songs. Much ink has been spilled in futile attempts to identify a definitive path for the triumphal parade. Ancient sources preserve few specifics beyond a starting area and terminus (fig. 6.1). From the Campus Martius outside the city's ritual boundary (*pomerium*), the procession moved south through the Fora Holitorium and Boarium (possibly also through the Velabrum), and then turned southeast to pass in front of the crowds seated in the Circus Maximus.[14] Continuing northward, the parade passed between the Palatine and the Caelian before turning west to climb up and over the Velian ridge. At the Forum Romanum the parade halted for special performances viewed from wooden stands (Plut. *Aem.* 32.2). With great fanfare, soldiers led the defeated enemy leader to the nearby Tullianum for execution (Cic. *Verr.* 5.77). In its final phase, the *triumphator* and a subset of the parade climbed up the steep slope of the Capitoline Hill and made solemn sacrifices before the temple of the most powerful god, Jupiter Optimus Maximus. After the parade ended, the streets were cleaned, the bleachers dismantled, and the floats put in storage. As individualized

[14] Wiseman 2007.

memories began to fade, collective memories gained strength, forged through kinetic engagement with a directed path, curated representations, and repeated reinscription.

3. A Directed Path

In A.D. 71, Vespasian and Titus commemorated their victories in the East with a glorious triumph procession through Rome. Josephus, a spectator at the event, described the parade as flowing like a river through the city (*BJ* 7.132). The imagery is telling. The Romans remembered the procession as animated, unvaried, and continuous in its directionality despite ebbs and flows and varied diversions. Like many rivers, the parade did not have a single point of origin. The general with his soldiers, captives, and wagons of booty scattered across the broad, flat Campus Martius to await senatorial approval of the triumph. Once an affirmative announcement was received, final preparations got under way with choreographers directing dancers, workers preparing floats, artists laboring on large descriptive paintings, and so on. The parade formally entered the city from the southwest Campus, passing through a (if not "the") *porta triumphalis*, and began its relentless progression toward the Capitoline Temple of Jupiter.[15]

The exact route cannot be fully reconstructed for even one of the more than three hundred documented Roman triumphs. No two were alike. In the competitive world of ancient Rome, each *triumphator* wanted to convey unique, personal messages calibrated for maximum political impact. In the Memory Walk System, a creator controlled the placement of *imagines*; in the living city symbols were already fixed in space; only a few artworks or ephemeral structures were quickly inserted before the pending event. Working with urban magistrates and event organizers, a *triumphator* laid out a route that, when possible, passed sites, buildings, and artwork of personal import, carefully stitching together memorable associations.[16] The challenge was to make such programming legible. Rome was filled with competing imagery. However, this kinetic event had an edge. Every corner of the capital reflected the Roman culture of triumph. Captured armor adorned the homes of successful generals, paintings of bloody battles hung on public display, inscriptions boasted of successful campaigns, and innumerable statues represented military figures.[17] Organizers probably enhanced the chosen *imagines* and *loci* to co-opt them into the new propaganda, adding bright paint to buildings, regilding statues, adorning all with fragrant garlands, and carefully placing musicians in key spots. The legibility of this stitching would have been obvious to organizers and to parade participants, who experienced the selected symbols and places in kinetic sequence. But who else could read (or imagine) this inscribed kinetic narrative?

Evidence on urban spectatorship in ancient Rome is limited.[18] Two points may be posited about viewer movement and the *pompa triumphalis* itself. First, observers did not sit still but were themselves in motion, especially as the parades expanded in length and duration. A minimum of five hours was required for the head of the parade to cover the 3.5 kilometers from the southern Campus Martius to the Capitoline.[19] The time required rapidly expanded depending on the parade's

[15] Beard 2007, 96–100.

[16] Aemilius Paullus observed that the organization of a triumphal parade required the same skills and mental toughness as a military campaign; Diod. Sic. 31.8.13. For more on the logistics of triumphal parades, see Künzl 1988, 66–84.

[17] Dillon and Welch 2006.

[18] Bergmann and Kondoleon 1999.

[19] One can imagine that the *triumphator* situated in the center of the parade entered the Circus Maximus as participants at the parade front entered the Forum.

scale, types of objects displayed, and crowd management. In 201 B.C., Scipio Africanus returned to Rome with so much booty that the procession was extended to three days in order to show it all (Livy 34.52). In addition, broken axles, irritable captives, elephants too big to pass through an arch, and other disruptions further lengthened the event (Plut. *Pomp.* 14.4). No wonder Cicero equated listless sauntering with the snail's pace of a *ferculum* (*Off.* 1.36.131). The ritual nature of the procession rendered complaints inappropriate, except for the emperor. Tired from the length and tediousness of the procession, Vespasian wished he had never desired a triumph (Suet. *Vesp.* 12). Some lucky spectators found seats in bleachers, theaters, and the Circus Maximus. Those standing on the sidewalks came and went, depending on biological needs and personal interests. Some rushed ahead to catch a second glimpse of notable features such as the *trimphator*, a grand display of booty, or rare animal; others hurried to the back of the parade to see family members among the soldiers.

Second, parade choreography, and thus viewing, varied. Ancient artistic and written depictions of the triumph have fostered the notion that the event had a fixed composition the same along its entire extent. The lived reality was different. The procession did not flow at an even pace. Rather it proceeded forward in fits and starts, changing its displays and character along the way. Some stops were spontaneous; others were planned. Mock battles, dance performances, and other set pieces briefly curbed the processional flow. These logically occurred in front of viewers seated in theaters and circuses, and on bleachers, and at processional nodal points where the parade slowed to change direction or rearrange parade components (see fig. 6.1). Towering displays several stories in height and large floats with live dioramas could not pass along streets that were narrow, blocked by construction, or encumbered with low overhangs.[20] Such enormous features probably moved only along the wide, straight segments of the route.[21] For example, the 110 ships in the triumph of Lucullus in 63 B.C. could have joined the procession at the docks by the Forum Boarium and peeled off from the parade before reaching the 10-meter rise up the Velia. These temporary pauses did not disrupt the relentless processional flow. Instead, they served as dividing chapters that facilitated remembrance, much like the rooms or spaces imagined in the Memory Walk System (Quint. *Inst.*11.2.27).

In antiquity all roads led to Rome, yet within the city many eyes, and memories, led to the Capitolium. The triumphal parade's relentlessness toward the Temple of Jupiter Optimus Maximus on the Capitoline ensured a cohesive memory.[22] This temple was arguably the most venerated, most memorable site in Rome, remarkable for its embellishments, hilltop site, visibility, and especially its rich religious history.[23] As a communal focal point, this *locus* was the touchstone of numerous urban narratives where ritual acts were initiated and others terminated in iterative succession.[24] Here each general made vows and offerings to the best and greatest god Jupiter before leaving Rome in pursuit

[20] For example, since large parade features could not pass through the arch at the curved end of the Circus Maximus, they had to be rerouted; Wiseman 2007, 446–447.

[21] After passing through the Forum Boarium, the *pompa triumphalis* moved along the two long valleys flanking the Palatine. Among the straightest passageways in Rome, these formed a notable urban armature that accommodated both ritual processions and the majority of heavy transport; MacDonald 1988, 30.

[22] On the importance of a true path as the means to virtue, see Sen. *Tranq.* 2.2.

[23] The Capitoline temple honored the triad of Jupiter, Juno,

and Minerva. When Rome's settlements coalesced into a single city, the Capitoline Hill was given a special status outside the four urban regions. Wheeled access to the hilltop was possible only on the east from the Forum below. The Forum linked directly with the river to the east through the so-called Velabrum Valley, but this approach was too short for civic processing and offered limited viewing opportunities; Wiseman 2007, 445–446. As a result, most processions took a longer route circumambulating the Palatine Hill before climbing up to Jupiter's temple.

[24] For example, the *pompa circensis* began on the Capitoline; Dion. Hal. 7.72.1–13. When Cicero returned to Rome from exile, he went immediately to the Capitoline Temple of Jupiter; *Att.* 4.1.4–5.

Fig. 6.2. Drawing of unrolled reliefs on a Julio-Claudian silver cup from Boscoreale showing a sacrifice in front of the Temple of Jupiter Optimus Maximus (?), and the triumphator *in a chariot (drawing by Marie Saldana).*

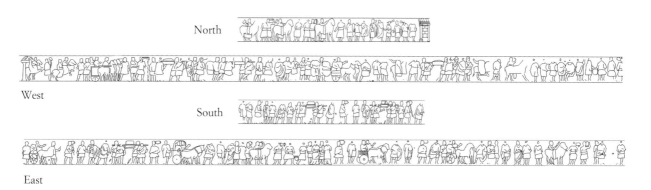

Fig. 6.3. Processional frieze, Arch of Trajan, Beneventum (drawing by Tim Callan).

of the greatest military honor—a triumph. If victorious and rewarded a triumph, he eventually attained glory with a return to the same spot for rites and sacrifices. The act of coming full circle back to the Capitoline brought the man close to the god. During the parade the *triumphator* processed through Rome in the garb of Jupiter Optimus Maximus (Livy 10.7.10). Smoke from his offerings before the god's temple wafted high above the city, signaling to everyone the culmination of the ritual event. The sacrifice occurred only a few meters northeast, and approximately 38 meters above the point where the procession had formally begun with the crossing of the *pomerium* into Rome (see fig. 6.1). The circularity of this story, its inevitability, is commemorated on the Boscoreale cups honoring the triumph of Tiberius in 8/7 B.C. (fig. 6.2).[25] On one side the artist depicted Jupiter's temple with an animal sacrifice in front, on the other the triumphant Tiberius riding through Rome. Turning the cup, a Roman viewer saw the general's circular path from the Capitoline Hill, to the battlefield, and back again eternally repeating.

Roman artists exploited the potency of the processional loop in public art as well. A frieze showing a triumphal procession encircles the memorial Arch of Trajan erected at Beneventum (fig. 6.3).[26] On the short, northern side artists carved a ritual scene with solemn sacrificial animals approaching a temple; continuing around to the west side the action became more animated with lively

[25] Kuttner 1995, Huet 1996. On Roman ideas of circular time, see Kondoleon 1999, 328–333.

[26] Ryberg 1955, 150–154; Pfanner 1983, 88–90. The arch commemorated not just Trajan's military successes but also his many other achievements, including the extension of the Via Appia, which it spanned.

Fig. 6.4. Northwest corner of frieze, Arch of Trajan,
Beneventum (drawing by Tim Callan).

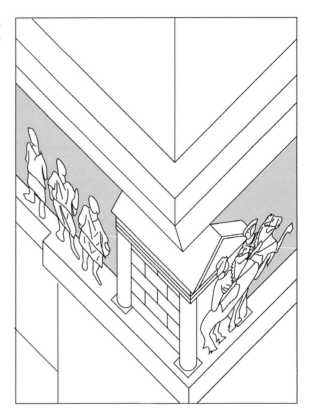

figures on horseback accompanying a *triumphator* in his chariot just as he approached an arch. A viewer at the northwest corner of Trajan's memorial simultaneously saw a sacrificial scene before a temple and the moving parade, the angled presentation emphasizing a kinetic link between the two (fig. 6.4). Modern scholars continuously debate what is being shown.[27] Is the overall procession a generic *pompa triumphalis* or a recreation of Trajan's specific event in A.D. 107? Is the temple that of Jupiter Optimus Maximus or one in the Campus Martius? Does the sacrifice represent the end or beginning of the ritual? Is the arch the *porta triumpalis* or a different urban memorial? Observers looking up approximately 12 meters could not readily read the details to provide an answer, but specificity may not have been the goal of ancient artists, who reveled in the conflation of identities that provoked enriching multiple readings. Regardless of how viewers interpreted the particular actions or structures depicted on arches, they all saw a continuously repeating processional movement that eternally ended (or began) at a temple.

Spectator reactions to ancient public events are notoriously difficult to determine, despite the importance accorded audiences by rhetoricians (Cic. *Brut.* 37). After all, individual and social memories constantly evolved. For example, a well-educated, foreign-born slave interpreted artistic imagery very differently from a plebian worker. Similarly, male viewers who had participated in the triumphal parades of the mid-republican period incorporated personal experiences of battles and processing into their readings. As fighting forces increasingly were drawn from outside Rome in the imperial period, spectators in the capital city drew upon secondary depictions in art, literature, and the theater.

[27] In eighteenth-century drawings of the frieze an arch stood before the *triumphator*'s chariot; today only traces remain. Adamo Muscettola argues the relief shows Trajan's actual triumph; in contrast Östenberg believes it is a generic depiction; Adamo Muscettola 1992, 13, passim; Östenberg 2009, 18.

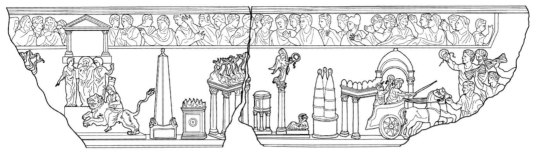

*Fig. 6.5. Now-lost relief depicting a magistrate of the games emulating a triumphator
processing through the Circus Maximus in Rome (image by Marie Saldaña after Étienne Dupérac).*

4. Curated Reproductions

The most direct way to evoke the directed movement of the triumphal parade was through reenactment. Simulations of processional kineticism entertained Roman viewers at theater and circus events performed long after a triumphal event. Horace described a play in which, "For four hours or more . . . troops of horse and files of foot [soldiers] sweep by . . . [and] with hurry and scurry come chariots, carriages, wagons and spoils."[28] At official games in the Circus Maximus disassociated from a specific triumphal celebration, the opening procession often exploited the imagery and processional dynamism of the triumph, with a magistrate in a two-horse chariot galloping before an animated cheering crowd (fig. 6.5). These restagings presented the triumphal parade as lively, fast-paced entertainments, an association underscored by depictions in art that included spectators and settings in theater and circus buildings.[29] While certainly memorable, such live recreations of the *pompa triumphalis* could not be continuously performed. Furthermore, these events emphasized energetic motion associated, at best, with military action and, at worst, with low-class activities.

Dynamic triumphal parades moving through Rome offered rich and memorable sensorial readings. The cheering crowds, saturated colors, blaring trumpets, incense, animal sweat, ground tremors from large floats, mouth-watering street food, jostling crowds, and other stimuli bombarded spectators' senses.[30] In this panoply of sensory stimuli, no two individuals had the same experiences. From Aristotle to Cicero, ancient authors acknowledged that the complex memory traces of sensorial perceptions formed the exclusive basis for remembering but explicitly identified sight as the keenest.[31] The power of sight derives not only from its importance in daily human activity but also from its operating largely on actions and tangible objects (things) that can be readily replicated; other senses deal with intangibles (smells, sounds, temperatures) that are not easily reproduced in stable forms.

Pictorial reproductions of the parade shaped post-event memories. The visual emphasis minimized remembrance of many senses but maintained a carefully curated and enduring presentation

[28] The full passage reads: *Quattuor aut pluris aulaea premuntur in horas dum fugiunt equitum turmae peditumque cateruae; mox trahitur manibus regum fortuna retortis, esseda festinant, pilenta, petorrita, naues, captiuum portatur ebur, captiua Corinthus* (Hor. *Epist.* 2.1.189–193).

[29] Versnel 1970, 101–104, 129–130; Lim 1999. An imperial funerary relief from Sant'Elia juxtaposes lively processions in both a theater and a circus; Vogel 1969, 155.

[30] Ov. *Tr.* 4.2. More research is needed to determine how sounds, colors, and other sensory factors impacted both remembrance and the interpretation of movement in antiquity. For a modern theorization, see Casey 2000, Schine accessed 2011.

[31] Cic. *De or.* 2.87.357–358. For a polysensory examination of ancient Rome, see Betts 2011.

of movement. Processional scenes appeared throughout Rome, on domestic objects, interior friezes and paintings, stone reliefs, and coins. In the public cityscape, Roman viewers directly associated the *pompa triumphalis* with commemorative arches. Architects initially developed this building type as a simple support elevating statuary to ensure visibility in the bustling urban environment. Soon, however, they transformed the arch into an effective billboard embellished with inscriptions, reliefs, and sculptures adorning the four sides.[32] As an architecture of passage spanning a street, these memorials became closely tied with urban processing. Their frequent use by generals, their supporters, and the state to commemorate both victories and the *pompa triumphalis* led to the post-antique labeling of all such forms as "triumphal arches" even though not all were connected with the formal ritual.[33] Large carved panels on the arches frequently depicted isolated set pieces from the triumph, while long friezes showed the procession eternally circling the honorific arch. Such artistic recreations reprogrammed remembrance by editing the content, composition, and reading of parade memories.

At the actual processional event, the forceful actions and consequences of war dominated the visual displays. Similarly, in post-event descriptions Roman writers carefully described the spoils, prisoners, floats, soldiers, and the *triumphator* in his grand chariot, all overt affirmations of military success and associated political stature. In contrast, artists carving the parade friezes presented the procession as a ritual act of communal civic piety. They showcased sacrificial animals, musicians, attendants, and ritual objects along with the *triumphator* while minimizing elite individuals.[34] Only three togate figures appeared on the Beneventum frieze (see fig. 6.3). Such curation was eternalizing, transferring the procession from the depiction of a specific event into a grand continuum of repeating contracts between the Romans and the gods.[35]

The placement of the processional friezes in specific urban contexts necessitated adjustments to the depicted choreography. Artists placed significant features on the primary façade of each triumphal arch and reordered the components to provide visual variety. On the Arch of Titus a large sacrificial ox is placed above the keystone of the arched opening. At Beneventum, the *triumphator* and notable spoils appeared on the west side facing the city and Rome; sacrificial animals appeared at modulated intervals throughout the length of the frieze.[36]

As befitting a ritual, the parade participants on arch friezes moved solemnly in a slow, modulated manner, usually left to right. To maintain decorum, Roman artists consistently avoided known artistic conventions that conveyed dynamic movement, such as compositional diagonals or twisting forms.[37] Throughout, a balanced modulation or *rhythmos* gave rational order to motion.[38] In most cases, the figures faced forward as if momentarily stopping to be seen, their distinctiveness emphasized by deep carving and limited overlapping; lumbering sacrificial oxen facing to the right indicated

---

[32] The commemorative arch appeared in the republic but proliferated under Augustus; Mansuelli 1979.

[33] The close connection of the arch form with triumphs may derive from the tradition of having enemies in the field pass under a "yoke" (*sub iugum missi*) made of spear (Livy 3.28) or from temporary versions erected during the triumphal celebration, though firm evidence is lacking for the latter. On the use of a triumphal arch to frame significant views, see Marlowe 2006.

[34] Östenberg 2009, 9–11, 18. The omission of large floats and other vertical elements may be due to the restrictions of the narrow frieze band.

[35] Ryberg 1955, 204.

[36] Ryberg 1955, 152–153.

[37] The ancients preferred to convey action through poses rather than graphical means; Pollitt 1972, 56–58; Cutting 2002, 1185. In the Severan period, architects in the eastern provinces and North Africa experimented with showing motion on architecture with windblown column capitals, which continued to be used in the Byzantine era.

[38] App. *Pun.* 66. The relationship of rhythms and movement through urban space is explored by Lefebvre 2004.

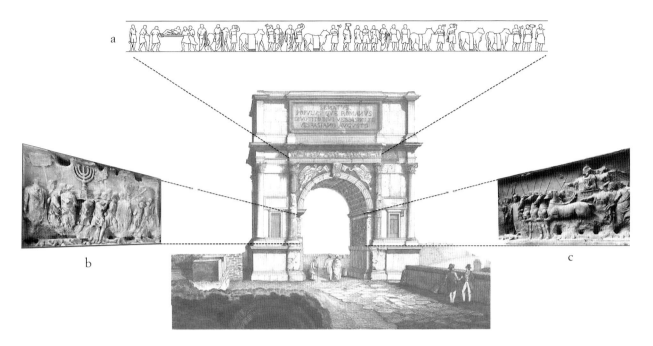

*Fig. 6.6. a. Arch of Titus, Rome, with drawing of reconstructed procession (images by Tim Callan and Diane Favro) (top);
b. Arch of Titus, Rome. Relief of booty from Jerusalem being carried in procession through an arch (left);.
c. Arch of Titus, Rome. Relief of Titus as* triumphator *in procession (right).*

directional movement as on the Arch of Titus (fig. 6.6a). Notably, references to the physical setting were few, with only a single temple or arch to indicate context. Movement in the real world was too specific and distracted. Instead, the frieze processions moved through a refined ritual world that seemed to exist outside time and place. The projected calm, controlled gravity of the movement in the triumphal friezes contrasted dramatically, and consciously, with the dynamism of war scenes on relief panels on the arch exterior or passageways. The reliefs of Roman battles showed a frenzy of action with numerous overlapping figures simultaneously moving in different directions in real-world settings indicated by buildings and plantings.[39]

The complicated art on triumphal arches called out for comment. Ancient speakers promoted *ekphrasis*, a mind-building rhetorical exercise involving the detailed description and commentary on a work of art or, less commonly, a place (Quint. *Inst.* 9.2.44). One can postulate that discussing artworks, especially those on public display, was not limited to the elite but became a pleasant, inexpensive pastime indulged in by city dwellers of all classes. The state encouraged close readings. Official artworks were both informing and operative. The carvings on triumphal arches conveyed specific information about the victories in distant lands. At the same time they stood as exemplars, cataloguing the proper movement for Romans according to status. Untamed actions on the battle reliefs contrasted with the slow, refined processing of the parade; the exertion of attendants pulling recalcitrant oxen contrasted with the stately poses of magistrates. The careful selection of the components and actions depicted conveyed a defining refined mood. The artists did not attempt to capture the live *pompa triumphalis* but rather to present current and future generations with a legible, defining image of how it should be remembered: as a well-ordered, decorous, slow-moving, timeless ritual.

[39] Hölscher 2004, 38–46.

5. Reinscribing the Parade

Artworks curated the memory of movement in triumphal parades. On a more physical level, their display in Rome also physically reconnected ancient occupants with the experience of the kinetic event in the cityscape. A parade is seductive even without a pied piper. Rome's residents began to formulate memories of the event weeks before it occurred. The exact pathway was made public in anticipation of a *pompa triumphalis* to allow other ritual parades, private processions, deliveries by heavy transport, daily traffic, construction projects, and other activities to be diverted or rescheduled.[40] Some residents walked along the proposed path searching for ideal viewing spots or locales for selling food to the hungry crowd. Such tracing bodily inscribed the motion of the triumphal parade into personal memories and the cityscape. In the aftermath of the celebrations, Romans reconnected with parade movement as they responded to processional artwork or repeatedly retraced the pathway of the *pompa triumphalis.*

FOLLOWING THE ART

Art is as significant for what it does as what it means.[41] Psychological motion studies affirm that depictions of moving humans compel observers to emulate the actions shown, following along in the same direction at the same pace.[42] The hundreds of figures solemnly processing in public art subliminally encouraged Roman observers to march in step.[43] In particular, the processional carvings on triumphal arches elicited bodily as well as conceptual readings. Of course, how a Roman observer responded to the activating, directional cues depicted in public artworks can never be proven. However, the diverse kinetic strategies repeatedly applied in representations on arches imply that ancient artists and architects had a reinforcing prescriptive agenda.

Climbing the Velia, ancient observers confronted the Arch of Titus (ca. A.D. 82). Facing this memorial to eastern campaigns, pedestrians naturally paused to catch their breath, taking the time to read the inscription and admire now-lost relief panels on the façade. The central passageway soon beckoned. Not only did it frame a view to the Capitoline Temple of Jupiter in the distance, but its interior sides boasted attractive, approximately life-size scenes from the triumph of Titus in A.D. 71. On the left side above head height, the well-known relief panels depicted the spoils from Jerusalem being carried toward a triumphal arch, literally echoing the kinetic movement of the viewers. The attendants carrying the heavily laden *ferculum* bent with the weight, their fluttering tunics indicating both directional movement and lower status (fig. 6.6b). On the right, the *triumphator* majestically rode in his chariot at a measured pace in order to be easily seen (fig. 6.6c). The legs of the horses are in march step to indicate control, but their nodding heads and open mouths conveyed strength and wildness tamed by the imperial driver.[44] Processing along the actual triumphal route, the carved

---

[40] The need for advance information is obvious. A long triumphal parade created a living wall around the Palatine, blocking access to the city center for hours. No sources indicate the Romans documented processional routes on maps.

[41] Gell 1998, 232–242.

[42] A powerful ancient example is found with the Ara Pacis, where Romans moving along the Via Flaminia from either the north or the south were encouraged by the direction of carved figures to move eastward toward a carefully constructed Augustan environment; Favro 1993.

[43] In Roman art, viewer movement is most studied for the Column of Trajan; Brilliant 1984, Torelli 1992, Huet 1996.

[44] These magnificent reliefs conveyed movement through the varied depth of carving, as well as through composition and directionality. Bronze statues of the *triumphator* in his chariot surmounted such arches, though there is scant evidence for how they faced. Did the general look down on the approaching parade or face in the same direction as the moving procession? In most cases, the orientation was probably determined by the context, as with the Arch of Septimius, where the emperor and his sons presumably faced toward the central Forum.

figures compelled viewers to fall into step and conceptually reengage with the original parade. For Romans approaching Titus's arch from the opposite direction, the powerful directionality of movement on the reliefs reinforced remembrance of the procession by overtly placing them in opposition to the potent triumphal flow.

Though the large panels lining the passageway of the Arch of Titus attracted attention, their location on a much-traveled thoroughfare did not accommodate lengthy perusal. Lower-status viewers in particular would have been pushed aside. They and others with time to spare could more readily examine the arch's exterior. The four-sided elaboration of urban arches affirms an original conceptualization as mid-space objects to be accessed on all sides. About 10 meters above ground pedestrians saw the triumphal procession in a frieze that originally wrapped around the structure (fig. 6.6). The small figures were not easy to read, though in antiquity paint may have enhanced viewing.[45] The movement, however, was clearly evident even to those with weak eyesight. The pedestrians' examination logically began with the sacrificial ox that held a place of honor over the central passageway. Facing right, he and other figures encouraged viewers to likewise move in that direction. Looking upward, Roman viewers walked slowly to read the frieze, emulating the ritual pace depicted. Confined within a narrow band, the figures were smaller and stockier than those on the reliefs in the archway; attendants and other lower-status individuals appeared frequently and at almost the same scale as individuals in togas. Such characteristics, as well as the parallel movement of walking observers, may have sparked a special empathetic engagement for ordinary Romans.[46]

The viewing and reviewing of such processional scenes reshaped memories of those who had seen a triumph and fostered pseudo-memories for those who had not. The recurrence of the *pompa triumphalis* varied widely over Rome's long history. During the republic, many Romans experienced several in a single lifetime. In the imperial period the honor was reserved to the emperor and his family; frequency plummeted. The essential connection among the triumph, the procession, and the honorific arch gradually began to warp. Ancient sources reflect this disintegration, in many cases disagreeing about when and if a triumph was awarded or if an arch related to a specific ritual.[47] When Septimius Severus erected his great arch in the Forum Romanum (dedicated A.D. 203), his confrontational relationship with the Senate complicated his receipt of a triumph. The looming memorial included small processional scenes under the large panels, but these were segmented rather than continuous. All four are roughly identical, with armed soldiers, heavily laden wagons, and personified provinces moving toward the goddess Roma (fig. 6.7a). Lacking a *triumphator*, *fercula*, priests, or other components essential for the ritual, these may represent the victorious emperor's convoy moving toward the capital or carrying materials for the celebrations associated with his anniversary (*decennalia*). None of the ancient sources specifically mentions that Septimius Severus was awarded a triumph. The segmentation and tight framing of the procession did not encourage viewers to replicate its directed movement. Furthermore, the siting of the arch on a slope with tangential structures and heavy traffic precluded circumambulation. Instead, other visual stimuli directed motion at ground level. On the long façades of the arch, over-life-size soldiers and Parthian prisoners moved along the three sides of the column pedestals. Those on the pedestal faces looked toward the central passageway, while those on the sides moved outward as if joining with the others

---

[45] The frieze was about 57 cm in height. Regarding the possibility of color on arch friezes, see Brilliant 1967, 223. Color research in Roman art and architecture is still in its infancy, especially in relation to spatial and kinetic analyses; Bradley 2011, 42–43.

[46] Ryberg considered the small relief to be close to popular art in contrast to the "Greek style" evident on the panel reliefs; Ryberg 1955, 147.

[47] Beard 2007, 322–323.

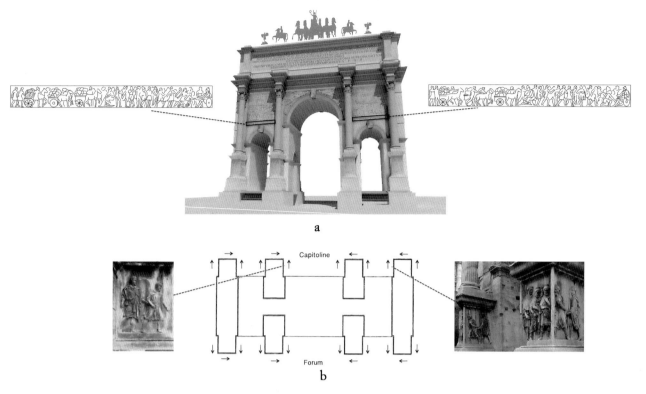

Fig. 6.7. a. Procession reliefs on Arch of Septimius Severus, Forum Romanum, Rome (images by Tim Callan and Diane Favro; digital model © Regents, University of California); b. Plan of Arch of Septimius Severus, Forum Romanum, Rome with arrows indicating direction of movement of carved figures on pedestal reliefs (image by Diane Favro).

to process through the arch (fig. 6.7b).[48] This directional configuration, however, was repeated on the opposite side toward the Capitoline Hill, thus subverting the kinetic reinscription of movement by a triumphal procession.

A similar subversion occurred on the arch erected to commemorate Constantine's victory over his fellow Roman, Maxentius, in A.D. 312. The monumental structure, embellished with *spolia* from other buildings, rose at the nodal point where the triumphal parade turned to move toward the Arch of Titus and Forum (see fig. 6.1). Among the reliefs specifically carved for this work were an encircling frieze and the pedestal bases.[49] On the latter, soldiers and victories followed a similar orientation as on the Arch of Septimius Severus, though being less animated in their directionality, did not as forcefully compel a specific movement.[50] Similarly, the war scenes on the large panels in the central passage and other reused carvings did not entice viewers along a particular path. In contrast, the frieze drew viewers to move around the arch looking at the figures carved in the artistic style of the day and wearing contemporary clothing.[51] At first glance, the relief band appeared to follow traditional models with a parade progressing around the building. On closer inspection,

[48] Brilliant 1967, 155. The evidence of game boards on the floor in the western passageway of the Severan Arch reinforces the primacy of the central opening for processing; Trifiló 2011, 315–317.

[49] Knudsen hypothesized that the small frieze was appro-priated from an earlier monument of Maxentius; Knudsen 1989, 313–314.

[50] Marlowe 2006, 235.

[51] Clarke 2003, 59–63.

South

West

Fig. 6.8. Arch of Constantine, Rome, seen from the south with arrows marking directional movement on frieze and drawing of processional friezes (image by Tim Callan and Diane Favro).

however, observers realized the scenes were not continuous. The large central passageway and the pilasters behind the columns disrupted the visual flow. In addition, the longer segments above the side passageways showed isolated, hieratic set pieces. All processing was pushed to the edges (fig. 6.8). The action began at the western end of the north façade, with a small frieze panel showing parading soldiers; their directed movement pulled viewers around the edge to join Constantine and his army on the march from Milan toward Verona (fig. 6.8). Continuing around the southwest corner, observers encountered a lone soldier moving toward the battle scenes in the longer panels on the southern façade. The processional action began again with another small scene of soldiers moving around the corner where Constantine was seen parading to Rome. The processing terminated on the north side with yet another small panel of mounted soldiers. Seen as a whole, the frieze simultaneously emulated and destabilized memories of the triumphal procession. The depiction clearly reflected essential transformations under way in the early fourth century. Though victorious, Constantine could not overtly celebrate a victory over other citizens. In addition, having allegedly won with the help of the Christian god, he could not complete a ritual that ended with sacrifices to Jupiter (Euseb. *Vit. Const.* 1.27–30). Roman observers following the frieze around the arch moved in fits and starts as the familiar, and the unfamiliar, continuously challenged kinetic expectations.

FOLLOWING THE PATH

De Certeau argued that by selecting and linking sites into an itinerary, a narrative becomes a spatial trajectory, thus implying the momentum of the trajectory predetermines pathways.[52] Reversing the formulation, an itinerary once inscribed in an environment has a narrative trajectory that projects a predetermined memory.[53] Especially in antiquity, movement inscribed memory and vice versa. Varro in the first century B.C. underscored the essential role of kinetics in mnemonics: "To remember derives from memory, since in this there is movement which is a return to what has remained in the mind."[54] Ancient writers did not refer to motion as the abstracted and quantified force familiar today in modern physics but as bodily action in space.[55] Again Varro is illuminating: "Nor is there motion where there is not place and body because the latter is that which is moved, the former is where to."[56] Once a cohesive public itinerary was inscribed in the cityscape of Rome, it had the capability of sparking journeys to the mind, provoking pedestrians to recall previous bodily actions as they moved along the original itinerary.

Current anthropological research and advances in the so-called archaeology of walking are moving beyond the analysis of social and spatial practices regarding mobility in urban contexts.[57] In Roman studies, these interdisciplinary approaches expand on semiotic analysis of *imagines* and *loci* to consider emplacement, the sensuous interrelationship of body-mind-environment in historical environments.[58] Roman writers were interested in the potent dialogue between action, place, and memory. Cicero, referring to Athens, wrote, "wherever we walk, we place our footprint in some history."[59] By attempting to walk in the footsteps of the past, scholars are interrogating how this bodily act stimulated memory by merging polysensory readings, past events, and places into lived experience.[60]

Rome's occupants were well familiar with the generalized route of the triumphal procession from posted descriptions, attendance at the ritual, literature, storytelling, and personal exchange.[61] This path was not a line on a map but a kinetic, embodied course of action. Over time, variations in the route of the *pompa triumphalis* and individual event experiences melded together into simplified schema that incorporated enduring features on the ground.[62] A majority of the triumphal itinerary was coincident with major urban arteries. As the most direct, flat circulation routes, the straight stretches of streets leading from the Forum Boarium and around the Palatine were firmly etched

[52] "Spatial Stories" in De Certeau 1984, 115–130.

[53] In Latin, *itinerarium* refers to written lists of places along a route such as the officially produced *Antonini Itinerarium* of the third century, as well as to planned and experienced individual journeys; the latter sense will be applied in the following discussion.

[54] *Meminisse a memoria, cum <in> id quod remansit in mente rursus mouetur; quae a manendo ut manimoria potest esse dicta* (Varro, *Ling.* 6.49); Spencer 2011, 71–72.

[55] Zeno's philosophical paradoxes referenced the motion of live animals as well as objects, from a philosophical rather than scientific viewpoint.

[56] *neque motis, ubi non locu et corpus, quod alterum est quod movetur alterum ubi* (Varro, *Ling.* 5.12); Newsome 2011, 20.

[57] Newsome 2011, Schine accessed 2011. The integration of perception and remembrance in current anthropological investigations is more operative than Aristotle's notion of perceptual memory traces as the exclusive base for creating memory; Casey 1979, 411.

[58] Howes 2005, 7. Such approaches are enlarging Roman studies of urban narrative encoding beyond the *genius loci* or *locus celeberrimus* to include a comprehensive analysis of embodied meaning.

[59] *Quamquam id quideminfinitum est in hac urbe: quacumque enim ingredimur, in aliqua historiavestigium ponimus* (Cic. *Fin.* 5.5).

[60] Casey 2000; Schine accessed 2011, 6.

[61] Larsen 1995.

[62] Casey 1979, 408–415.

into the minds of all Rome's occupants. Even more traveled was the processional way leading to the Forum. The cultural significance of this populated path was reinforced by repeated use for diverse state and private processions (as well as daily occupations), yet the triumphal imprint was prevailing. In addition to the numerous statues, reliefs, inscriptions, and buildings touting military victories along the path, arches continuously affirmed connection with military victories.

Rome was the only legitimate *locus* for the triumph. The existence of an arch in the teeming capital immediately caused viewers to ponder how it related to the triumphal parade itinerary. Operating as urban doorways, triumphal arches drew people forward along a dynamic urban trajectory. Passing through a triumphal arch, pedestrians rejoined the original procession flanked, as at the Arch of Titus, by other parade participants (see fig. 6.6). Such movement gave male residents of Rome who had never known battle a fleeting opportunity to engage in military success and action. Relief scenes showing the triumphal parade likewise moving through an arch literalized the pedestrians' actions, establishing an eternal, kinetic *mise en abyme* (see fig. 6.6b–c). As thousands of Romans engaged with the triumphal path each day, their bodily motion etched the event into individual and collective memories, affirming a triumph-sensitive mobility.[63]

Of course urban occupants did not recall the ritual procession with each step. However, the embodied act of walking along the potent triumphal path was a powerful mnemonic that enriched the journey while reinforcing culturally constituted ideas about motion. Romans did not have to follow the entire extent of the route, as its directed flow and terminus maintained the overall narrative and kinetic trajectory. Along the way, visual presentations reinforced culturally constituted notions about the movement and status of individuals while compelling physical emulation. The arches, art, and places encountered along the way operated as *imagines* and *loci*, conveying specifics about Rome's culture of triumph. But it was the bodily motion, the inscription and reinscription of processional memories that provided a strong mnemonic glue.

[63] Triumph-sensitive mobility adds a polysensory kinetic dimension to Elsner's notion of ritual-sensitive visuality; Nelson 2000, 54.

7 ◆ Memory and the Roman Viewer:
Looking at the Arch of Constantine

Jessica Hughes

History is to the nation rather as memory is to the individual. As an individual deprived of memory becomes disorientated and lost, not knowing where he has been or where he is going, so a nation denied a conception of its past will be disabled in dealing with its present and its future. As the means for defining national identity, history becomes a means for shaping history.

Schlesinger 1992, 51

quae acciderunt in pueritia, meminimus optime saepe.

Rhetorica ad Herennium 3.22

In many ways, the Arch of Constantine in Rome is an obvious choice of subject for an exploration of Roman memory.[1] Not only was its primary function commemorative (it celebrated Constantine's tenth year of rule and his victory over Maxentius in A.D. 312), but it was also constructed from pieces of sculpture and architecture that had, at some point, been taken from the monuments of earlier Roman rulers. Indeed, much of the existing scholarship on the arch already addresses the topic of memory, although the word *memory* itself is not always explicitly invoked.[2] These earlier discussions deal primarily with themes that might come under the heading of "Cultural Memory" or "Collective Memory," since they consider how the arch's makers selected, preserved, and re-presented elements of a "usable past" to serve their own, contemporary purposes.[3] Most commentators now agree that the decision to recycle old sculptures was motivated by an ideological agenda rather than a (purely) financial one, taking it to be deeply significant that the older reliefs come from the monuments of the "good emperors," Trajan, Hadrian, and Marcus Aurelius. The fact that these scholars go on to offer rather different interpretations of the arch's program reflects the inherent ambiguity of reused images, which can simultaneously indicate both change *and* continuity, and which can assert supremacy over the past at the same time as appropriating its numinous power.

The present chapter builds on this rich tradition of scholarship on the Arch of Constantine. However, in contrast with most earlier commentators, here I am particularly interested in memory as a human, cognitive faculty. The figure of the Roman viewer is thus central to my analysis, and one aim of this chapter is to show how work in the interdisciplinary field of memory studies can bring us closer to understanding the dynamics of viewing monuments in antiquity. I focus principally

[1] My research into *spolia* and memory was generously funded by a grant from the Memoria Romana project. I am grateful to Karl Galinsky, Adam Gutteridge, Janet Huskinson, Maggie Popkin, and Hugo Spiers for their comments on an earlier draft of this chapter.

[2] On the Arch of Constantine, see the following selective bibliography, with further references: Faust 2011; Gutteridge 2010; Marlowe 2006; Liverani 2004a; 2009; 2011; Holloway 1985; 2004, 19–54; Elsner 1998; 2000; 2003; Wilson Jones 2000; Pensabene and Panella 1999; Kleiner 1992, 444–455 with bibliography on 464; Peirce 1989; Brilliant 1984, 119–123; Ruysschaert 1963; Giuliano 1955; Berenson 1954.

[3] For the concept of "usable past," see Zamora 1998.

Fig. 7.1. The Arch of Constantine in Rome, seen from the north (Koppermann, neg. D-DAI-Rom 61.2297).

Fig. 7.1. The Arch of Constantine in Rome, seen from the north (Koppermann, neg. D-DAI-Rom 61.2297).

on two aspects of the complex and mutually formative relationship that existed between the arch and the Roman viewers who contemplated it. First, I emphasize the fact that viewers approached the monument with a suite of existing memories, which shaped their own unique responses to the imagery and configured its meaning in ways that could both consolidate and subvert the intentions of its creators. Secondly, I suggest that the arch actively impacted the memory of viewers, shaping the way in which they thought about the past, in the future. This idea of a two-way relationship between a monument and viewer dovetails with those theories that describe memory as *distributed* between individuals and the physical or social environment in which they operate.[4] Finally, I will propose a third way in which the monument relates to memory, suggesting an analogy between individual memory and national history similar to that described by Schlesinger in the citation above.

1. The Arch as "Monumentum"

The Arch of Constantine stands at the southern edge of the Colosseum valley (figs. 7.1 and 7.2). It was probably dedicated in A.D. 315, having taken approximately two and a half years to build. The duplicate inscriptions that appear on the north and south fronts of the arch state its *raison d'être*: it was a gift from the Senate and people of Rome to the emperor Constantine after he delivered the state from an unnamed tyrant (Maxentius).[5] A visual narrative of Constantine's victory is depicted on the continuous frieze that winds in chronological sequence around the arch's middle. This story begins with the departure of Constantine's army from Milan, then continues with the siege of Verona and the battle of the Milvian Bridge, before representing the emperor's victorious entry into Rome

[4] See, e.g., Wertsch 2002. Notably, this is a different view from the one presented by Roman writers, who often imply that monuments provide a direct, unmediated link to the people and events of past eras. Cf. Varro, *Ling.* 6.49; Cic. *Epist. ad Caes.* fr. 7.

[5] "To the emperor Caesar Flavius Constantinus, the greatest, pious, and blessed Augustus: because he, inspired by the divine, and by the greatness of his mind, has delivered the state from the tyrant and all of his followers at the same time, with his army and just force of arms, the Senate and people of Rome have dedicated this arch, decorated with triumphs."

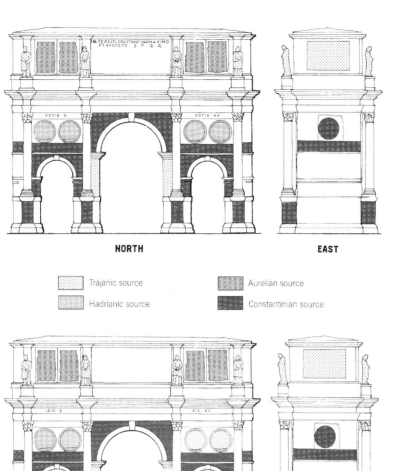

Fig. 7.2. Schematic plan of the four faces of the Arch of Constantine, with the arrangement of the reliefs and their sources, Rome, ca. A.D. 312–315 (original at Elsner 1998, 188 fig. 126; used with kind permission of Jaś Elsner).

and his subsequent activities in the city—his address from the rostra in the Roman Forum (*oratio*) and the distribution of gifts to the people (*liberalitas*). Other fourth-century carvings on the arch include images of Victories and the Genii of the Seasons on the spandrels, the Victories and captives that decorate the pedestal bases, and the sculpted roundels of the sun and moon placed above the frieze on the arch's short sides (fig. 7.3).[6] As Adam Gutteridge has noted in his exploration of the depiction of time on the Arch of Constantine, these roundels evoke cosmic time "and its synchronization with the more historical and human events with which it is depicted."[7]

In addition to these fourth-century sculptures, the arch also incorporates reused material, including architectural elements (capitals, bases, column shafts, and entablature) as well as figurative reliefs. Sculptures from the Trajanic period include the eight freestanding statues of Dacian prisoners that dominate the arch's attic and eight slabs of a large relief frieze showing the historic Roman victory

[6] L'Orange and von Gerkan 1939.

[7] Gutteridge 2010, 166.

Fig. 7.3. Arch of Constantine, east side with section of Constantinian frieze and roundel (neg. D-DAI-Rom 3134).

over the Dacians at the beginning of the second century A.D. These slabs are displayed in pairs, two in the central passageway and two in the attic above the sun and moon roundels; both these and the prisoner statues are thought to have been taken from the Forum of Trajan.[8] Eight sculpted medallions from the Hadrianic age decorate the north and south fronts of the arch. These show scenes of hunting and sacrifice and may originally have been part of an imperial hunting monument.[9] Meanwhile, eight large rectangular reliefs on the attic represent the civic, religious, and military deeds of the emperor Marcus Aurelius.[10] These Aurelianic reliefs may have come from a lost commemorative arch for that emperor, along with four similar panels in the Capitoline Museums.[11]

The juxtaposition of old and new sculptures on the arch results in an eclectic, dynamic appearance, which would have been even more striking in antiquity. As Mark Wilson Jones has explained, "the original effect has to be mentally reconstructed, since the accumulated centuries of wear has made white and colored marbles alike converge towards a dull buff."[12] Besides the *giallo antico* column shafts, the arch incorporated red porphyry (for the paneling around the tondi), purple *pavonazzetto* (for the cloaks of the Dacian prisoners), greenish gray *cipollino* (the prisoners' bases), and perhaps also a deep green porphyry (for a now-lost frieze in the main entablature). In addition to these colored marbles, bronze was used for the letters of the inscription and for the now-vanished sculptures on the arch's top.[13] This array of contrasting materials would have combined with the different shapes, sizes, and styles of the figurative sculptures to produce a powerful sense of variety and heterogeneity. In recent years, scholars have demonstrated the centrality of *varietas* as an aesthetic principle in late antiquity and the Middle Ages, thereby helping us to reconstruct the positive valency of *spolia* monuments in these periods.[14] But in the context of the Arch of Constantine, one wonders whether *varietas* might also have had a more particular symbolic resonance. Descriptions

---

[8] On the Great Trajanic Frieze, see Leander Touati 1987; Kleiner 1992, 220–223, 264. On the statues of prisoners, see Waelkens 1985, 645 nos. 3–9; Packer 1997, 1:437–438.

[9] Boatwright 1987, 190–192; Evers 1991; Kleiner 1992, 251–253, 265.

[10] Ryberg 1967; Angelicoussis 1984; Kleiner 1992, 288–295, 314.

[11] De Maria 1988, 316; Pensabene 1988.

[12] Wilson Jones 2000, 63. See Wilson Jones 2000, 54 fig. 7 for a diagram showing the locations of the different marble types.

[13] Marlowe 2006, 240 n. 52.

[14] Brenk 1987; Hansen 2003, 173–178; Carruthers 2009.

Fig. 7.4. Detail of the head of Constantine, recut from a head of Trajan, from the Trajanic frieze now on the west wall of the passageway in the central opening (Schwanke, neg. D-DAI-Rom 82.1106).

Fig. 7.5. Arch of Constantine, Rome. Trajanic panel from central passageway of arch with inscription FUNDATORI QUIETIS (Faraglia, neg. D-DAI-Rom 37.329).

of the Roman triumphal procession frequently emphasize the visual variety and cumulative effect of the spectacle, using contrast, volume, and heterogeneity to communicate the totality of Roman victory and control (cf. Favro in this volume). Josephus's description of the Flavian triumph is one example: he notes "the variety (*poikileia*) and beauty of the dresses" of the captives and "the beasts of many species" before claiming that "it is impossible adequately to describe the multitude of these spectacles and their magnificence under every conceivable aspect, whether in works of art or diversity of riches or natural rarities."[15] Many of the individual images on the Arch of Constantine evoke the material culture of the triumph (the victories, captives, personifications, and the narrative images of battle, for instance), but we might also see the overall aesthetic of the procession as referenced by, and crystallized in, the monument's busy eclecticism.[16]

Despite its appearance of vibrant chaos, however, the choice of sculptures and their arrangement on the arch suggest a careful and deliberate decision-making process on the part of the arch's makers. In particular, scholars have drawn attention to how the design of the monument reinforced the links between the emperors represented on it. One way in which this was achieved was by altering and annotating the spoliated second-century sculptures. Several of the older emperors' heads were recarved with the portrait features of Constantine (fig. 7.4), as well as with those of another tetrarch (either his co-ruler Licinius or his father Constantius Chlorus).[17] The Trajanic reliefs in the side arches were also inscribed with the textual epithets of Constantine: LIBERATORI VRBIS ("to the liberator of the city") on the western side of the bay, and FVNDATORI QUIETVS ("to the founder of tranquillity") on the eastern side (fig. 7.5). Notably, the dative case makes it clear that these phrases

[15] Joseph. *BJ* 7.132–133, 136, 138.

[16] On the imagery of the Roman triumphal procession, see Östenberg 2009.

[17] Galinsky 2008, 14; Kleiner 1992, figs. 185 and 186. On the Trajanic panels, see Leander Touati 1987, 91–95; for the Hadrianic roundels, see Wilson Jones 2000, 70–72; L'Orange and Van Gerkan 1939, 165–169; Rohmann 1998. On the later recarving of the heads on the Aurelianic panels, and on the post-antique reception of the arch in general, see Punzi 1999.

Fig. 7.6. Arch of Constantine, Rome, north side with oratio *(photo Alinari/Art Resource, New York, 17326).*

applied to Constantine, the recipient of the arch, and thus reminds the viewer of the arch's status as a gift. Roman audiences were acutely aware of the reciprocal nature of gift giving, and many of the images on the arch can be understood in the light of a *do ut des* philosophy—that is, not only as demonstrating the traditionalism of the Senate and people who awarded the monument but also as a public reminder to Constantine of the type of behavior that was expected of him in return.[18]

Besides these modifications of the second-century reliefs, the tight links between Constantine and his three chosen predecessors were also emphasized in the design and placement of the new fourth-century sculptures. For example, both Constantine and Trajan appear fighting and entering the city in triumph, while both Constantine and Marcus Aurelius distribute largesse to the people. The physical placement of the reliefs encouraged viewers to recognize the parallels in their content; it has been noted, for instance, that the walled city represented in the Aurelian "Rex Datus" panel "lends itself to assimilation with the similarly-walled city of Verona shown in the narrative frieze below," while Constantine's triumphant march toward Rome on the east end of the arch "echoes the equally triumphant scenes in the Trajanic relief above it on the Attic."[19] Meanwhile, the "Oratio" scene on the fourth-century frieze shows Constantine flanked by statues of Hadrian and Marcus Aurelius (fig. 7.6). Unlike the panels with the recarved heads, this scene acknowledges the bodily boundaries between the emperors but nevertheless emphasizes their contiguity.

Not all Roman viewers would necessarily have perceived and recognized (all) the emperors on Constantine's arch.[20] For those who *did*, however, these repeated typological links would have impinged on their understanding of each individual and era involved in the comparison. On the one hand, the arch's imagery shaped the viewer's ideas about Constantine and the present by showing the traditionalism and antiquity of the new ruler's actions. This served to legitimate Constantine but also (as James Young has remarked of monuments in a different historical context) "to elevate and mythologize current events" by erasing their particularity.[21] At the same time, the parallels between the spoliated and new reliefs also had the potential to transform the viewer's perspective on the older emperors by presenting them in the context of a teleological narrative. As Jaś Elsner has noted, this sort of typological exegesis "displayed the past only in so far as the past is validated by,

[18] Cf. Elsner's comments at 2000, 171. The arch's relationship to the future has been discussed by Gutteridge 2010, 165–166, who draws attention to the proleptic significance of the Constantinian scenes of *liberalitas* and *adlocutio* and of the Votis X and Votis XX inscriptions, which "reflect a promise and a control over the times that were yet to come." See also Brilliant 1984, 121 and Peirce 1989, 415.

[19] Wilson Jones 2000, 69; Elsner 2000, 173.

[20] Liverani 2004. Like most previous interpretations of the arch, some aspects of my own reading postulate a viewer who was able to identify the emperors represented on the arch. However, the methodology outlined here emphasizes the multivalency of the monument and suggests ways in which memory might be used to reconstruct discrepant as well as idealized responses to the arch's imagery.

[21] Young 1993, 10.

fulfilled in, and made meaningful through the present."[22] In other words, in their new context these scenes became prototypes for, or anticipations of, Constantine, taking on a proleptic significance that was entirely absent at the moment of their manufacture.[23]

2. Remembering at the Arch of Constantine

What did viewers remember when they looked at the Arch of Constantine? Monuments can cue many different kinds of memories, as a brief personal anecdote can help to clarify. On a recent trip to central London, I encountered a statue and discovered, upon reading the inscription, that it represented George VI (the current queen of England's father). Immediately, I remembered who he was—or rather, what I *actually* remembered was the highly successful 2010 film *The King's Speech* starring Colin Firth. This film, which was about the life of George VI and particularly his speech impediment, provided me with a concrete visual image of the king, along with a limited set of stories about his reign, some of which sprang to mind as I looked at this statue. At the same time, I also recalled "episodic" memories associated with the film, such as the evening that I went to the cinema to watch it and the conversations that I had with friends afterward. As well as these relatively recent events, I found myself thinking about earlier memories of my grandmother telling me stories about the British royal family. All of these memories—but particularly the older memories from childhood—contributed to the vague sense of nostalgia that I experienced when viewing this statue, the "positive affect" that arguably predisposed me to have a sympathetic reaction to the monument and the subject it represented.

This modern example underlines a very simple fact that is nevertheless often obfuscated in modern discussions of monuments: that is, what a monument cues its viewer to recall is *not* "firsthand" memories of the people and events being commemorated (which often occurred long before their lifetimes) but other, "mediating" representations and experiences.[24] Importantly, these mediating representations can impinge on viewers' interpretation of the monument, predisposing them to respond in a certain way to its imagery as well as its ideological message. Some of these representations are unique to certain individuals, as is the case with the stories told to me by my grandmother. Others can be shared by much larger groups of people: *The King's Speech,* for instance, was a box-office phenomenon, and I was probably not the only person who looked at this statue in 2011 and "remembered" the face of Colin Firth. This second type of "shared" memory is central to the view of collective memory put forward by writers like James Wertsch, who notes that groups "share a representation of the past because they share textual resources."[25] As Wertsch goes on to explain, the use of these textual resources "may result in homogeneous, complementary, or contested collective memory, but in all cases, it is the key to understanding how distribution [of memory] is possible."

How can this kind of analysis be brought to bear on the ancient viewer of monuments like the Arch of Constantine? The personal "episodic" or "communicative" memories of Romans are, for the most part, out of our reach—it is impossible to retrieve what Romans talked about with their

[22] Elsner 2000, 176; cf. Brilliant 1970, 78; and Gutteridge 2010, 164–165.

[23] Parallel to the process of intertextuality; see Rosati in this volume.

[24] Cf. Quintilian's observation that "When we return to a place after considerable absence, we not merely recognize the place itself but remember things that we did there, and recall the persons whom we met and even the unuttered thoughts that passed through our minds when we were there before" (*Inst.* 1.2.17).

[25] Wertsch 2002, 26.

grandmothers (although presumably stories of earlier rulers would have featured somewhere in the repertoire). However, we do have access to at least some of the mediating texts and images that were accessible to Roman viewers and that may have conditioned their reception of the monument. In her 1997 article in the *Memoirs*, Dale Kinney uses such a methodology to reappraise the recarved portrait heads on the second-century reliefs in the light of other Roman image-making practices. Noting that "since H.P. L'Orange published his seminal book on the Arch of Constantine in the 1930s, most scholars have accepted some version of his thesis that this was a panegyrical gesture to all four emperors," Kinney points out that, as far as *imperial* portraits are concerned, this use of recarving to convey a positive message was very unusual—perhaps even unprecedented. Normally, the reworking of emperor portraits happened in a context of "penury, hubristic appropriation, or *damnatio memoriae*," negative practices that, Kinney argues, would have determined the viewer's reaction to the recarved heads on the Arch of Constantine.[26] In other words, while the designers of the arch may have intended the recarving to be read as a panegyrical gesture, the "remembering viewer" would have found it difficult to escape the negative connotations of this practice.

Kinney's interpretation of the reworked portrait heads shows the power of memory to complicate the intentions of a monument's designers by indicating counter-hegemonic readings. Of course, monuments could also—deliberately or "accidentally"—cue other memories that were entirely coherent with their makers' ideological program. In fact, Jaś Elsner and Karl Galinsky have both pointed out that the reworking of portrait heads occurred in a much wider range of contexts than the negative ones mentioned by Kinney (for instance, the honorific reuse of statues and the later insertion of portrait heads into mythological scenes on Roman sarcophagi), thereby alerting us to the possibility that the heads on the arch might have cued positive or neutral as well as negative memories for their viewers.[27] Further similarities might be drawn between the recarved heads and (non-recarved) images such as the "theomorphic" or "allegorical" portraits that were so beloved by imperial patrons. These are visually and conceptually similar to recarved portraits, insofar as they present one subject's head on another subject's body. Seeing the reworked figures on the Arch of Constantine in the light of these allegorical portraits would have emphasized the divine or quasi-mythological status of the earlier emperors by showing them as equivalent to the gods or mythical figures who were normally used as allegorical "costumes." Then, there are the stories and images of bodily metamorphosis, which saturated Roman culture and which were often set in bucolic landscapes similar to those on the arch's Hadrianic roundels. While modern academic interpretations of the arch's recarved figures prefer formal terms such as *analogy, typology,* and *prototype,* we need to remain open to the possibility that the Roman viewer—who was used to the idea of people and things taking on new forms—might have perceived these images as representing a genuine bodily transformation. Such a reading implies a very literal continuity in the imperial office: the emperors might look slightly different from one another, but they were essentially made from the same substance—they were (to use a term current in Constantine's lifetime) *homoousioi.*

The discussion so far indicates the fundamental role of memory as a source of meaning and discrepant viewer experience. Other aspects of the arch's imagery would have cued different memories, and all of these would have nuanced the viewer's reception of the monument in subtly different ways. For instance, the formal similarities between the Arch of Constantine and earlier arches like those of Titus and Septimius Severus may have underlined the conservatism of Constantine's monument and

[26] Kinney 1997, esp. 58. Note that *damnatio* is a modern term of convenience and as such should be used with caution. See Flower 1998, esp. 156.

[27] Elsner 2000, 174; Galinsky 2008, 15.

the traditional values of its makers while at the same time showcasing the novel aspects of its design and use of *spolia*.[28] Viewers who remembered Constantine's interventions in the nearby building projects of his rival Maxentius may have been primed to read the recarved portrait heads in the negative light suggested by Kinney; meanwhile, memories of the original (and now dismembered) contexts of the second-century reliefs would have undoubtedly impinged on their interpretation of the Arch of Constantine.[29] And so on. Of course, in one sense this whole discussion is simply a reframing of existing theories of intertextuality and reception in which "knowledge" is preferred to the word *memory*. But insisting that *memory* is at stake in viewing is important for at least two reasons. First, as indicated earlier, it reminds us that all viewers' experiences of a monument drew on their unique, episodic, autobiographical memories as well as the "semantic" memories (knowledge) that they shared with the rest of their "textual community." Secondly, framing the analysis in terms of memory also brings art-historical work into dialogue with other scholarship in the interdisciplinary field of memory studies—a dialogue that potentially holds benefits for all of its participants.

3. Remembering after the Arch of Constantine

So far, this discussion has implicitly focused on a viewer standing in front of the Arch of Constantine who is prompted by the arch's imagery to recall other objects and experiences. But we might also think about what happened to those viewers once they had walked away from the monument. How did their encounter with the Arch of Constantine transform the way in which they thought about the past (and the present), in the future?

One possible approach to this question involves highlighting the agency of the arch's makers, whose choices in selecting and presenting material for display influenced what future audiences—including ourselves as historians—were (collectively) enabled to remember.[30] We might note, for instance, that Roman history according to the Arch of Constantine is an *imperial* history—there is no room for regal or republican episodes in this coherent story of emperors and their victories over men and beasts. Such ellipses are significant because, as Eviatar Zerubavel has pointed out, "The extent to which our social environment affects the "depth" of our memory is also manifested somewhat more tacitly in the way we conventionally begin historical narratives. . . . After all, by defining a certain moment in history as the actual beginning of a particular historical narrative, it implicitly also defines for us everything that preceded it as mere 'pre-history' which we can practically forget."[31]

Along these same lines, we might emphasize that the version of Roman history presented by the Arch of Constantine is a relentlessly male one. Diana Kleiner has already pointed out that in the Constantinian scene of *oratio* the Roman population is represented solely by men and their male children (see fig. 7.6).[32] A quick count of the extant, recognizable figures on the arch reveals more than 370 mortal men, including soldiers and emperors (although the latter category straddle the mortal-divine boundary), and at least twenty divine or allegorical male figures, including statues of gods and male personifications. Divine and allegorical females also number approximately twenty; again, these include statues of goddesses, Victories, and personifications like Virtus, Honos, and

[28] On the "mimesis of the Arch of Septimius Severus," see Wilson Jones 2000, 65–67.

[29] On the arch's interplay with Maxentian building projects and other nearby buildings, see Marlowe 2006. On the provenance of the spoliated sculptures, see Kinney 1997, 127–128.

[30] This is familiar territory for scholars working within the field of cultural memory studies; see for instance Fowler 2007.

[31] Zerubavel 1996, 287.

[32] Kleiner 1992, 450 and 462.

the Via Flaminia. But besides these idealized, fetishized figures, only *one* "real" mortal woman can be found on the arch, waiting for a handout from her emperor on one of the Aurelianic reliefs. The creation of this *spolia* monument might thus exemplify the multilayered process through which women have often been written out of their national histories. Here, the process began when the second-century sculptures were made and decisions were taken about who and what was worth commemorating. The fourth-century makers of the Arch of Constantine then made their own selections from the supply of available sculpture, tilting the gender balance even further in the process. The elision of women from this version of Roman history was completed by the passage of time, which disposed of the real individuals who could supply alternative narratives or "counter-memories,"[33] and whose physical presence would highlight the gaps in this monumental account of the past. Clearly, these various stages of "filtering" the past leave no trace on the monument itself, which continues to be invoked as a totalizing compendium of Roman sculpture and history. Such comprehensive erasure from the historical record is arguably more damning than acts of normative inversion like *damnatio memoriae*, which tend to recast the past rather than negate it and to confirm memory even as they dishonor it.[34]

In addition to interrogating the contents of the arch(ive),[35] we can also ask how the visual format in which these contents were presented might have impacted how—and how effectively—they were remembered. Such an approach is, in fact, suggested by the Roman rhetorical texts on the *ars memoriae*—an artificial memory system that relied on its practitioners equating "to-be-remembered" items with visual images (*imagines*), and then placing these images in fixed places (*loci*), which often took the form of architectural backgrounds ("for example, a house, an intercolumnar space, a corner, an arch, and other things that are similar to these").[36] The writers of these Roman texts, and in particular the anonymous author of the *Rhetorica ad Herennium,* demonstrate a palpable awareness of the differing mnemonic potential of visual images, acknowledging the fact that some images are more easily stored in and retrieved from memory than others. Indeed, we might examine the Arch of Constantine in the light of the ancient texts themselves, noting, for instance, the use of "great and good images," of "purple cloaks" (the Dacian prisoners), and the "tainting of images with red" (the porphyry around the Hadrianic panels).[37] These elements of the arch's design would all—so the Roman art of memory suggests—enhance the monument's visual saliency and the successful encoding and easy retrieval of its contents.

New research on human memory in the cognitive sciences might also give some fresh insights into how Roman viewers perceived and subsequently remembered the arch's imagery. In her 1997 book *Wax Tablets of the Mind,* Jocelyn Penny Small showed how modern psychological research might be used to provide empirical support for the ideas of the ancient authors on *ars memoriae*.[38] But cognitive research on memory can also draw attention to other mnemonic features of Roman monuments that do not appear in the ancient texts on memory.[39] We might take as an example the concept of "cued retrieval"—the idea that a piece of information such as a word, image, or odor can be used to access memory traces. The classic experiments investigating this phenomenon were

[33] Foucault's contre-mémoire; see the introduction to this volume, note 38.

[34] Galinsky 2008, 20; Hedrick 2000, xii and 113–130.

[35] "Archive" has been an operative notion in memory studies; cf. A. Assmann 1999, 343–347 with reference to Derrida and, similarly, Frischer in this volume.

[36] On the *ars memoriae*, see Small 1997, 95–116 and Onians 1999, 177–205.

[37] These examples are drawn from *Rhet. Her.* 3.22.

[38] Small 1997.

[39] Cf. Brilliant 1984, 110.

conducted by Canadian psychologist Endel Tulving and his colleagues in the 1960s and 1970s. These involved presenting subjects with lists of words to be retained and then recalled ("target" words), some of which were accompanied by a partner ("cue" words).[40] When subjects were asked to recall a target word—either unaided *or* prompted by the relevant cue word—Tulving found that the presence of the appropriate cue significantly increased the chance of subjects recalling the target. Notably, he also discovered that for a cue to function efficiently, it must already have some semantic association with the target word (a phenomenon known as "feature overlap") and that the target and cue must have been presented at the same time ("encoding specificity"). The effect of cued retrieval suggests that the presentation of pairs of words together shortens or strengthens the neural pathways between them, meaning that it takes less energy to pass from one to another. Since their description by Tulving, these ideas about cued retrieval have been given practical applications in fields such as law, politics, and television advertising. But how might they be relevant to the Arch of Constantine?

The hypothesis offered here involves thinking about the act of viewing the arch as analogous to the first stage of Tulving's experiments, in which the pairs of words were first presented together. This time, however, the pairs are images of emperors: Constantine and Trajan, Constantine and Hadrian, Constantine and Marcus Aurelius—figures who are already semantically related by virtue of the fact that they are all emperors (thus fulfilling Tulving's criterion of "feature overlap"). As we have already seen, the arch's designers linked these pairs of emperors in different ways, namely through the addition of portrait features and epithets to the spoliated reliefs, the drawing of parallels between Constantine's deeds and those of his predecessors, and the representation of Constantine in the vicinity of the earlier emperors' statues. The viewer scanning the monument would thus find several repetitions of the links between Constantine and his chosen predecessors, each of which would consolidate and shorten the semantic pathways between these men in the viewer's memory. Significantly, the psychological evidence raises the possibility that one partner in the pair could subsequently function as a retrieval cue for the other, and that contemporary viewers who examined the imagery on the Arch of Constantine and then went on to encounter other images of Trajan, Hadrian, and Marcus Aurelius on display elsewhere in the city might be cued automatically to recall their own emperor. Scholars are already aware that Constantine was a master of appropriating the past, reusing earlier images to a greater extent than any previous emperors.[41] However, the cognitive work on memory adds another dimension to this discussion by suggesting that Constantine (or rather, the makers of his arch) might have appropriated the images of his predecessors without ever laying a chisel on them.

Cued retrieval represents just one of several ways in which cognitive work on memory resonates with the Arch of Constantine and its imagery. Other areas that might be explored include the saliency of visual images (a theme already present in the texts on the *ars memoriae*), theories about "levels of processing" (the idea that complex images are more memorable than simple ones), and Ebbinghaus's discoveries about "spaced repetition" (which here may shed light on the effect of repeat encounters between a moving viewer and fixed monument).[42] Of course, in all of these cases, the broad insights that cognitive science allows into the workings of viewer memory need to be balanced, supplemented, and problematized by historical analysis of individual cases. If many of the

[40] See, for instance, Tulving and Pearlstone 1966, Tulving and Osler 1968.

[41] Prusac 2011.

[42] Ebbinghaus 1885. Accessible introductions to cognitive work on memory include Schacter 2001; Baddeley, Eysenck, and Anderson 2009; and Boyer and Wertsch 2009.

existing readings of the arch's imagery postulate (as Dale Kinney has objected) "an ideal viewer with historically-specific knowledge," the cognitive approach outlined here postulates an ideal viewer with *no* historically specific knowledge—one who exists in silent, experimental test conditions rather than the noisy and visually crowded environment of ancient Rome.[43] Even the example of cued retrieval offered here needs to be tempered with the caveat that each imperial portrait seen on the viewer's "post-arch" journeys around Rome would have had its own peculiar set of viewing conditions, which may have overwritten the idealized reading described here. But despite such caveats, the different questions and perspectives that are suggested by modern cognitive work on memory can only enrich our work on historical case studies and underline the formative power that ancient images have over how we think about the past. Moreover, it is worth noting that the effect of cued retrieval proposed here is often simply assumed as a matter of course in discussions of typological and allegorical imagery, which take for granted the capacity of this type of representation to construct long-lasting associative links between pairs of people or narratives.

4. Postscript: Memory, History, and Autobiography

This chapter has explored some aspects of the relationship between the Arch of Constantine and its viewers. It has also investigated the relationship between individual and "collective" memory, thinking about how far individual viewers' experience of the arch might be in line with—or different from—those of the people around them. For instance, we have seen how viewers' reception of the arch may have been influenced by their memories of other cultural resources, many of which would also have been available to their contemporaries; at the same time, I have argued that the arch itself worked on the memories of those who saw it, with the result that many of the monument's viewers came to share a homogenized set of images and narratives with which to internally visualize the past. These are broad conclusions that might be applied to any monument, but I would like to end this chapter by suggesting one additional and quite unique way in which the Arch of Constantine brought individual and group memory into dialogue with each other. This suggestion involves taking a fresh look at the relationship between the second-century *spolia* and fourth-century frieze, whose contrasting appearances have been the focus of so much of the scholarly literature on the arch. While previous studies have normally paid attention to the different artistic *styles* of the sculptures, here I want to focus on the strikingly different ways in which they present historical narrative.

Jaś Elsner has already noted of the Constantinian frieze that "What seems aesthetically the odd choice of having the frieze spill over the end-corners of the Arch, beyond the last projecting pilaster on each of the long sides, is an effective visual marker of the continuity of the frieze's narrative action around the Arch, by contrast with the self-contained icons above."[44] This observation draws attention to the structural disparity between the spoliated reliefs (the Trajanic segments, as well as the Hadrianic roundels and Aurelianic panels), all of which present single "snapshots" of history that appear as "discrete icons," and, on the other hand, the wrap-around fourth-century frieze, which presents history in the form of a long, sequential narrative, whose continuity was emphasized by the insistent forward movement of the participants, as well as by their "spilling" around the corners.[45]

[43] Kinney 1995, on the view of L'Orange and his successors.

[44] Elsner 2000, 165–166; cf. Gutteridge 2010, 167.

[45] "Discrete icons" is Elsner's phrase: 2000, 165. A differ-

ent view is presented by Kleiner 1992, 466: she describes the *frieze* as representing "discrete historical episodes," in contrast to the earlier, encircling friezes of the Arch of Titus in Rome and Trajan in Beneventum.

This juxtaposition between a *historic past* in the form of single, fragmentary images and a *recent past* presented in the form of a continuous narrative is deeply interesting in the present context because of the analogy that it suggests with the structures of human autobiographical memory. Writers on memory from antiquity to the present often draw attention to the different qualities of childhood and adult memories (see, for instance, the citation from the *Rhetorica ad Herennium* at the opening of this chapter). In both autobiographical literature and cognitive science studies, childhood memories are frequently described as stronger and more intensely visual than adult memories. Crucially, for the present argument, they also have a fragmentary quality, appearing as single moments excised from their broader narrative context. Biologist Stephen Rose's book on *The Making of Memory* contains one fairly typical example of this: "Another snapshot—a moment at my fourth birthday party, racing with my guests, around a circular rosebed, arms outstretched, making aeroplanes. But what came before or after this frozen moment in time? Who were my party guests? Did I have a birthday cake? I have no idea."[46] These "eidetic" and fragmentary qualities of childhood memory contrast with adult memories for recent events, which can be stitched with ease into a continuous narrative, albeit one that is constantly reconstructed and reshaped in the process of remembering.

In this case, looking at descriptions of individual memory draws attention to the fact that the presentation of history on the Arch of Constantine echoes the narrative structures of human autobiographical memory, with the continuous, linear narrative of recent events contrasting sharply with the fragmented and jumbled images of the city's early life. In noting this analogy I am by no means suggesting that it reflects a conscious decision on the part of the arch's designers; rather, I see it as a useful but probably unintended consequence of the incorporation of spoliated sculptures, which by definition represent the past in the form of fragments hewn from a larger picture. Other commentators have drawn attention to the ways in which the arch creates analogies between different timescales (such as the cosmic and historical—see above p. 105). In this way, the monument's evocation of the human lifespan simply adds another dimension to its rich multitemporality.[47] While the sun and moon roundels may elevate the historical events depicted on the arch to the cosmic, universal level, the form and content of the *spolia* bring them down to a more intimate and personal scale—that of the remembered human life. Of course, both the cosmic and the autobiographical analogies have a powerful naturalizing function, but the evocation of human memory has the added power to engender in the viewer a sense of ownership of, and personal identification with, the history of the Roman state. This conflation of the boundaries between individual and state has obvious ideological implications, but it also resonates with modern debates about the usefulness and precision of the term "collective memory." Many scholars have criticized what they see as the inaccurate and potentially pernicious metaphorical use of memory as a paradigm for understanding history.[48] The reading of the Arch of Constantine proposed here does nothing to counter those objections, but it does suggest that our own modern analogies between individual memory and group history might, in fact, have a very long ancestry.

[46] Rose 1993, 41.

[47] See in particular Gutteridge 2010.

[48] E.g., Kansteiner 2002; Novick 1999, 267–268; Wertsch 2002, 37.

8 ◆ Remembering with Greek Masterpieces: Observations on Memory and Roman Copies

Anna Anguissola

1. Introduction: A Look at Roman Copies

In 1933, the Metropolitan Museum of Art announced the acquisition of a Roman marble copy of the *Diadoumenos* of Polykleitos, a work that, as is widely known, was one of the most highly esteemed masterpieces of antiquity (fig. 8.1). The statue has been variously dated from the Flavian to the Antonine age but should probably be assigned to the last quarter of the first century A.D.[1] Unfortunately, when the statue of the youth reached its new home in New York, it was in a much poorer state of preservation than what we see today. The missing torso and the upper part of his legs had to be supplied from a plaster cast of a Hellenistic replica of the same work, from Delos, dating to the turn of the second to first century B.C. (fig. 8.2).[2] Although separated by about two centuries, the pair shares their dimensions to the point that the patchwork proves perfectly consistent.

Few other examples show as conspicuously how the shape and details of certain classical Greek works of art had survived unaltered for centuries after their original, which, in the case of Polykleitos's athlete, goes back to the second half of the fifth century B.C. Although the practice of replicating renowned classical masterpieces had already been well established in mid-Hellenism, mass copying became a distinctive feature of the Romanized world as early as the first century B.C. By then, the production and trade of plaster casts of entire statues (both "ancient Greek" masterpieces and "recent Roman" creations) and parts of their bodies were thriving, a fact that allowed sculptors throughout the Mediterranean to manufacture exact replicas as well as endless variations on the theme.

Notwithstanding their striking similarity in size and proportion, the New York and Athens *Diadoumenoi* differ in a manner that should not pass unnoticed. The former bears traces of a peculiar abundance of heavy supports that joined the left hand to the shoulder, both elbows to the body, the right shoulder to the right hand or fillet, and the two legs.[3] The fact that the dimensions coincide with those of the Athenian marble, fully preserved until our day with only a tiny strut under the left foot, rules out static constraints. Moreover, the quality of the New York *Diadoumenos* suggests that it is the work of an accomplished copyist. Clearly, therefore, contemporary viewers were not as disturbed by these obtrusive companions as we are. Nor were those who purchased other overly supported marbles such as the beautiful copy of Myron's *Diskobolos* from Castel Porziano (with a long joint between the right hip and the wrist/hand holding the disk) (fig. 8.3) or that of the *Apoxyomenos* by Lysippos found in Trastevere (fig. 8.4).[4] In the latter's case, the huge strut running from

[1] Fletcher Fund, 1925 (25.78.56). Richter 1935 and Kreikenbom 1990, 188 no. V.2.

[2] Athens, National Archaeological Museum, 1826. Kreikenbom 1990, 188 no. V.1.

[3] Richter 1935, 49 and 50 fig. 6.

[4] Respectively in Rome, Museo Nazionale Romano, 56039 (Anguissola 2005, 319–320 no. 2) and at the Museo Pio-Clementino, Gabinetto dell'Apoxyomenos, 1185 (Moreno 1995, 197–205).

Fig. 8.1. Copy of the Diadoumenos *of Polykleitos, restored with casts from the Delos* Diadoumenos *(fig. 8.2). New York, Metropolitan Museum of Art (photo ARTstor).*

Fig. 8.2. Copy of the Diadoumenos *of Polykleitos, from Delos. Athens, National Archaeological Museum (E.-M. Czakó, neg. D-DAI-Athen 5321).*

the youth's right wrist down to his thigh even prevents the view of the instrument and gesture that gave him the name: the strigil to scrape away sweat and dust after exercise. At the time when this replica was set up in the first century A.D., its bronze prototype was in Rome too and had, in recent years, been in the spotlight because of the scandal of its removal from public display by Tiberius, who, Pliny the Elder says (*HN* 34.62), had to return the statue to the Baths of Agrippa under public pressure. The fame of the original must have rendered immediately recognizable the copy and, with it, its two main differences: material and the strut.

In light of these circumstances, it is difficult to escape a radical challenge to our ideas about the taste that lies beneath the spread and display of copies. It has long been held that structural supports in Roman marble statuary, while indicating the translation of lighter Greek bronze originals into another medium, denote the inferiority of the former to the latter. Certainly, struts served the practical purpose of stabilizing marble sculptures with a view to their transport. As these few examples show, however, the presence of supports seems to indicate a more complex interaction between prototypes and the artist's own interpretation. Did perhaps the taste for works that plainly stated their status as accurate marble translations from Greek bronzes lie at the root of this taste for eye-catching additions?[5]

Even today, one of the most widely practiced scholarly efforts is that of dismantling Furtwängler's *Kopienkritik* and its positivistic premises, such as: copies were made to meet the demand for substitutes of Greek masterpieces and needed to be as faithful as possible; workshops developed

---

[5] For supports in Roman marbles, see Hollinshed 2002.

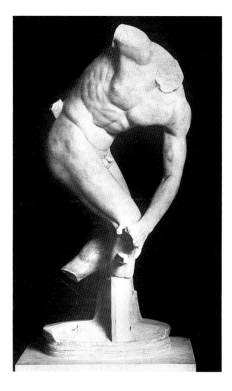

Fig. 8.3 (far left). Copy of the Diskobolos *of Myron, from Castel Porziano. Rome, Museo Nazionale Romano (neg. D-DAI-Rom 1706).*

Fig. 8.4 (near left). Copy of the Apoxyomenos *of Lysippos. Vatican City, Museo Pio-Clementino, Gabinetto dell'*Apoxyomenos*, inv. 1185 (Sansaini, neg. D-DAI-Rom 57.898).*

technologies for copying with the highest degree of precision; the fame of an image could be deduced from the number of its copies.[6] Certainly, the idea of "Roman copies after Greek originals," as posed by nineteenth- and early twentieth-century art historians, revolves around a simplistic view of the relation between Greek and Roman cultures. That this approach fails to account for the pervasive formularity that permeated Roman art at a much deeper level is certainly true.

That said, however, the conceptual framework within which we consider imitation in the Roman visual arts should not neglect to account for the spread and success of true copies—intended, manufactured, and displayed to establish a clear relationship to a given Greek masterpiece. With all of the emphasis that Roman culture seems to have put on the artists' ability to play with tradition, a few sources reveal a radically different attitude. Lucian, for instance, confidently resorts to a replica to present a famous classical Greek painting, the *Centaurs* by Zeuxis.[7] The original was lost long before, when it was shipped to Italy in the aftermath of Sulla's seizure of Athens. However, Lucian, who lived six centuries after the Greek painter and over two centuries after his work had sunk off of Cape Maleas, takes it for granted that a copy he had seen in Athens provides means to judge not only the original's subject and iconography but also the precision of Zeuxis's line, his mastery of the palette, the quality of his brushwork, and his management of shadows. Again, among the many accomplishments of Zenodorus, a fashionable sculptor of Pliny the Elder's time, was his successful emulation of two silver cups chased in the fourth century B.C. by the Greek engraver Kalamis.[8] The similarity

[6] An annotated bibliography on ancient copying is provided in Anguissola 2012b. For broad overviews, see Ridgway 1984, Perry 2005, Marvin 2008, and Anguissola 2012a. Excellent shorter introductions are Zanker 1992, Gasparri 1994, Cain 1998, Geominy 1999, and Brilliant 2005. In addition, several collections of studies address a variety of issues from both

Greek and Roman perspectives: Preciado 1989, Gazda 2002, Trimble and Elsner 2006, Junker and Stähli 2008.

[7] Lucian, *Zeuxis* 3. Perry 2005, 91–94.

[8] Plin. *HN* 34.47. Anguissola 2006, 561–563.

of their metalwork was such that, according to Pliny, the two deserved to be held as equal in terms of artistic achievements (*ars*). If the capacity to vary on a given repertoire was a much-esteemed quality for rhetoricians, poets, and artists alike, the skill to reproduce an illustrious prototype with exactitude was by no means marginal even in the eyes of skilled viewers.

Within Roman visual culture both "real copies" and "free imitations" held a central role in collective imagery, everyday practice, and art criticism. The ubiquity of repeated images, as a consequence of diverse demands, invites different responses from scholars. This chapter aims at exploring one possibility for the understanding of Roman copies after Greek *opera nobilia*, namely their use as catalysts of individual and collective memories. As the following pages will argue, copies could be exceptionally effective in broadcasting socially relevant information because of their capacity to evoke multiple memories and associated narratives. As widely repeated and highly recognizable figures, copies were among the most efficient *aides-mémoires* in the visual practice of the Romans. The "mnemonic" use of copies allows for varying degrees of *attention*, from high-quality "true" replicas to schematic quotations.[9] Yet the *intention* remained to call to mind a given masterpiece in all its features and meaningful associations.

The potential of copies as instruments for communication may partly explain the reasons for their spread in the homes and cities of the Romans. Undoubtedly, repeated images and standardized bodies were often chosen because they belonged to a widespread language of clichés that filled architectural spaces as conventional commonplaces. Nonetheless, their potential for manipulating collective memory constitutes one fundamental aspect in the Roman ethos of visual repetition. Thanks to two well-known case studies, this chapter will show how the collective memories of famous artworks could be used to construct personal identities and memories through connecting the individual history of a contemporary person to concepts, stories, and persons of the past. In addition, this chapter will discuss the interaction of image and text for the purpose of memory retrieval and social communication. With all their potential for immediate recollection, quotations of ancient masterpieces seem to have relied heavily on the power of words to enhance memory, all the while guiding its retrieval.

2. Greek Masterpieces as Conceptual Identities

The works of Polykleitos—and above all his most famous athletes, the *Doryphoros* and the *Diadoumenos*—provide an ideal test case with which one can approach the issue of copies from this point of view. The fortune and penetration of Polykleitos's art into the visual culture of the Romans pose thorny problems for distinguishing between the different types of citation. As is widely known, the schemes and style of Polykleitos were exploited in an extraordinary variety of contexts: as elements for new compositions as well as stereotypes associated with a set of Roman values revolving around the general concept of décor.[10] In both the *Doryphoros* and *Diadoumenos* was vested an extraordinary evocative power, the rhetoric of which had largely been exploited by Greek and Latin literature.[11] Like Myron with his *Diskobolos* (the Discus-Thrower) and Lysippos with his *Apoxyomenos* (the Scraper), Polykleitos was the author of images whose gesture had become synonymous with the statue

[9] Koortbojian 2002, 204 describes as "forms of attention" the attitudes behind the phenomenon of copying in response to different purposes and expectations.

[10] Quint. *Inst.* 5.12.20–21 and 12.10.7. For the meaning-

ful association between certain Greek masters and a tight semantics of Roman concepts, see Hölscher 2004, 47–57, 93, 97 on Polykleitan style.

[11] Neumeister 1990.

itself.[12] The Greek title (cf. Wiseman in this volume on *tituli*) and the gesture combined to create both a visual and conceptual unity that indelibly fixed those statues in the minds of Roman viewers. The coincidence of gesture and title proved invaluable to nineteenth-century archaeologists in their task of recognizing the prototypes behind these replica series. That insight, however, is accompanied by a lack of information on the identity of the portrayed. Indeed, it remains impossible to identify the real or fictional character depicted by those statues (a god, a hero, or a winner in the pan-Hellenic games), a detail systematically overlooked (and probably ignored) by the written sources.

Seneca, when summarizing Aristotle's theory on causes, illustrates the concept of "form" through Polykleitos's *Doryphoros* and *Diadoumenos*, two universally recognized examples of how form not only provided titles for images but also became their ultimate content.[13] The exact nature of this content is referred to by Pliny the Elder (*HN* 34.55), who describes the *Spear-Bearer* and the *Youth Binding the Fillet* as a *viriliter puer* and a *molliter iuvenis* respectively—a "manly-looking boy" and a "soft-looking man." As visual translations of the opposite poles of *mollitia* and *virilitas*, canonized by rhetorical and ekphrastic traditions, the statues embodied the whole imagery of athletic youth (and the entire span of their author's artistic capacity).[14]

The semantics attached to the image of Polykleitos's *Diadoumenos* are condensed in a peculiar object: the funerary altar erected in honor of a man called Ti. Octavius Diadumenus, which was found in the Vigna Sinibaldi near the Colosseum and is now on display in the Vatican Cortile Ottagono (fig. 8.5). The altar has variously been dated from the Julio-Claudian to the Hadrianic period, although stylistic and paleographic details seem to point to the first decades of the second century A.D.[15] The relief portrays the full-length figure of a naked youth frontally positioned in the act of tying a ribbon around his forehead, his weight displaced in the characteristic Polykleitan "contrapposto." The *cognomen* of the dead person, Diadumenus, is written in large characters beneath the image. The lack of individual features, as well as the placement of the figure on a pedestal, makes it all the more unequivocal that what is represented is Polykleitos's statue rather than a "real" portrait of the deceased.[16]

Here, unlike any other funerary relief known to us from the Roman world, a person is portrayed through the statue that had his same name, becoming virtually an ideogram. Within the funerary realm, there is a large amount of evidence for other "onomastic images" in which a person bearing the name of a certain deity was presented through a well-known iconographic type for that member of the Graeco-Roman pantheon. Nowhere else, however, do a name and the title of an individual work of art make such a perfect match and become mutual illustration. What the quotation implies

---

[12] About the widespread knowledge of the *Diskobolos* by Myron, see Anguissola 2007. Although other statues of a youth *se destringens* existed (Plin. *HN* 34.55 mentions one by Polykleitos), only the one created by Lysippos was known with the title of *Apoxyomenos* (*HN* 34.62). For similar remarks on the images of athletes tying a ribbon around their heads, see below note 16.

[13] Sen. *Ep.* 65.5–7. Settis 1992, 60–63.

[14] Settis 1992, 63–68.

[15] Museo Pio-Clementino, Cortile Ottagono, 1142 (*CIL* 6.10035). E. Simon in Helbig 1963, 1:174–175 no. 229 (early imperial); Varner 2006, 292–295 (Augustan); Ritti 1977, 313 no. 74 (Julio-Claudian); Kleiner 1986, 127–128 and 1987,

97–98 no. 1 (Augustan/Julio-Claudian), Kreikenbom 1990, 197 no. V.36 and in Beck, Bol, and Bückling 1990, 559 no. 73 (A.D. 100–130); Spinola 1996, 43–44 no. PE 29; and Boschung 1987, 115 no. 975 (first half of second century A.D.).

[16] Kleiner 1986, 127 observes that although the general stance is based on Polykleitos's statue, in the arms and head the figure seems closer to another type of fillet-binder, attributed by some to Phidias. According to Kleiner, the relief version is probably a conflation of both prototypes. It must be noted, however, that although Phidias was credited (Paus. 6.4.5) with a statue of a victor at Olympia in the act of tying a ribbon around his head, this composition never achieved the fame of Polykleitos's statue, nor had it ever been identified with the "title" of *Diadoumenos*.

*Fig. 8.5. Funerary altar of Ti. Octavius Diadumenus. Vatican
City, Museo Pio-Clementino, Cortile del Belvedere,
inv. 1142 (Singer, neg. D-DAI-Rom 72.587).*

goes beyond generic recognition. First, the viewer is expected to recall the statue's exact title (not just a description of its iconography), which serves as an onomastic visual for the deceased's *cognomen*. The inscription strengthens the connection, as the *cognomen* beneath the statue identifies both the man and Polykleitos's athlete—a further visual aid to those who may, at first, have missed the link (cf. Wiseman in this volume). Although the altar is not explicit in this respect, the combination of a Latin onomastic cue with a Hellenic *cognomen* points to the possibility that Diadumenus may have been a well-to-do freedman who, therefore, derived his personal and family names from the former owner while retaining his ancient slave name as *cognomen* on manumission. As a personal name, Diadumenus (and the derivate Diadumenianus) seems to have enjoyed a great prominence in Roman times, often in conjunction with boys of remarkable beauty.[17] Once in use, however, it passed on from father to son like any other family tradition (as might have been the case with a descendant of Ti. Octavius Diadumenus).[18] If, indeed, this latter individual had been named Diadumenus by his former owner as a play on his beauty, graceful composure, or athletic talents, the link to the ancient Greek work of art and what this implied seem to have been clear both to the name-giver and, most meaningfully, to the nominated. Unfortunately, the lack of a clear statement about the

[17] Mart. 3.65, 5.46, 6.34 and *Thesaurus Linguae Latinae. Onomasticon* 3.1:123–124. See also Settis 1992, 58–60.

[18] On the back, the word *Patris* seems to have been written in a later period, perhaps to distinguish Diadumenus from a son bearing his same name (Spinola 1996, 43–44; *Bildkatalog* 1998, pl. 237). A few inscriptions attest the handing down of this name inside the family (*CIL* 6.12660, 13780).

person's social standing (such as the abbreviation for *libertus*) prevents us from making any further determination on this point and decision on the origin of the name.

The memory of Polykleitos's masterpiece played a major role in shaping the imagery and self-presentation of the person that was portrayed. The quotation, of course, hinted at his beauty and virtue, bestowing on him the physical and moral qualities embodied *par excellence* by Polykleitos's youths. It is obvious that, in this case, there was no need to reproduce the chosen prototype with particular care (increasing the production costs for the monument) as long as it remained recognizable. However sketchy, the outline on the funerary stone retains the full set of aesthetic and ideal values attached to the model. The reference is just as effective and the transmission just as faithful as those in any major marble copies.[19]

An artifact such as Diadumenos's stone has to be contextualized within the language for funerary art and its conventions. Reliefs on sarcophagi and other funerary monuments were, first and foremost, vehicles for remembrance. By means of reference to a well-known repertoire, the virtues and values by which the deceased wished to be remembered were played out on a heroic scale.[20] The mutual identification and reciprocity between the deceased's life and the fiction on his or her monument rested on well-established conventions for the reading of images and on shared practices for memory.

As we know, the ancients emphasized the visual quality of memory, as well as the fact that it primarily resulted from the creation and retrieval of images (as stressed by Cicero, who recognized the role of the senses, in particular of sight, in the formation of durable impressions in the human mind).[21] The process had been systematized, and memory, according to the theories that the rhetorical treatise known as *Rhetorica ad Herennium* recounts, was divided into two parts: natural and artificial. The former is inherent to human thought, complemented and aided by the latter. Artificial memory, on the other hand, is strengthened by training, that is, by sharpening one's ability to form new mental images of those things to be remembered:

> The artificial memory includes backgrounds and images (*constat igitur artificiosa memoria ex locis et imaginibus*). By backgrounds (*loci*) I mean such scenes as are naturally or artificially set off on a small scale, complete and conspicuous, so that we can grasp and embrace them easily by natural memory [. . .] An image (*imago*) is, as it were, a figure, mark, or portrait (*formae, notae, simulacra*) of the object we wish to remember.[22]

While the elaborate structure of this rhetorical system may have little to do directly with the creation of individual works of art, certain details help explain the role of stories, iconographies, and quotations in the establishment of the repertoire they drew upon. Images on funerary monuments complemented natural memories of the dead (in the case of Ti. Octavius Diadumenus, by stating his—true or aspirational—qualities) and, in this sense, functioned as activators of artificial memory. A further step is to consider the rules about what kind of images to choose for memorizing facts, places, and people. Both Cicero and the author of the *Rhetorica ad Herennium* advance

[19] The point has been made by Bartman 1992 with regard to miniature copies. Small-size replicas can hardly be discarded as secondary evidence. They retain the same evocative power as their larger counterparts and provide an exceptional insight into the tastes and visual literacy of a wide public.

[20] Koortbojian 1995, 114–126.

[21] Cic. *De or.* 2.87.357. The main sources for the Roman

theories on memory are three texts from the first century B.C. and the first century A.D.: the treatise known as *Rhetorica ad Herennium*, contemporary with Cicero but wrongly attributed to him in the Middle Ages (3.16–24), the dialogue *De oratore* by Cicero (2.86.351–352), and Quintilian's *Institutio Oratoria* (11.2.17–22). Yates 1966, 1–26; Coleman 1992, 39–59; Small and Tatum 1995.

[22] Trans. H. Caplan, The Loeb Classical Library, 1954.

psychological reasons (which are confirmed by modern research in neuropsychology) to explain how memory could be helped by arousing emotional effects through striking images that could both be called to mind easily and implant themselves in the repository of memory: "We ought, then, to set up images of a kind that adhere longest in the memory. And we shall do so if we establish likenesses as striking as possible (*si maxime notatas similitudines constituemus*); if we set up images that are not many or vague, but doing something (*agentes imagines*); if we assign to them exceptional beauty or singular ugliness."[23]

The immediacy of standardized episodes of the myth or, as in our case, the surprise generated by famous masterpieces in unexpected contexts, with its inherent tension between familiarity and displacement, functioned as an efficient means to evoke the life, values, accomplishments, and character of the dead. The choice to portray oneself or a deceased relative through an ancient and illustrious masterpiece projects the whole semantics of that work onto the person depicted, an act that turns the image into an effective "icon of/for the memory."[24] The *Youth Binding the Fillet* of Polykletos, both as a statue whose principal aspect lay in its gesture and as an aesthetic paradigm, was particularly apt to imprint itself on memory as an *imago agens* as well as one of exceptional beauty. The correspondence between the names ensured accuracy and guaranteed that the relationship was understood at once.

At the time when Ti. Octavius Diadumenus lived, information on the original subject of the bronze cast by Polykleitos many centuries before was long lost. Its content had come to be identified primarily with its form, style, and the ideal meanings evoked in the minds of contemporary viewers. In other words, when Diadumenus was named after this Greek masterpiece and when he decided to be portrayed as such, that particular image was burdened with a rich cluster of values and concepts but lacked any permanent reference to a person, place, or history. Open to new associations, Polykleitos's *Diadoumenos* could turn into the portrait of any man who possessed or aimed at possessing the physical and moral characteristics embodied by that statue. In this light, we understand the seeming indifference to the deceased's individual features and a "true" physiognomic representation. The *Diadoumenos* provided, instead, an ideal instrument to create a "conceptual" portrait stressing a standardized set of outward and inner qualities. The "real" identity of the man Diadumenus was eclipsed and effaced as it became one and the same with the Greek athlete of Polykleitos.

These considerations can be further explored when one considers the mutual role of image and the name. Although the statue created by Polykleitos many centuries before was famously vested with a largely known set of values, the identification between man and statue depended primarily on the shared name. Therefore, in order to cement the association and to make it patent to the viewers, the altar had to be completed with a written label. On the one hand, few figures in Roman imagery were as *agentes* (and therefore as easily memorized) as the *Diadoumenos* of Polykleitos, whose gesture had even become the title of the statue, dropping a curtain of shadows on the name of the person portrayed. On the other hand, for the *similitudo* to be as close as possible (*maxime notata*) the stone carver and his client had to devise a solution—namely, the addition of a written *nota*—to illuminate the reasons for the choice and to allow the ancient Greek statue to become a moral and psychological portrait of the deceased. Cognitive research on art has recognized the combination of visual and written messages as a major factor in the correct understanding of an

[23] *Rhet. Her.* 3.22 (trans. H. Caplan, The Loeb Classical Library, 1954). Cicero (*De or.* 2.87.358), too, calls for "*imaginibus* [. . .] *agentibus, acribus, insignitis.*"

[24] Varner 2006, 290 comments similarly upon the reuse of

famous Greek body types within the realm of Roman funerary portraiture: "These body types do not merely function as divine signifiers; they also reduplicate known works of art and in so doing they transform the deceased into works of art with an historical past and into memorial icons."

artwork and its continued remembrance in the future. A label or title constitutes one of the most important semantic contextual cues for an image, providing the public with an alternative instrument for comprehension. The attachment of a verbal label, while allowing viewers not to rely on their visual competence entirely, influences not only the quantity of information grasped but also how deeply the new object implants itself in the repository of memory.[25] The name written under the silhouette of the Polykleitan youth has a fundamental informative function: it states the subject and makes the image recognizable as both a celebrated ancient statue and a portrait of the deceased. More important to this discourse is the performative function of the title, which accomplishes the socially significant act of creating a link between the qualities of artwork and person. Finally, as a persuasive device the title functions as a pledge of truthfulness for the connection between the two Diadoumenoi (the statue and the dead).[26]

3. Greek Masterpieces for Multiple Identities

This perspective, recognizing the narrative and associative potential of copies, provides a method, complementary to other approaches, for dealing with both the retention of a given repertoire and its new uses (the *attention* and the *intention*). This discourse becomes clear with another case study from Rome, this one later in time and from a much different social milieu: a replica of the *Resting Hercules* of the so-called Farnese-Pitti type. The heroically scaled figure depends on an original that has been attributed to one of the leading Greek sculptors of the fourth century B.C., Lysippos.[27]

Two copies were found during the mid-sixteenth century in the ruins of the Baths of Caracalla, both of which were dedicated in A.D. 216. They stood next to each other and flanked the entrance to a large hall.[28] One of them, the so-called *Hercules Farnese*, is now in Naples (fig. 8.6), while the other, known as *Latin Hercules*, stands in the Palazzo Reale of Caserta (fig. 8.8).[29] A crucial detail distinguishes the colossal twins. Only the former, in fact, had been signed by its author (that is, the copyist): Γλύκων Ἀθηναῖος ἐποίει ("Glykon the Athenian made [it]").[30] Clearly one of the sculptors who manufactured a *Resting Hercules* for the Thermae Antoninianae wished to make an explicit link between himself and that piece—whether out of personal pride or following his customary business practice, which may have required that marbles leaving the workshop be labeled. A third version, carved some thirty years earlier, around A.D. 180, and found in Rome as well, now decorates a niche in the courtyard of the Palazzo Pitti in Florence (fig. 8.9).[31] Here, too, a Greek signature runs on the rock under the club but refers to the putative author of the original, the fourth-century

[25] Solso 1994, 253–255.

[26] On the informative, performative, and persuasive function of a title, see Hoek 1981, 273–281. For artworks and titles, see also Dyson 2010, 12–13.

[27] On the sculptural type and its replica series, see Moreno 1995, 242–250; S. Ensoli in Moreno 1995, 294–295; and Brilliant 2005, 19–21.

[28] Moreno 1982, 389–390; Marvin 1983, 355; DeLaine 1997, 75.

[29] On the *Hercules Farnese* (Naples, Museo Archeologico

Nazionale, 6001), see F. Rausa in Gasparri 2010, 17–20 no. 1; Krull 1985, 10–22 no. 1; and Moreno 1995, 244–246. On the Caserta replica, see Krull 1985, 191–197 no. 2; Moreno 1982, 379–397; and Schneider 2005, 151–152. The differences in the stance and support (Krull 1985, 305–312, 332–334, 337–339, 349–350) have been interpreted as dating back to two distinct Hellenistic elaborations of the same Lysippean archetype, conventionally known as Farnese-Pitti and Side-Caserta.

[30] Images of the signature are provided by Marvin 2008, 126 fig. 7.10 and Donderer 2010, 187 fig. 3b (DAIR 80.2917).

[31] Krull 1985, 22–27 no. 2 and Moreno 1974, 140–141.

Fig. 8.7. Resting Hercules *(so-called* Hercules Farnese*)*
from the Baths of Caracalla, rear view. Naples,
Museo Archaeologico Nazionale, inv. 6001
(Schwanke, neg. D-DAI-Rom 80.2913).

Fig. 8.6. Resting Hercules *(so-called* Hercules Farnese*)*
from the Baths of Caracalla, front view. Naples, Museo
Archaeologico Nazionale (from Anguissola 2012, fig. 61).

B.C. artist Lysippos: Λυσίππου ἔργον ("the work of Lysippos").[32] The label chooses a different path than its counterpart in Naples by ignoring who actually carved the statue and would have been mentioned with a Greek verb for "made" (such as ἐποίει or ἐποίησε). What we read instead is the name of the man who devised the *inventio* and was responsible for the ἔργον itself.

It remains unclear whether the signature was carved when the statue first left the workshop or after it underwent a crucial modification: the head was replaced by a portrait of the emperor Commodus, which was of a slightly smaller scale than the colossal body.[33] The marble was found in 1540 on the Palatine, near the Domus Augustana, complete but for a hand and remarkably well preserved. It is likely that the colossus may have been displayed in the imperial residence, at the very least during Commodus's reign. Notwithstanding the *damnatio memoriae* following his overthrow, the statue

[32] Moreno 1995, 243. On the inscription (*IG* 14.1254), see Loewy 1885, 334–336 no. 506; Marcadé 1953, 1:70; and Moreno 1974, 141–143.

[33] Lippold 1923, 247–248 n. 19 thinks that the statue must be the result of an ancient restoration involving the replace-ment of the head. The label with the name of Lysippos, he argues, would never have been carved on an imperial portrait. The language of Commodus's visual propaganda and the implications of a Lysippean replica, however, make all but unlikely the contemporaneity of the statue as a whole (Moreno 1974, 140–141).

Fig. 8.8. Resting Hercules *(so-called* Latin Hercules*)*
from the Baths of Caracalla. Caserta, Reggia
(from Anguissola 2012, fig. 62).

Fig. 8.9. Resting Hercules *with a portrait-head*
of the emperor Commodus. Florence, Palazzo Pitti
(from Anguissola 2012, fig. 63).

was not destroyed, though it seems to have been buried (which explains the good preservation of the surface, the traces of color on the lion's skin, as well as the sharp cut of the inscription).[34] In any case, with the transformation of Hercules into Commodus (whether contemporary with the label or subsequent), the narratives that the statue conveyed changed radically. Obviously, the emperor was presented as the new, invincible Hercules.

We know how meaningful this association was to Commodus's propaganda and his visual program.[35] His assimilation to Hercules matured during the last years of his reign. Coinage from the year A.D. 191 presents the icons of the emperor and Hercules on opposite sides, labeled as *Herculi*

[34] Moreno 1974, 140–141; Loewy 1885, 334–335; and Hekster 2002, 126–128.

[35] The emperor claimed for himself the name Hercules

(Dio Cass. 73.15.2) and as such he was hailed by the Senate (SHA *Comm.* 8.9). On the ideology of Commodus's self-presentation as Hercules: Gagé 1981; Jaczynowska 1981; Hekster 2002, 117–136.

comiti or *Herculi Commodiano.* The fusion between the two characters was completed within a few months, and on coins minted shortly before his death the emperor was presented in Hercules's clothing and with his attributes.[36] Certainly a statue like the Pitti colossus would have easily recalled the emperor's predilection for Hercules and what such a comparison was meant to stress, reinforcing his image as a demigod, a physical giant, and a victorious battler against beasts and men. Moreover, this particular iconography projected not only a mythological dimension but also a precise story: the hero is represented after his eleventh labor and holds the Hesperidean apples behind his back (fig. 8.7). The properties attached to the immortality-giving golden apples from Hera's orchard subtly hint at a central theme of Commodus's propaganda as articulated by his coinage: the stress on the *aeternitas,* the perpetuity, of his power. A further detail of the myth enhances the range of suggestions, opening up another favorite aspect of Commodus's communication, the cosmic nature of his destiny as a ruler, elsewhere symbolized by the sphere of the heavens. According to one version of the legend, Hercules tricked Atlas, father of the Hesperides, into retrieving the golden apples for him by offering to hold up the heavens in his place for a little while.

The choice to turn a copy of this particular prototype into a portrait of Commodus summarized a variety of key elements of imperial imagery. The colossus would readily call to mind the plethora of similar images that contemporary viewers were exposed to in everyday life, from the emperor *sub specie Herculis* on coins to his statues that crowded cities and homes. Cassius Dio, who wrote his history of Rome a few decades after the death of Commodus, explicitly mentions the "vast numbers of statues [that] were erected representing him in the garb of Hercules."[37] In addition, according to his account, at least another—and much better known—colossal image of the emperor in the guise of Hercules (and similarly provided with an explicative label) was on display in Rome. Determined to turn into a stately self-portrait the famous colossus that Nero had built representing himself and Vespasian had transformed into a statue of the Sun, Commodus changed its features yet again so that it now resembled himself as Hercules. He had the god's head replaced with his own while equipping the giant with a club and a bronze lion at its feet. On the pedestal ran an inscription that listed the emperor's titles and his purported achievements as a gladiator.[38] The resulting image must have resembled closely the Pitti colossus: a gigantic body of Hercules completed with the emperor's portrait and a caption clarifying the reasons for the *similitudo* between the two.

Commodus's most famous portrait today, a bust in the Palazzo dei Conservatori, itemizes exactly the same elements (fig. 8.10).[39] The statue, discovered in December 1874 together with other marbles, belonged to the sculptural decoration of the Horti Lamiani on the Esquiline—which was imperial property. As in the case of the Pitti colossus, the fine state of preservation of the shiny polished surfaces seems to have depended on the bust's removal from view and storage in a *crypto-porticus* after Commodus's death.[40] Here, too, the *novus Hercules* wears a lion's skin knotted on his chest and holds a club in his right hand with the apples of the Hesperides in his outstretched left. The size of the bust and the addition of arms make the piece unique within the frame of Roman portraiture. The pedestal emphasized the emperor's universal rule and his struggles as the *pacator*

---

[36] Kaiser-Raiß 1980, 45–56 and Jaczynowska 1981, 639.

[37] Dio Cass. 73.15.6.

[38] Dio Cass. 73.22.3. The same circumstance is mentioned, with minor variations, in the relevant chapter of the *Historia Augusta* (17.10). Galinsky 2008, 10–11; Hekster 2002, 122–125; and Hallett 2005, 253.

[39] The bust (Palazzo dei Conservatori, 1120) dates to A.D. 191–192 and replicates the fifth and last portrait type of Commodus. K. Fittschen in Fittschen and Zanker 1985, 85–90 no. 78 and von den Hoff 2005.

[40] Varner 2004, 141–142 and Hekster 2002, 121.

Fig. 8.10. Portrait of the emperor Commodus with Hercules's attributes. Rome, Musei Capitolini, Palazzo dei Conservatori, inv. 1120 (Faraglia, neg. D-DAI-Rom 6303, inv. 6001).

orbis. The portrait rests on a *pelta*-shaped shield with a *gorgoneion*; two cornucopias supported by a globe with zodiacal signs surround the shield, flanked by a pair of kneeling Amazons, only one of which is preserved. Obviously, the cornucopias are the emblem of the peace and abundance that Commodus's reign brought, while the globe symbolizes the eternity of this "golden age." Upon the band encircling the globe are inscribed signs of the zodiac. As a consequence of Commodus's stress on his mastery over time, stars and the seasons of the year acquired a central place in the imperial propaganda. All twelve months were renamed according to the emperor's choices in self-presentation and heroic assimilation. Recent studies have suggested that the arrangement of the signs on the globe beneath the Capitoline bust may refer to the month of October, which Commodus ordered to be renamed Hercules, further enforcing the Herculean imagery of the portrait.[41] Besides, just as the emperor added Amazonius (or Conqueror of the Amazons) to the list of his own names toward the end of his life, the month of December, too, came to be known by that epithet.[42] While perhaps reasserting the link to Commodus's new calendar, the Amazons on both sides of the portrait refer to a plurality of meanings. Certainly, the fierce female warriors functioned as an apt symbol for the barbarism that both Hercules and the emperor had conquered (with an allusion to the hero's ninth

[41] Hannah 1986, 337–340. On the renaming of the month of October as Hercules, see Dio Cass. 73.15.3 and SHA *Comm.* 11.13.

[42] Dio Cass. 73.15.3–4 and SHA *Comm.* 11.8. Kaiser-Raiß 1980, pl. 26 figs. 4, 10 presents two medallions minted in A.D. 192 where a *pelta*-shaped shield under the bust of Commodus hints at his new name, *Amazonius*. See also Gagé 1981, 672–673.

labor of obtaining the girdle of Hippolyta, queen of the Amazons). Moreover, for viewers familiar with mythical geography, the depiction of the golden apples and of the Amazons together must have immediately signified the universality of Commodus's power, reaching from one end of the world to another: from the blissful garden of the Hesperides in its western corner to the eastern borders of Scythia, where the Amazons were thought to have lived.

To return to the copy of the *Resting Hercules* now in Florence: what role did Lysippos play in this system of references? Crucially, Lysippos was the only sculptor, together with the painter Apelles and the gem-engraver Pyrgoteles, entrusted with portraying Alexander the Great, who remained the highest exemplum of regality throughout antiquity.[43] Copies of the works by Lysippos undoubtedly made a widely comprehensible reference to the Macedonian king. In addition, Alexander the Great had been the first ruler to be explicitly portrayed as Hercules (followed by most of his successors throughout the Hellenistic world and, later, by the Roman *principes*). The meaning of such an association in the context of the emperor's iconographic choices was clear to his contemporary Athenaeus, who comments: "What wonder, then, that the emperor Commodus of our time also had the club of Hercules lying beside him in the chariot, with the lion's skin spread beneath him, and desired to be called Hercules, seeing that Alexander, Aristotle's pupil, got himself up like so many gods, to say nothing of the goddess Artemis?"[44]

Perhaps, on a further fictional level, a subtle yet perspicuous connection may have been evoked between that Greek artist and Commodus, hinting, in a conscious deception, that the subject of the Lysippaean masterpiece might have always been the future emperor of Rome, within a dimension that (as frequently in Commodus's portraiture) eludes the natural course of time and historical truth. This suggestion may be further investigated in light of the Roman semantics of sculptural styles as described by Tonio Hölscher.[45] Lysippos, although the author of many excellent statues of gods and heroes, was credited with an unsurpassed ability to transmit truth and beauty rather than divine characteristics. He enjoyed universal fame as a creator of faithful portraits, repeatedly praised for their close resemblance to their human prototypes. He was especially remembered as the only portraitist able to convey Alexander's "manliness and lion-like quality."[46] To those (few) competent enough to recognize Lysippos as the Greek master who succeeded more than anyone else in depicting human figures, Commodus may have sent out a further, indirect message. While disguising himself as the demigod son of Jupiter, at the same time, the emperor advertised his awareness of being an exceptional mortal—one who, like Alexander, deserved to be depicted with perfect adherence to reality by the unrivaled master of portraiture.

A replica of this prototype allowed for a dense network of connections between past and present, myth and history, as it projected the fame of a mythic hero, an artist, and a great king into the person of the contemporary Roman ruler. The *Hercules* of Lysippos is a good example of *agens imago*: his bending on the club and the golden apples in his hand reveal that the demigod has performed his next-to-last labor. It is likely that most viewers knew the number and content of Hercules's labors and would easily link the image to its mythological context. The *similitudo* is manufactured through the addition of an individual portrait, which transformed the body of Hercules into an attribute of the emperor. The effectiveness and reliability of the identification depends on the name of a master who famously excelled in portraiture. The *nota* with a "signature" of Lysippos cemented these multiple

---

[43] See Pliny the Elder (*HN* 7.125), Cicero (*Fam.* 5.12.7), and Horace (*Ep.* 2.1.237–241).

[44] Ath. *Deipn.* 12.537, trans. C. Burton Gulick, The Loeb Classical Library, 1933.

[45] Hölscher 2004, 94–97. On the link between the Roman appropriation of Lysippos's style and its congruency to the portrait of Commodus, see also Hekster 2002, 128.

[46] Plut. *De Alex. fort.* 2.2.

associations. The reuse of a Greek masterpiece and the label are both fundamental to the effort of integrating Commodus's kingdom and his personal image into the continuity of myth and history.[47]

As a combination of image and text, the Herculean Commodus conflates two distinct aspects: functional and storage memory.[48] As modern neuropsychology has pointed out, images have a primacy over other forms of communication in the manipulation of collective memory. The reason for the superiority of images for the purpose of advertising and political propaganda is that they can convey a larger amount of information than is possible with written or oral language.[49] While language imparts notions in a sequence, images broadcast a quantity of diverse information simultaneously. The effort to steer public perception with the aid of images relies heavily on the power of automatic cognition and the repetition of widely available cultural schemata.[50] While delivering information, these schemata simplify the content of what is being communicated and structure the process of recollecting. An image such as the Herculean Commodus was designed to communicate both a set of articulated narratives and a wide array of abstract concepts. Nonetheless, a textual label was required in order to mitigate the arguably greater vagueness of recollections excited by visual stimuli alone. Unlike the altar of Diadumenus, the label does not inform directly about the content (i.e., the identity of masterpiece and contemporary man). Instead, it provides the name of a Greek sculptor of many centuries before, thereby triggering a more complicated chain of recollections. Multiple—yet carefully guided—levels of comprehension were offered to the refined public who had the chance to see the colossus in the imperial palace. The choice of combining the replica of an *opus nobile* of the Greek past and a label providing context for it ensured that the artwork retained the full communicative potential of both images and texts.

4. Conclusion: The Visual Language of Memory

These case studies address the issue of how self-presentation could be affected by quoting an ancient masterpiece. The practice aligns imperial propaganda with monuments of a much lower rank. In both cases, references to the "ancient" Greek *opera nobilia* (chronologically distant) were layered over links to "modern" Roman artifacts or places (closer to the ultimate recipient), as well as to a rhetoric of styles that had become commonplace among contemporary viewers. Here, the quality of copies relative to one another is of little historical value without the consideration of other factors. What matters is neither (only) faithfulness nor (only) the ideal content associated with the styles of Polykleitos and Lysippos; instead, the importance lies in the narratives that certain relationships recalled.

Attention to memory provides an alternative tool to complement other approaches and to read a number of contexts that invite recollections at multiple levels. It was well known to the ancients themselves that meaningful things are easier to remember than nonsensical information. Indeed, we reconstruct past events so that they make sense and become as intelligible as possible both in terms of cause and effect and through chronological concatenation.[51] This process often takes the

[47] As observed by Zerubavel 2003, 46, "imitating entails repetition, thereby helping to create an illusion of actual *replication*."

[48] See A. Assmann 1999, 138–142 for the distinction between *Funktionsgedächtnis* (functional memory) and *Speichergedächtnis* (storage memory).

[49] Meusburger, Hefferman, and Wunder 2011, 4.

[50] As pointed out by DiMaggio 1997, 269, these cultural schemata "represent objects or events and provide default assumptions about their characteristics, relationships, and entailments."

[51] As remarked by the memory researcher Frederick Bartlett, remembering is in fact making an "effort after meaning" (see Anders et al. 2010, 12).

form of narrative, and past occurrences become part of a logical chain of events—that is, a *story*. From this perspective, the copies of widely known artworks possessed an extraordinary potential for narrative constructions, relieving viewers from the effort of making sense and enabling them to concentrate on less direct messages. Central to this discourse is the double process that determines the consolidation and retrieval of memory.

Memory consolidation is a set of processes by which newly obtained memories make a transition from an initially labile state to their permanent, long-term fixture.[52] Consolidation involves a time-consuming effort of organizing new memories through a psychological process of repetition and association. Until these associations are fixed and permanently established, memory remains susceptible to disruption and unreliable for the long term. In the sphere of visual communication, few other images are as open to meaningful associations as the copies of famous artworks known by (almost) the whole community of viewers. At the same time, copies referred not only to their famous original but also to other items from the same replica series, thereby broadening the choice of associations to the purpose of memory consolidation. As the ancient *ars memorativa* did not fail to notice, mnemonic devices are based essentially on repetition and reference points—all qualities that copies possess to the largest extent.[53]

The usefulness of copies for social communication might have equally depended on the mechanisms of memory retrieval. Experimental research has demonstrated that the process of understanding and contextualizing a probe item requires a serial search through memory: stored items are compared with the probe item one at a time. Correctness and quickness of retrieval depend upon the number and availability of matching features found in the repository of memory. Clearly, according to this explanation, the more features an item has, the longer it will take to perform the comparative search through memory.[54] The other side of the coin is that the more features an item has, the slower will be the processing, but the more resilient the trace will be after the exertion of memory search. Artworks such as the *Diadoumenos* of Polykleitos or the *Resting Hercules* of Lysippos fulfill both requirements. Profusely replicated throughout the Mediterranean, these images must have been so widely known that only a quick search through memory was required in order to find appropriate matches for the portraits of Ti. Octavius Diadumenus and Commodus. At the same time, both figures were anything but uncharacterized, thereby allowing prompt addition of the new item to the memory storage.

As part of a series, copies could broadcast a message that transcended their original. A "vertical" (diachronic) memory of the masterpieces by Polykleitos and Lysippos intersected with a "horizontal" (synchronic and genuinely "Roman") memory of their sculptural styles, as embodied by their replicas. Copies functioned as true palimpsests, resulting in multiple layers of understanding and meaningful reuse. This becomes clear when considering another peculiar process of memory retrieval known as "pattern completion": together with the sought-after information, other facts can be recalled as a consequence of similarities in form or meaning.[55] Images that establish a link to a tradition automatically trigger this process: some features will prompt the viewer to remember certain elements of the prototype or of the replica series and will awaken a chain of recollections to further objects, contexts, and circumstances that might bear a connection to any of them. This system of layering, intrinsic to memory, enables richness of allusions and determines the twofold nature of the experience: its individual quality and the possibility of its channeling through a series of inputs.

[52] Eichenbaum 2012, 315.

[53] A. Assmann 1999, 158–162, 298–339.

[54] Underwood 1976, 147–148, 160.

[55] For an introduction to "pattern completion" and the retrieval of memory, see Dodson and Schacter 2002, 344–345.

On the one hand, we cannot know what reactions the view of those masterpieces aroused in any individual Roman at any given point in time. On the other hand, statues and paintings were (and are) created and exhibited both to act as stimuli to a broad group of individuals of the same culture and to activate a similar process of perception and appreciation. More than any other image a masterpiece is likely to generate similar recollections. The adherence to conventions and the repetition of forms familiar to the public draw viewers into an immediate engagement with the monument. All those who marveled at the Lysippean colossus in a public bath or met with a multitude of identical athletes of Polykleitos in their everyday life would at once recognize these images as familiar, although each of the viewers relied on different interpretive instruments derived from his or her own background and artistic literacy. Images that belong to widespread replica series provide viewers with a schematic visual template and function as accessible receptacles of information. As such, they force their public into the process of repeatedly retrieving names (Polykleitos, Lysippos, Alexander the Great), titles (*Diadoumenos*), facts (the achievements of Ti. Octavius Diadumenus, the deeds of Alexander and Commodus), stories (the myth of Hercules), and contemporary Roman concepts shared by both the portrayed and the viewer (the qualities embodied by Polykleitos's youths or the Herculean, universal, and eternal dimension of Commodus's rule).[56]

From the point of view of "memory studies," attention to copies in the visual arts contributes to the debate over social boundaries in fashioning collective memory (i.e., the collective frame within which memory is individually constructed).[57] The literary sources on which we rely to gain an image of Roman culture and life were written by an educated, male, and privileged elite for the benefit of others belonging to the same group. At the level of "high" literary communication the evidence for other social strata remains extraordinarily impalpable. When moving from the consumption of literature to the sphere of figural art, we approach a field that allows far greater social interaction. The exhibition of art implies, in principle, that various categories of the public may experience the same object simultaneously, even if differently.[58] Unlike reading, the simple act of viewing a statue or a painting does not require any particular competence to be acquired through schooling and education. All those who belong to the same larger community already share a general knowledge of the basic patterns and conventions of oral, visual, and behavioral communication that allow them to decipher these codes, at least at their simplest level. That works of art were able to communicate to a wide audience and on a variety of levels, thus forming a shared sphere of consensus and integration within the community, was clear to our elite sources too. Cicero, for instance, recognized that all men have "a sort of subconscious instinct" that allows them to form a judgment upon works of art "without having any theory of art of their own."[59] The use of Greek visual syntax, so well known throughout the Mediterranean, extended the power of visual stimuli to a larger and ethnically diverse audience.

More than any other artworks, copies expedite the process of remembering and allow a highly efficient visual communication. In the case of Ti. Octavius Diadumenus and his stone, the prototype was perceived as void of individual content, yet it was an exceptional container of dignifying concepts. The colossus attributed to Lysippos, instead, provided the emperor with the exceptional chance to summarize the cornerstones of his visual (and political) program, due to a

---

[56] Roediger, Zaromb, and Butler 2009, 145–146 and www.pattern-completion.net.

[57] On the "collective" dimension of memory, see Erll 2005 and the essays collected in Olick, Vinitzky-Seroussi, and Levy 2011.

[58] On the nuances inherent in ancient Roman viewing, see Elsner 1995.

[59] Cic. *De or.* 3.50.195 (trans. H. Rackham, *Cicero De Oratore Book III*, The Loeb Classical Library, 1982). See Rutledge 2012, 79–82.

set of inescapable connections between subject(s) and biography(-ies). Because of their evocative and associative potential, copies provide an exceptional instrument for the manipulation of collective memory since they simplify the process of memorizing and retrieval. Replicas and quotations of famous masterpieces are perfect, conventional vehicles of socially relevant and rapidly intelligible contents.[60] These remarks help to dismiss an outdated idea of memory as a passive process of data collection into a repository to be searched when necessary. Instead, copies demonstrated that memory was a process integral to and coincident with image production.

[60] Fentress and Wickham 1992, 47.

PART IV

ANCIENT AND

MODERN MEMORIES

9 ◆ Remembering a Geography of Resistance: Plebeian Secessions, Then and Now

Lisa Marie Mignone

¿Se acuerda Vd. cuando fuimos juntos al Monte Sacro en Roma
a jurar sobre aquella tierra santa la libertad de la patria?

S. Bolívar, 1824

1. Introduction: United Socialism, Plebeian Hill

On 16 October 2005 a large gathering collected at the Parco della Libertà in Monte Sacro (ancient Mons Sacer), part of the flood plain of the Anio River, just 5 kilometers outside Rome's *centro storico*. Beneath a waning moon, Benvenuto Salducco, the president of the IV Municipio Roma, bound the event to both time and space in a complex transaction of ritual, memory, and ideology.[1] The nonviolent political protest served as a rallying call for global populism and for international solidarity against the oppressive forces of capitalism and hegemonic imperialism. That evening staged the dynamic, if grandiloquent, sermon of Venezuelan president Hugo Chávez on the very site where, over two and a half millennia earlier, plebeian members of Rome's newly established *res publica* were believed to have thrown off the political, economic, and legal shackles of their patrician rulers.[2] According to the ancient historical tradition, three times during the fifth and third centuries B.C., secessions of the plebs demanded an end to patrician tyranny. Legal equality and access to political magistracies, military command, and religious authority were eventually extended to all Roman citizens. On Chávez's commemoration, the official national press release of Venezuela explained: "In the year 494 B.C., this hill takes on a starring role in the first popular rebellion recorded in Roman history. It represents an icon of the resistance (*ícono de la resistencia*) and was a place of refuge for the commoners who were oppressed. After 200 years, many Latin American countries are subject to the will of a foreign power."[3] Chávez's location at Monte Sacro, the very destination of the plebeian secessions, reactivated the ancient precedent and dramatically reasserted the ongoing need to oppose the tyranny of the elite. The combined power of place and memory gave vitality and authority to the Venezuelan's mobilization of the populace.

2. Place and Memory

This contribution explores the transformative capacity of place and memory: how does space become imbued with ideological meaning and cultural memory so that a plot of land becomes a political

---

[1] *Chavez a Roma (Montesacro)* 2011. On the unification of "place, society, actions, and memory," see Bastide 2011, 161.

[2] Ramírez Salas 2005.

[3] Ramírez Salas 2005. All translations are my own.

landmark?[4] How do later reactivations of geographical memory both reassert and reframe past associations and, at the same time, lend aged authority to contemporary agendas? Leaving aside Mons Sacer and Chávez (if momentarily), this piece focuses on the plebeian secessions and the Aventine Hill, for it is this Roman mount that became the modern reference point for populist resistance. It is the Aventine that has consistently served as an ideological command post for modern sociopolitical revolutionaries whose recollection of the fifth- and third-century plebeian secessions has integrated their own actions into a historic framework of social struggles and, at the same time, fortified their identification of the republican Aventine with the plight of the oppressed rabble.

This chapter calls into question some of the fundamental assumptions underpinning sociocultural topography and examines one of the ways in which the Aventine Hill became recognized as the quintessentially plebeian quarter of republican Rome, and, more specifically, the location of anti-tyrannical revolution and constitutional reform. The authenticity and details of the traditional histories are less my concern than the topography mapped therein. My ultimate questions are how and why and when *in antiquity* did the Aventine become associated with the secessions and thereby imbued with a cultural meaning and social identity so inexorably linked to the plebeian cause, and how have modern reactivations retrofitted our perception of both the ancient historiography and the topography itself? After exploring some modern restagings of the secessions, this chapter works its way back through the ancient historiographical record to the first plebeian secession of 494 B.C.

3. Modernization: Commemoration, Reactivation, Redefinition

30 May 1924. Rome, Italy. The outspoken socialist deputy Giacomo Matteotti denounced the Fascists' use of force in securing parliamentary elections. Matteotti called upon members of the Camera to abrogate the April elections. The Fascists' retaliation followed quickly and brutally. On 10 June five members of the Fascist secret police clandestinely assassinated Matteotti and tossed his corpse in a remote part of the Roman Campagna. Though they had executed the socialist leader, they had not slain his *idea*.[5] On 27 June, Socialist and Catholic parliamentary members opposed to the tactics of the Fascist party withdrew from the Chamber of Deputies. Secluded in Aula B of the Parliamentary Palace, they refused to carry on the work of government. Instead, they inaugurated the first session of their "secession" with a commemoration of Matteotti.

Filippo Turati, the founder of Italy's United Socialist Party and the occasion's official orator, declared, "We talk of this parliamentary chamber, while there is no longer a Parliament. The representatives who were properly elected stand on the Aventine of their consciences (*sull'Aventino delle loro coscienze*), whence no enticement will remove them, until the sun of Liberty dawns, the rule of law is restored, and the representation of the people ceases to be so heinously reduced."[6]

---

[4] Because this study focuses more on the ideological power of a toponym than on an actual physical landscape, the observations of Halbwachs 1992, 193–235 apply only in a general way.

[5] Among Matteotti's dying words are recorded: "Kill me, but the idea (*idea*) that is in me you will never kill. . . . My idea will not die." *L'Unità* 15 June 1924. His *idea* was socialist revolution. Abstracted from the time and place of their utterance, the sentences have become an oft-cited slogan among Italian socialists. The deputy's alleged dying words were

first reported—with great rhetorical flourish—in *L'Unità* (Gramsci's communist newspaper). The article reported the eye-witness account of Albino Volpi, a member of the *Ceka* charged with Matteotti's murder, but contains no byline. The newspaper's source for Volpi's confession was also protected. Thus this fourth-hand account traces back to Matteotti circuitously. On 27 June Turati recited Matteotti's alleged last words in his own commemoration of the fallen deputy; hearsay was inscribed into history.

[6] Scotti 1984, 116.

It was the first challenge to Italian unification, *l'Italia unita* (1861); and in contrast to the National Fascist Party's corruption and thuggery, this oppositional body chose nonviolent, symbolic revolution. They hailed their withdrawal as the *secessione dell'Aventino* ("Aventine secession"), but the designation and destination were ideological rather than geographical. Recalling plebeian protests against tyranny and violence in archaic Rome, the opposition used the toponym to indicate their refusal to participate in governmental business. As Turati's words indicated, being on the Aventine had become a moral and psychological claim.

The Aventiniani aimed to convince King Vittorio Emmanuele III to restore civil liberty and the preeminence of law and to force the resignation of Mussolini and the other Fascists, who had been elected through corruption and violence.[7] Their general strike, however, backfired; as happened in Livy's account of the plebeians' secession to the Aventine, "nothing was achieved."[8] The predominantly Fascist government continued to operate without them. While some members of the opposition were frustrated by the ineffectiveness of the Aventiniani's self-isolation and inaction, Mussolini not only enjoyed governmental harmony[9] but even engaged the ideology of those *sull'Aventino* directly in proclaiming: "The parliamentary opposition has withdrawn itself to the Aventine, where no Fascist Menenius Agrippa will go to recite the famous apology."[10] In the first plebeian secession (494 B.C.) the patricians' emissary, Menenius Agrippa, brought the seceding plebeians back into Rome by offering them various concessions, including full recognition of their magistrates. Mussolini chose to rewrite rather than replay history and thus paralyzed the efforts of the Aventiniani. From 1925 to 1926, the tyrannical "Special Laws" (*leggi fascistissime*) of the Fascist State outlawed the secession as unconstitutional. Members of the opposition went into exile, redirected their efforts towards other anti-Fascist organizations, or were imprisoned. By 1926, the Aventine movement had completely collapsed.

Though the *secessione dell'Aventino* failed, the cultural memory of the event continues to garner ideological power. The room to which the Aventiniani had withdrawn retains the name Sala dell'Aventino, and when Italian Parliamentary proceedings meet gridlock, the left threatens *l'Aventino!* For example, on 13 October 2011, the day prior to the vote of confidence for Silvio Berlusconi and his center-right political party, delegates from three major oppositional parties boycotted Berlusconi's parliamentary address, thereby leaving the prime minister to address a hall that was half-empty.[11] Yet this protest was only a "semi-Aventine movement"; oppositional deputies were sure to return the next day to register their vote. Nevertheless, the Aventiniani once again failed. Berlusconi received the necessary votes and, with a botched recitation of a well-known aphorism,[12] fired back: "In as much as the Aventine, the first time—in 1929—was a tragedy; the second time—now—it was a farce."[13] Reporters and oppositional politicians alike swiftly pointed out the prime minister's historical gaffe: 1929 for 1924. Berlusconi and the majority of the news media, however,

---

[7] Carcaterra 1946, 56; Scotti 1984, 116.

[8] Livy 3.52.1: *nihil transigi.*

[9] Contemporary complaints speak to these issues. A Roman wood carver branded the secession nothing more than a "gesture" and accused the opposition of collaborating with the Fascists: see E. P. of Rome 1924. An article in the same newspaper insisted that the inactivity of the Aventine secession was insufficient and urged workers to prepare for action in order to reclaim their government. "Nei Comuni come al Governo" 1924. See also E. P. of Venice 1924.

[10] Mussolini 1934, 4:212. See also Kemechey 1930, 217.

[11] "Opposizioni diserteranno" 2011.

[12] Marx 1979: "Hegel remarks somewhere that all great world-historic facts and personages occur twice, so to speak. He forgot to add: *the first time as tragedy, the second time as farce.*" On the matter of Hegel's "forgetfulness" and Marx's confabulation, see Mazlish 1972.

[13] "Goberno/ Berlusconi" 2011.

universally identified "the first Aventine" as that of Matteotti's successors. What had happened to the plebeians of the early Roman republic?

The ideological use of Rome's Aventine is not restricted to Italian politics. In the late nineteenth century in another European capital, the Paris Commune used the Aventine to symbolize the plight and the empowerment of the urban working class. By winter's end in 1871, Napoleon III had fallen, and urban discontent continued to spread throughout Paris. In order to pay reparations to the victorious Prussians, Louis-Adolphe Thiers's new government passed restrictive financial laws, but it feared armed insurrection from the National Guard: Paris's democratically organized citizen militia populated by urban workers and led by radical republicans and socialists. On 18 March Thiers's attempt to disarm the National Guard by seizing and removing 150 canons from Paris's Montmartre met disaster. The urban population so supported the National Guardsmen that one of Thiers's infantrymen later recalled he was "stopped by a crowd of several hundred local inhabitants, principally children and women."[14] The Parisians expelled Thiers's men and installed their own government.

For two months the Paris Commune served as the prototypical "Dictatorship of the Proletariat."[15] The Commune's membership included tradesmen, urban workers, and radical bourgeois. The Commune's "authentic proclamation" was published in a manifesto named *Le Mont-Aventin*. It took aim at economic reforms and demanded the immediate resignation of Thiers's Chamber under penalty of defenestration.[16] By the end of May, however, the Commune had been dismantled and the Communards slaughtered. The Paris Commune was the only socialist government[17] Karl Marx and Fredrick Engels witnessed, and it has long since taken on romantic stereotypes of its own. The revolution first began, however, in Montmartre, the hilltop headquarters, which the Communards nicknamed *Mont Aventin*.

These episodes from the last century and a half are more than mere cultural asides; they demonstrate how engrained the idea of a "plebeian Aventine" is—culturally and ideologically. As a rallying cry against tyranny, the Aventine and its history have been co-opted into the political programs of revolutionaries demanding governmental reform and social equality.

4. Plebeian Secessions: Aventini (Sacrique Montis) Admonebat![18]

The Aventine serves as an archetypal seat of socialist resistance. Because the antecedent is ancient, the plebeian secessions of the early republic, it is worth revisiting the topography of those secessions as they were remembered and used in ancient literature. The following focuses on the geography of the three canonical secessions of 494, 449, and 287 in the context of the interests and motivations

[14] Gluckstein 2006, 4. See also Michel 1981, 64–65.

[15] See Engels, at the close of his introduction to the fifth edition of Marx's *The Civil War in France* (1891), published in commemoration of the twentieth anniversary of the Commune: "Look at the Paris Commune. That was the Dictatorship of the Proletariat."

[16] Fetridge 1871, 96.

[17] Note that unlike the secessions of antiquity or 1924 Rome, the Paris Commune was active. The toponym (Aventine) was not only plucked from its specific geographical location but also stripped of its association with inactive protest—as if in reaction to the 1834 concerns of Blanqui (1971, 82) regarding Aventine withdrawal. This maintenance of the topographical label and select aspects of sociopolitical ideology in the face of spatial recontextualization fits Bastide's notions regarding the survival of the past through adaptability to the present; Bastide 2011.

[18] See Livy 3.61.5, wherein the popular consul L. Valerius Potitus encourages his troops to remember the recent secession to the Aventine and Mons Sacer as the place where they acquired their freedom: *Aventini Sacrique montis admonebat, ut ubi libertas parta esset paucis ante mensibus . . .*

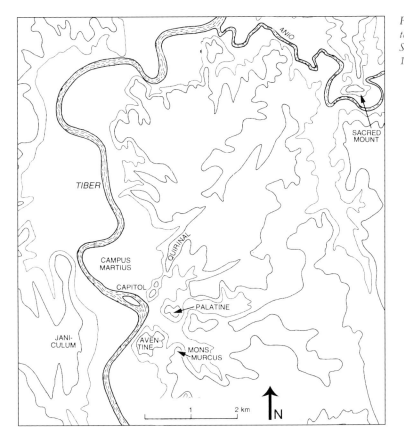

Fig. 9.1. Map of Rome, showing the Janiculum, Aventine, and Sacred Mount (after Wiseman 1995, fig. 12).

of the Greek and Roman authors who treated them (fig. 9.1). Where did the plebeians retreat? Or rather, how "Aventine" were the secessions?[19]

The final plebeian secession (287 B.C.) is obscure in detail. Three fleeting references survive: Pliny the Elder's note on a grove in the Campus Martius, a chapter in the *Digest* on the circumstances provoking the *lex Hortensia*, and an epitomator's summary of Livy's since lost eleventh book.

> Plin. *HN* 16.15: When the plebs had seceded to the Janiculum, the dictator Q. Hortensius passed a law in the oak grove, that any law ratified by the plebs would be binding over all the citizens of Rome.

> *Dig.* 1.2.2.8: Then when the Law of Twelve Tables, the civil law, and the law of statutory actions were in effect, it came about that strife beset the relations of the plebs with the senators, and the plebs seceded and enacted laws for themselves. . . . Soon after, when the plebs had been brought back, because much strife was born of these plebiscites, it was agreed through a Hortensian Law that the plebiscites would be observed as laws; and thus it came about that the manner of their establishment differed, but the force of the plebiscites and law were the same.

> *Per.* 11.16: On account of debt, the plebs, after severe and protracted insurrection, finally seceded to the Janiculum, whence they were brought back by the dictator Q. Hortensius.

---

[19] For an analysis of the objectives and the results of the plebeian secessions, see Raaflaub 2005. The current study intends to examine the mapping of the received tradition onto the city's landscape.

In sum, debt crisis and inter-ordinal discord led to secession. Upon the return of the plebeians to Rome, a law of the dictator Q. Hortensius gave plebeian resolutions, *plebis scita*, the full authority and legal sanction of proper Roman *leges*.[20] Concord was restored.

The consensus of the sources makes the destination of the secession clear: both Pliny and the epitomator report the Janiculum, the city's only hill across the Tiber River. The walk from the Forum to its steeply vaulted peak runs about 2 kilometers, and even in the late republic, the Janiculum was considered *longe* ("far off") from the center of town.[21] It was excluded from Rome's fourth-century B.C. fortification wall,[22] and in the middle of the fifth century B.C., *trans Tiberim* seems to have been a technical term for "outside of Rome."[23] In the plebeian secession of 287, the plebeians did not withdraw to the Aventine; they left the city altogether.[24]

Before turning to the secessions of the fifth century, it is worth standing our ground on the Janiculum with those seceding plebeians of the early third century B.C. Gary Forsythe has recently revived Eduard Meyer's theory that the third plebeian secession, occurring within a generation of the first Roman annalists, was in fact the only authentic, historical secession of the three.[25] In this reconstruction, the secession of 287 served as the model for the fictive and retrojected first and second secessions of 494 and 449. Historical events and historiographical reconstructions do not always align; but the fact that no ancient source places the third and potentially only historic secession on the Aventine significantly undermines the identification of the hill as the quintessential headquarters for plebeian resistance—be it in the ancient Roman experience or in the ancient historiographical record.

Accounts of the second secession make the Aventine associations hard to dismiss, much less forget.[26] Cicero claimed (*Rep.* 2.63.2): "The story, of course, is well known and famous through very many memorable works (*monumentis*) of literature." A generation later, Livy and Dionysius offered their own extended accounts filled with dynamic and rhetorical flourishes. In 449 B.C., Rome's plebeian soldiers did, in fact, withdraw to the Aventine. Two years prior, all regular magistracies had been suspended at Rome. A board of ten men, the decemvirate, was vested with full consular *imperium* and commissioned to compile and publish a full law code. In 450, the second board grew increasingly tyrannical and, upon publishing the laws, refused to dissolve their office and to restore the traditional constitution. Though all of Rome—Senate, patricians, and plebeians alike—were similarly victims of the decemvirate's despotism, it was a secession of

[20] For the *lex Hortensia*, see Rotondi 1912, 238–241. Only Pliny, Livy's epitomizer, and Pomponius report the secession.

[21] Hor. *Sat.* 1.9.18.

[22] Livy (1.33.6) claims Ancus Martius constructed fortifications to prevent the hill's occupation by a foreign enemy. See, however, Ogilvie 1965, 137. Archaeological studies suggest that the Janiculum stood outside the urban enceinte until 87 B.C. (Säflund 1998, 188–190).

[23] Ungern-Sternberg 2005, 79.

[24] Florus (1.25) seems to record a secession to the Janiculum in connection with the *lex Canuleia* (445 B.C.). Though Florus's catalogue of secessions does not align with the one that has become canonical, his topographical sequence does: first secession/Mons Sacer (1.23), second secession/

Aventine? (1.24), third secession/Janiculum (1.25). Von Fritz 1950, 25 dismisses Florus's Janiculan secession as an exaggeration. Regardless of the factuality of the event itself, Florus's placement of the plebs on the Janiculum complements the traditional secessions and counteracts a strictly Aventine geography for plebeian resistance in the ancient literary record.

[25] Forsythe 2005, 170–177, 230–233, 344–349. See also Raaflaub 2005, 209. Previously, Meyer 1921 = 1895. For a counter-response, see von Fritz 1950, 22–23 and Ridley 1968, 538.

[26] Cic. *Rep.* 2.63; Sall. *Iug.* 31.17; Diod. Sic. 12.24; Livy 3.43–54, 7.40.11, 9.34.4; Dion. Hal. *Ant. Rom.* 11.25–44; Sen. *Brev. Vit.* 13.8; Florus 1.24; App., *B Civ.* 1.1.2; Festus 422L; Dig. 1.2.2.20, 24. Strangely, Florus's account features Verginius dragging the tyrants *from* the Aventine into chains.

the plebs that forced the restoration of the traditional Roman government, including both the consuls and the plebeian tribunes.

The catalyst for the secession was a double tragedy, which triggered the rapid movement of narrative players across a landscape in which the Aventine was only one setting. First, on campaign, henchmen of the decemvirate ambushed and murdered the outspoken military hero and former plebeian tribune L. Siccius. Second, in the Roman Forum, Verginius killed his own too-beautiful daughter lest she be forced into slavery and a decemvir's bed. Dionysius dramatically celebrates the maiden's public funeral throughout the streets of Rome as her blood-drenched father, butcher-knife still in hand, galloped off alone to the military camp.[27] Livy, in turn, sets a sort of urban secession: nearly 400 citizens escorted Verginius 20 kilometers to Mt. Algidus. After various impassioned speeches, the bereaved father, his civilian supporters, and the soldiers marched to Rome:

> Livy 3.50.13: They marched in file to the city and occupied the Aventine, and each one encouraged whatever plebeian he met to seek back his freedom and to appoint tribunes of the plebs. No other appeals to violence were heard.

> Dion. Hal. *Ant. Rom.* 11.43.6: For the soldiers, passing through the alleys, called out that they were friends and had come for the good of the commonwealth; and they made their words match their deeds, as they did no harm to anyone. Then, proceeding to the hill called the Aventine—which of all the hills included in Rome is the most suitable for an encampment—they put down their arms near the temple of Diana. The following day they strengthened their camp, and having appointed ten tribunes . . . to take care of their common interests, they remained quiet.

The plebeian troops had taken the Aventine. Soon the remaining legions, led by Verginia's betrothed, Icilius, abandoned their post in Sabine country, marched to Rome, and set up on the Aventine. It was an act of complete nonviolence (*nulla vox violenta*/ἡσυχία), but a danger to the young republic hemmed in by advancing enemies and now lacking an army to defend itself.[28] It was also the only military boycott in Roman history that did not settle outside of Rome, across a river. The soldiers abandoned their battle stations and far-off military camps for Rome itself, and the perceived alarm of the city's civilian population upon seeing the soldiers march through their streets to the Aventine serves as an indication that this was not a secession. For the city of Rome, it was a sit-in.

If the second plebeian secession had ended at the Aventine Hill, it would have failed. Dionysius's manuscript breaks off abruptly,[29] but Livy's story continues. The Senate effectively refused to entertain any plebeian demands, despite the plebeians' encampment on one of the city's hills. An extreme move was necessary. Livy explains (3.52.1–2): "The plebs were further assured that . . . the senators would not concern themselves with the plebs until they saw the City deserted; the Sacred Hill would remind (*admoniturum*) them of the firm determination once shown by the plebs."[30] It was only after Rome had been abandoned to the Senate and the feeble elderly,[31] only after the entire population had relocated to Mons Sacer, three miles outside of Rome and across the Anio River,

---

[27] Dion. Hal. *Ant. Rom.* 11.39, 40–43.

[28] On the composition of the fifth-century army and the effectiveness of *secessio*, see Raaflaub 2005, 185–222.

[29] Likewise, the text of Cicero's *De republica* breaks off precisely when the seceding soldiers arrive on the Aventine. Cicero, however, reports the soldiers initially seceded to Mons Sacer and then relocated to the Aventine (*Rep.* 2.63.2):

"And first Mons Sacer, as they had done previously in a similar circumstance, then the Aventine." Although Livy and Dionysius may have drawn from older sources, Cicero's is the oldest extant text on the second secession.

[30] Livy 3.52.1–2.

[31] Livy 3.52.5. The scene prefigures the emptiness of Rome at the arrival of the Gauls, Livy 5.39–42.

that the Senate finally met the plebeians' demands, dissolved the tyrannical decemvirate, and reestablished both the consulship and the plebeian tribunate. The secession of 449 proved successful only when the plebeians actively, physically, and geographically reminded the patricians of plebeian constancy and determination—that is, only when they retreated to Mons Sacer.

The Sacred Mount had been, after all, the destination of the first plebeian secession (494).[32] Sixteen years after the kings had been expelled from Rome, a different tyranny pervaded Rome. Foreign wars and uneven land distribution resulted in a debt crisis so crushing that the plebeian masses quit both their military service and their city. After careful negotiations, managed on the patricians' part by Menenius Agrippa, the plebeians returned to Rome. There are several discrepancies in the historical tradition, not least of which that the demand for economic reform led to a new political constitution, including the establishment of the plebeian tribunate.[33] The place of the secession, however, is mostly consistent throughout the extant record. In his brief and direct treatment, Dionysius provides directions (6.45.2): "They occupied a certain mount situated near the River Anio, not far from Rome, which from the circumstances is still called the Sacred Mount." The Greek antiquarian acknowledges the etymology and the contemporary survival of the toponym as indices of the authority of the geographical tradition.[34] Livy likewise reports Mons Sacer and explicitly rejects the mistaken Aventine version in favor of the more recognized, *frequentior*, tradition that named the Sacred Mount (2.32.2–3): "[it is said] that they seceded to Mons Sacer with a certain Sicinius as the instigator and without the authorization of the consuls. It is across the Anio River, three miles from the city. This is a more generally accepted tradition than the one which Piso authored, that the secession was made to the Aventine." When Livy picks up his narrative with Menenius Agrippa's "famous apology," the backdrop is undeniably Mons Sacer, not the Aventine.[35]

When we tally the destinations of the three canonical secessions, the ideological distinction of the Aventine begins to lose ground. The secessions of 494 and 287 withdrew to the Sacred Mount and Janiculum respectively. The secession of 449 seems to have passed through the Aventine, but this retreat failed, forcing the plebeians to take Mons Sacer once again. How, then, are we to explain the preeminence of the Aventine in the modern tradition of popular protest? Why have modern political parties of the left repeatedly withdrawn to a place—be it in the physical landscape or in their conscience—that they have labeled "Aventine"? To put the question another way, how did a temporary and initially unsuccessful occupation of the Aventine in the second of three plebeian secessions render the hill the dominant site in the cultural geography of proletariat resistance? Taken together with Roman historiographical methods, memory studies help provide an explanation.

Already in ancient Rome, theories of memory recognize that the new (*novum*), marvelous (*admirabile*), and striking (*insigne*) proved more memorable than the quotidian. The author of the *Rhetorica ad Herennium* explains (3.22): "But if we see or hear anything that is remarkably base or honorable, uncommon, great, unbelievable, laughable, then we are wont to remember it for a long time." As the accounts of the second plebeian secession attempted to reconcile divergent

[32] Cic. *Rep.* 2.58, *Brut.* 54, *Corn.* 1 fr. 49; Livy 2.32–33, 2.57.4, 3.15.2, 3.54.12, 9.34.4; Dion. Hal. *Ant. Rom.* 6.45.2, 10.35.1; Val. Max. 8.91; App. *B Civ.* 1.1; Festus 422L; Plut. *Cor.* 6.1; Flor. 1.17, 1.23; *Dig.* 1.2.2.20; Oros. 2.5.

[33] For a sober overview of the first secession, see Ridley 1968.

[34] On the naming of the hill "Mons Sacer" as a credit to the authenticity of accepting the Mons Sacer tradition over the Aventine tradition, see Niccolini 1932, 29. All references to

Mons Sacer in the extant literary-historical record connect the hill to the plebeian secessions. Dismissing any relationship of Mons Sacer and the secessions simply on the accusation of false etymologizing not only seems arbitrary but also dismisses ancient attestations in favor of silence or modern speculations, *pace* Ogilvie 1965, 311 and Forsythe 2005, 282–283, both following Asc. *Corn.* 1 fr. 49.

[35] Livy 2.33.3. On the fame of the apology, see note 10 above.

geographical traditions, they did so through some of the most dramatic Roman historical prose that has survived to the modern era. The stories of the ambush of Sicinius and the sacrifice of Verginia have nearly all the criteria—"images that do something"—recommended in the *Rhetorica ad Herennium*: "outstanding beauty" (the ill-fated beauty of Verginia), "singular depravity" (the lasciviousness and blood crimes of Appius), "some deformation so that it becomes gory to the point that its form is more striking" (the mangled corpses of Sicinius and Verginia, and the blood-drenched toga of Verginius).[36] In the mechanics of memory, furthermore, the sensational replaces the irrelevant.[37] Despite Menenius Agrippa's parable on Mons Sacer, and never mind any vague detail from the "historic" third secession on the Janiculum, the riveting stories of the second secession are simply the most memorable. It is the Aventine, furthermore, that anchors the second secession's shifting geographies. It is the first site to which the plebeians resolutely secede in 449, and, when the decemvirate is overthrown, the plebeians return to the hill and elect their tribunes. The vividness and narrative dynamism of Livy's and Dionysius's treatments guaranteed the episode's implantation into cultural memory for generations to follow.[38] Surely the works of Augustan authors did not stand alone; as noted above, Cicero already considered the episode so widely published and collectively known that it required no further rehearsing on his part.

It is the popular memory of the "Aventine" secession, then, that modern reactivations of the plebeian secessions have grabbed hold of. It is this episode that furnishes the icon promoted by the Italian Socialists of 1924 and by the Communards of 1871. Yet two questions remain: why and when was the Aventine introduced into the ancient historiographical record?

5. An Ancient Reenactment or "Frugal" Revisionism? Gracchus on the Aventine

The footnote of Livy in the secession of 494 B.C. proves suggestive (2.32.2–3). Livy directly identifies Piso as the source (*auctor*) of the Aventine myth of plebeian secession.[39] The historian L. Calpurnius Piso Frugi was plebeian tribune in 149 B.C., consul in 133, and censor in 120; in creating and constructing history, Piso was not only a conservative moralist, hence Frugi, but also a confirmed enemy, *inimicus capitalis*, of Gaius Gracchus.[40] Between Piso and Gracchus our sources record nothing but profound enmity—both political and personal. To what extent might this hatred have affected Piso's reconstruction of the archaic social struggles?

It has been well demonstrated that historical events of the early republic were not only

---

[36] The catalogue derives from various sentences in *Rhet. Her.* 3.22: *aliquid agentes imagines, egregia pulcritudo, unica turpido, aliqua re deformatum ut cruenta [fit] quo magnis insgnita sit forma.* Absent from the Verginia episode is the comic (*ridiculum*). (For a similar argument regarding narrative memory and scenic memory, see J. Assmann 2006, 3). Generic influences other than rhetoric can be traced in the texts of Livy and Dionysius. The melodramatic narrative style and its enhancement by pathetic or licentious elements seem to have been fashionable among some Hellenistic historians (see Polybius's twelfth book for indictments of Theopompus, Callisthenes, and especially Timaeus), and Roman accounts may have been influenced by stage performances. The passage from the *Rhetorica ad Herennium* demonstrates that those trained in Roman rhetoric actively recognized, sought out, and deployed narrative elements that served as memory hooks.

[37] *Rhet. Her.* 3.22: prohibition against *vagae imagines*. Also, Fentress and Wickham 1992, 73–74; J. Assmann 2011. On the importance of memory cues, see Schacter 2001, esp. 41–60.

[38] Their sources were likely responsible for the narrative embellishments (and any fabrications): Mommsen 1864, 287–318 and Wiseman 1979.

[39] Livy's repetition of *auctor (Sicinio quodam auctore . . . Piso auctor)* further encourages reading the verb as not simply indicating Piso wrote the history but that he was possibly the source of the story as well.

[40] *Schol. Bob.* In Cic. *Flac.* f10 p.96St. As late as the seventh century A.D., the scholiast had access to Gracchus's vitriolic speech against Piso.

reconstructed but also redesigned—even fabricated—as false precedents by the politically minded second-century annalists who crafted their accounts of the past according to their own contemporary ideology and political propaganda.[41] Traditions regarding the archaic social struggles were not only filtered through the dramatic events of the second century but also framed in terms of them. The literary reconstruction of the plebeian secessions may have been particularly susceptible to manipulation, for these secessions successively established and reinstalled the plebeian tribunes in response to patrician tyranny and the problems of land management and personal debt bondage. These were, of course, boilerplate issues in the second century, when Gracchus aimed his policies at alleviating the plight of the urban poor, reassessing the distribution of public lands, and relieving debt bondage, some of which was acquired through ongoing military service. Such points are well taken, but what do they have to do with the geography of the secessions, and how do they get the plebeians on the Aventine?

When writing his own history of the early republic, Piso had, in his own lifetime, witnessed a very real Aventine secession; but this withdrawal was no peaceful protest march or occupy movement on the part of disquieted plebeian soldiers seeking liberty and equality. It was a flight—and a hunt. In the year 121 B.C., the consul L. Opimius assembled the Senate to abrogate all of Gracchus's measures; Gracchus and his once fellow tribune M. Fulvius Flaccus assembled their supporters on the Capitoline. A riot ensued, and Opimius had passed a *Senatus Consultum Ultimum*, the always-controversial decree to save the republic at all costs. The cost was clear: the execution of the insurrectionists. The next morning, Gracchus and Flaccus with their supporters retreated to the Aventine in the hope that the Senate would come to some sort of agreement with them.[42]

Here one finds oneself in an interpretive circle. The conventional argument is that this Aventine flight served as an attempt to rally popular support by recalling and reenacting the plebeian secessions. I would suggest that such a reading reverses the flow of influence and likely historiographic reality. Accounts of the plebeian secessions, which were thought to have established the tribunate, served as historiographic foils or at least retrojected antecedents for the flight of Gracchus. One notes that like the secession of 449, Gracchus's Aventine rally failed. Onward the former tribune fled: across the river, to the Janiculum. The destination of the secession of 287 became the site of Gracchus's death. The final location on the Janiculum may be a matter of coincidence. The insertion of the Aventine into the traditional secession legend, on the other hand, was likely influenced, if not wholly inspired, by the flight of Gracchus, Flaccus, and their followers. When they decided to *salire l'Aventino*, their move may have been a novel one. Their retreat to the Aventine may not have evoked the archaic social struggles, but now it should be clearer why we have chosen to remember it that way.

6. A Preliminary Conclusion

There was little agreement in antiquity as to where the seceding plebeians withdrew at any given moment in the early republic: the Aventine, Mons Sacer, the Janiculum, and even *in alios colles*.[43]

[41] See Cornell 2005 and 1986; Forsythe 2005, 172; Rawson 1991 = 1976; Ogilvie and Drummond 1990; Wiseman 1981; and especially Ungern-Sternberg 2005, who uses the history of the decemvirate as his case study in his discussion of the formation of the annalistic tradition. For the opposite, the resuscitation of some representation (or memory) of the past to legitimate contemporary propaganda and ideology, see Marx 1979 and Halbwachs 1992, 193–235.

[42] Cic. *Phil.* 8.14; App. *B Civ.* 1.3.26; Oros. 5.13.6–8.

[43] Livy 2.34, 3.61, 3.67, 7.40, 9.30, 34.7 (cf. 38.51–52: Scipio's secession to the Capitol from the plebeian tribunes). See also Sall. *Hist.* 1.11M. Ampelius lists four secessions, retreating in turn to Mons Sacer, the Aventine, the Janiculum, and the Forum; these secessions are matched by four urban seditions, the second of which is C. Gracchus's on the Aventine (*Lib. Mem.* 25–26).

Additional references to the plebeian secessions, including rhetorical uses, demonstrate that the historical record was hardly uniform.[44] The Aventine was not the unique destination in the ancient literary tradition of the plebeian secessions. The historic flight of Gracchus to the Aventine may have relocated the geography of the secessions to southwestern Rome. The highly embellished passages of Livy and Dionysius helped provide a lasting impression. Modern reactivations of the secessions, finally, seem to have retrofitted the ancient secessions to support the narrative of contemporary political and social discourse. Legacy has reshaped history.

Ancient accounts and modern ideological treatments of the archaic social struggles each write their reconstructions on different maps; the characterization of the Aventine in ancient literature differs from that in modern scholarship. In Paris of 1906, when Alfred Merlin published his seminal monograph, *L'Aventin dans l'Antiquité*, the ghosts of the Commune had not been exorcised.[45] In Merlin's reconstruction, the ancient secessions marked the Aventine as the plebeian hill *par excellence*.[46] The Sacred Mount, a vague toponym for a hill located outside Rome's imperial and papal walls, disappeared into relative obscurity; only close philological readings of the texts rescue the site—and even the name itself—from oblivion.

7. Afterword: Forgetting, Remembering, and Myth-making

In the modern period, Gaius Gracchus has regularly appeared as a revolutionary hero and the revolutionary's hero.[47] The ongoing manipulation of his political legacy has promoted popular agendas, particularly in France of the late eighteenth and nineteen centuries.[48] It is plausible that Gracchus's final stand influenced the Communards' use of the toponym for their own headquarters' nickname. In many respects, Gracchus seems the type of cultural hero Hugo Chávez would claim as his own model and whose social legacy the Venezuelan could readily put to use as his own ideological ancestor. Yet in his Roman secession of October 2005, Chávez did not ascend the Aventine. He did not stand shoulder to shoulder with the ghosts of the Paris Commune, the Aventiniani of the 1920s, or Gracchus and Flaccus. Rather, he stood on Mons Sacer of Menenius Agrippa. Chávez's reading of the landscape does not indicate a revived critical reading of ancient texts. His is a powerful ideological maneuver and a dual act of memory and forgetfulness.

The year 2005 was the bicentennial of the arrival of another Venezuelan to Rome: Simón Bolívar, the man who would be *Libertador*. Not long after Napoleon's imperial coronation in Paris and triumphal entry into Milan, Bolívar arrived in the Eternal City with his mentor, Simón Rodríguez.[49] Young Bolívar found Rome blessed with the spirits of austere republicans and haunted by

[44] Cicero's various accounts are inconsistent: *Mur.* 15; *Brut* 54; *Rep.* 2.58.1, 2.63.2; *Corn.* 1 fr. 49. See also the speech of Cicero in Cassius Dio (44.25.3).

[45] For the Commune's ongoing psychological effects on modern French politics, see Shortliffe 1949.

[46] Merlin 1906, esp. 81: "The second secession takes place on the Aventine, which became the 'people's mountain' *par excellence*," and p. 268: "The Aventine was permanently cemented to the memory (*mémoire*) of the secessions."

[47] See Malamud 2009, 46–61 and 80–89, for views of the Gracchi in antebellum America.

[48] See, for example, the sociopolitical impact of the 1793 performance of Marie-Joseph de Chénier's *Caïs Gracchus: Tragédie en trois actes* (Maslan 1995 and Wiseman 1998). In 1794 the revolutionary François-Noël Babeuf adopted the name Gracchus. For the manufacture of tradition and propagation of cultural memories from the Paris Commune to World War I, see Hobsbawm 1983, 263–307.

[49] Rodríguez dedicated his life to education as a teacher, administrator, and reformer. When we recognize Rodríguez primarily as an educator and man of letters, Bolívar's oath on Mons Sacer, rather than on the Aventine, becomes intelligible.

the ghosts of depraved emperors.[50] On 15 August a postprandial walk took Bolívar and Rodríguez to Mons Sacer. Mindful of both the legendary struggles of the republic's plebeians and of his own America's suffering under imperial Spain, Bolívar was wholly caught up with the *genius loci* of the Sacred Mount.[51] He solemnly declared: "I swear before you; I swear by the God of my fathers; I swear by them, I swear by my honor, and I swear by my country, that I shall not give my arm rest nor repose to my soul until the chains that oppress us by the will of the Spanish have been broken."[52]

It was Mons Sacer—the hill "whither Sicinius led the plebeians of Rome, exasperated as they were by the taxes, the injustices, the arrogance, and the violence of their masters, the patricians"[53]—that catalyzed the launch of Bolívar's revolutionary campaign to liberate Latin America from the tyranny of imperial Spain. Years later, Daniel O'Leary, Bolívar's general, aide-de-camp, and biographer, recalled the fateful event in his own memoirs: "Much was spoken in Rome at the time of that oath; but the Spanish residing there hardly imagined that the oath would be anything more than youthful outbursts produced as a result of the memories (*recuerdos*) evoked by those sites."[54] His contemporaries underestimated the power of the place, inexorably chained to the memory of the ancient plebeian secessions.

Early in 1824, Bolívar wrote a letter to his mentor and asked: "Do you remember (*se acuerda*) when we went together to Monte Sacro in Rome to swear on that blessed land the freedom of our country? Certainly you have not forgotten that day of eternal glory for us; the same day which was anticipated, so to say, by a prophetic oath of the very hope that we ought not have."[55] Two decades had seen the oath's gradual fulfillment, and the *Libertador* himself recognized his visit to Mons Sacer as the flint sparking the conflagration of revolution. A century after Bolívar's death, the critical moment was memorialized in a painting on the ceiling of the National Pantheon in Caracas, the grand mausoleum entombing Bolívar and other heroes of the revolution.[56] The icon represents "El Patriotismo" and features Bolívar standing with one arm outstretched in his oath toward his future, his other arm resting upon the ruins of the past.[57] The memory of Bolívar on Mons Sacer serves as a "foundational scene of Latin American identity."[58] The so-called *Juramento de Roma* or *Juramento en el Monte Sacro* became "one of the cornerstone texts of the myth of Bolívar."[59] Both the episode and the oath itself also underpin Chávez's Bolivarismo.[60]

[50] Uribe 1884, 74. Bolívar prefaced his oath with a lengthy reflection on the virtues and crimes of Rome from Romulus through Caracalla. Some of the rhetorical features, including the republican/imperial antithesis, are analyzed in Rotker 1998.

[51] Uribe 1884, 74. In setting the geographical context and emotional tone for the oath, Rodríguez recalls Bolívar's physiognomy as marked by a "certain air of considerable preoccupation and concentrated thought" and his actions as conveying a "certain unforgettable solemnity."

[52] Uribe 1884, 74.

[53] O'Leary 1952, 67; see also O'Leary 1970, 19. The moment of the oath is deemed so important as to have been included in the abridged version of O'Leary's memoirs as well as the thirty-four-volume original.

[54] O'Leary 1952, 68. O'Leary claims to have learned of the event from Bolívar himself and others who were in Rome at the time.

[55] Lecuna 1929, 32.

[56] Tito Salas's allegorical and historical paintings of Bolívar's life, triumph, and eventual apotheosis were part of a sweeping redesign of the mausoleum and its decoration in the 1930s. For the iconographical program, see Darias Príncipe 1996.

[57] Salas's work dates to 128 years after Bolívar's visit to Rome. Any attempt to reconstruct the oath's location based on Salas's painting is misguided. The painting's background is an evocative pastiche of *Romanitas*, and Bolívar's placement on the Capitoline is in keeping with the ideology of Salas's overall visual program in the Pantheon (cf. Darias Príncipe 1996).

[58] Conway 2003, 152.

[59] Conway 2003, 151. It is the first text produced in Bolívar 1985, 3–4, for example.

[60] On Chávez's manipulation of and reliance upon the oath, see Conway 2003, 151–153.

Throughout his paramilitary and political career, Chávez consistently recited Bolívar's oath. Seven of the thirty-three published speeches Chávez delivered in 2005, the bicentennial of Bolívar's visit to Rome, contain verbatim recitations of the "Juramento de Roma."[61] One of those speeches was delivered 16 October in Rome's Parco della Libertà, the site where the *Libertador* first uttered his prophetic vow.[62] Chávez seized upon the importance of the site: "here on this hill, on this Mons Sacer, the *Libertador* Símon Bolívar was born 200 years ago."[63] Chávez's impassioned commemoration, a speech of 105 minutes, is full of literary, philosophical, spiritual, and historical references. Something, however, is missing from his commemoration. As he stood there on the Sacred Mount— twice the legendary rallying point of the seceding plebeians—Chávez never recalled the ancient Roman antecedent that had so inspired his beloved Bolívar's "youthful outbursts." The roots of the new cult of Chavismo reached only so deep as Bolivarian revolution. The archaic social struggles and plebeian secessions, it would seem, had not simply been supplanted but altogether forgotten.[64]

Exploring the history of the "Juramento en el Monte Sacro" further exposes the deep complexity of historical memory and at the same time problematizes the relationship of history, memory, and past reality. Bolívar's oath, at least in the form so often reprinted in collections of the *Libertador*'s works and recited by Chávez, may itself be a fiction.

Bolívar's reference in the aforementioned letter of 1824 confirms the historicity of the episode and highlights its fateful potential. O'Leary's claim that the event was much discussed in contemporary Rome, if it is to be believed, likewise suggests the occurrence itself cannot be challenged. What remains far from certain, however, is the authenticity of the account's details and the very words of Bolívar's extended speech. O'Leary's memoirs, collated and edited by his son—and thus at multiple removes from the Libertador—were published nearly a century and a half after Bolívar visited Mons Sacer. The only extended firsthand account of that afternoon in 1805 derives from recollections Rodríguez himself shared forty-five years later with Manuel Uribe Angel, a Colombian doctor and geographer. Uribe published the interview in 1884, seventy-nine years after the oath would have originally taken place.

Does the "Juramento de Roma" faithfully represent the words so solemnly uttered by the *Libertador* on that providential August afternoon? Was the highly rhetorical and emotive text concocted by his tutor, Rodríguez? To what extent did Uribe enhance or altogether manufacture the account before he published it in the Colombian national *Gedenkschrift* honoring the first centennial of the hero's death? In untangling the various *testimonia* for the oath as well as its performance, content, audience, style, and emotional and psychological qualities, Susana Rotker has concluded:

> If [the oath] did not happen, it is not important: *it should have happened . . .* The *Juramento en el Monte Sacro* produces an effect of recognition. How many footnotes belie its content is not important, since it has the resistance of an icon; as such the category of Truth should be totally secondary. As an emblem or as an icon, *it produces a feeling*.[65]

[61] Chávez 2005.

[62] For the controversy over the actual site of Bolívar's oath, see Filippi 1987, 45–55.

[63] Chávez 2005, 526.

[64] I have already noted how Berlusconi and Italian media alike forgot (and thereby obliterated) the archaic social struggles in their identification of the 1924 *secessione dell'Aventino* as the first secession.

[65] Rotker 1998, 42; emphasis is her own. On confabulations, see J. Assmann 2006, 2–3. What Rotker proposes is a sort of collective confabulation or the triumph of social memory over historical uncertainty. For this conflict between history and memory, see Connerton 1989, 3–12 and Megill 2011.

Icons have the quality of resistance and of solemn endurance, and they also serve as memory cues locked into a network of semantic values.[66] Rotker's approach to the emotional and ideological potential of the past, unhinged from reality or "Truth" but granted meaning and value in the present so as to retrofit the past, reminds us why, ultimately, it need not matter to Livy, Dionysius, or other historians of Rome whether the plebeians withdrew to the Aventine or to Mons Sacer or to both (or elsewhere). Over time, both hills became icons continually remembered and integrated into a sequence of revolutionary reactivations in the ongoing struggle of the people against tyranny.

[66] Rotker's (1998) concept of resistant icons pertains less to iconic memory (visual in nature) than to semantic memory (laden with meaning).

10 ◆ Cultural and Digital Memory:
Case Studies from the Virtual World Heritage Laboratory

Bernard Frischer

This chapter will discuss how, in the light of neuroscientific research, the new interactive 3D technologies that have developed in the last three decades can be useful for the preservation and transmission of cultural memory by archaeologists working in the new subdiscipline of virtual archaeology.[1] This is a vast topic and can only be addressed in general terms and illustrated with select examples of recent work by the virtual heritage laboratory I direct.

It goes without saying that I write as a humanist, not a neuroscientist. For the neuroscience of memory, I rely on two recent books as well as on the collection of thirty-nine essays in the *Oxford Handbook of Memory*. The books are Kurt Danziger's *Marking the Mind: A History of Memory*, which was published by Cambridge in 2008; and Eric Kandel's *In Search of Memory: The Emergence of a New Science of Mind*, published in 2006. Danziger is a distinguished historian of psychology; Kandel won the Nobel Prize in Physiology or Medicine in 2000 for his work on how short-term memory is converted to long-term memory.

The research programs embodied in these books are very different: Kandel is interested in how the brain processes memory, while Danziger is concerned with the history of explanations of memory from ancient Greece until the late twentieth century. But in another sense, the books intersect. Kandel alternates accounts of his discoveries with recollections of his life; Danziger reminds us that memory has a history, and one that is not simply dusty and irrelevant background for today's memory scientists. The topics where both authors find common ground are thus, appropriately enough, familiar to us humanists: autobiography (cf. Flower in this volume) and the history of ideas.

I begin with a painting located in Rome called *The Archaeologist* by Giorgio de Chirico (fig. 10.1). It is a late work, dating to 1973, but it reprises similar works from the 1920s.[2] In *The Archaeologist* and related works, we see a manikin figure that is typical of de Chirico's metaphysical works.[3] Enthroned and seated in the pose of a thinker, the figure in *The Archaeologist* is set in front of a building and an arcade, which give it an implicit monumental dimension. More than by its vacant facial expression, the figure is defined by its attributes. These are found precariously poised on its

I wish to acknowledge the help of all those involved in the Digital Hadrian's Villa Project, especially Matthew Brennan, John Fillwalk, Lynne Kvapil, and Lee Nelms. A detailed listing of all the many contributors to the project will be posted on the project website. I thank an anonymous donor for helping us to start the project in 2007 and the National Science Foundation for giving us the funding to complete it (grant no. IIS-1018512). For her helpful comments about an earlier version of this chapter, I thank Jane Crawford. Finally, I thank Karl Galinsky for inviting me to speak at the conference on Memoria Romana held at the American Academy in Rome from 14 to 16 October 2011, and I also thank conference participant and neuroscientist Alessandro Treves for his friendly feedback about the neuroscientific matters discussed in my chapter.

[1] On the subdiscipline, see, in general, Lock 2003.

[2] Cf. the painting in the Museo Bilotti entitled *Gli archeologi* and the statue called *L'archeologo—pensatore* in the same museum.

[3] On the manikin figure in de Chirico's work, see Bohn 1975.

lap and consist of a heap of two books and some random architectural and sculptural fragments. In the 1973 painting, the archaeologist's right hand holds a pen, and his left hand holds a text he has written that says: *sum sed quid sum* ("I am, but what am I?").

This enigma is a good place to start. What is the archaeologist? Is he de Chirico's expressionless figure who collects and piles up whatever the past happens to have left to us? Is he someone who does not know himself as a unique being living his life in his own time and place but who instead rummages affectless through the boneyard of the past assembling, and perhaps at best sorting and classifying, whatever happens to turn up?

This is precisely the image of the archaeologist one not infrequently finds in the public mind. How often have we seen covers of the popular archaeological magazines that feature skulls, bones, desiccated mummies, and the like? We might well ask with de Chirico who is this vacuous person who collects but does not recollect, who brings back the skulls and bones of the dead to the living but who seems incapable of bringing back old things to life? In this sense, the painting could almost be taken as an illustration of a challenge issued in Ernst Cassirer's *Essay on Man*: "In man, we cannot describe [memory] as a simple return of an event, as a faint image or copy of former impressions. It is not simply a repetition but rather a rebirth of the past; it implies a creative and constructive process. It is not enough to pick up isolated data of our past experience; we must really re-collect them, we must organize and synthesize them."[4]

Kandel has explained why the isolated fragments of personal memory, if left unintegrated as they appear to be in de Chirico's painting, are psychologically disruptive and dangerous:

> Memory provides our lives with continuity. . . . Without the binding force of memory, experience would be splintered into as many fragments as there are moments in life. Without the mental time travel provided by memory, we would have no awareness of our personal history. . . . We are who we are because of what we learn and what we remember.[5]

The observations of Cassirer and Kandel about personal memory can be applied as well to the collective, or historical, memory with which the archaeologist must deal. Indeed, Kandel makes this point explicitly when he writes that "memory is essential not only for the continuity of individual identity, but also for the transmission of culture and the evolution and continuity of societies over centuries."[6]

Kandel and Cassirer might interpret de Chirico's painting and the archaeologist's enigmatic text as an illustration of what it would mean to preserve the fragments of experience without "the binding force of memory," to collect without also recollecting. Someone who did this would not have an identity but could state nothing about himself except the enigma of identity itself: "I am, but what am I?"

The implicit challenge of de Chirico's metaphysics is to consider how the random fragments left by our collective past can be reassembled into a meaningful whole so that we can understand and possess a cultural identity by knowing our past. The painting even suggests that the past was a much more interesting place than the present. Contrast the rounded, detailed forms of the architectonic elements and the classical head on the lap of the archaeologist with the dull, flat forms and featureless pavement of the present. De Chirico invites us to imagine that we can enrich and enhance the present not simply by hoarding up bric-a-brac from the past but by revivifying the present through the inspiration of our cultural heritage.

---

[4] Cassirer 1953, 74.

[5] Kandel 2011, location 354.

[6] Kandel 2011, location 364.

In Kandel's terms, by collecting his fragmentary relics, de Chirico's archaeologist has taken the first step of short-term, or working, memory.[7] But to achieve his true end, the archaeologist must take another, and more difficult, step of converting short-term memory into long-term memory, first for himself, then for his contemporaries and, ultimately, for future generations. To do this, Kandel's research would suggest, the archaeologist must reassemble the fragments into a whole—supplemented where necessary by his informed historical imagination—so that the picture he gives us of the past has salience and grabs the attention of not only his fellow scholars but also children and the general public. Only then can the archaeologist's work result in memory that is long in cultural as well as individual terms.

For centuries archaeologists have tended to divide into two groups, those who see themselves as fact-gatherers unbiased by theory, and those who seek to take the accidental remnants of the past and reconstruct them with the help of tools, methods, and theories into a living whole. This contrast can be seen in one of the very first professional publications in the field: the inaugural issue of *Archaeologia*, published by the Society of Antiquaries of London in 1770. It contains two articles by important members of the society: Martin Folkes, the president; and his sworn foe, William Stukeley, famous for his monumental studies of Stonehenge and Avebury. Folkes was a fact-gatherer *par excellence*. Writing about Trajan's Column in Rome, he is relentlessly descriptive and quantitative, giving us nothing but measurement after measurement accurate to the inch. In contrast, Stukeley is high-flying. In his short, six-page article on a little church that was a mere 75 square feet in size, he ranges far and wide, concluding with a discussion of the origin of architecture itself, which he traces to Abraham.[8]

The perennial division exemplified in *Archaeologia* between empiricists and rationalists reflects the inevitable dilemma faced by the archaeologist—that the past almost always survives with gaps and imperfections. Moreover, archaeologists who do fieldwork face the additional irony that they must kill to dissect: the very process of excavating a site leads to its irreversible destruction. The thesis of this chapter is that the new subdiscipline called virtual archaeology can provide precisely "the mental time travel provided by memory" that Kandel implicitly saw as the correct response to de Chirico's metaphysical enigma.

What is virtual archaeology? Danziger observed that "the practices and institutions of social memory are historically embedded."[9] Despite the great variety of commemoration implied by this statement, Danziger then goes on to note a certain constant pervading all known cultures of *homo sapiens* back to the Palaeolithic: the presence of *external memory*, which Danziger defines as "the use of materials outside an individual's body for purposes of representation."[10] In the earliest times, the materials might be rock surfaces, tree bark, or (as in prehistoric China) ox bones and turtle shells. Eventually they came to include writing implements and still later even more advanced symbol-creating and recording devices. Danziger notes that "external memory constitutes a kind of technology, and like all technology it exhibits historical change and improvement that depend on the social conditions of its employment but also affect those conditions in turn."[11]

In the first book ever written on the subject of virtual archaeology, Forte and Silotti defined the field as "the most faithful representation of the ancient world possible, highly realistic in information

[7] Some psychologists distinguish between short-term and working memory; see Dehn 2008, 3.

[8] Frischer 2001, 73–74.

[9] Danziger 2008, location 58; cf. Nelson and Fivush 2000.

[10] Danziger 2008, location 84.

[11] Danziger 2008, location 90.

and with a high scientific content."[12] To achieve this faithful representation virtual archaeology cooperates with a number of disciplines, including electrical engineering, information science, and archaeology. It uses the new digital tools for digital data capture, representation, and dissemination for two related ends: representing the physical remains of the past and analyzing or interpreting them. Thus understood, virtual archaeology has a strong and obvious relationship to the topic of cultural memory: if memory is a recalling of the past of either an individual or a group, then virtual archaeology can provide a new way to evoke memory. How these ways are better and what inevitable risks they entail are the topics to be addressed in this chapter.

Evaluating the strengths and weaknesses of these forms of external memory depends on a criterion, something that Danziger called a mnemonic value.[13] For example, Danziger points out that in the Middle Ages, monks were urged to memorize the religious texts not only accurately but with appropriate emotional engagement.[14] Starting in the Enlightenment and especially the nineteenth century, the leading mnemonic value was precise reproduction as emblematized by external memory aids such as photographs and phonographs.[15] As Danziger suggests, in both cultures, the mnemonic values resonated with the forms of external memory, memory performance, and the very concept of memory itself.[16]

If the forms of external memory that interest us are the new 3D digital technologies, then to which mnemonic values, memory performances, and scientific concepts of memory do they respond today? To answer this question, the work of Daston and Galison on objectivity is helpful. The book charts the emergence of the value of objectivity in the nineteenth century and examines its afterlife in the last century. It shows that the value of objective recording gave way to what is called "interpreted" recording, where the correct understanding of a seemingly objective record such as a map, x-ray, or other scientific image depends on the active engagement of a trained expert who views the image.[17]

In our age, we are acutely aware both of our Enlightenment duty to be as precise as possible in our acts of remembering and of our twentieth-century insight into the way in which the recording of memory is, or can be, inventive even to the point of falsehood. So our concept of memory is a combination of the objective and subjective as sublated through a notion of professional best practice and conventions of intersubjectivity. We see this concept operationalized in our culture forensically in the courts, where the potential unreliability of even eyewitnesses is well understood,[18] and in the physics of a Niels Bohr who saw "no strict rule about the . . . demarcation between the measurer and the measured."[19] We see the notion embedded within the neuroscience of memory, where it has become commonplace to say, as Bartlett stated as early as 1932, that "memory is not the re-excitation of innumerable fixed, lifeless and fragmentary traces. It is an imaginative reconstruction, or construction, built out of the relation of our attitude towards a whole active mass of organized past reactions of experience."[20] This point of view—revolutionary in its day—is now commonplace. Thus in 2007 Kandel wrote that "perception is creative . . . built into neural pathways of the brain are complex rules of guessing," and "sensation is an abstraction, not a

[12] Forte and Silotti 1997, 10.

[13] Danziger 2008, location 128, 162.

[14] Danziger 2008, location 128.

[15] Danziger 2008, location 168.

[16] Danziger 2008, location 172.

[17] Daston and Galison 2007, 311, 313, 315, passim.

[18] See Bartlett 1932, Roediger and McDermott 2000, Mitchell and Johnson 2000.

[19] Sachs 2007, 111.

[20] Bartlett 1932, 213.

Fig. 10.1. Giorgio de Chirico, The Archaeologist. *Rome, Fondazione Giorgio de Chirico (photo courtesy Giorgio de Chirico Foundation).*

Fig. 10.2. Rome Reborn, aerial view of version 2.2 of the digital model (Frischer Consulting; image Bernard Frischer).

Fig. 10.3. *Digital model of the cast of* Augustus of Prima Porta *in the Erlangen Antikensammlung*
(Virtual World Heritage Laboratory; image Matthew Brennan).

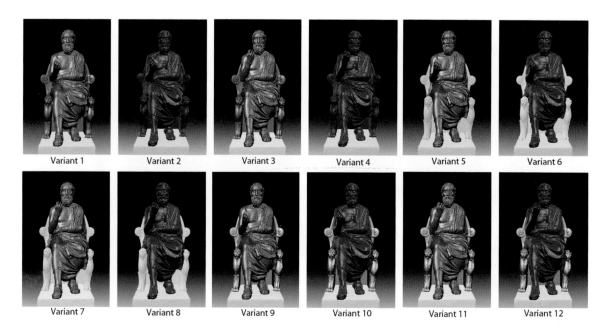

Variant 1 Variant 2 Variant 3 Variant 4 Variant 5 Variant 6

Variant 7 Variant 8 Variant 9 Variant 10 Variant 11 Variant 12

Fig. 10.4. Twelve hypotheses of reconstruction of the portrait statue of Epicurus (Frischer Consulting).

Fig. 10.5. Reconstruction of the lower rotunda of Roccabruna at Hadrian's Villa at sunset, 21 June A.D. 130 (Julian calendar) (Virtual World Heritage Laboratory; image Matthew Brennan).

replication of the real world."[21] Practitioners of virtual archaeology are acutely aware of the need to differentiate objective from subjective knowledge. The field strives for precision, but precision as applied both to the object of study and to the subjectivity of the experts whose opinions are solicited in interpreting the object.

How do virtual archaeologists make highly realistic and scientifically faithful representations of 3D archaeological artifacts? These artifacts may differ in scale from the potsherd to the statue, building, or entire settlement or landscape, but the techniques we use are the same and can be divided into four categories. Scanning is used when the object exists fairly well intact. Using a device such as a laser or structured light scanner, the 3D data of the object can be captured with submillimeter accuracy. Hand modeling is used when the object has disappeared or is so damaged that there is little point in scanning it. Software such as Google's free Sketchup, Autodesk's 3D Studio Max or a host of other software packages is commonly used to create hand models. Procedural modeling is used when a scene must be populated with many variations on the same theme—for example, the houses of a Roman colony or the apartment buildings of imperial Rome itself. In procedural modeling a set of rules is developed about the design features of the object: how wide and high it can be, what materials it is made of, how close it can be set next to its neighbor, and so on. For each rule there are appropriate variants so that, for example, if several dozen procedural models of temples in ancient Rome are needed, column types can be varied among Doric, Ionic, Corinthian, and composite. Once the rules have been defined, the software can automatically generate as many instances of the artifactual models as are required.

Finally, there is a hybrid fourth category in which two or more of the simple types are combined. The Rome Reborn project (fig. 10.2) exemplifies such a hybrid since it was made by scanning Gismondi's great physical model of Rome in the Museum of Roman Civilization,[22] proceduralizing the resulting scan model and inserting hand-made models of buildings such as the Colosseum and Pantheon about which we have enough information to justify detailed modeling inside and out.[23]

Whatever the technique used for modeling, two basic distinctions are important: the general difference between a model and replica (cf. Anguissola in this volume) and the specifically archaeological difference between a model showing an artifact's current state and one restoring it to the way it looked at some earlier stage in its history, usually its condition when newly made.

To begin with the first distinction, a replica is, or strives to be, an exact copy of an original. In contrast, a model is a reduction of the characteristics of the original to the bare minimum needed to capture its essential characteristics. Three-dimensional models of cultural heritage monuments are sometimes criticized because they are not realistic enough—perhaps because they make the structures depicted appear too new and perfect.

This criticism reflects the fact that the incidental imperfections have been intentionally left out and betrays a confusion between a model and a replica. Almost all sciences work with this distinction, whether we think of physics, chemistry, economics, logic, or even philology. In the case of textual criticism, for example, the stemma of a text is not literally—that is to say, photorealistically—that same thing as the history of its transmission. Most of the time, no one objects that the model is not a replica, but that is because most scientific models are abstract or formal. In contrast, the models made by the virtual archaeologist are what we call literal or empirical: they actually resemble the thing they represent. But despite this surface resemblance, they are no less an abstraction and reduction.

---

[21] Kandel 2011, locations 4541, 4630.

[22] On Gismondi, see Filippi 2007.

[23] For more information, see the project's website at www.romereborn.frischerconsulting.com.

In making the reduction of a complex reality to a model, virtual archaeologists always have to ask themselves what phase in the life of the artifact is to be represented. If the purpose is to model the current condition of the artifact, we call the result a "state model." If the goal is to show how the artifact looked at an earlier phase—typically, when it was first created—we call that a "restoration model."[24]

But why make models in the first place? In the terms of cultural memory, I would answer that we are either trying to preserve, recover, or create memory. A state model clearly preserves the memory of how an object looked in our lifetime. This may help people in the future to understand that the life of an artifact does not end when the culture that produced it disappears. The relics of the past, once brought back to a later culture, continue to change and evolve.

A restoration model serves the purpose of letting us experiment with different hypotheses of reconstructing the artifact to an earlier condition without having to physically intervene on the object, something that—with all the best intention and chemistry in the world—always runs the risk of irreversibly damaging it. In the case of a statue, a digital 3D restoration model can in this sense be said to be a new and improved version of the cast.

As an example I would cite our project to create a restoration model of the *Augustus of Prima Porta* in the Vatican Museums.[25] Discovered in 1863 just north of Rome in the Villa of Livia at Prima Porta, the statue shows a barefoot—which is to say, heroized—Augustus wearing a breastplate that celebrates his famous diplomatic triumph of 20 B.C., when the Parthians restored to Rome the standards lost by Crassus at the battle of Carrhae. When the statue was found, traces of paint on its surface were clearly visible. From 1999 to 2002, conservators at the Vatican used new techniques to add still more documentation of the five colors applied to the clothing, armor, hair, and eyes. A cast was made of the statue, and it was painted to reflect the evidence of the paints across the surface of the statue.[26]

In 2010–2011, with the generous support of the National Endowment for the Humanities, our lab scanned the cast of the statue in the Antikensammlung of the University of Erlangen. This state model—which is available on our website[27]—was then used to create the state and restoration model (for the latter, see fig. 10.3). New studies of the statue are planned using the hitherto untried technique known as UV-VIS absorption spectroscopy.[28] This has the potential to reveal whether, for example, the emperor's skin was painted—something that would not be at all surprising. Once the new studies have been completed, a new version of the restoration model will be created, this one perhaps more audacious and based on the idea that much of the paint that is preserved comes from a preparatory layer that was covered with secondary layers and highlighting, all of which has disappeared.

Anyone who has seen the show on the polychromy of ancient art, which in recent years has made its way from Munich to Rome to Los Angeles, may have a memory of the painted cast of Augustus—indeed, if s/he is like most visitors to the show, s/he may have a bad memory of the cast, whose painting has been called "aesthetically unpleasing."[29] Its use of polychromy is so schematic and the style of decoration so evocative of "paint-by-numbers" that we find it hard to imagine that an imperial portrait in an empress's villa could have been so lacking in artistic quality. If we think

[24] On terminology for models, see Frischer and Stinson 2007.

[25] Vatican Museums, Braccio Nuovo, inv. no. 2290.

[26] See Liverani 2003 and 2004b, Santamaria and Morresi 2004.

[27] http://www.digitalsculpture.org/augustus/index.html.

[28] See http://en.wikipedia.org/wiki/UV-vis_spectroscopy.

[29] See Bradley 2009 for a review of the catalogue of the show at the J. Paul Getty Museum in Los Angeles.

of even an average Fayum portrait,[30] we have higher expectations of the painter responsible for the *Augustus of Prima Porta*. But the painted cast that has been publicly exhibited has already contributed to our collective memory of how Augustus looked and how the Romans used polychromy.

The fact that this memory is unpleasant for those who visited the exhibition, and from a scientific point of view almost certainly misleading, shows us that restoration, whether physical or virtual, is a risky undertaking that places great responsibility on the restorer. If we restore at all, we need to go all the way: we shouldn't leave the garment red when we strongly suspect that it was probably mixed with Egyptian blue to yield purple. The blue on the metallic standard being handed by the Parthian to the Roman was probably gilt since we know that blue could be used as a base for gold foil.[31] What seems fairly certain is that the standard was not blue, nor was Augustus's garment red. So we should show these features as we have done in our first restoration model, but we need to make it clear to the end users of our website that this is a model of the state of the statue and its colors not in antiquity but in the period 1863–2002. Indeed, it does not even show the state of the statue in that period but the state of mind of its modern conservators as they imagined how the random surviving bits of pigment could be integrated.

At a certain point in their discussion of interpreted recording, Daston and Galison cite a striking statement of Frederick and Erna Gibbs made in the preface to the second edition of their classic *Atlas of Electroencephalography* (1951): "Accuracy should not be sacrificed to objectivity."[32] In making restoration models such as the *Augustus of Prima Porta*, we must not sacrifice an accurate reconstruction of how the statue was originally painted to an objective representation of what traces of paint happen to be recoverable on the surface today.

In daring to go from the state to restoration model, virtual archaeologists must be aware of the danger of creating misleading memory. This can happen when the evidence does not warrant a single, unequivocal restoration but supports two or more variants, each considered equally likely by the consulting experts. As a case in point, I would cite our laboratory's work on the portrait statue of Epicurus.

The principal problems in reconstructing this lost portrait are, first of all, that we have many copies of the head without the body attached and several copies of the torso preserved without any heads, so we must determine the most accurately copied head and torso, scale them to each other, and merge them digitally. Then we have the problem of the right arm: there is no sculpted right arm that is preserved, but a mosaic in Autun, France, seems to reproduce the statue and shows the arm outstretched and possibly uplifted in a gesture of greeting or teaching. Next, there is the matter of materials: was the whole statue made of marble or bronze; or was the throne on which the philosopher sits perhaps of marble, while the body was made of bronze? There is also the question of how the bronze was finished: was it left in its natural state, or was it patinated? Similarly, was the marble left plain, or was it gilded?

The interaction of these different variants, all considered equally possible by our scholarly consultants, dictated that we produce twelve hypotheses of reconstruction. These were generated by the matrix of possibilities about the appearance of the original statue: the bronze of Epicurus's body might have been left untreated, or it might have had a dark patination with an applied blackening sulfide. The right arm may have been outstretched in a gesture of greeting or angled up in a gesture of teach-

---

[30] Cf. *Portrait of the Boy Eutyches* in the Metropolitan Museum (acc. no 18.9.2); illustrated at http://www.metmuseum.org/Collections/search-the-collections/100004780?rpp=20&pg=1&ft=Fayum%2c+Portrait+of+a+Boy&pos=4 (accessed 1 June 2012).

[31] Giovanni Verri, personal communication, 11 May 2011.

[32] Daston and Galison 2007, 324.

ing. The throne might have been made of the same bronze as Epicurus's body, or it might have been carved of marble. Either way, it might have been gilded. The resulting 3D models, based on 3D data capture of a bust from Herculaneum and the torso in Florence,[33] can be seen in figure 10.4.

This example brings up something that is crucial on a scientific and ethical level: the need in virtual archaeology to present all legitimate viewpoints when it comes to reviving the memory of an artifact; and in the user interface to reveal, along with the 3D restoration models, all the evidence and hypotheses behind those viewpoints. There is even a term of art for such evidence and hypotheses: *paradata*. And there is an initiative called The London Charter to set an international standard for making such digital restorations in a responsible way.[34] The charter is a case in point of expert best practice or intersubjectivity.

The third and final activity of the virtual archaeologist is the creation of memory. In a limited sense, when we make digital restorations of Epicurus's portrait and post them on the web, we are creating memories for the end users of our website. But this is a rather weak, passive, and random way for us to discharge our responsibility to the public we serve.

There is a stronger, more focused approach to memory creation that is exemplified by our laboratory's Digital Hadrian's Villa project.[35] The purpose of the study was to determine whether a virtual world coupled with Problem-based Learning (PBL) can facilitate archaeological understanding by students and the general public. In terms of the neurobiology of memory, it is relevant to the topic of cultural memory because it shows how digital technology can be not merely a new form of Danziger's external memory tool but something new: a memory-creating device by taking a number of restoration models of the bric-a-brac on the lap of de Chirico's archaeologist and putting them back into their full ancient spatial context.

Let us first unpack all the terms and concepts behind this claim. Hadrian's Villa is, of course, the World Heritage site in Tivoli built by Hadrian during his twenty-year reign from A.D. 117 to 138.[36] The site covers over 100 hectares of land and consists of over thirty major building complexes. Though there is still a great deal of new fieldwork to be done, the site has been the subject of a large number of scholarly monographs.[37]

Our project took advantage of this previous research and had four phases: (1) creating 3D models of the elements constituting the villa—the terrain, gardens and groves, buildings, fountains and water features, as well as furnishings, including sculpture; (2) combining these elements in a virtual world with the addition of avatars and Non-playing Characters representing the members of the imperial court in Hadrian's day; (3) using the virtual world in two PBL-based undergraduate classes on Hadrian's Villa at the University of Virginia and Xavier University; (4) analyzing the data collected from the students and writing the final report. We are currently in the fourth phase of summative assessment, and so only anecdotal results can be related here.[38]

[33] Naples Archaeological Museum inv. 5465; Florence Archaeological Museum inv. 70990.

[34] For details, see www.londoncharter.org.

[35] National Science Foundation grant no. IIS-10158512.

[36] http://whc.unesco.org/en/list/907/.

[37] For a survey of recent work on the villa, see Mari 2010.

[38] Work undertaken during the first phase was largely done by Matthew Brennan, an architect and 3D modeler employed by the Virtual World Heritage Laboratory at Indiana University. The task of converting Brennan's 3D model of the site to the game engine Unity3D with all that entails (e.g., the creation of avatars and Non-playing Characters) was the responsibility of the IDIA Lab at Ball State University under the direction of John Fillwalk. In the third phase we benefited from a close collaboration with Lynne Kvapil, an archaeologist based at Xavier University who specializes in applying Problem-based Learning to archaeological education. The fourth phase of summative assessment is being conducted by Lee Nelms, a specialist in the use of virtual world technology in education.

Our goal was to test the idea that archaeological education—that is, the creation of long-term memory—could be improved by making it possible for today's students to do virtual time travel to the villa in the time of Hadrian and, once there, to engage in PBL exercises that entail playing the roles of people in the court.

Virtual worlds are computer simulations that allow physically separated users to interact, often as avatars engaged in role-playing.[39] PBL was first developed for medical education[40] and asks students to develop answers to ill-defined problems with many possible solutions. Instructors facilitate the process of problem solving instead of presenting facts in a lecture-style class.[41] PBL is new to archaeological education, and our study extended the previous work done by Kvapil 2009 while also applying virtual world technology to PBL for the first time.

We used PBL to challenge the students to solve a series of problems that were intentionally only vaguely defined, leaving it to the students, who worked together in small teams, to determine the right approach to finding the answer. One example of such a problem was: you are one of the duoviri of Ostia and are sent on an embassy to the villa, where you must persuade the emperor to make a benefaction to the city. This left it to the students to decide when to go, what to wear, to whom to talk when they arrived, what benefaction to request, and what case to make to Hadrian when admitted to his presence. In another exercise, students were asked to organize an Isiac festival on the occasion of the summer solstice. They had to choose where in the villa to hold the festival, what rites to perform, how to dress, and what to say.

Note that such exercises required the students to spatialize knowledge: by playing an avatar with the identity of an historic personage, the student not only had to behave appropriately but also learn how to walk through the villa. In the case of the second example, the students had to understand the function of the various spaces at the villa, and they had to understand the interaction of sunlight and shadow on buildings by using a solar tracker created as part of the user interface that gives the exact position of the sun in the sky for any hour of the day and any day of the year A.D. 130.

Why did we believe that such an approach could facilitate learning? This question could be answered by looking at educational research on the successful use of virtual worlds and PBL at various levels in K–16.[42] Instead let us look at the question in terms of neuroscientific research on memory.

First, one might note the obvious point that there is a close relationship between memory and learning.[43] Thus throughout his book Kandel uses the phrase "learning and memory" as a hendiadys.[44] Sometimes he is more specific and talks about learning and long-term memory. Learning involves memory, but neuroscientists have identified several kinds of memory, including, for example, episodic memory, semantic memory, short-term (or "working") memory, implicit memory, and explicit memory.[45] For learning, it is declarative long-term memory that is most important.[46] What has neuroscience taught us about how long-term memory of space operates, and how do these lessons relate to our Hadrian's Villa project?

---

[39] See Bartle 2003.

[40] Savin-Badin and Major 2004.

[41] Hmelo-Silver 2004, Hmelo-Silver and Barrows 2006.

[42] Cf. the following educational research on PBL showing that it (1) results in a higher retention rate (de Vries, Schmidt, and de Graaff 1989; Schmidt, Dauphnee, and Patel 1987); (2) offers a more effective way to develop critical-thinking and communication skills as compared to

a traditional, lecture-based model (Lieux 1996).

[43] Bahrick 2000.

[44] Cf. Kandel 2011, locations 3023, 3189, 3259, 3708, 4150, 4235, etc.

[45] Schacter, Wagner, and Buckner 2000, 630–637.

[46] Zola and Squire 2000, 486.

Pioneering work on this was done in the 1970s by John O'Keefe, who discovered that the processing and memorization of spatial information from all the senses occur in the hippocampus.[47] He furthermore showed "that the hippocampus of rats contains a . . . map of space and that the units of that map are the pyramidal cells of the hippocampus, which process information about place."[48] He called these neurons the "place cells." If we want to teach people about space, we clearly need to understand the mechanism whereby short-term memory processing of new spatial information is converted to long-term memory, or what is called long-term potentiation. Kandel, who was one of the contributors to the solution of this problem, summarized it in the following succinct, if technical, way: "neuromodulators are usually recruited to switch short-term homosynaptic plasticity into long-term heterosynaptic plasticity."[49]

In 1992, Kandel and his team identified the gene that is responsible for linking long-term potentiation in a pathway of the hippocampus and spatial memory.[50] Subsequent work showed how under repeated electrical stimulation, the brain "switch[es] a short-term, homosynaptic into long-term, heterosynaptic change."[51] As he pursued this research, Kandel worked out the key role of attention in determining when short-term memories are converted to long-term memory.[52] Fortunately for us, of all the kinds of memory he might have used in his research, he used his own earlier research on spatial mapping to address this issue. He found that people who must learn about space, such as London taxi drivers who must master the so-called "knowledge" of the enormously complex street system of London, develop larger hippocampi.[53]

The importance of space to the life of animals whose chief characteristic is precisely locomotion is clear to neuroscientists. O'Keefe wrote that "space plays a role in all our behavior. We live in it, move through it, explore it, defend it."[54] The relationship between space and human memory has been clear since the ancient Greeks. Here one thinks of the memorization technique known as mnemotechics attributed to Simonides. In the anonymous *Rhetorica ad Herennium* is a passage whose long-lasting influence down to the seventeenth century was traced by Frances Yates.[55] In it we are told that:

> Now nature herself teaches us what we should do . . . ordinary things easily slip from the memory while the striking and the novel stay longer in the mind. A sunrise, the sun's course, a sunset are marvelous to no one because they occur daily. But solar eclipses are a source of wonder because they occur seldom, and indeed are more marvelous than lunar eclipses, because these are more frequent. . . . We ought, then, to set up images of a kind that can adhere longest in memory.[56]

O'Keefe in fact found neuroscientific support for mnemotechics. He found that "many forms of explicit memory (for example, memory for people and objects) use spatial coordinates—that is, we typically remember people and events in a spatial context."[57] Kandel's work confirmed that the author of the *Rhetorica* was correct to highlight the key role of salience, or attention-grabbing

[47] Kandel 2011, location 4320.

[48] Kandel 2011, location 4320.

[49] Kandel 2011, location 4332.

[50] Kandel 2011, location 4463.

[51] Kandel 2011, location 4487.

[52] Kandel 2011, location 4555.

[53] Kandel 2011, location 4696.

[54] *Apud* Kandel 2011, location 4706.

[55] Yates 2001.

[56] *Rhet. Her.* 3.22 *apud* Yates 2001, 9–10. Cf. Mignone in this volume.

[57] Kandel 2011, location 4711.

elements, in initiating the constant stream of stimuli that result in long-term memory. In this context it is relevant to note that the first of Robert Gagné's nine instructional events is "gaining attention." And Gagné stressed the value of matching the stimulus arousing attention to the content of the lesson.[58]

Mnemotechnics gradually lost favor because it is an artificial way of linking information to space: it works by encouraging us to associate new information with specific spots in places that are well known to us. In our Hadrian's Villa project, we used the digital villa to link information to space in two *natural* ways: first as a place where its many features could be digitally restored and spatially recontextualized in an exercise that Daston and Galison would call expert image interpretation. This allowed us to go beyond de Chirico's archaeologist who simply collects random bric-a-brac. Secondly, once we finished our digital restoration, we used the resulting product as a learning device so that our students could benefit from what Kandel called "the binding force of memory" by going on a trip of virtual time travel to recapture the lost memories of a culturally significant place. But this was not to be a matter of the kind of usual knowledge acquisition that occurs in K–16 education but rather a hybrid that also included a large measure of episodic memory formation.[59] This occurred because the learning device we created involved historic role-playing by avatars in the virtual world. So students did not simply travel to the court of Hadrian at Tivoli; they became part of the court.

Episodic memory is autonoetic; that is, it involves "conscious recollection of personal happenings and events from one's personal past. . . . At the core of autonoetic awareness is a sense of a personal self and the subjective experiences associated with that self."[60] In the virtual world, history became personal and part not only of our cultural but also of our individual memory. This made the study of history more engaging, and there is some neuroscientific research that suggests that it resulted in more effective learning since knowledge encoded in reference to the self is more likely to be remembered.[61]

How this worked can be illustrated with the exercise of playing the role of a priest of Isis in a ceremony on the summer solstice. Following the lead of a recently published book on the villa,[62] we placed the sanctuary of Isis in the rotunda of Roccabruna (fig. 10.5). In the statue niche at the end of the main axis was placed a statue of Isis from the villa, now in the Capitoline Museums. We made a state model of the statue and then the restoration model seen in figure 10.5. Finally, by a happy coincidence that had nothing to do with the recommendation of the author of the *Rhetorica ad Herennium*, we studied the lighting of the rotunda in relation to an odd feature of the building's design: several conduits punctuate the cupola to focus light from the outside on certain spots of the interior dome. Mangurian and Ray speculated that at least one of these conduits may have been oriented to align with the path of the sun through the sky on the summer solstice.[63] Working with physicist-archaeastronomer David Dearborn, we tested and confirmed this hypothesis by calculating the exact time of the summer solstice in the reign of Hadrian and made it possible to simulate the solstice with our virtual world software. Figure 10.5 shows the dramatic effect of the setting sun illuminating the statue of the goddess at sunset on the summer solstice of A.D. 130.

Of course, we did not tell the students where the sanctuary of Isis was located, only that research suggests that there was an Isaeum somewhere on the site. All but one of the student PBL groups were able to find the right spot by exploring the virtual world of the villa while using the solar tracker to

[58] Gagné 1965.

[59] Cf. Wheeler 2000.

[60] Moscovitch 2000, 611.

[61] Moscovitch 2000, 619.

[62] De Franceschini and Veneziano 2011.

[63] Mangurian and Ray 1993.

look for alignments between the light of the setting sun on the solstice and the built environment. Anecdotal evidence collected from the students shows that the experience of seeing the sun light up the area in and above the statue niche in Roccabruna at sunset on the summer solstice was a salient and memorable experience.

In conclusion, in this chapter I have tried to show how virtual archaeology exploits digital technology as a new form of external memory. The products of virtual archaeology are images that show either the current or earlier state of the archaeological artifact. In both the act of creation and of perception these are interpreted, interactive, dynamic images that do not sacrifice accuracy to objectivity. Very often we arrive not at a single image but several variants reflecting the different visions of contributing experts. Our responsibility as keepers of memory is to present all valid interpretations of which we are aware and to make available to our users not only the images but also the paradata—or the process of evidence-gathering and thinking—that went into making them.

Finally, besides passive publication of interactive images, we also engage our users in the evocation of their own episodic memories through the use of virtual world technology. This technology exploits the fact that spatialization facilitates learning and memory, and virtual world technology allows us to reintegrate the individual 3D models from a site into their original context. Immersed in a dynamic, interactive image of a lost world of the past, viewers become participants in what Kandel described as "mental time travel provided by memory," and they can make the archaeologist's professional memory of the cultural past a part of their own personal stock of memories, which is to say a part of their own sense of self-identity. In this respect, we might consider virtual world technology an updated form of mnemotechnics.

EPILOGUE

11 ◆ Memorials and Their Voices*

Daniel Libeskind

Two days ago [on 12 October 2011] I opened the Military History Museum in Dresden, and I had to make a speech. As I spoke spontaneously, I finished with an Emily Dickinson poem that I had memorized:

> Water, is taught by thirst.
> Land—by the Oceans passed.
> Transport—by throe—
> Peace—by its battles told—
> Love, by Memorial Mold—
> Birds, by the Snow.
>   (Poem 135, 1859)

And I think it was particularly interesting to have a poet summarize what is really the intent of architecture because I think architecture does deal with memory, the city, and spiritual aspects that are not often associated with stone, steel, and glass. Yet, being in Rome, in this beautiful place, I am with people who have studied in depth that connection between history and the human desire to understand, to transcend, to be part of the past, and at the same time be part of something that is still to come. I have put together a few of my past projects to share with you, projects that I believe deal with the issue of memory. Memory is not a footnote in my work—I think all architecture is guided by memory, informing our sense of space, of orientation, and of our relationships with one another.

The first building I completed opened in 1998. It was the Felix Nussbaum house (fig. 11.1) in Osnabrück, a museum dedicated to the painter who lived there, Felix Nussbaum. In German, I called it *Das Museum ohne Ausgang*, "The Museum without an Exit," because there was no exit from Nussbaum's life. He was a Jewish artist caught up in the horrors that began in 1933, and unfortunately he did not survive. He was deported on the last train to Auschwitz while trying to document, with his paintings, what was happening in the world around him. In 1933, he had been in Rome, with a Prix de Rome, but the government had taken the prize away. He had then moved to Belgium but was arrested and deported to a camp in France. He managed to escape and make his way back to Belgium, and he lived there with his wife in hiding, in an attic, until they were discovered by Nazi soldiers. I was able to design the extension of the museum directly across from the great ancient walls of Osnabrück, Nussbaum's hometown. The Schlikker'sche Villa is part of the museum complex—it was one of the first headquarters of the Nazi Party in Germany. Nearby is the Kunsthistorische Museum, and around the corner, in a strange collision of vectors relating

*Transcribed by Sarah Davies from Daniel Libeskind's concluding address; edited for publication by S. Davies and K. Galinsky.

Fig. 11.1. Felix Nussbaum Museum Extension, Osnabrück, Germany (photo Bitter Bredt).

to the site, is Roland Strauss's synagogue, which was burned down during the war. These were the architectural lines in Nussbaum's life, evident in a moving self-portrait, in which he shows himself holding his identity card, walls behind him (fig. 11.2). I decided that the museum project should be about the look in that portrait. That look, and what Nussbaum wrote about his work—that if anyone ever found it, he wanted it to be treated as if a message in a bottle, thrown into the ocean of history. He wrote that the message should be read, and lessons learned from it, because it has a story to be told.

What was so different about the small-scale Osnabrück museum was that it was a public project, dedicated to a single individual and his life, deportation, and death. In the courtyards, it is possible to sense a history that is only partially known, with pieces still left to be discovered. I tried to create a series of spaces that travel slowly through a small area with three structures: one wooden, one concrete, and the third connecting them via a metal bridge called the Nussbaum *Gang*, or "Walk." Nussbaum painted while he was in hiding, in an attic with his wife Felka Platek, and he was thus in very close proximity to his paintings, which are very detailed and dense with impending death. I wanted those feelings to be part of the experience of the museum, which is intended to seem close and personal—more like an attic than a set of expansive galleries. And so the Nussbaum *Gang* is really a space that opens the gap between the known paintings of the artist and those that are yet to be rediscovered. There's also a collision and a connection, without hiding the differences, between the Kunsthistorische Museum, which is a nineteenth-century museum, and this metal bridge. When I designed the bridge, and I gave it the subtitle "For the future knowledge of Nussbaum," people

Fig. 11.2. Felix Nussbaum, Self-portrait
*(1943), Felix-Nussbaum-Haus Osnabrück
mit der Sammlung der Niedersächsischen
Sparkassenstiftung (© 2013 Artists Rights
Society [ARS], New York / VG Bild-
Kunst, Bonn).*

thought it was a waste of time since there was not going to be any "future knowledge" of Nussbaum. But as a result of this museum being built, two collections of Nussbaum's work were acquired: one from Tel Aviv and the other from New York, in which his signature had been painted over.

Recently, I was able to plan another building for the museum, in order to connect the complex more emphatically to the Kunsthistorische Museum and add a café and auditorium. The windows might seem slightly odd, but they are designed to look as if the geometry of the three other structures—those colliding lifetimes—pierced the building, and a negative light and space was left open between them. From the street, the building is like a blank canvas—the largest unpaintable panorama of Nussbaum's life. It's a large, concrete building, with a very narrow doorway. I had sunflowers, Nussbaum's favorite flower and frequent subject in his paintings, planted in front. Originally, the city authorities did not like this idea because sunflowers die and are not necessarily attractive in the winter, but I thought that such a transformation was the point. Schoolchildren have since created a Sunflower Society in order to learn about what happened in their city, to all of history during those years. It's quite a popular phenomenon now, and it has created a network of young people communicating about the city's dark past, its future, and how these both relate to the Osnabrück in which Felix Nussbaum spent his childhood.

Just a few years after the Nussbaum Museum, I opened the Jewish Museum in Berlin (fig. 11.3). The issue here was not to design a museum but to design a space that subverted the original concept, of creating a *Jüdische Abteilung*, a "Jewish Department," as part of a larger municipal museum complex. I thought it wrong to compartmentalize Jewish history and to use the term *Abteilung* to do so. For *Abteilung* was the word used by Eichmann as a euphemism for the deportation and extermination of Jews. So I believed that I should do everything possible to make the building

Fig. 11.3. Jewish Museum, Berlin: aerial view (photo Günter Schneider).

respond by radiating the hidden, invisible Berlin—a Berlin in which the story of the Jewish people is a long one, and not just one with a recent past.

The building took many years to complete. It went through six different governments, the reunification of Germany, and it had five different names. It is a museum organized around not only the apparent but also the less apparent: the visible and invisible, the audible and its echoing. And the new structure is connected in an unusual way to the baroque-style Altbau, which was the original location of the museum on Lindenstraße. The Lindenstraße curves eastward in this location—it is the spot where the great architect Hans Scharoun changed the course of the street in his reconstruction of postwar Berlin. I violated city ordinance here with my building and had to get special permission in order to have the new museum extend beyond the façade of the historic Altbau and point to this location on Lindenstraße, a marker of the transformation of Berlin.

The museum consists of an area known as The Void, the Holocaust Towers, and behind the main building, an addition made a few years ago, named the Sukkah. This last is a space for public events and gatherings based on a number of concepts. Its plan goes beyond the history of Berlin, the city streets, or the visual elements of the city. On a structural level, it is comparable to the unfinished opera by Schoenberg (who lived in Berlin)—*Moses and Aaron*. The third libretto of this opera has no music. And I liked the thought that it could not be completed as a result of the *aporia* in the conversation between Moses and God, and in the search for meaning in history. Like the opera, the museum could be completed only in the *Gedenkbuch*, in the Book of Memory, and through the echoes of the shuffling footsteps of museum visitors.

In this way, I used many "meta-architectural" concepts, creating a program for the museum around the space of the *Einbahnstraße*, Walter Benjamin's beautiful text that serves as a sort of Berlin topography. I wanted to bring back this map of the invisible Berlin because the museum

Fig.11.4. Jewish Museum, Berlin: detail (photo Michele Nastasi).

deals not only with the physical remains of Berlin architecture but also with the spaces created in
the mind and soul of the city. I also drew inspiration from the poetry of Paul Celan. In the poem
"Oranienburger Straße No. 1"—the address is directly south of the museum's location—Celan
actually references another layer, of Prussian history. For the site for the museum originally housed,
in the eighteenth century, the Prussian Court of Justice building. So I used unusual means to
inform the spatial, geometric, and functional structure of the museum, creating an overture but
without a bridge between the Altbau and the Neubau. Instead, visitors travel underground; they
explore Berlin in a more visceral way, through acoustics and temperature. I wanted to evoke the
sense of fragments of a lost world. And so the Holocaust Towers and The Void run in an interrupted path throughout the museum. The Void itself cannot be accessed like an atrium and was
difficult to get approved since it does not contain an exhibit, is not heated in the winter or cooled
in the summer, and serves no ostensible purpose. Instead, I thought it important to have a space
simply for emptiness—a space not functionally or rationally accessible but very much present in
everyone's experience of Berlin.

The same was true for the Garden of Exile, which distorts the urban space with its geometry
and provides a different angle from which to view the city. There are forty-nine columns in the
garden, filled with earth and fed by water, with plants growing from the tops. It's a symbolic space
because the central column contains the earth of Jerusalem, and the other forty-eight—in a reference to the year 1948—contain the earth of Berlin. Moving from here to the main staircase inside,
one is connected to a future, to an open space, and a sense of hope because buildings cannot only
deal with the irreversibility of catastrophe.

There are no traditional windows in the museum. Instead, there are slices cut through the walls
(fig. 11.4), forming an unfolded map of the Jewish star that also exists in the plan of the building

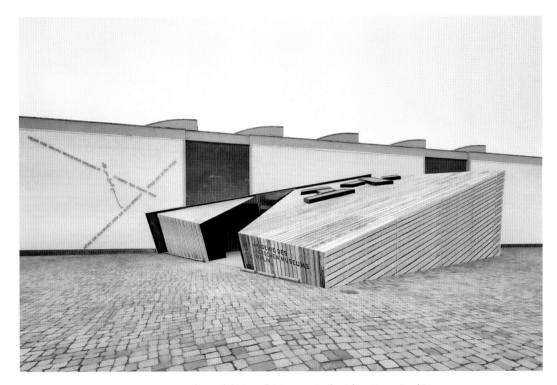

Fig. 11.5. Academy of the Jewish Museum, Berlin (photo Bitter Bredt).

itself. I wanted the contours of this unwrapped star to shine like intermarriage lines, connecting individuals, like Rahel Varnhagen, the *grande dame* of Berlin who ran the Jewish literary salon that brought German literature into focus, with Friedrich Schleiermacher, who is buried in alignment with one of the lines of the building, or E.T.A. Hoffmann and Jean-Paul Salon, or Mies van der Rohe. And so I drew these marriage lines, expanded them, and made them radiate throughout the building, across a void of memory, which is in some ways inaccessible but in others is detectable. There's nothing in the space, but at the same time there's everything in it. And I am happy to say that this museum has succeeded in becoming a building not just for the Jewish people but also for Germany and a whole new generation, a future that should know something about the story it can tell. For it is not simply a didactic museum. Visitors are given the chance to make interpretations as they wish since there is no singular message. The addition of the glass court of the Sukkah has testified to the continuing expansion and resonance of the museum—one of the most visited in Berlin, which is a city with an impressive, world-class roster of museums.

The Jewish Museum project has also taught me that it can take only a single building to change the character of an entire city and the manner in which that city is perceived. There is now a construction project happening across the street, in the Blumenhalle, a 1960s flower market, to convert the area into an academy for the museum, with an auditorium, library, and office space (fig. 11.5). It is slated to open next year. I designed the addition to the original structure as a tilted cube passing through the old building's frame, like a crate of lost knowledge having come crashing down. The crate in turn references the shapes repeated throughout the museum across the street—in the Garden of Exile and the Sukkah. There will also be a text carved across the façade of the academy building—a text that I selected from Maimonides, originally written in Arabic and Judeo-Arabic, and then translated into Hebrew, German, and English. It reads: "Hear the truth—believe the truth,

Fig. 11.6. Imperial War Museum, Manchester, UK: view from across ship canal (photo Bitter Bredt).

from those who tell it to you." It is an interesting thought—that there is a universal truth, which cannot be bound by barriers, even cultural ones.

And part of this truth is trauma—something that goes beyond the voices of a particular history. We have all lived in the twentieth century, and we are what we are—we have become something— through the trauma of catastrophes. And this observation brings me to my next project—the Imperial War Museum in Manchester (fig. 11.6). I had a chance here to base a building on the idea that the globe of the modern world has been shattered. I took this concept of a shattered globe and re-erected the fragments in all directions to build the shape of the museum, with segments like metallic shards, directed vertically, horizontally, on the water, and in the exhibition spaces themselves. Entering the museum, visitors thus view the city beyond while looking through the open web of the building. Outside, they can see the waterfront area of Manchester—an area that was severely devastated during the war, became a place that people did not want to live in or come visit, but has since come back to life and experienced new development, in great part because of the new museum there.

For this museum, I probably created the smallest door to a large museum, simply because I felt that when it comes to the concept of conflict, it is not merely something seen on television or read about in news articles—it is something that is felt on the scale of a single human being, one at a time. Upon entering, the visitor is confronted by a vast, enveloping panorama of fires, smoke, and a multitude of sensory experiences. For this is not so much a museum filled with weaponry but a series of large-scale sound and light installations. The space itself is slightly curved, like the earth, and its horizon guides the visitor through the ambient darkness around these video presentations. They are divided into thematic zones—and I designed the space to allow this—with themes like "Women and War" and "Children and War." These themes center upon the idea that any group of people, even children, could create such presentations, using selections from their family albums. This then highlights the fact that, just around the Manchester area, there are tens of thousands of people who have fought or who are currently fighting in wars. And so behind the video projections, visitors can enter silos and interact with artifacts—for example, handling the heavy weight of a Gatling gun, which teenagers would somehow carry during World War I.

There is also a temporary exhibition space, at the point where the vertically placed segment of the building cuts through the horizontal. Here, artworks that have been produced during times of war and conflict are displayed. It is truly amazing to see how much art and how many things of beauty have been drawn out of traumatic events. There is a quote from Winston Churchill that lingered with me throughout the Manchester project. It was: "We shall draw from the heart of suffering itself the means of inspiration and survival." I found this very compelling. The idea then is that perhaps there will never be a time without conflict, and that we as human beings need to know how to steer the evils of conflict into a better place and be able to learn from the past. In some ways, this is a pessimistic view, but I believe it remains relevant in a world in which conflicts are ongoing.

This view—that conflict cannot and should not be hidden—also influenced my design of another museum, the Military History Museum in Dresden (fig. 11.7). The original building in this location was an armory, built in the 1870s and subsequently serving as the Saxony Military Museum, later as a Nazi museum, a Soviet museum, and lastly an East German museum. It sits in the Albertstadt and overlooks the historic district, in what was once the military quarter of Dresden. In 1989, after the reunification of Germany, there was some debate about what to do with this immense building. It was the largest museum in the country at the time, measuring a total of about 95,000 square meters. When I first visited, the building was in ruins, the front was covered up, and the windows were boarded. Inside, the collections were a jumble of Soviet-era kitsch. But even then, I thought that there was a possibility of bringing back the old armory in a radically new way. Other designs for the project had suggested a simple update, placing a new building directly behind the old. I broke with this concept and decided to highlight rather than to obscure the need, especially in a democracy, to expose the military rather than to hide it behind walls of the past. And so I cut through the façade of the original building and added a wedgelike formation that disrupts the rigid, neoclassical lines of the original and creates a very different space, without the solidity of columns and arches.

The wider context is of course Dresden, that beautiful city on the Elbe that was completely obliterated in the bombings of 1945. But it is not a straightforward story—it has many layers. For example, in the diaries of Victor Klemperer, we get a very poignant perspective, of Victor and his wife praying for the bombs to come, if only to bring an escape from their life of hiding in fear of deportation. I wanted to convey this complexity in the structure of the new building, by adding a wedge to represent an aerial vector slicing through the order and symmetry of the armory. The

Fig. 11.7. Military History Museum, Dresden, Germany (photo by Bitter Bredt).

angle of this vector also has meaning. It points to the stadium, creating a 41-degree angle—the same angle at which the Allied bombs fell onto Dresden. Within the larger wedge, there are then smaller versions of the same angle, crisscrossing the space to create splintered windows. In this way, the horizontal plane of an ordered, chronological history is thus interrupted, again and again, just like the city, and Germany as a whole, which were dislocated, transformed, and reoriented many times over.

The Dresden museum is a space that neither celebrates war nor acclaims peace. As part of the *Bundeswehr*, the institution where soldiers come to learn about military history, it projects a degree of ambivalence. And the design reflects this ambivalence, openly presenting the visitor with issues of tradition and the ways in which traditions can be, and have been, subverted. At the top of the building, the visitor emerges from an elevator onto a sloping and doubly tilted floor. It's a slightly disorienting experience, and it leads to a space called the Dresden *Blick*, or the Dresden "View." In this space there are images of the destructions of several cities—Coventry, Rotterdam, Wielun—and then of Dresden itself. Having viewed these destructions, the visitor stands at the end, at a point that extends up and out, beyond the line of the museum below. From here, the visitor can view the panorama of the rebuilt Dresden but only through the grid of a metallic grille. And so the visitor is caged and pulled in several directions at once: outward to the city, upward to the sky, and downward by vertigo. It is a very dramatic space, one that can truly be understood only through personal experience, via the physical language of architecture. One thus travels through the metal, steel, and

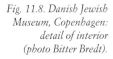

*Fig. 11.8. Danish Jewish
Museum, Copenhagen:
detail of interior
(photo Bitter Bredt).*

glass structure in what becomes an adventure of the mind, turning away from the more authoritarian ideals of society and reaching an opaque space at the very apex of the building. Military history is never an easy subject, but the Dresden museum was perhaps the first to not celebrate war—and, daringly, to present the Shoah—the Holocaust—as part of military history.

My design for the Danish Jewish Museum in Copenhagen also deals with the Shoah, incorporating the Hebrew word *mitzvah* as a central concept. *Mitzvah*, or "good deed," is a term with important symbolic and spatial value in Talmudic literature since each individual letter carries special meaning. I worked these symbols into the structure and lighting of the building, as a reference to the intersections of history and Jewish culture in Denmark. During the war, the Danes, by a stroke of almost inexplicable good luck, were able to save most of their Jewish population by putting them on boats to Sweden. This *mitzvah* stands out as a rare occurrence in wartime Europe, for only two other countries—Albania and Bulgaria—were able to save portions of their Jewish populations, and to a much lesser extent. So I wanted to highlight the good deed accomplished in Copenhagen, using Talmudic text inside the library of the museum. The library itself is the Royal Library—a new building constructed over the former boathouse of Danish King Christian IV. In this location, then, there resides a deep set of historical connections: between the boats of a king, the books and sacred writing of a library, and the boats that saved the Jews of Denmark.

Throughout, the structure is made of wood set in panels at different angles (fig. 11.8). These panels leave an impression of rocking back and forth in a rowboat. Ahead, there seems to be a horizon, but then the windows are at angles, and they leave traces of light at different points, providing a sense of motion and hinting at the continuity and integration of Jewish people in Denmark. For rather than a story of destruction, Denmark presents us with a story of integration—both the Tuborg and Carlsberg beer companies are Jewish establishments. The museum allows the visitor to reenact a series of good deeds, with the latest being the government's funding of a building intended mainly to spark dialogue about what anyone can do when faced with dark times.

The Danish museum has a diminutive entryway, introduced by a small piazza, which looks across the street to the grand Parliament Building. With its rather unassuming entry, the Danish museum is similar to the one in Berlin, whose small doorway was first opened to the public on 11 September 2001. That morning, after the opening, I remember commenting that I no longer needed to think closely about communicating a particular history because the public could now enter the museum and see it for themselves. But by 2:30 that afternoon, the doors of the museum had closed again, for a period of three days, because New York had been attacked and there was so much uncertainty. It was really at that time that it became clear to me that nothing is ever disconnected. For I was ultimately the one chosen to design the overall rebuild project at the site of Ground Zero—a site that is not just about the real estate and physical infrastructure but is also about profound and powerful memories and the foundation for new ones.

I made a number of decisions in the design for Ground Zero that differed from other ideas at the time. I did not want to rebuild the towers as they originally were or to keep the structures to a low profile. Instead, I decided not to build anything on the building sites where people had died. This left half of the 16-acre site open, pushing the new constructions to the periphery. I designed the new towers to form a crown, reflecting that of the Statue of Liberty, which faces the site from the south. I thereby sought a symbolic encounter between a memorial for 9/11 and a resurgence of life in the city.

The project consists of a vast array of structures: a museum, seven towers, the footprints of the old World Trade Center, and a transportation hub (fig. 11.9). Tower 1, Freedom Tower, will be the tallest, at 1,776 feet high—a symbolic number in the timeline of American history. Below these structures, there are additional, below-ground levels of complexity: subway trains running and the remains from 9/11 left deep in the ground, some 75 feet down. The design highlights the contrast between these subterranean levels, of the memorial and the very bedrock of New York, with the continuing energy of the city, its business and civic infrastructures as well as its need for cultural and green space. In many ways, I only came to fully understand the site of Ground Zero when I visited it and went down to the level of the bedrock. For it is there that one can see the scars where the buildings collapsed, where three thousand people from ninety different countries lost their lives. And then there is the slurry wall, which functions as an immense dam, holding back the Hudson River. Miraculously, on 9/11, it held, keeping the subways of New York from becoming flooded. I decided to keep the slurry wall as it was, as part of the memorial, a testament to the quality of construction in New York and a stark witness to the catastrophe of 9/11.

Fig. 11.9. Design for Ground Zero Memorial by D. Libeskind (image Silverstein Properties).

I also suggested the idea of waterfalls—with a sense of a river rushing in—to mark the footprints of the towers. These waterfalls now add a uniquely intimate, soothing, and yet powerful incorporation of nature to the experience of the memorial. There is the sound of the water yet also the social experience of hearing people talking, and even laughing. These human sounds then fade as one nears the edge, and the water gets louder where names of the deceased are listed. And around these waterfalls is an added public space, shaped by angles of sunlight coming through the streets and creating a wedge of light that marks the two times—8:46 and 10:28—when the planes struck the towers. A central skylight in the PATH terminal designed by Calatrava allows this wedge of light to pass through, into the subway. And so the entire complex is in many ways a memorial written in the symbolic rhythms of nature—a place that is memorable rather than horrifying to visit and signals the ways in which New York as a whole has changed.

I was an immigrant to New York. I came from Poland, by boat. And I had that iconic experience, on the Hudson River, first seeing the Statue of Liberty through the mists—I did not relate to the city from the air. For these reasons, my designs for Ground Zero incorporated a particular, quintessential New York, and American, experience. Looking from Ellis Island, the skyline will have a new proof of liberty, of ambition and struggles. It is a project that, like the others, is ultimately about memory—the values we share and the final victory of life and hope over death and destruction.

Bibliography

Adamo Muscettola, S., "Per una riedizione dell'arco di Traiano a Benevento: appunti sul fregio trionfale," *Prospettiva* 67 (1992) 2–16.

Alcock, S., *Archaeologies of the Greek Past: Landscape, Monuments, and Memories* (Cambridge 2002).

Anders, J., Joyce, S., Love, B., Raussert, W., and Wait, A. R., "Introduction" in *Remembering and Forgetting: Memory in Images and Texts*, ed. W. Raussert, B. Love, J. Anders, and S. Joyce (Bielefeld 2010) 7–20.

Angelicoussis, E., "The Panel Reliefs of Marcus Aurelius," *Mitteilungen des Deutschen Archäologischen Instituts (Rom)* 91 (1984) 167–178.

Anguissola, A., "Roman Copies of Myron's Discobolus," *Journal of Roman Archaeology* 18 (2005) 317–335.

———, "Parole e contesto nel discorso pliniano sull'imitazione artistica," *Rendiconti. Accademia Nazionale dei Lincei* ser. 9, 17 (2006) 555–572.

———, "Fama, tema, forma: fortuna antica e moderna del Discobolo di Mirone," *Prospettiva* 128 (2007) 26–42.

———, *Difficillima imitatio. Immagine e lessico delle copie tra Grecia e Roma* (Rome 2012a).

———, "Greek Originals and Roman Copies" in *Oxford Bibliographies Online: Classics*, ed. D. Clayman (New York 2012b) 1–45, www.oxfordbibliographies.com.

Ash, R., *Tacitus: Histories*, vol. 2 (Cambridge 2007).

Assmann, A., *Erinnerungsräume. Formen und Wandlungen des kulturellen Gedächtnisses* (Munich 1999) = *Cultural Memory and Western Civilization. Arts of Memory* (Cambridge 2011).

———, "From 'Canon to Archive'," in Olick, Vinitzky-Seroussi, and Levy 2011, 334–337.

Assmann, J., *Das kulturelle Gedächtnis. Schrift, Erinnerung, und politische Identität in frühen Hochkulturen* (Munich 1992).

———, *La memoria culturale. Scrittura, ricordo e identità politica nelle grandi civiltà antiche* (Turin 1997).

———, *Religion und kulturelles Gedächtnis. Zehn Studien* (Munich 2000).

———, *Religion and Cultural Memory: Ten Studies* (Palo Alto 2006).

———, *Cultural Memory and Early Civilization* (Cambridge 2011).

Baddeley, A., Eysenck, M. W., and Anderson, M. C., *Memory* (Hove 2009).

Badian, E., "Caepio and Norbanus: Notes on the Decade 100–90 B.C.," *Historia* 6 (1957) 318–346.

———, "The Early Historians," in *Latin Historians*, ed. T. A. Dorey (London 1966) 1–38.

———, "The Death of Saturninus: Studies in Chronology and Prosopography," *Chiron* 14 (1984) 101–147.

Bahrick, H., "Long-term Memory Maintenance of Knowledge," in Tulving and Craik 2000, 347–362.

Baier, T., "Autobiographie in der späten römischen Republik," in *Antike Autobiographien: Werke—Epochen—Gattungen*, ed. M. Reichel (Cologne 2005) 123–142.

Barchiesi, A., "Learned Eyes: Poets, Viewers, Image Makers," in *The Cambridge Companion to the Age of Augustus*, ed. K. Galinsky (Cambridge 2005) 281–305.

———, "Roman Perspectives on the Greeks," in *The Oxford Handbook of Hellenic Studies*, ed. G. Boys-Stones, B. Graziosi, and P. Vasunia (Oxford 2009) 98–113.

Bardon, H., *La littérature latine inconnue,* vol. 1: *L'époque républicaine* (Paris 1952).

Bartle, R., *Designing Virtual Worlds* (Indianapolis 2003).

Bartlett, F., *Remembering: A Study in Experimental and Social Psychology* (Cambridge 1997; orig. publ. 1932).

Bartman, E., "Sculptural Collecting and Display in the Private Realm," in *Roman Art in the Private Sphere*, ed. E. Gazda (Ann Arbor 1991) 71–88.

———, *Ancient Sculptural Copies in Miniature* (Leiden, New York, and Cologne 1992).

Bastide, R., "From the African Religions of Brazil: Toward a Sociology of the Interpenetration of Civilizations," in Olick, Vinitzky-Seroussi, and Levy 2011, 157–162.

Beacham, R. C., *Spectacle Entertainments of Early Imperial Rome* (New Haven 1999).

Beard, M., "The Triumph of the Absurd: Roman Street Theatre," in *Rome the Cosmopolis*, ed. C. Edwards and G. Woolf (Cambridge 2003) 21–42.

———, *The Roman Triumph* (Cambridge, MA 2007).

Beard, M., North, J., and Price, S., *Religions of Rome* (Cambridge 1998).

Beck, H., and Bol, P. C., eds., *Polykletforschungen* (Berlin 1993).

Beck, H., Bol, P. C., and Bückling, M., eds., *Polyklet. Der Bildhauer der griechischen Klassik* (Frankfurt am Main 1990).

Beck, H., and Walter, U., *Die frühen römischen Historiker*, vol. 1 (Darmstadt 2001).

Bell, A., *Spectacular Power in the Greek and Roman City* (Oxford 2004).

Berenson, B., *The Arch of Constantine and the Decline of Form* (London 1954).

Bergmann, B., "The Roman House as Memory Theater," *Art Bulletin* 76.2 (1994) 225–256.

Bergmann, B., and Kondoleon, C., eds., *The Art of Ancient Spectacle*. CASVA Studies in the History of Art, Symposium Papers (Washington, DC 1999).

Bernstein, F., "Complex Rituals: Games and Processions in Republican Rome," in *A Companion to Roman Religion*, ed. J. Rüpke (Malden, MA 2007) 222–234.

Bessone, F., *La Tebaide di Stazio; epica e potere* (Pisa and Rome 2011).

Betts, E., "Towards a Multisensory Experience of Movement in the City of Rome," in *Rome, Ostia, Pompeii: Movement and Space*, ed. R. Laurence and D. J. Newsome (Oxford 2011) 118–134.

Bildkatalog der Skulpturen des Vatikanischen Museums, vol. 2: *Museo Pio Clementino. Cortile Ottagono*, ed. B. Andreae (Berlin and New York 1998).

Blanqui, A., *Textes Choisis* (Paris 1971).

Blänsdorf, J., *Fragmenta Poetarum Latinorum*, 3rd ed. (Stuttgart 1995).

Bloch, M., "The Past and the Present in the Present," *Man* 12.2 (1977) 278–292.

Boatwright, M., *Hadrian and the City of Rome* (Princeton 1987).

Bodel, J., "Monumental Villas and Villa Monuments," *Journal of Roman Archaeology* 10 (1997) 5–35.

Bohn, W., "Apollinaire and de Chirico: The Making of the Mannequins," *Comparative Literature* 27.2 (1975) 153–165.

Bolívar, S., *Doctrina del Libertador* (Caracas 1985).

Bonadeo, A., *L'Hercules Epitrapezios Novi Vindicis. Intr. e comm. a Stazio. silvae 4,6* (Naples 2010).

Boschung, D., *Antike Grabaltäre aus den Nekropolen Roms* (Bern 1987).

Boyer, M. C., "The City of Collective Memory," in Olick, Vinitzky-Seroussi, and Levy 2011, 378–381.

Boyer, P., and Wertsch, J., eds., *Memory in Mind and Culture* (Cambridge 2009).

Bradley, M., *Colour and Meaning in Ancient Rome* (Cambridge 2011).

———, Rev. of R. Panzanelli, E. D. Schmidt, and K. Lapatin, eds., *The Color of Life: Polychromy in Sculpture from Antiquity to the Present* (Los Angeles 2008) in *Bryn Mawr Classical Review* 2009.04.5, http://bmcr.brynmawr.edu/2009/2009-04-55.html.

Brenk, B., "Spolia from Constantine to Charlemagne: Aesthetics versus Ideology," *Dumbarton Oaks Papers* 41 (1987) 103–109.

Brilliant, R., "The Arch of Septimius Severus in the Roman Forum," *Memoirs of the American Academy in Rome* 29 (1967) 5–271.

———, "Temporal Aspects in Late Roman Art," *L'Arte* 10 (1970) 64–87.

———, *Visual Narratives: Storytelling in Etruscan and Roman Art* (Ithaca 1984).

———, "Let the Trumpets Roar! The Roman Triumph," in Bergmann and Kondoleon 1999, 221–229.

———, "Roman Copies: Degrees of Authenticity," *Source* 14.2 (2005) 19–27.

Brizzi, G., "*Honos et uirtus, Fortuna Huiusce Diei*. Idéologies et propagande au dernier siècle de la République," in *État et société aux deux derniers siècles de la république romaine. Hommage à François Hinard*, ed. Y. le Bohec (Paris 2010).

Burke, P., "History as Social Memory," in *Memory: History, Culture, and the Mind*, ed. T. Butler (New York 1989) 97–113.

Cain, H.-U., "Copie di *mirabilia* greci," in *I Greci. Storia cultura arte società*, ed. S. Settis, vol. 2.3 (Turin 1998) 1221–1244.

Camps, W. A., "A Second Note on the Structure of the *Aeneid*," *Classical Quarterly* 53 (1959) 53–56.

———, *An Introduction to Virgil's Aeneid* (London 1969).

Cancik, H., "Rome as a Sacral Landscape: Varro and the End of Republican Religion in Rome," *Visible Religion* 4/5 (1985–86) 250–265.

Candau, J. M., "Republican Rome: Autobiography and Political Struggles," in *Political Autobiographies and Memoirs in Antiquity: A Brill Companion*, ed. G. Marasco (Leiden 2011) 121–159.

Canobbio, A., *M. Valerii Martialis. Epigrammaton liber quintus* (Naples 2011).

Carandini, A., *Giornale di scavo: pensieri sparsi di un archeologo* (Turin 2000).

———, *La casa di Augusto dai "Lupercalia" al natale* (Rome and Bari 2008).

Carcaterra, A., *Storia dell'Aventino* (Rome 1946).

Carney, T. F., *A Biography of C. Marius* (Assen 1961).

Carruthers, M., "*Varietas*: A Word of Many Colours," *Poetica: Zeitschrift für Sprach- und Literaturwissenschaft* (Munich 2009) 33–54.

Casey, E. S., "Perceiving and Remembering," *The Review of Metaphysics* 32.3 (1979) 407–436.

———, *Remembering: A Phenomenological Study* (Bloomington 2000).

Cassirer, E., *An Essay on Man: An Introduction to a Philosophy of Human Culture* (New York 1953).

Castelli, E., *Martyrdom and Memory: Early Christian Culture Making* (New York 2004).

Cerutti, S. M., "The Location of the Houses of Cicero and Clodius and the *Porticus Catuli* on the Palatine Hill in Rome," *American Journal of Philology* 118 (1997) 417–426.

Chassignet, M., *Les origines de Caton* (Paris 1986).

———, *L'annalistique romaine*, vol. 1: *Les annales des pontifes et l'annalistique ancienne* (Paris 1996).

———, *L'annalistique romaine*, vol. 3: *L'annalistique récente, l'autobiographie politique* (Paris 2004).

Chávez a Roma (Montesacro), YouTube video, 1:25:18, from a video televised by arcoiris.tv of the 16 October 2005 visit of Hugo Chávez, posted by "illupetto," 20 May 2011, http://youtu.be/QiuNb0UpXBY.

Chávez, H., "Discurso del Presidente de la República Bolivariana de Venezuela, Hugo Chávez Frías, con Montivo de su Visita al Monte Sacro," in *Selección de Discursos del Presidente de la República Bolivariana de Venezuela*, ed. H. Chávez Frías, 7.7 (Caracas 2005) 521–536.

Claridge, A., *Rome: An Archaeological Guide*, 2nd ed. (Oxford 2010).

Clark, A., *Divine Qualities: Cult and Community in Republican Rome* (Oxford 2007).

Clarke, J. R., *Art in the Lives of Ordinary Romans: Visual Representation and Non-elite Viewers in Italy, 100 B.C.–A.D. 315* (Berkeley, Los Angeles, and London 2003).

Coarelli, F., *Il foro romano: periodo archaico* (Rome 1983).

———, *Il Campo Marzio: dalle origini alla fine della repubblica* (Rome 1997).

———, *Rome and Environs: An Archaeological Guide* (Berkeley 2007).

Coarelli, F., and Sauron, G., "La tête Petini. Contribution à l'approche méthodologique du néo-atticisme," *Mélanges de l'École française de Rome, Antiquité* 90 (1978) 705–751.

Corbeill, A., *Nature Embodied: Gesture in Ancient Rome* (Princeton 2003).

Coleman, J., *Ancient and Medieval Memories: Studies in the Reconstruction of the Past* (Cambridge 1992).

Confino, A., "Collective Memory and Cultural History: Problems of Method," *American Historical Review* 102 (1997) 1386–1404.

Connerton, P., *How Societies Remember* (Cambridge 1989).

Conway, C., *The Cult of Bolívar in Latin American Literature* (Gainesville 2003).

Cornell, T., "The Formation of the Historical Tradition of Early Rome," in *Past Perspectives*, ed. I. S. Moxon, J. D. Smart, and A. J. Woodman (Cambridge 1986) 67–86.

———, "The Value of the Literary Tradition Concerning Archaic Rome," in Raaflaub 2005, 47–74.

———, "Cato the Elder and the Origins of Roman Autobiography," in Smith and Powell 2009, 15–40.

Coudry, M., and Späth, T., eds., *L'invention des grands hommes de la Rome antique. Die Konstruktion der grossen Männer Altroms* (Paris 2001).

Courtney, E., *The Fragmentary Latin Poets* (Oxford 2003) 75–78.

Crawford, M., "Reconstructing What Roman Republic?," *Bulletin of the Institute of Classical Studies* 54.2 (2011) 105–114.

Cugusi, P., *Epistolographi Latini Minores*, 2 vols. (Turin 1970).

Cutting, J. E., "Representing Motion in a Static Image: Constraints and Parallels in Art, Science, and Popular Culture," *Perception* 31.10 (2002) 1165–1193.

Danziger, K., *Marking the Mind: A History of Memory* (Cambridge 2008), e-book.

Darias Príncipe, A., "Iconografía Bolivariana en el Panteón de Caracas: la necesidad de un mito," *Norba-Arte* 16 (1996) 277–298.

Daston, L., and Galison, P., *Objectivity* (New York 2007).

David, J.-M., "*Maiorum exempla sequi*: l'*exemplum* historique dans les discours judiciaires de Cicéron," *Mélanges de l'École française de Rome, Antiquité* 92 (1980) 67–86.

De Certeau, M., *The Practice of Everyday Life* (Berkeley 1984).

De Franceschini, M., and Veneziano, G., *Villa Adriana. Achitettura celeste. I segreti dei solstizi* (Rome 2011).

Degrassi, A., *Inscriptiones Italiae, XIII Fasti et elogia,* fasc. 1: *Fasti consulares et triumphales* (Rome 1947).

Dehn, M., *Working Memory and Academic Learning: Assessment and Intervention* (Hoboken, NJ 2008).

DeLaine, J., *The Baths of Caracalla: A Study in the Design, Construction, and Economics of Large-scale Building Projects in Imperial Rome.* Journal of Roman Archaeology suppl. 25 (Portsmouth, RI 1997).

De Maria, S., *Gli archi onorari di Roma e dell'Italia romana* (Rome 1988).

De Vries, M., Schmidt, H. G., and de Graaf, E., "Dutch Comparisons: Cognitive and Motivational Effects of Problem-based Learning on Medical Students," in *New Directions for Medical Education: Problem-based Learning and Community Oriented Medical Education*, ed. H. G. Schmidt et al. (New York 1989) 230–240.

Diefenbach, S., *Römische Erinnerungsräume. Heiligenmemoria und kollektive Identitäten im Rom des 3. bis 5. Jahrhunderts n. Chr.* (Berlin and New York 2007).

Dillon, S., and Welch, K. E., eds., *Representations of War in Ancient Rome* (Cambridge 2006).

DiMaggio, P., "Culture and Cognition," *Annual Review of Sociology* 23 (1997) 263–287.

Dixon, S., *Cornelia, Mother of the Gracchi* (London 2007).

Dodson, C. S., and Schacter, D. L., "The Cognitive Neuropsychology of False Memories: Theory and Data," in *The Handbook of Memory Disorders*, ed. A. D. Baddeley, M. D. Kopelman, and B. A. Wilson (Chichester 2002) 343–362.

Donderer, M., "Nicht immer wörtlich zu verstehen. Wie Bildhauer mit griechischen Inschriften Werbung betrieben," *BABESCH. Annual Papers in Mediterranean Archaeology* 86 (2010) 185–207.

Dugan, J., "Rhetoric and the Roman Republic," in *The Cambridge Companion to Ancient Rhetoric*, ed. E. Gunderson (Cambridge 2009) 178–193.

Dyson, B., "Aesthetic Appreciation of Pictures," in *Encyclopedia of Perception*, ed. E. B. Goldstein (Los Angeles 2010) 11–13.

Ebbinghaus, H., *Über das Gedächtnis. Untersuchungen zur experimentellen Psychologie* (Leipzig 1885).

Eden, P., *A Commentary on Virgil: Aeneid VIII* (Leiden 1975).

Edwards, C., *Writing Rome: Textual Approaches to the City* (Cambridge 1996).

Edwards, C., and Liversidge, M., *Imagining Rome: British Artists and Rome in the Nineteenth Century* (London 1996).

Eichenbaum, H., *The Cognitive Neuroscience of Memory: An Introduction* (Oxford 2012).

Elsner, J., *Art and the Roman Viewer: The Transformation of Art from the Pagan World to Christianity* (Cambridge 1995).

———, *Imperial Rome and Christian Triumph* (Oxford 1998).

———, "From the Culture of Spolia to the Cult of Relics: The Arch of Constantine and the Genesis of Late Antique Forms," *Papers of the British School at Rome* 68 (2000) 149–184.

———, "Iconoclasm and the Preservation of Memory," in *Monuments and Memory, Made and Unmade*, ed. R. S. Nelson and M. Olin (Chicago 2003) 209–231.

Engels, F., "Introduction," in K. Marx, *The Civil War in France* (London 1891).

E. P. of Rome, "A proposito di coincidenze," "Gli operai e I contadini a 'l'Unità': le risposte al nostro 'referendum'," *L'Unità* 1.126 (9 July 1924) 2.

E. P. of Venice, "Che Cosa Fanno Sull'Aventino," "Gli operai e I contadini a 'l'Unità': le risposte al nostro 'referendum'," *L'Unità* 1.128 (11 July 1924) 2.

Erll, A., *Kollektives Gedächtnis und Erinnerungskulturen* (Stuttgart 2005).

———, *Memory in Culture* (Palgrave Macmillan 2011).

Evers, C., "Remarques sur l'iconographie de Constantin: à propos du remploi de portraits des 'bons empereurs'," *Mélanges de l'École française de Rome, Antiquité* 103 (1991) 785–806.

Fabbrini, D., *Il migliore dei mondi possibili. Gli epigrammi ecfrastici di Marziale per amici e protettori* (Florence 2007).

Fantham, E., *The Roman World of Cicero's* De Oratore (Oxford 2004).

Farrell, J., "The Phenomenology of Memory in Roman Culture," *Classical Journal* 92 (1997) 383–393.

Faust, S., "Original und Spolie. Interaktive Strategien im Bildprogramm des Konstantinsbogens," *Römische Mitteilungen* 117 (2011) 377–408.

Favro, D., "The Roman Forum and Roman Memory," *Places* 5 (1988) 17–24.

———, "Reading the Augustan City," in *Narrative and Event in Ancient Art*, ed. P. J. Holliday (New York 1993) 230–257.

———, "The Street Triumphant: The Urban Impact of Roman Triumphal Parades," in *Streets: Critical Perspectives on Public Space*, ed. Z. Çelik, D. Favro, and R. Ingersoll (Berkeley, Los Angeles, and London 1994) 151–164.

———, *The Urban Image of Augustan Rome* (Cambridge 1996).

Febvre, L., "Sur une forme d'histoire qui n'est pas le nôtre: l'histoire historisante" (1947), in idem, *Combats pour l'histoire* (Paris 1953) 114–118.

Fentress, J., and Wickham, C., *Social Memory: New Perspectives on the Past* (Cambridge, MA 1992).

Fetridge, W. P., *The Rise and Fall of the Paris Commune in 1871* (New York 1871).

Filippi, A., *El Libertador en la historia italiana: ilustración, 'risorgimento', fascismo* (Caracas 1987).

Filippi, F., ed., *Ricostruire l'antico prima del virtuale. Italo Gismondi. Un architetto per l'archeologia (1887–1974)* (Rome 2007).

Fittschen, K., and Zanker, P., *Katalog der römischen Porträts in den Capitolinischen Museen und den anderen kommunalen Sammlungen der Stadt Rom*, vol. 1: *Kaiser- und Prinzenbildnisse* (Mainz am Rhein 1985).

Flaig, E., "Politisierte Lebensführung und ästhetische Kultur. Eine semiotische Untersuchung am römischen Adel," *Historische Anthropologie* 1 (1993) 193–217.

———, "Die *pompa funebris*. Adlige Konkurrenz und annalistische Erinnerung in der römischen Republik," in *Memoria als Kultur*, ed. O. G. Oexle (Göttingen 1995) 115–148.

———, *Ritualisierte Politik. Zeichen, Gesten und Herrschaft im Alten Rom* (Göttingen 2003).

Flammini, G., "Marco Emilio Scauro e i suoi frammenti," *Annali della Facoltà di Lettere e Filosofia, Università di Macerata* 10 (1977) 37–56.

Flower, H. I., *Ancestor Masks and Aristocratic Power in Roman Culture* (Oxford 1996).

———, "Rethinking 'Damnatio Memoriae': The Case of Cn. Calpurnius Piso Pater in A.D. 20," *Classical Antiquity* 17.2 (1998) 155–187.

———, "Spectacle and Political Culture in the Roman Republic," in *The Cambridge Companion to the Roman Republic*, ed. H. I. Flower (2004) 322–343, 394.

———, *The Art of Forgetting: Disgrace and Oblivion in Roman Political Culture* (Chapel Hill, NC 2006).

———, "The Tradition of the *spolia opima*: M. Claudius Marcellus and Augustus," in *The Roman Historical Tradition (Regal and Republican Rome)*, ed. J. Richardson and F. Santangelo (Oxford forthcoming).

Flower, M. A., *Xenophon: Anabasis or the Expedition of Cyrus* (Oxford 2012).

Forsythe, G. A., *Critical History of Early Rome: From Prehistory to the First Punic War* (Berkeley 2005).

Forte, M., and Silotti, A., *Virtual Archaeology: Recreating Ancient Worlds* (New York 1997).

Foucault, M., *Dits et écrits*, vol. 2: *1976–1988* (Paris 2001).

Fowler, B., *The Obituary as Collective Memory* (New York 2007).

Fredrick, F. D., "Beyond the Atrium to Ariadne: Erotic Painting and Visual Pleasure in the Roman House," *Classical Antiquity* 14 (1995) 266–287.

Freud, S., *Civilization and Its Discontents*, trans. J. Strachey (New York 1961).

Frischer, B., "Ramsay's 'Enquiry': Text and Context," in *Allan Ramsay and the Search for Horace's Villa*, ed. B. Frischer and I. G. Brown (London 2001) 73–104.

Frischer, B., and Stinson, P., "The Importance of Scientific Authentication and a Formal Visual Language in Virtual Models of Archaeological Sites: The Case of the House of Augustus and Villa of the Mysteries," in *Interpreting The Past 2: Heritage, New Technologies & Local Development*, ed. N. A. Silberman and D. Callebaut (Brussels 2007) 49–83.

Fritz, K. von, "The Reorganisation of the Roman Government in 366 B.C. and the So-Called Licinio-Sextian Laws," *Historia* 1 (1950) 3–44.

Fuchs, M., *"In hoc etiam genere Graeciae nihil cedamus": Studien zur Romanisierung der späthellenistischen Kunst im 1. Jhr. v. Chr.* (Mainz am Rhein 1999).

Gagé, J., "La mystique impériale et l'épreuve des jeux. Commode-Hercule et l'anthropologie héracléenne," in *Aufstieg und Niedergang der römischen Welt* 2.17.2, ed. H. Temporini and W. Haase (Berlin 1981) 662–683.

Gagné, R., *The Conditions of Learning and Theory of Instruction* (Fort Worth 1965).

Galinsky, K., "Recarved Imperial Portraits: Nuances and Wider Contexts," *Memoirs of the American Academy in Rome* 53 (2008) 1–25.

———, *Augustus: Introduction to the Life of an Emperor* (Cambridge 2012).

Gasparri, C., "Copie e copisti," in *Enciclopedia dell'Arte Antica*, suppl. 2 (Rome 1994) 267–280.

———, ed., *Le Sculture Farnese*, vol. 3: *Le sculture delle Terme di Caracalla. Rilievi e varia* (Milan 2010).

Gazda, E. K., ed., *The Ancient Art of Emulation: Studies in Artistic Originality and Tradition from the Present to Classical Antiquity* (Ann Arbor 2002).

Gedi, N., and Elam, Y., "Collective Memory—What Is It?," *History and Memory* 8.1 (1996) 30–50.

Geertz, C., *The Interpretation of Cultures* (New York 1973; repr. London 1993).

———, *Local Knowledge* (New York 1983; repr. London 1993).

Gell, A., *Art and Agency: An Anthropological Theory* (New York 1998).

Geominy, W., "Zwischen Kennerschaft und Cliché. Römische Kopien und die Geschichte ihrer Bewertung," in *Rezeption und Identität. Die kulturelle Auseinandersetzung Roms mit Griechenland als europäisches Paradigma*, ed. G. Vogt-Spira and B. Rommel (Stuttgart 1999) 38–58.

Giacchero, M., ed., *Edictum Diocletiani et collegarum de pretiis rerum venalium: pubblicazioni dell'Istituto di storia antica e scienze ausiliarie dell'Università di Genova* 8 (Genoa 1974).

Giardina, A., "*Metis* in Rome: A Greek Dream of Sulla," in *East and West: Papers in Ancient History Presented to Glen W. Bowersock*, ed. T. C. Brennan and H. I. Flower (Cambridge, MA 2003) 61–83.

Gibbon, E., *The Decline and Fall of the Roman Empire*, ed. J. B. Bury, 2 vols. (London 1897).

Gibson, B., *Statius,* Silvae 5 (Oxford 2006).

Giuliano, A., *Arco di Costantino*. Istituto Editoriale Domus (Milan 1955).

Gluckstein, D., *The Paris Commune: A Revolution in Democracy* (Chicago 2006).

"Governo/ Berlusconi sbaglia data Aventino: In '29 fu tragedia . . . ," *Wall Street Italia,* TMNews (15 October 2011), Internet.

Gowers, E., "The Anatomy of Rome from Capitol to Cloaca," *Journal of Roman Studies* 85 (1995) 23–32.

Gowing, A., *Empire and Memory: The Representation of the Roman Republic in Imperial Culture* (Cambridge 2005).

Grüner, A., *Venus ordinis. Der Wandel von Malerei und Literatur im Zeitalter der römischen Bürgerkriege* (Paderborn 2004).

Gutteridge, A., "The Depiction of Time on the Arch of Constantine," in *Archaeology and Memory*, ed. D. Boric (Oxford 2010) 158–170.

Habinek, T. N., *The Politics of Latin Literature: Writing, Identity, and Empire in Ancient Rome* (Princeton 1998).

Halbwachs, M., *Les cadres sociaux de la mémoire* (Paris 1925).

———, *La topographie légendaire des Évangiles en Terre Sainte* (Paris 1941; repr. 2008).

———, *La mémoire collective* (1950).

———, *On Collective Memory*, trans. L. Coser (Chicago 1992).

Hallett, C. H., *The Roman Nude: Heroic Portrait Statuary 200 B.C.–A.D. 300* (Oxford and New York 2005).

Hannah, R., "The Emperor's Stars: The Conservatori Portrait of Commodus," *American Journal of Archaeology* 90 (1986) 336–342.

Hansen, M. F., *The Eloquence of Appropriation: Prolegomena to an Understanding of Spolia in Early Christian Rome* (Rome 2003).

Hardie, A., *Statius and the 'Silvae': Poets, Patrons and Epideixis in the Graeco-Roman World* (Liverpool 1983).

Hardie, P., *Virgil's Aeneid: Cosmos and Imperium* (Oxford 1986).

———, "Statius' Ovidian Poetics and the Tree of Atedius Melior (*Silvae* 2.3)," in *Flavian Poetry*, ed. R. Nauta, H.-J. van Dam, and J. J. L. Smolenaars (Leiden, Boston, and Cologne 2006) 207–221.

Harris, W., *Ancient Literacy* (Cambridge, MA 1989).

Häusle, H., *Das Denkmal als Garant des Nachruhms. Eine Studie zu einem Motiv in lateinischen Inschriften* (Munich 1980).

Hedrick, C., Jr., *History and Silence: Purge and Rehabilitation of Memory in Late Antiquity* (Austin 2000).

Hekster, O., *Commodus: An Emperor at the Crossroads* (Amsterdam 2002).

Helbig, W., ed., *Führer durch die öffentlichen Sammlungen klassischer Altertümer in Rom*, vol. 1 (Tübingen 1963).

Hemelrijk, E. A., *Matrona Docta: Educated Women in the Roman Élite from Cornelia to Julia Domna* (London 2004).

Heusch, C., *Die Macht der* memoria. *Die 'Noctes Atticae' des Aulus Gellius im Licht der Erinnerungskultur des 2. Jahrhunderts n. Chr.* (Berlin and New York 2011).

Hillard, T. W., "Popilia and the *'Laudationes Funebres'* for Women," *Antichthon* 35 (2001) 45–63.

Hinard, F., "Sur une autre forme d'opposition entre *virtus* et *fortuna*," *Kentron* 3 (1987) 17–20.

Hinds, S. E., "Cinna, Statius and 'Immanent Literary History' in the Cultural Economy," in *L'histoire littéraire immanente dans la poésie latine*, ed. E. A. Schmidt. Entretiens Hardt 47 (2001) 221–265.

Hmelo-Silver, C., "Problem-based Learning: What and How Do Students Learn?," *Educational Psychology Review* 16 (2004) 235–266.

Hmelo-Silver, C., and Barrows, H. S., "Goals and Strategies of a Problem-based Learning Facilitator," *The Interdisciplinary Journal of Problem-based Learning* 1.1 (2006) 21–39.

Hobsbawm, E., and Ranger, T., eds., *The Invention of Tradition* (Cambridge 1983).

Hoek, L. H., *La marque du titre: dispositifs sémiotiques d'une pratique textuelle* (The Hague 1981).

Hölkeskamp, K.-J., "Capitol, Comitium und Forum. Öffentliche Räume, sakrale Topographie und Erinnerungslandschaften" (2001), in Hölkeskamp 2004a, 137–168.

———, "*Oratoris maxima scaena*. Reden vor dem Volk in der politischen Kultur der Republik" (1995), in Hölkeskamp 2004a, 219–256.

———, "Exempla und *mos maiorum*. Überlegungen zum kollektiven Gedächtnis der Nobilität" (1996), in Hölkeskamp 2004a, 169–198.

———, *Senatvs Popvlvsqve Romanvs. Die politische Kultur der Republik—Dimensionen und Deutungen* (Stuttgart 2004a).

———, *Rekonstruktionen einer Republik. Die politische Kultur des antiken Rom und die Forschung der letzten Jahrzehnten* (Munich 2004b).

———, "History and Collective Memory in the Middle Republic," in *A Companion to the Roman Republic*, ed. N. Rosenstein and R. Morstein-Marx (Malden, MA 2006a) 478–495.

———, "Rituali e cerimonie 'alla romana'. Nuove prospettive sulla cultura politica dell'età repubblicana," *Studi Storici* 47.2 (2006b) 319–363.

————, "Konsens und Konkurrenz. Die politische Kultur der römischen Republik in neuer Sicht," *Klio* 88.2 (2006c) 360–396.

————, "Der Triumph—'erinnere Dich, daß Du ein Mensch bist'," in *Erinnerungsorte der Antike: die römische Welt*, ed. E. Stein-Hölkeskamp and K-J. Hölkeskamp (Munich 2006d) 258–276.

————, "Hierarchie und Konsens. Pompae in der politischen Kultur der römischen Republik," in *Machtfragen. Zur kulturellen Repräsentation und Konstruktion von Macht in Antike, Mittelalter und Neuzeit*, ed. A. Arweiler and B. Gauly (Stuttgart 2008) 79–126.

————, "Eine politische Kultur (in) der Krise? Gemäßigt radikale Vorbemerkungen zum kategorischen Imperativ der Konzepte," in *Eine politische Kultur (in) der Krise? Die "letzte Generation" der römischen Republik*, ed. K.-J. Hölkeskamp and E. Müller-Luckner (Munich 2009a) 1–25.

————, "Mythos und Politik—(nicht nur) in der Antike. Anregungen und Angebote der neuen, historischen Politikforschung," *Historische Zeitschrift* 288 (2009b) 1–50.

————, *Reconstructing the Roman Republic: An Ancient Political Culture and Modern Research* (Princeton 2010).

————, "Self-serving Sermons: Oratory and the Self-construction of the Republican Aristocrat," in *Praise and Blame in Roman Republican Rhetoric*, ed. C. Smith and R. Covino (Swansea 2011a) 17–34.

————, "The Roman Republic as Theatre of Power: The Consuls as Leading Actors," in *Consuls and Res Publica: Holding High Office in the Roman Republic*, ed. H. Beck, A. Duplà, M. Jehne, and F. Pina Polo (Cambridge 2011b) 161–181.

————, "Im Gewebe der Geschichte(n). Memoria, Monumente und ihre mythhistorische Vernetzung," *Klio* 94.2 (2012) 380–414.

————, "Raum, Präsenz, Performanz. Prozessionen in politischen Kulturen der Vormoderne—Forschungen und Fortschritte," in *Medien der Geschichte in den griechisch-römischen Altertumswissenschaften*, ed. O. Dally, S. Muth, and R. M. Schneider (Berlin 2013a) 359–395.

————, "Friends, Romans, Countrymen. Addressing the Roman People and the Rhetoric of Inclusion," in *Community and Communication: Oratory and Politics in Republican Rome*, ed. H. van der Blom and C. Steel (Oxford 2013b) 11–28.

Hölkeskamp, K.-J., and Stein-Hölkeskamp, E., "Erinnerungsorte (in) der Antike—Programm eines Projektes," *Geschichte in Wissenschaft und Unterricht* 62.1/2 (2011) 37–49.

Hollinshed, M. B., "Extending the Reach of Marble: Struts in Greek and Roman Sculpture," in Gazda 2002, 117–152.

Holloway, R. R., "The Spolia of the Arch of Constantine," *Numismatica e Antichità Classica* 14 (1985) 261–273.

————, *Constantine and Rome* (New Haven 2004).

Hölscher, T., "Die Anfänge römischer Repräsentationskunst," *Mitteilungen des Deutschen Archäologischen Instituts (Rom)* 85 (1978) 315–357.

————, "Die Geschichtsauffassung in der römischen Repräsentationskunst," *Jahrbuch des Deutschen Archäologischen Instituts* 95 (1980) 265–321.

————, *Staatsdenkmal und Publikum. Vom Untergang der Republik bis zur Festigung des Kaisertums in Rom* (Constance 1984).

————, *Römische Bildsprache als semantisches System* (Heidelberg 1987) = *The Language of Images in Roman Art* (Cambridge 2004).

————, "Römische Nobiles und hellenistische Herrscher," in *Akten des 13. Internationalen Kongresses für Klassische Archäologie Berlin 1988* (Mainz 1990) 74–84.

————, "Bilderwelt, Formensystem, Lebenskultur. Zur Methode archäologischer Kulturanalyse," *Studi italiani di filologia classica* ser. 10, 3a (1992) 460–484.

————, "Bildwerke. Darstellungen, Funktionen, Botschaften," in *Klassische Archäologie. Eine Einführung*, ed. A. H. Borbein, T. Hölscher, and P. Zanker (Berlin 2000) 147–165.

————, "Die Alten vor Augen. Politische Denkmäler und öffentliches Gedächtnis im republikanischen Rom," in *Institutionalität und Symbolisierung. Verstetigungen kultureller Ordnungsmuster in Vergangenheit und Gegenwart*, ed. G. Melville (Cologne 2001a) 183–211.

————, "Vorläufige Überlegungen zum Verhältnis von Theoriebildung und Lebenserfahrung in der Klassischen Archäologie," in *Posthumanistische Klassische Archäologie. Historizität und Wissenschaftlichkeit von Interesse und Methoden*, ed. S. Altekamp, M. R. Hofter, and M. Krumme (Munich 2001b) 173–192.

————, *The Language of Images in Roman Art*, trans. A. Snodgrass and A. Künzl-Snodgrass (Cambridge 2004).

Hornblower, S., *Thucydides and Pindar* (Oxford 2004).

Horsfall, N., "The 'Letters' of Cornelia: Yet More Problems," *Athenaeum* 65 (1987) 231–234.

————, *Cornelius Nepos: A Selection Including the Lives of Cato and Atticus* (Oxford 1989).

————, "The Cultural Horizons of the Plebs Romana," *Memoirs of the American Academy in Rome* 41 (1996) 101–119.

————, *The Culture of the Roman Plebs* (London 2003).

Howes, D., *Empire of the Senses: The Sensual Culture Reader* (Oxford 2005).

Huet, V., "Stories One Might Tell of Roman Art: Reading Trajan's Column and the Tiberius Cup," in *Art and Text in Roman Culture*, ed. J. Elsner (Cambridge 1996) 9–31.

Hutton, P. H., "Collective Memory and Collective Mentalities: The Halbwachs-Ariès Connection," *Historical Reflections/Réflexions Historiques* 15.2 (1988) 311–322.

————, *History as an Art of Memory* (Hanover 1993).

Itgenhorst, T., *Tota illa pompa. Der Triumph in der römischen Republik* (Göttingen 2005).

Jaczynowska, M., "Le culte de l'Hercule romain au temps du Haut-Empire," in *Aufstieg und Niedergang der Römischen Welt*, 2.17.2, ed. H. Temporini and W. Haase (Berlin 1981) 629–661.

Jaeger, M., *Livy's Written Rome* (Ann Arbor 1997).

Jehne, M., "Methods, Models, and Historiography," in *A Companion to the Roman Republic*, ed. N. Rosenstein and R. Morstein-Marx (2006) 3–28.

Jordan, H., "Der Brief des Quintus Catulus *de consulatu suo*," *Hermes* 6 (1872) 68–81.

Junker, K., and A. Stähli, eds., *Original und Kopie. Formen und Konzepte der Nachahmung in der antiken Kunst* (Wiesbaden 2008).

Kaiser-Raiß, R., *Die Stadtrömische Münzprägung während der Alleinherrschaft des Kommodus. Untersuchungen zur Selbstdarstellung eines römisches Kaisers* (Frankfurt am Main 1980).

Kandel, E., *In Search of Memory: The Emergence of a New Science of Mind* (New York 2006; e-book 2011).

Kansteiner, W., "Finding Meaning in Memory: A Methodological Critique of Collective Memory Studies," *History and Theory* 41.2 (2002) 179–197.

Kemechey, L., *"Il Duce": The Life and Work of Benito Mussolini* (New York 1930).

Kennedy, G. A., *The Art of Rhetoric in the Roman World: A History of Rhetoric* (Cambridge 1972).

Kierdorf, W., *Laudatio funebris. Interpretationen und Untersuchungen zur Entwicklung der römischen Leichenrede* (Meisenheim am Glan 1980).

Kinney, D., "Rape or Restitution of the Past? Interpreting *Spolia*," in *The Art of Interpreting*, ed. S. C. Scott (University Park, PA 1995) 53–67.

————, "*Spolia. Damnatio* and *Renovatio Memoriae*," in *Memoirs of the American Academy in Rome* 42 (1997) 117–148.

Klein, K., "On the Emergence of Memory in Historical Discourse," *Representations* 69 (2000) 127–150.

Kleiner, D. E. E., "Private Portraiture in the Age of Augustus," in *The Age of Augustus*, ed. R. Winkes (Providence and Louvain-la-Neuve 1986) 107–135.

————, *Roman Imperial Funerary Altars with Portraits* (Rome 1987).

————, *Roman Sculpture* (New Haven 1992).

Knudsen, S. E., "Spolia: The So-called Historical Frieze on the Arch of Constantine," *American Journal of Archaeology* 93 (1989) 313–314.

Kondoleon, C., "Timing Spectacles: Roman Domestic Art and Performance," in Bergmann and Kondoleon 1999, 321–342.

Koortbojian, M., *Myth, Meaning, and Memory on Roman Sarcophagi* (Berkeley, Los Angeles, and London 1995).

————, "Forms of Attention: Four Notes on Replication and Variation," in Gazda 2002, 173–204.

Koselleck, R., *Vergangene Zukunft. Zur Semantik geschichtlicher Zeiten* (Frankfurt 1979) = *Futures Past: On the Semantics of Historical Time* (Cambridge, MA 1985; New York 2004).

Krause, C., "*In conspectus prope totius urbis* (Cic. *Dom.* 100): il tempio della Libertà e il quartiere alto del Palatino," *Eutopia* 1 (2001) 169–201.

——, "Das Haus Ciceros auf dem Palatin," *Numismatica e antichità classiche* 33 (2004) 293–316.

Kreikenbom, D., *Bildwerke nach Polyklet. Kopienkritische Untersuchungen zu den männlichen statuarischen Typen nach polykletischen Vorbildern* (Berlin 1990).

Krull, D., *Der Herakles vom Typ Farnese. Kopienkritische Untersuchung einer Schöpfung des Lysipp* (Frankfurt am Main and Bern 1985).

Kruschwitz, P., *Carmina Saturnia Epigraphica. Einleitung, Text und Kommentar zu den saturnischen Versinschriften* (Stuttgart 2002).

Künzl, E., *Der Römische Triumph: Siegesfeiern im Antiken Rom* (Munich 1988).

Kuttner, A. L., *Dynasty and Empire in the Age of Augustus: The Case of the Boscoreale Cups* (Berkeley 1995).

——, "Roman Art during the Republic," in *The Cambridge Companion to the Roman Republic*, ed. H. I. Flower (2004) 294–321; 391–393.

Kvapil, L. A., "Teaching Archaeological Pragmatism through Problem-based Learning," *Classical Journal* 105.1 (2009) 45–52.

Lada-Richards, I., "Was Pantomime 'Good to Think With' in the Ancient World?," in *New Directions in Roman Pantomime*, ed. E. Hall and R. Wyles (Oxford 2008) 285–313.

Lai, C., Franke, T., and Gan, W.-B., "Opposite Effects of Fear Conditioning and Extinction on Dendritic Spine Remodelling," *Nature* 483 (2012) 87–91.

La Penna, A., "Sulla *communis historia* di Lutazio," in *Studi su Varrone, sulla retorica, storiografica e poesia latina. Scritti in onore di Benedetto Riposati* (Milan 1979) 229–240.

La Rocca, E., and Tortorella, S., eds., *Trionfi Romani* (Milan 2008).

Larsen, S., "Remembering without Experiencing: Memory for Reported Events," in *Remembering Reconsidered: Ecological and Traditional Approaches to the Study of Memory*, ed. U. Neisser and E. Winograd (Cambridge 1995) 326–355.

Leander Touati, A. M., *The Great Trajanic Frieze* (Stockholm and Göteborg 1987).

Lecuna, V., *Cartas del Libertador*, vol. 4 (Caracas 1929).

Lefebvre, H., *Rhythmanalysis: Space, Time and Everyday Life* (London 2004).

Le Goff, J., *History and Memory* (New York 1992).

"L'eroismo di Matteotti nella confessione del Volpi," *L'Unità* 1.106 (15 June 1924) 1.

Lewis, R. G., "Catulus and the Cimbri 102 B.C.," *Hermes* 102 (1974) 90–109.

——, "Sulla's Autobiography: Scope and Economy," *Athenaeum* 79 (1991a) 509–519.

——, "Suetonius' *Caesares* and Their Literary Antecedents," in *Aufstieg und Niedergang der Römischen Welt* 2.33.5 (1991b) 3623–3674.

——, "Imperial Autobiography: Augustus to Hadrian," in *Aufstieg und Niedergang der Römischen Welt* 2.34.1 (1993) 629–706.

——, "Scope for Scaurus," *Athenaeum* 89 (2001) 345–354.

Lieux, E. M., "A Comparative Study of Learning in Lecture versus Problem-based Format," *About Teaching* 50 (1996) 25–27.

Lim, R., "'In the Temple of Laughter': Visual and Literary Representations of Spectators," in Bergmann and Kondoleon 1999, 343–365.

Linke, B., *Die römische Republik von den Gracchen bis Sulla* (Darmstadt 2005).

Lippold, G., *Kopien und Umbildungen griechischer Statuen* (Munich 1923).

Liverani, P., "Die Polychromie des Augustus von Prima Porta, vorläufiger Bericht," in *Neue Forschungen zur hellenistischen Plastik. Kolloquium zum 70. Geburtstag von Georg Daltrop (27 April 2002)*, ed. G. Zimmer (Eichstätt and Ingolstadt 2003) 121–140.

——, "Reimpiego senza ideologia: la lettura antica degli spolia dall'arco di Costantino all'età carolingia," *Mitteilungen des Deutschen Archäologischen Instituts (Rom)* 111 (2004a) 383–434.

————, "L'Augusto di Prima Porta," in *I colori del bianco. Policromia nella scultura antica* (Rome 2004b) 235–242.

————, "The Fragment in Late Antiquity: A Functional View," in *The Fragment: An Incomplete History,* ed. W. Tronzo (Los Angeles 2009) 23–36.

————, "Reading Spolia in Late Antiquity and Contemporary Perception," in *Reuse Value: Spolia and Appropriation in Art and Architecture, from Constantine to Sherrie Levine*, ed. R. Brilliant and D. Kinney (Farnham 2011) 33–51.

Lock, G., *Using Computers in Archaeology: Towards Virtual Pasts* (London 2003).

Loewy, E., *Inschriften Griechischer Bildhauer* (Leipzig and Teubner 1885).

L'Orange, H. P., and von Gerkan, A., *Der Spätantike Bildschmuck des Konstantinsbogens* (Berlin 1939).

Lowrie, M., *Writing, Performance, and Authority in Augustan Rome* (Oxford and New York 2009).

MacDonald, W. L., *The Architecture of the Roman Empire: An Urban Appraisal* (New Haven 1988).

Malamud, M., *Ancient Rome and Modern America* (Hoboken 2009).

Malcovati, E., ed., *Oratorum Romanorum Fragmenta liberae rei publicae*, 4th ed. (Turin 1976).

Mangurian, R., and Ray, M. A., "A Modern Survey of an Ancient Roman Villa. 1993 Data Collector Survey," *Point of Beginning* 18.6 (1993) 10–20.

Mansuelli, G. A., "Fornix e Arcus. Note di terminologia," in *Studi sull'arco onorario romano*, ed. G. A. Mansuelli (Rome 1979) 15–19.

Marcadé, J., *Recueil des signatures de sculpteurs grecs*, 2 vols. (Paris 1953).

Mari, Z., "Villa Adriana. Recenti scoperte e stato della ricerca," *Ephemeris Napocensis* 20 (2010) 7–37.

Marincola, J., "Genre, Convention, and Innovation in Greco-Roman Historiography," in *The Limits of Historiography: Genre and Narrative in Ancient Historical Texts*, ed. C. Kraus (Leiden 1999) 281–324.

Marlowe, E., "Framing the Sun: The Arch of Constantine and the Roman Cityscape," *Art Bulletin* 88.2 (2006) 223–242.

Marszal, J. R., "Ubiquitous Barbarians: Representations of the Gauls at Pergamon and Elsewhere," in *From Pergamon to Sperlonga: Sculpture and Context*, ed. N. T. de Grummond and B. S. Ridgway (Berkeley, Los Angeles, and London 2000) 191–234.

Marvin, M., "Freestanding Sculptures from the Baths of Caracalla," *American Journal of Archaeology* 87 (1983) 347–384.

————, *The Language of the Muses: The Dialogue between Roman and Greek Sculpture* (Los Angeles 2008).

Marx, K., "The Eighteenth Brumaire of Louis Napoleon," in *Collected Works of Marx and Engels*, vol. 11 (New York 1979) 99–197.

Maslan, S., "Resisting Representation: Theater and Democracy in Revolutionary France," *Representations* 52 (1995) 27–51.

Mattingly, D., *Imperialism, Power, and Identity: Experiencing the Roman Empire* (Princeton 2011).

Mazlish, B., "The Tragic Farce of Marx, Hegel, and Engels: A Note," *History and Theory* 11 (1972) 335–337.

McDonnell, M. A., *Roman Manliness:* virtus *and the Roman Republic* (Cambridge 2006).

Megill, A., "From 'History, Memory, Identity'," in Olick, Vinitzky-Seroussi, and Levy 2011, 193–197.

Meier, C., *Das Gebot zu vergessen und die Unabweisbarkeit des Erinnerns. Vom öffentlichen Umgang mit schlimmer Vergangenheit* (Munich 2010).

Mellor, R. "The New Aristocracy of Power," in *Flavian Rome: Culture, Image, Text*, ed. A. J. Boyle and J. W. Dominik (Leiden 2003) 69–101.

Merlin, A., *L'Aventine dans l'antiquité* (Paris 1906).

Meusburger, P., Heffermann, M., and Wunder, E., "Cultural Memories: An Introduction," in *Cultural Memories. The Geographical Point of View*, ed. P. Meusburger, M. Heffermann, and E. Wunder (New York 2011) 3–14.

Meyer, E., "Die Sezessionen von 494 und 449," *Kleine Schriften* 1 (1921) 333–361 = "Der Ursprung des Tribunats und die Gemeinde der Vier Tribus," *Hermes* 30 (1895) 1–24.

Michel, L., *The Red Virgin, Memoirs of Louise Michel* (Tuscaloosa 1981).

Miller, J. F., "Ovidian Allusion and the Vocabulary of Memory," *Materiali e Discussioni* 30 (1993) 153–164.

Misch, G., *Geschichte der Autobiographie*, 3rd ed., vol. 1 (Frankfurt 1949).

Mitchell, K. J., and Johnson, M. K., "Source Monitoring," in Tulving and Craik 2000, 179–195.

Mommsen, T., *Römische Forschungen* (Berlin 1864).

Moreno, P., *Lisippo* (Bari 1974).

———, "Il Farnese ritrovato ed altri tipi di Eracle in riposo," in *Mélanges de l'École française de Rome, Antiquité* 94 (1982) 379–526.

———, *Lisippo: l'arte e la fortuna* (Milan 1995).

Morstein-Marx, R., *Mass Oratory and Political Power in the Late Roman Republic* (Cambridge 2004).

———, "Political History," in *A Companion to Ancient History*, ed. A. Erskine (Malden and Oxford 2009) 99–111.

Moscovitch, M., "Theories of Memory and Consciousness," in Tulving and Craik 2000, 609–625.

Mussolini, B., *Scritti e discorsi di Benito Mussolini*, vol. 4 (Milan 1934).

"Nei Comuni come al Governo: i fascisti mantegono il potere contro la volontà della popolazione," *L'Unità: Cronache Milanesi* 1.126 (9 July 1924) 3.

Nelson, K., and Fivush, R., "Socialization of Memory," in Tulving and Craik 2000, 283–295.

Neumeister, C., "Polyklet in der römischen Literatur," in *Polyklet. Der Bildhauer der griechischen Klassik*, ed. H. Beck, P. C. Bol, and M. Bückling (Frankfurt am Main 1990) 428–449.

Newlands, C., "Statius' Self-Conscious Poetics: Hexameter on Hexameter," in *Politics and Power in Imperial Literature*, ed. W. J. Dominik, J. Garthwaite, and P. Roche (Leiden 2009) 387–404.

Newsome, D., "Making Movement Meaningful," in *Rome, Ostia, Pompeii: Movement and Space*, ed. R. Laurence and D. J. Newsome (Oxford 2012) 15–19.

Niccolini, G., *Il Tribunato della Plebe* (Milan 1932).

Nora, P., *Constructing the Past: Essays in Historical Methodology* (Cambridge 1984).

———, ed., *Les lieux de mémoire* (Paris 1984–1992) = *Realms of Memory: Rethinking the French Past* (New York 1996–1998).

Novick, P., *The Holocaust in American Life* (Boston 1999).

Oakley, S. P., *A Commentary on Livy: Books VI–X*, vol. 1 (Oxford 1997).

———, *A Commentary on Livy: Books VI–X*, vol. 2 (Oxford 1998).

Ogilvie, R., *A Commentary on Livy, Books 1–5* (Oxford 1965).

Ogilvie, R., and Drummond, A., "The Sources for Early Roman History," in *Cambridge Ancient History*, 2nd ed., vol. 7.2 (Cambridge 1990) 1–29.

O'Keefe, J., and Nadel, L., *The Hippocampus as a Cognitive Map* (Oxford 1978).

O'Leary, D., *Memorias del general Daniel Florencio O'Leary: narración* (Caracas 1952).

———, *Bolívar and the War of Independence* (Austin 1970).

Olick, J., and Robbins, J., "Social Memory Studies: From 'Collective Memory' to the Historical Sociology of Mnemonic Practices," *Annual Review of Sociology* 24 (1998) 105–140.

Olick, J., Vinitzky-Seroussi, V., and D. Levy, eds., *The Collective Memory Reader* (New York 2011).

Onians, J., *Classical Art and the Cultures of Greece and Rome* (New Haven and London 1999).

"Opposizioni diserteranno discorso del premier, Venerdì voteranno la sfiducia," in *Repubblica Pubblico* (12 October 2011), Internet.

Östenberg, I., *Staging the World: Spoils, Captives and Representations in the Roman Triumph* (Oxford 2009).

O'Sullivan, T. M., *Walking in Roman Culture* (Cambridge 2011).

Packer, J. E., *The Forum of Trajan in Rome* (Berkeley, Los Angeles, and London 1997).

Parker, E. S., Cahill, L., and McGaugh, J. L., "A Case of Unusual Autobiographical Remembering," *Neurocase* 12 (2006) 35–49.

Pavan, A., *La gara delle quadrighe e il gioco della guerra (Theb. VI 238–549)* (Alessandria 2009).

Peirce, P., "The Arch of Constantine: Propaganda and Ideology in Late Roman Art," *Art History* 12 (1989) 387–418.

Pelikan Pittenger, M. R., *Contested Triumphs: Politics, Pageantry, and Performance in Livy's Republican Rome* (Berkeley 2008).

Pelling, C. B. R., "Was there an ancient genre of 'autobiography'? Or did Augustus know what he was doing?," in Smith and Powell 2009, 41–64.

———, *Plutarch Caesar* (Oxford 2011).

———, "Xenophon's and Caesar's Third Person Narratives—or Are They?" (forthcoming).

Pensabene, P., "The Arch of Constantine: Marble Samples," in *Classical Marble: Geochemistry, Technology and Trade*, ed. N. Herz and M. Waelkens (Dordrecht 1988) 411–418.

Pensabene, P., and Panella, C., *Arco di Costantino: tra archeologia e archeometria* (Rome 1999).

Perry, E. E., *The Aesthetics of Emulation in the Visual Arts of Ancient Rome* (Cambridge 2005).

Perutelli, A., "Lutazio Catulo poeta," *Rivista di filologia e di istruzione classica* 118 (1990) 257–281.

Peter, H., *Historicorum Romanorum Reliquiae*, 2 vols., 2nd ed. (Leipzig 1914–1916).

Petrocelli, C., "Cornelia the Matron," in *Roman Women*, ed. A. Fraschetti (Chicago 2001) 34–65.

Pfaffel, W., "Wie modern war die varronische Etymologie?," in *The History of Linguistics in the Classical Period*, ed. D. J. Taylor (Amsterdam 1987) 207–227.

Pfanner, M., *Der Titusbogen* (Mainz am Rhein 1983).

Pittenger, M. P., *Contested Triumphs: Politics, Pageantry, and Performance in Livy's Republican Rome* (Berkeley 2008).

Pollitt, J. J., *Art and Experience in Classical Greece* (Cambridge 1972).

Popkin, M., "The Triumphal Route in Republican and Imperial Rome: Architecture, Experience, and Memory" (Ph.D. diss., New York University 2012).

Preciado, K., ed., *Retaining the Original: Multiple Originals, Copies and Reproductions* (Washington, DC 1989).

Prusac, M., *From Face to Face: Recarving of Roman Portraits and the Late-Antique Portrait Arts* (Leiden and Boston 2011).

Punzi, R., "Fonti documentarie per una rilettura delle vicende post-antiche dell'Arco di Constantino," in Pensabene and Panella 1999, 185–228.

Purcell, N., "The City of Rome and the *plebs urbana* in the Late Republic," in *Cambridge Ancient History*, 2nd ed., vol. 9 (Cambridge 1994) 644–688.

Raaflaub, K., ed., *Social Struggles in Archaic Rome: New Perspectives on the Conflict of the Orders* (Malden 2005).

Ramírez Salas, T., "Principios del Juramento de Monte Sacro siguen más vigentes que nunca," in *Ministerio del Poder Popular para la Comunicación y la Información, Gobierno Bolivariano de Venezuela,* posted 16 October 2005, http://www.minci.gob.ve/noticias-prensa-presidencial/28/8522/principios_del_ juramento.html.

Rawson, E., *Intellectual Life in the Late Roman Republic* (Baltimore 1985).

———, "The First Latin Annalists," in *Roman Culture and Society, Collected Papers* (New York 1991) = *Latomus* 35.4 (1976) 689–717.

Raymond, E., "Forsan et haec olim meminisse iuvabit: recherches sur les formes et aspects de la mémoire dans l'Énéide de Virgile" (Thèse du doctorat, Université Jean Moulin-Lyon 2011).

Revell, L., *Roman Imperialism and Local Identities* (Cambridge 2009).

Richardson, L., *A New Topographical Dictionary of Ancient Rome* (Baltimore 1992).

Richter, G. M. A., "Another Copy of the Diadumenos by Polykleitos," *American Journal of Archaeology* 39 (1935) 46–52.

Ridgway, B. S., *Roman Copies of Greek Sculpture: The Problem of the Originals* (Ann Arbor 1984).

Ridley, R., "Notes on the Establishment of the Tribunate of the Plebs," *Latomus* 27 (1968) 535–554.

Ritti, T., "Immagini onomastiche sui monumenti sepolcrali di età romana," *Memorie. Accademia Nazionale dei Lincei* 21 (1977) 257–397.

Roediger, H. L., III, and McDermott, K. B., "Distortions of Memory," in Tulving and Craik 2000, 149–162.

Roediger, H. L., III, Zaromb, F. M., and Butler, A. C., "The Role of Repeated Retrieval in Shaping Collective Memory," in Boyer and Wertsch 2009, 138–170.

Rohmann, J., "Die spätantiken Kaiserporträts am Konstantinsbogen in Rom," *Mitteilungen des Deutschen Archäologischen Instituts (Rom)* 105 (1998) 259–282.

Roller, M., "Exemplarity in Roman Culture: The Cases of Horatius Cocles and Cloelia," *Classical Philology* 99 (2004) 1–56.

———, "Culture-based Approaches," in *The Oxford Handbook of Roman Studies*, ed. A. Barchiesi and W. Scheidel (Oxford 2010) 234–249.

Rosati, G., "Luxury and Love: The Encomium as Aestheticisation of Power in Flavian Poetry," in *Flavian Poetry*, ed. R. Nauta, H.-J. van Dam, and J. J. L. Smolenaars (Leiden, Boston, and Cologne 2006) 41–58.

———, *Ovidio. Metamorfosi, Vol. III (Books V–VI)* (Milan 2009).

———, "I *tria corda* di Stazio, poeta greco, romano e napoletano," in *Filellenismo e identità romana in età flavia*, ed. A. Bonadeo, A. Canobbio, and F. Gasti (Pavia 2011) 15–34.

———, "Muggiti nel foro. Su un'immagine di Stazio, *Silvae* 1.1.69," in *Per Roberto Gusmani. Studi in ricordo*, vol. 1, ed. G. Borghello and V. Orioles (Udine 2012) 443–449.

Rose, S., *The Making of Memory: From Molecules to Mind* (London 1993).

Rotker, S.,"El evangelio apócrifo de Simón Bolívar," *Estudios: revista de investigaciones literarias y culturales* 6.12 (1998) 29–44.

Rotondi, G., *Leges Publicae Populi Romani* (New York 1912).

Royo, M., "Catulus et les infortunes de la *virtus*," *Kentron* 5 (1989) 151–160.

Rutledge, S. H., *Ancient Rome as a Museum: Power, Identity, and the Culture of Collecting* (Oxford 2012).

Ruysschaert, J., "Unità e significato dell'Arco di Costantino," *Studi Romani* 11.1 (1963) 1–15.

Ryberg, I. S., *Rites of the State Religion in Roman Art* (Rome 1955).

———, *Panel Reliefs of Marcus Aurelius* (New York 1967).

Sachs, M., *Concepts of Modern Physics: The Haifa Lectures* (London 2007).

Säflund, G., *Le mura di Roma repubblicana* (Uppsala 1998).

Sampson, G. C., *The Crisis of Rome: The Jugurthine and Northern Wars and the Rise of Marius* (Barnsley, UK 2010).

Santamaria, U., and Morresi, F., "Le indagini scientifiche per lo studio della cromia dell'Augusto di Prima Porta," in *I colori del bianco. Policromia nella scultura antica* (Rome 2004) 243–248.

Sauron, G., "Le suicide de Catulus et la naissance du 'deuxième style' théâtral," *Helmantica* 50 (1999) 677–696.

———, "La révolution iconographique du 'deuxième style'," *Mélanges de l'École française de Rome, Antiquité* 113 (2001) 769–786.

Savin-Baden, M., and Major, C. H., *Foundations of Problem-based Learning* (New York 2004).

Schacter, D., *How the Mind Forgets and Remembers: The Seven Sins of Memory* (Boston and New York 2001).

Schacter, D., Norman, K., and Koutstaal, W., "The Cognitive Neuroscience of Constructive Memory," *Annual Review of Psychology* 49 (1998) 289–318.

Schacter, D. L., Wagner, A. D., and Buckner, R. L., "Memory Systems of 1999," in Tulving and Craik 2000, 627–643.

Schine, J., "Movement, Memory, and the Senses in Soundscape Studies," *Sensory Studies*, http://www.sensorystudies.org/sensorial-investigations-2/movement-memory-the-senses-in-soundscape-studies/ (accessed 10 September 2011).

Schlesinger, Jr., A. M., *The Disuniting of America: Reflections on a Multicultural Society* (New York 1992).

Schmidt, H. G., Dauphnee, W. D., and Patel, V. L., "Comparing the Effects of Problem-based and Conventional Curricula in an International Sample," *Journal of Medical Education* 62.4 (1987) 305–315.

Schneider, R. M., "Der Hercules Farnese," in *Meisterwerke der antiken Kunst*, ed. L. Giuliani (Munich 2005) 136–157.

Scotti, I., "Il fascismo e la Camera dei Deputati: I.—La Costituente fascista (1922–1928)," in *Bollettino di Informazione Costituzionali e Parlamentari* (Rome 1984).

Sehlmeyer, M., *Stadtrömische Ehrenstatuen der republikanischen Zeit. Historizität und Kontext von Symbolen nobilitären Standesbewusstseins* (Stuttgart 1999).

———, "Die kommunikative Leistung römischer Ehrenstatuen," in *Moribus antiquis res stat Romana. Römische Werte und römische Literatur im 3. und 2. Jh. v. Chr.*, ed. M. Braun, A. Haltenhoff, and F.-H. Mutschler (Leipzig 2000) 271–284.

Seider, A., "Competing Commemorations: Apostrophes of the Dead in the *Aeneid*," *American Journal of Philology* 133 (2012) 241–269.

———, *Memory in Vergil's* Aeneid: *Creating the Past* (Cambridge 2013).

Senie, H., and Webster. S., eds., *Critical Issues in Public Art: Content, Context, and Controversy* (New York 1992).

Settis, S., "Fortuna del Diadumeno: i testi," *Quaderni Ticinesi di Numismatica e Antichità Classiche* 21 (1992) 51–68.

Short, W., "Thinking Places, Placing Thoughts: Spatial Metaphors of Mental Activity in Roman Culture," *I Quaderni del Ramo d'Oro* 1 (2008) 106–129.

Shortliffe, G., "Class Conflict and International Politics," *International Journal* 4 (1949) 95–108.

Siegel, D. J., "Entwicklungspsychologische, interpersonelle und neurobiologische Dimensionen des Gedächtnisses. Ein Überblick," in *Warum Menschen sich erinnern können. Fortschritte in der inter-disziplinäre Gedächtnisforschung*, ed. H. Welzer and H. J. Markowitsch (Stuttgart 2006) 19–49.

Skinner, Q., ed., *The Return of Grand Theory in the Human Sciences* (Cambridge 1985; repr. 1990).

Small, J. P., *Wax Tablets of the Mind: Cognitive Studies of Memory and Literacy in Classical Antiquity* (London 1997).

Small, J. P., and Tatum, J., "Memory and the Study of Classical Antiquity," *Helios* 22.2 (1995) 149–177.

Smith, C., "Sulla's Memoirs," in Smith and Powell 2009, 65–85.

Smith, C., and Powell, A., eds., *The Lost Memoirs of Augustus and the Development of Roman Autobiography* (Swansea 2009).

Solso, R. J., *Cognition and the Visual Arts* (Cambridge, MA 1994).

Spencer, D., "Movement and the Linguistic Turn," in *Rome, Ostia, Pompeii: Movement and Space*, ed. R. Laurence and D. J. Newsome (Oxford 2011) 57–80.

Spinola, G., *Il Museo Pio-Clementino*, vol. 1 (Vatican City 1996).

Stamper, J., *The Architecture of Roman Temples: The Republic to the Middle Empire* (Cambridge 2005).

Steinby, E. M., ed., *Lexicon Topographicum Urbis Romae*, 6 vols. (Rome 1993–2000).

Stewart, A., "Pergamo Area Marmorea Magna: On the Date, Reconstruction, and Functions of the Great Altar of Pergamon," in *From Pergamon to Sperlonga: Sculpture and Context*, ed. N. T. de Grummond and B. S. Ridgway (Berkeley, Los Angeles, and London 2000) 32–57.

Stroup, S. C., *Catullus, Cicero, and a Society of Patrons* (Cambridge 2010).

Suerbaum, W., ed., *Die Archaische Literatur. Von den Anfängen bis Sullas Tod.* Handbuch der Lateinischen Literatur der Antike 1 (Munich 2002).

Sumi, G. S., *Ceremony and Power: Performing Politics in Rome between Republic and Empire* (Ann Arbor 2005).

Thein, A., "*Felicitas* and the Memoirs of Sulla and Augustus," in Smith and Powell 2009, 87–109.

Timpe, D., "*Memoria* und Geschichtsschreibung bei den Römern," in *Vergangenheit und Lebenswelt*, ed. H. J. Gehrke (Tübingen 1996) 277–299.

Todorov, T., *Les abus de la mémoire* (Paris 1995).

Torelli, M., *Typology & Structure of Roman Historical Reliefs* (Ann Arbor 1992).

Trifiló, F., "Movement, Gaming, and Use of Space in the Forum," in *Rome, Ostia, Pompeii: Movement and Space*, ed. R. Laurence and D. J. Newsome (Oxford 2011) 312–221.

Trimble, J., and Elsner, J., eds., *Art and Replication: Greece, Rome and Beyond. Art History* 29.2 (2006).

Tulving, E., and Craik, F. I. M., eds., *The Oxford Handbook of Memory* (Oxford 2000).

Tulving, E., and Osler, E., "Effectiveness of Retrieval Cues in Memory for Words," *Journal of Experimental Psychology* 77.4 (1968) 593–601.

Tulving, E., and Pearlstone, Z., "Availability versus Accessibility of Information in Memory for Words," *Journal of Verbal Learning & Verbal Behavior* 5.4 (1966) 381–391.

Underwood, G., *Attention and Memory* (Oxford and New York 1976).

Ungern-Sternberg, J. von, "The Formation of the 'Annalistic Tradition': The Example of the Decemvirate," in Raaflaub 2005, 75–97.

Uribe, M., "El Libertador, Su Ayo Y Su Capellán," in *Homenaje de Colombia al Libertador Simón Bolívar En Su Primer Centenario*, ed. M. E. Corrales (Bogota 1884) 72–74.

Van den Hout, M. P. J., *M. Cornelii Frontonis Epistulae* (Leipzig 1988).

———, *A Commentary on the Letters of M. Cornelius Fronto* (Leiden 1999).

Varner, E. R., *Mutilation and Transformation. "Damnatio Memoriae" and Roman Imperial Portraiture* (Leiden and Boston 2004).

———, "Reading Replications: Roman Rhetoric and Greek Quotations," *Art History* 29.2 (2006) 280–303.

Vasaly, A., *Representations: Images of the World in Ciceronian Oratory* (Berkeley, Los Angeles, and London 1993).

Vernant, J.-P., *Mythe et pensée chez les Grecs: études de psychologie historique* (Paris 1965).

Versnel, H. S., *Triumphus: An Inquiry into the Origin, Development and Meaning of the Roman Triumph* (Leiden 1970).

Veyne, P., "L'histoire conceptualisante," in *Faire de l'histoire,* vol. 1: *Nouveaux problèmes*, ed. J. Le Goff and P. Nora (Paris 1976) 62–92.

Vogel, L., "Circus Race Scenes in the Early Roman Empire," *Art Bulletin* 51.2 (1969) 155–160.

Von den Hoff, R., "Commodus als Hercules," in *Meisterwerke der antiken Kunst*, ed. L. Giuliani (Munich 2005) 115–135.

Waelkens, M., "From a Phrygian Quarry: the Provenance of the Statues of the Dacian Prisoners in Trajan's Forum in Rome," *American Journal of Archaeology* 89 (1985) 641–653.

Wallace-Hadrill, A., "Mutatas Formas: The Augustan Transformation of Roman Knowledge," in *The Cambridge Companion to the Age of Augustus*, ed. K. Galinsky (Cambridge 2005) 55–84.

———, *Rome's Cultural Revolution* (Cambridge 2008).

Walter, U., "*Natam me consule Romam*: historisch-politische Autobiographien in republikanischer Zeit: ein Überblick," *Altsprachl. Unterricht* 46.2 (2003) 36–42.

———, Memoria *und res publica. Zur Geschichtskultur im republikanischen Rom* (Frankfurt am Main 2004).

———, "Die *Communes Historiae* des Lutatius. Einleitung, Fragmente, Übersetzung, Kommentar," in *Göttinger Forum für Altertumswissenschaft* 12 (2009) 1–15.

Welzer, H., *Das kommunikative Gedächtnis. Eine Theorie der Erinnerung* (Munich 2005).

Wertsch, J., *Voices of Collective Remembering* (Cambridge 2002).

West, D., *The Imagery and Poetry of Lucretius* (Edinburgh 1969).

Wheeler, M., "Episodic Memory and Autonoetic Awareness," in Tulving and Craik 2000, 597–608.

Wilson Jones, M., "Genesis and Mimesis: The Design of the Arch of Constantine in Rome," *Journal of the Society of Architectural Historians* 59.1 (2000) 50–77.

Wiseman, T. P., *Clio's Cosmetics: Three Studies in Greco-Roman Literature* (1979).

———, "Practice and Theory in Roman Historiography," *Historia* 66 (1981) 375–393.

———, "Monuments and the Roman Annalists," in *Past Perspectives: Studies in Greek and Roman Historical Writing*, ed. I. S. Moxon, J. D. Smart, and A. J. Woodman (Cambridge 1986) 87–101.

———, "*Conspicui postes tectaque digna deo*: The Public Image of Aristocratic and Imperial Houses in the Late Republic and Early Empire," in *L'Urbs: Espace urbain et histoire, 1er siècle avant J.-C.–IIIe siècle après J.-C.* Collection de l'École française de Rome 98 (Rome 1987) 395–413.

———, "Rome and the Resplendent Aemilii" (1993), in Wiseman 1998, 106–120.

———, *Historiography and Imagination: Eight Essays on Roman Culture* (Exeter 1994).

———, *Remus: A Roman Myth* (Cambridge 1995).

———, "The Minucii and Their Monument" (1996), in Wiseman 1998, 90–105.

———, *Roman Drama and Roman History* (Exeter 1998).

———, *The Myths of Rome* (Exeter 2004).

———, "Three Notes on the Triumphal Route," in *Res bene gestae: ricerche di storia urbana su Roma antica in onore di Eva Margareta Steinby*, ed. A. Leone, D. Palombi, and S. Walker (Rome 2007) 445–449.

———, *Unwritten Rome* (Exeter 2008).

———, *Remembering the Roman People: Essays on Late-Republican Politics and Literature* (Oxford 2009).

Wuttke, D., ed., *Aby Warburg, Ausgewählte Schriften und Würdigungen* (Baden-Baden 1979).

Yates, F. A., *The Art of Memory* (Chicago 1966; repr. 2001).

Yerushalmi, Y., *Zakhor: Jewish Memory and Jewish History* (Seattle 1982).

Young, J. E., *The Texture of Memory: Holocaust Memorials and Meaning* (Yale 1993).

Zamora, L. P., *The Usable Past: The Imagination of History in Recent Fiction of the Americas* (Cambridge 1998).

Zanker, P., *Augustus und die Macht der Bilder* (Munich 1987).

———, "Nachahmen als kulturelles Schicksal," in *Probleme der Kopie von der Antike bis zum 19. Jahrhundert: vier Vorträge*, ed. C. Lenz (Munich 1992) 9–24.

Zeiner, N. K. *Nothing Ordinary Here: Statius as Creator of Distinction in the* Silvae (New York and London 2005).

Zerubavel, E., "Social Memories: Steps to a Sociology of the Past," *Qualitative Sociology* 19 (1996) 283–300.

———, *Time Maps: Collective Memory and the Social Shape of the Past* (Chicago 2003).

Zola, S., and Squire, L., "The Medial Tempora Lobe and the Hippocampus," in Tulving and Craik 2000, 485–500.